A WORLD SAFE FOR DEMOCRACY

POLITICS AND CULTURE

James Davison Hunter and John M. Owen IV, Series Editors

A World
Safe for
Democracy

Liberal Internationalism and
the Crises of Global Order

G. JOHN IKENBERRY

Yale

UNIVERSITY PRESS

NEW HAVEN AND LONDON

Published with the assistance of the Institute for Advanced Studies in Culture, University of Virginia, and with assistance from the foundation established in memory of Calvin Chapin of the Class of 1788, Yale College.

Yale University Press books may be purchased in quantity for educational, business, or promotional use. For information, please e-mail sales.press@yale.edu (U.S. office) or sales@yaleup.co.uk (U.K. office).

Set in Electra type by Westchester Publishing Services.
Printed in the United States of America.

Library of Congress Control Number: 2020936946
ISBN 978-0-300-23098-7 (hardcover: alk. paper)

A catalogue record for this book is available from the British Library.

This paper meets the requirements of ANSI/NISO Z39.48-1992 (Permanence of Paper).

10 9 8 7 6 5 4 3 2 1

To Lidia, Jackson,
and the loving memory of Tessa
fiat lux

I will begin by speaking about our ancestors, since it is only right and proper on such an occasion to pay them the honor of recalling what they did. In this land of ours there have always been the same people living from generation to generation until now, and they, by their courage and their virtues, have handed it on to us, a free country. They certainly deserve our praise.

Pericles' Funeral Oration, as recorded by Thucydides

Come, my friends,
'Tis not too late to seek a newer world.
. . . .
Tho' much is taken, much abides; and tho'
We are not now that strength which in old days
Moved earth and heaven, that which we are, we are;
One equal temper of heroic hearts,
Made weak by time and fate, but strong in will
To strive, to seek, to find, and not to yield.

Alfred, Lord Tennyson, "Ulysses," 1833

We are living and shall live all our lives now in a revolutionary world. This means among other things a world of restless experiment.

Walter Lippmann, New Republic, April 1917

The world goes a little by peaks and valleys, but on the whole the curve is upward; on the whole, . . . over these thousands of years human life is on a great deal better scale than it was then.

Franklin Delano Roosevelt, press conference, 22 December 1944

CONTENTS

PREFACE

On 2 April 1917, President Woodrow Wilson went before Congress to call for a declaration of war against imperial Germany, proclaiming as the war's purpose that the world "be made safe for democracy." These famous words are widely seen to embody the essence of liberal internationalism. The phrase is typically understood as an idealist appeal to spread democracy worldwide. Wilson seemed to be calling for a great campaign to remake the world in America's image and bring the blessing of democracy to all corners of the earth. This is how his words—and liberal internationalism—have been handed down to us.

But the statement can also be read literally, as a plea for safety. Rather than an idealist appeal, it is a call to reform the postwar international order so as to allow Western liberal democracy to survive. If the United States, western Europe, and other established democracies hope to protect their democratic institutions and traditions, Wilson is saying, they must reorganize the international setting in which they live. This is a very different take on Wilson's intent. He is calling on us to confront the dangers that imperil the survival of democracy, not to promote it on distant shores. As I argue in this book, this second reading best captures the longer tradition of liberal internationalism, which begins a century before Wilson and unfolds in the century after him. The essential element and guiding impulse of this tradition is the cooperative organization and reform of international order so as to protect and facilitate the security, welfare, and progress of liberal democracy—in short, to make the world safe for democracy.

A century after Wilson, people across the liberal democratic world are again worried about whether their way of life can be made safe, and even whether it will survive. Great powers—China and Russia—are offering forceful illiberal challenges to the Western liberal order. Equally profound challenges are coming from within the liberal democratic world itself—reactionary nationalism, populist authoritarianism, and attacks on openness and the rule of law. Today's liberal internationalists are once again forced to return to the most basic questions. What are the prospects for liberal democracy? How can capitalism and liberal democracy be reconciled, reformed, and put on a solid foundation? How can the conflicting values at the heart of liberal order— liberty and equality, openness and social solidarity, sovereignty and interdependence—be brought back into balance? Most important, in our unraveling world order, is there a future for liberal internationalism as a way of organizing global relations and making the world safe for democracy? On what geopolitical and intellectual foundation can liberal internationalism plant its flag?

In grappling with these questions, I take the long road: looking back at the crooked trajectory of liberal internationalism's long and uncertain passage to the twenty-first century. This book recounts two centuries of its rise, spread, crises, and transformation. Liberal internationalism can be understood as a cluster of ideas on how to think about and act in the world, which emerged out of the Enlightenment and the Western liberal democratic experience. In the twentieth century it became a political project. At its core are convictions about how liberal democracies—and the wider world—should cooperate to organize their common relations. Liberal internationalists see cooperation driven by shared values and interests, but this cooperation is also a defense against the existential dangers and mutual vulnerabilities that arise out of modernity itself. It is this impulse—a response to the dangers and vulnerabilities that come with the rise of modernization and interdependence— that I emphasize in this portrait of the liberal international project.

Liberal internationalism is not in its essence a utopian project to make the world a better place. It is a pragmatic, opportunistic, and reform-oriented approach aimed at "making safe" liberal democracy in a world that is riven by tyranny, brutality, and intolerance. To be sure, Enlightenment sensibilities and progressive narratives of Western society lurk at the heart of the liberal tradition. But liberal internationalists actually have quite diverse views about modernity, and their ideas and projects over the past two centuries tend to reflect a surprisingly practical, even world-weary cast of mind. Progress is possible but not inevitable. Modernity has a split personality: the modern world is continuously creating capacities for great advances in human welfare but also for monumental disaster and civilizational catastrophe. Liberal internationalists share with political realists—their great intellectual rivals—a suspicion of the power-seeking and despotic aspects of human nature. This is why they view constitutions, legal restraints, and institutional checks and balances as essential features of political order. Unlike realists, who see cycles of power and order across history, liberal internationalists are heirs of the Enlightenment project of scientific and technological advance and societal transformation that open new possibilities for both progress and disaster. Liberal internationalism is a cluster of ideas about how to build world order—starting with the liberal democracies—to realize the gains from modernity and guard against its dangers.

What is this book arguing against? Realism provides the most coherent "other" to the arguments that follow. But the book is not written as a battle between "realism" and "liberalism." Instead, I see the two traditions as different types of intellectual and political enterprises. One difference is in the core problems they seek to understand. Realism is a school of thought that focuses on how states cope with the problems of anarchy, and liberal internationalism, while concerned with anarchy, focuses on how states cope with the problems of modernity. They are looking at different aspects of the modern world, asking different questions, and offering different solutions. Liberals acknowledge the bleak world that realists depict in their theories, even as they debate among themselves how and to what extent it is possible for liberal democracy to escape this inhospitable setting. Realism claims to explain the character of international politics everywhere across the ancient and modern worlds, wherever there is anarchy. Liberal internationalism is focused on the rise of liberal democracies and the types of international space that they seek to build in order to make their polities safer and more prosperous. Liberal internationalism makes sense only in a world where liberal democracies exist. It is thus different from realism in two respects: it is historically contingent, and it is in important respects normative. Liberal internationalists seek not only to explain the world as it exists but also to bring into being a world they would like to live in. I am in sympathy with these efforts.

This book also argues against revisionist critiques of liberal internationalism that implicate the liberal project in the racist, imperial, and militarist features of Western power. Critics note that Western democracies often proclaim a commitment to liberal values and universal rights, but they argue that these ideals have largely served as a facade or legitimating cover for traditional realpolitik policies that perpetuate racial and imperial hierarchies. In this book, I acknowledge the deep entanglement of liberal internationalism in the sordid history of Western empire, racism, and military interventionism. But I also show the ways in which liberal internationalism, particularly in the twentieth century, has helped to crystallize opposition to these dark impulses. No liberal state has ever acted in international affairs solely on the basis of liberal principles. Hypocrisy is inherent in the rhetoric of liberal democracy and human rights. But the spaces opened up within even a deeply flawed liberal international order create opportunities for political struggles that can bring the order closer to its founding ideals.

Lastly, I am arguing against a view that reduces liberal internationalism to a particular thinker, such as Woodrow Wilson, or a particular historical moment, such as the American postwar hegemonic era. In my account, liberal internationalism is a long-evolving, diverse, and internally contested set of ideas. Its DNA contains multiple strands of "internationalism" that have combined, frayed, and recombined over the centuries. I seek to decenter liberal internationalism away from Wilson and to look back to founding ideas and breakthroughs of the nineteenth century as well as forward to the Rooseveltian moment and the post–Cold War era. This portrait seeks to avoid the appeal to purity, the "no true Scotsman" fallacy of defining a tradition by excluding inconvenient ideas and counterexamples. It is the diversity of thinkers and projects and its ongoing debates that marks the tradition, not an unchanging dogma.

This book is centrally preoccupied with the historical moments when liberal internationalists have lost—and then found—their way. The rise of multiple varieties of internationalism in the nineteenth century set the stage for modern liberal internationalism. World War I and Wilsonian peacemaking constituted an important turning point, the moment when liberal internationalism crystallized as a political project and yet, as it was turned into the Versailles settlement, revealed its limits and vulnerabilities. In the 1930s and during World War II, liberal internationalism again struggled to pick up the pieces. In the hands of Franklin Delano Roosevelt and his contemporaries, it was redefined for a world divided between competing great powers with competing ideological projects. In the postwar decades—such as the 1970s, when liberal capitalism was again in crisis—and today, debates over liberal internationalism's future have returned yet again.

Throughout this history, despite its diversity, the liberal tradition has retained a glimmering of continuity. In the mid-nineteenth century, the British parliamentarian and political activist Richard Cobden was the epitome of the liberal internationalist. A leader of the movement to repeal the Corn Laws, Cobden spent his life championing free trade, arms control and disarmament, and the peaceful settlement of disputes. A French colleague called him "an international man." In 1919, John Hobson, a leading internationalist of his day, looked back at Cobden as a forerunner of his generation's liberal internationalism. In the mid-twentieth century, Secretary of State Cordell Hull, a former congressman from Tennessee, carried the flag of free trade into debates on the post-1945 world order, earning the nickname "Tennessee's Cobden." When Hull won the Nobel Peace Prize in 1945, it was seen as a deliberate echo of the 1920 award of the prize to Woodrow Wilson. A half century later, when the World Trade Organization was launched, its official organizational history looked back to Hull's words from 1937: "I have never faltered, and I will never falter, in my belief that enduring peace and the welfare of nations are indissolubly connected with . . . the maximum practicable degree of freedom in international trade." These words could have been spoken by Cobden.

If we look back over the past two centuries, the euphoria of the post-1989 period, when liberal democracy seemed to be the only political idea left standing, stands out as an anomalous moment. The rest of the period has been marked by crisis, uncertainty, and close-run contests with rival ideologies and political projects. Liberal internationalists have repeatedly been forced to pick up after a disaster and rethink their grand theories and order-building ideas. Repeatedly, the liberal imagination has found itself as T. S. Eliot found it in 1922, "only a heap of broken images." But it has always returned, out of moral conviction and the practical imperatives of creating the conditions for liberal democracy.

ACKNOWLEDGMENTS

This book began as a series of lectures at the University of Virginia in November 2016, presented under the title "The Crooked Arrow of History: The Origins, Triumph, and Crisis of Liberal Internationalism." I am grateful to John Owen and James Davison Hunter and the Institute for Advanced Studies in Culture at the University of Virginia for hosting me. I am also thankful for the comments and suggestions from its many participants, including Dale Copeland, Jackson Lears, Melvyn Leffler, and Philip Zelikow.

Whatever the weaknesses of this book, they would have been much greater without the assistance of many friends and colleagues: Alan Alexandroff, Robert Cooper, Michael Doyle, Gareth Evans, Martha Finnemore, Orfeo Fioretos, Suzanne Fry, Kiichi Fujiwara, Yoichi Funabashi, James Goldgeier, David Gordon, William G. Gray, Joseph Grieco, John A. Hall, Takashi Inoguchi, Ash Jain, Robert Jervis, Robert Johansen, Bruce Jones, Miles Kahler, Peter Katzenstein, Paul Kennedy, Jonathan Kirshner, Thomas Knock, Charles Kupchan, David Lake, Phillip Lipscy, Michael Mastanduno, Hanns Maull, Kate McNamara, John Mearsheimer, Nuno Monteiro, Jonathan Monten, Daniel Nexon, Vittorio Parsi, Stewart Patrick, Louis Pauley, Patrick Porter, Barry Posen, Karoline Postel-Vinay, Chris Reus-Smit, Gideon Rose, Cheryl Schonhardt-Bailey, Randy Schweller, Tony Smith, Doug Stokes, Jake Sullivan, Hidemi Suganami, Trygve Throntveit, Steve Walt, Stephen Wertheim, James Lindley Wilson, William Wohlforth, and Thomas Wright. I have benefited enormously over the years from ongoing conversations with many friends and colleagues at Princeton University, including Jeremy Adelman, Gary Bass, Miguel Centeno, Tom Christensen, Aaron Friedberg, Michael Gordin, Harold James, Robert Keohane, Atul Kohli, Steve Kotkin, Helen Milner, Andy Moravscik, Jan-Werner Muller, Philip Pettit, Kris Ramsey, Anne-Marie Slaughter, and Deborah Yashar. At Princeton, I have been fortunate to work with and learn from many talented doctoral students, including Adam Liff, Darren Lim, and Audrye Wong. I am grateful as well to Tolya Levshin, who has been a wonderful source of ideas and inspiration. I owe a special debt to Daniel Deudney, who through many years of conversation and collaboration has contributed to the core arguments of the book.

I also want to thank Sir John Vickers, the Warden of All Souls College, Oxford University, and the fellows of All Souls for a wonderful sabbatical year as a visiting fellow in 2018–19, during which I finished a draft of the book. All Souls provided an intellectual setting as rarefied as it was congenial in which to work, and I enjoyed my many encounters with its faculty, including Cecile Fabre, David Gellner, Cecilia Heyes, Roger Hood, Stathis Kalyvas, Noel Malcolm, Edward Mortimer, Avner Offer, Kevin O'Rourke, and Nicholas Rodger. I also benefited from conversations at Oxford with other old friends and colleagues, including Timothy Garton Ash, Rosemary Foot, Jeffrey Holzgrefe, Andrew Hurrell, Edward Keene, Elizabeth Kiss, Margaret Macmillan, Neil and Fusa McLynn, Rana Mitter, Kalypso Nicolaidis, Justine Potts, Adam Roberts, and David Vines. At Chatham House in London, I enjoyed exchanging ideas with Robin Niblett and Leslie Vinjamuri. At the London School of Economics (LSE), I had stimulating conversations with Mary Kaldor, Kori Schake, Linda Yueh, and many others. At Kings College London, I have benefited from exchanges with John Bew, Andrew Ehrhardt, and Nick Kaderbhai, and at the University of Wales I enjoyed conversations with Richard Beardsworth, Ken Booth, and Jan Ruzicka.

I am indebted to Mick Cox, George Lawson, and Peter Trubowitz for hosting a day-long manuscript workshop at the LSE in October 2019. I benefited enormously from their comments, as well as from those of the other participants: Duncan Bell, Barry Buzan, Janina Dill, Beate Jahn, Emma MacKinnon, Jeanne Morefield, Inderjeet Parmar, and John Thompson. My old friend

Joe Barnes also gave the manuscript a careful reading, and the book is better for it.

I offer a special thanks to Inwon Choue, the chancellor of Kyung Hee University, who has supported my research over the years. I also want to thank two dear colleagues who passed away during the writing of this book: John Peterson, who took interest in my project and hosted me on two occasions at the University of Edinburgh, and James Huntley—my old comrade-in-arms who truly embodied the liberal internationalist sensibility.

William Frucht, my editor at Yale University Press, has been a constant source of editorial and intellectual insight. I appreciate his patience and good humor as the manuscript made its intrepid journey from lecture notes to scholarly monograph. Karen Olson also provided able assistance in the preparation of the manuscript. I also want to acknowledge Bill Nelson for his preparation of the book's figures. Let me also thank the thoughtful comments from two anonymous reviewers for the press. Research and writing on this book was also supported by the Project on the Future of Multilateralism at Princeton University. Lindsay Woodrick has provided cheerful and efficient support.

My greatest debt is to my family, Lidia and Jackson. Their love and support have been the rock on which I stand. It is to them that I owe the most.

Shakespeare put it best in *Twelfth Night*: "I can no other answer make, but, thanks, and thanks, and ever thanks."

ONE

Cracks in the Liberal World Order

For two hundred years, the grand project of liberal internationalism has been to build a world order that is open, loosely rules-based, and oriented toward progressive ideas. As the twentieth century came to an end, that order appeared to be at hand. The democratic world was expanding. Across regions, civilizations, and developed and developing worlds, states were choosing to integrate into an open global order girded by a multilateral system of rules and institutions. A worldwide consensus seemed to have arrived on the virtues and accomplishments of market capitalism and liberal democracy. This global turn was marked by dramatic moments—the fall of the Berlin Wall, the collapse of Soviet communism, the peaceful end of the Cold War. As old geopolitical and ideological divides collapsed, a new global era beckoned. For most of the century, the world had been convulsed by a great contest between rival ideologies and movements—communist internationalism, revolutionary socialism, fascism, authoritarian nationalism, and liberal internationalism. In the century's last decade, it appeared the contest was over.

This global turn seemed sudden, but it had deep roots. In the aftermath of World War II, the United States and its partners built a new type of international order, organized around open trade, cooperative security, multilateralism, democratic solidarity, and American leadership. Regional and global institutions were established to facilitate cooperation, enshrine shared norms, and bind societies together. Western Europe overcame centuries of division to launch a project of integration and political union. West Germany and Japan reinvented themselves as "civilian" powers and became stakeholders in the postwar liberal order. Across the industrial world, the postwar period was a golden era of economic growth and social advancement. When the Cold War ended and the Soviet Union collapsed, this Western liberal order expanded outward across the globe. Countries on the edges of this order made political and economic changes to integrate into it. Russia and China joined the World Trade Organization. Moscow was enfeebled. Beijing had yet to emerge as an economic superpower. Great power rivalry and ideological competition were at a low ebb. Everything that Western liberal internationalists believed in and promoted seemed to be on the move.

Today, this grand project is in crisis—a crisis most profoundly manifest in a lost confidence in collective solutions to common problems. Surprisingly, the retreat from liberal internationalism is coming from the very states that had been the postwar order's patrons and stakeholders. The two great powers that have done the most to give the modern international order a liberal character—Great Britain and the United States, the world's oldest and most venerated democracies—now seem to be pulling back from this leadership. Britain's referendum in June 2016 to leave the European Union (EU) shocked observers and raised troubling questions about the future of the European project—the long-standing postwar effort, enshrined in the EU's founding treaty, to build a "more perfect union." The EU has been the silent bulwark of the Western liberal order. In each decade of the postwar era, it was Europe's political advance—its efforts to bind together its liberal democracies and diminish old geopolitical and nationalist divides—that most fully embodied the liberal international vision. But that advance has now come to a halt, and the wider challenges that beset the EU—refugee flows, monetary imbalances, stagnant economies, reactionary nationalism—reinforce the sense of crisis.

In the United States, the election of Donald Trump has triggered even more doubt about the future of the liberal international order. For the first time since 1945, the United States found itself led by a president who is actively hostile to the core ideas of liberal internationalism. In areas such as trade, alliances, multilateralism, human rights, immigration, rule of law, and democratic solidarity, the Trump administration has actively undermined the American-led postwar order.[1] In the name of "America First," the American president has abandoned commitments to fight climate change, defend democratic institutions, and uphold the multilateral agreements of an open and rules-based global system. He presents the remarkable spectacle of an American president systematically undermining the institutions and partnerships that the United States created and has led over the past seventy years.[2] As Donald Tusk, the president of the European Council, put it: "The rules-based international order is being challenged, not by the usual suspects, but by its main architect and guarantor, the U.S."[3]

The profound danger of this political moment is greater still because it occurs amid a nationalist and populist revolt unfolding across the democratic world. The centrist and liberal governing coalitions that built the postwar order have weakened. Liberal democracy itself appears fragile, vulnerable in particular to far-right populism.[4] Some date these troubles to the global financial crisis of 2008, which widened economic inequality and fueled grievances across the advanced democracies that first championed and benefited from the liberal order. In the meantime, China and Russia have begun to push back on the American-led order, cracking down on Western influences in their countries and seeking to expand their spheres of influence. Russia is actively attempting to undermine the legitimacy and operation of democratic institutions in Europe and the United States. China has begun to advance its own vision of modernity: capitalism without liberalism or democracy. Authoritarian states across the world are actively promoting dark narratives and illiberal visions of civilization, politics, and modernity.[5]

In all these ways, the old Western-led liberal order looks more troubled today than at any time since the 1930s. Observers are now forced to ask first-order questions about the future of liberal democracy, liberal internationalism, the West, and the trajectory of the modern global order. Writing at the end of 2015, *New York Times* columnist Ross Douthat captured this turn in the global zeitgeist: "Here in the dying days of [the year] . . . something seems to have shifted. For the first time in a generation, the theme of this year was the liberal order's vulnerability, not its resilience. 2015 was a *memento mori* moment for our institutions, a year of cracks in the system, of crumbling fire walls, of reminders that all orders pass away."[6] Across the Western world, something fundamental seems to have been lost: a sense of possibility, a belief that the future can be made better. Decline, decay, and backsliding are the new catchphrases of the old order.

What has happened? What are the underlying sources of these troubles? To say that a political order is in crisis is to argue that its institutions and relationships are not sustainable—that something has to give.[7] But how deep does the crisis run? It might simply be a momentary dip in our economic and political fortunes, something that renewed growth and new leadership can turn around. The Western liberal democracies have gone through disruptions and downturns before. After all, the early decades of the postwar Western order were not as halcyon as they are often remembered. The Suez crisis, France's departure from the NATO command structure, disputes about the US dollar, protest movements over civil rights and the Vietnam War, political assassinations—these were all defining markers of a turbulent era. Inside Europe, Spain and Portugal were both ruled by authoritarian regimes and France and Italy had large communist parties.[8] In the 1970s, the foundations of the Western capitalist system were shaken by soaring oil prices, stagnant economies, transatlantic disputes, and a constitutional crisis in the United States. But in the years that followed, growth returned and new political leadership emerged on both sides of the Atlantic.[9]

The troubles today are surely deeper. Many observers see the crisis as the faltering of American hegemony. The United States played an outsized role in organizing and running the liberal order, but its ability and willingness to do so have diminished under the pressure of rising states and the inevitable redistribution of wealth and power. If this is the case, the problems might be a "crisis of transition" in which the leadership, institutions, and bargains within the postwar liberal order are being renegotiated toward some post-American order—still relatively open and rules-based, but less Western. This is a crisis of governance that can be remedied by a redistribution of authority and roles across the system.[10]

Others argue that liberal internationalism cannot be separated from American hegemony. When the world is "less American," they argue, it will also be less liberal. If this is so, the current crisis runs deeper. It calls into question the underlying logic of liberal internationalism itself. In this view, the open and loosely rules-based order is an artifact of the past two centuries of Anglo-American global dominance, and when that dominance fades, the liberal international characteristics of the old order will disappear and the long Western liberal ascendancy will give way to a postliberal order organized around some other set of principles and institutions.[11] Some observers think China will become the organizational center of a post-Western liberal system.[12] Or there might be a decentralized system composed of regions, blocs, and spheres of influence dominated by great powers.[13] Or it might be that fracture, discord, and disorder will become a permanent feature of world politics.

If this were not enough, the crisis might be even more epochal—reflecting a breakdown of Enlightenment principles and liberal modernity. Some observers see the forces of liberal modernity—where economic growth, social advancement, and liberal democracy are seen to move forward together, driven by the powerful "engines" of rationalism, science, and modernization—giving way to a new postmodern age. The Enlightenment underpinnings of the modern world system, understood as an unfolding story of human progress and betterment, are artifacts of a departing era. Pankaj Mishra, for instance, argues that behind the liberal vision of modernity—with its anticipation of "gradual progress under liberal-democrat trustees"—is a rapacious capitalist system that has generated only disorder, dislocation, and rage.[14]

These accounts agree that the liberal order is in trouble but disagree as to its causes. To glimpse liberal internationalism's future, we must look into its past and trace its long road to the present. Liberal internationalism did not begin in 1989 or even 1945. It is a tradition of thought and action that emerged out of the Enlightenment and the age of democratic revolutions, and it has traveled a rocky pathway of success, failure, struggle, and reinvention into today's world. Its two-hundred-year journey has been marked by a succession of crises in which it was repeatedly upended and set back by wars, depressions, and reactionary movements. Yet it has always found its way back to the center of world politics. In his book *Desolation and Enlightenment*, Ira Katznelson eloquently chronicles how, even in the face of history's worst assault on liberal democracy in the modern age—witnessed in the 1930s and 1940s with the collapse of the world economy, the rise of fascism and totalitarianism, the unprecedented violence of world war, the Holocaust, and the dropping of the atomic bomb—the "Enlightenment values" that underpin the liberal vision remained alive, waiting to be revived and reaffirmed by a postwar generation.[15]

If liberal internationalism is to remain at the center of twenty-first-century struggles over world order, the world-weary and agonistic side of its past must be recovered and brought forward. In the chapters that follow, I explore the logic and changing character of liberal internationalism across the past two centuries, through its many turning points, entanglements, crises, and renewals. I pose the question: What is liberal internationalism and how has it made an impact on modern international relations—and what is its future?

The Argument

Liberal internationalism, as a way of organizing the world, still has a future. The ideas and impulses of an open, rules-based, and progressively oriented international order run deep in world politics. The liberal tradition of order-building emerged with the rise and spread of liberal democracy, and its ideas and agendas have been shaped as democratic countries have confronted the opportunities and dangers of modernity. Creating an international "space" for liberal democracy, reconciling the dilemmas of sovereignty and interdependence, seeking protections and preserving rights within and between states—these are among the core aims that have propelled liberal internationalism through the upheavals of the past two centuries. In a world of rising economic and security interdependence, it remains the most coherent, functional, and widely acceptable way of organizing international relations. Liberal internationalism has not failed so much as it has been a victim of its own success. In its post–Cold War transition from a Western liberal order to a globalized order, it effectively overran its political foundations and undermined its social purposes. As they did in earlier eras, liberal internationalists today will need to rethink and reinvent their project.

6

In this book I make three sets of arguments. First, I offer a portrait of liberal internationalism as a set of ideas about how the world works. I look at its claims about the underlying character of international relations, the sources of order, and the problems that liberal internationalism seeks to solve.

—Liberal internationalism is best understood as a set of ideas and projects for organizing the world of liberal democracies. "Making the world safe for democracy," as Woodrow Wilson put it, is its raison d'être. It is a tradition of thought and action that seeks to organize and reform the international order in ways that strengthen and facilitate liberal democracy's security, welfare, and progress. It seeks to create an ordered environment in which liberal democracies can cooperate for mutual gains, manage their shared vulnerabilities, and protect their way of life. In this sense, unlike political realism—the other great tradition of international theory, which presents itself as a reductionist and universal explanation of the behavior of states—liberal internationalism is normative and historically contingent, an artifact of the rise of Western nation-states, liberal democracy, and Anglo-American hegemony. It is realized in practice through rules, institutions, and partnerships within a modernizing world system. But its deeper ambitions are to shape the political-institutional and normative environment—the international ecosystem—in which liberal democracies operate.

—Liberal internationalism has evolved as liberal democracies have encountered the problems and opportunities of modernity, by which I mean the ongoing transformation of societies and international relations driven by science, technology, and the industrial revolution. Modern societies, led by the liberal democracies, are becoming more complex and interdependent as they develop. As liberal internationalists have learned and relearned over the nineteenth and twentieth centuries, modernity has two faces. There is the face of human advancement—technological change, economic growth, rising standards of living, and the constant revelation of shared interests and fates across societies. But there is also modernity's other face: economic depression, war, totalitarianism, reactionary backlashes, violent revolution, and sudden vulnerability. Liberal internationalism can be understood as a response to modernity's upside and downside. It involves cooperation between states to capture the benefits of modern interdependence and guard against its perils. At critical turning points—1918, 1945, 1991, and today—liberal internationalists have been forced to rethink their understanding of modernity and recast their ambitions and goals.

—Liberal internationalism was brought into the twentieth century on the backs of other powerful forces and movements. Nationalism, imperialism, capitalism, great-power politics, and Anglo-American hegemony are all parts of the moving terrain on which liberal internationalism was shaped and reshaped. It is a tradition with a grand vision of liberal democracy and the modern world but without a fixed set of ideas. This has been both its weakness and its strength. Its thin and shape-shifting character has allowed it to affiliate with other forces and movements, including empire, imperialism, racism, and great-power order-building projects. This property has given liberal internationalism salience and influence in shaping the modern world order, but it has also put it in the company of forces and agendas that seek to move the world in other directions.

Second, I look at liberal internationalism as a political project: the programs and agendas that liberal internationalists have devised and pursued over the past two centuries.

—Liberal internationalism's impact on international relations in the nineteenth and twentieth centuries has been accomplished through a variety of agents—activists, thinkers, diplomats, planners, and political leaders—as they have navigated the political, economic, technological, and great-power revolutions of their times. Four ongoing transformations have been most important in shaping the terms on which liberal internationalism was brought into the modern world: the rise and evolution of liberal democracy, the transition from a world of empire to a world of nation-states, the intensification of economic and security interdependence, and the rise and decline of British and American hegemony. These great transformations have provided the setting—the shifting geopolitical landscape and modernizing circumstances—within which individuals and groups have defined and pursued the liberal international project.

—Liberal internationalism emerged in the nineteenth century as a family of internationalisms. In the West, internationalism and nationalism emerged together as historical Siamese twins. Not all internationalism was liberal, and we can identify imperial and Westphalian varieties as well as more liberal forms of internationalism—trade, law, arbitration, and the peace movement—that came together to form the modern liberal international tradition. Seen in this way, Wilson-era liberal internationalism was not the "beginning" of the tradition, but the culmination and consolidation of a long nineteenth-century ascendancy. By looking at liberal internationalism as a composite of several strands—some classical and laissez-faire, others more progressive and social democratic—we can see how they have combined, recombined, and come apart over the past two centuries. For example, we can see how neoliberalism emerged in the 1990s and separated itself from earlier postwar strands.

—Liberal internationalism has been deeply connected to progressive political movements. Its greatest moments have come when its international agenda was defined in ways that strengthened the ability of national governments to carry out

9

progressive socioeconomic goals. In these instances, the building of international rules, institutions, and partnerships has been designed to strengthen—not undermine—the capacities of national governments. The Bretton Woods institutions of the post-1945 era can be understood in this way: they created policy instruments with which governments could stabilize and manage their economies. As modern liberal democracies have grown in their social purposes, complexity, and connectivity, the "functionality" of the international order has taken on increasing importance. To accomplish their goals at home, liberal democracies and other states have found themselves wanting a congenial international environment within which to operate.

—Between the late 1930s and late 1940s, a grand shift occurred in liberal internationalist ideas. The Great Depression, the rise of fascism and totalitarianism, World War II, and the geopolitical and ideological struggles of the Cold War reshaped the ambitions of the liberal project. It came to embrace New Deal notions of economic security as well as Cold War notions of national security. Out of the ravages of the 1930s and 1940s, liberals increasingly saw modernity as empowering both liberal and illiberal states—and generating an ever more complex set of dangers and opportunities. The racial, religious, and civilizational hierarchies and discriminations contained in earlier notions of internationalism did not disappear, but they lost legitimacy. Liberal internationalism acquired a more expansive and progressive agenda, incorporating more universal notions of rights and protections and tied more closely to the solidarity of the Western democratic world. A distinctive type of international order—liberal hegemony— emerged within the bipolar Cold War system.

Finally, I turn to the contemporary crisis of liberal internationalism—how the seeming triumph of the liberal international project after the Cold War came undone and how it might be put back together. Here the question is: On what intellectual and political foundation can liberal internationalism build its endeavors?

—The seeds of the current crisis were planted at the moment of apparent triumph. The collapse of the great ideological and geopolitical challenge to American-led liberal internationalism seemed to open up a new golden era. The Western liberal order had existed inside the bipolar Cold War system, but now this inside order became the outside order. Countries everywhere in the world made economic and political transitions in order to integrate into this expanding system. But the globalization of the liberal order was not really successful, and its failures have undermined that order's governance foundations and eroded its legitimacy and social purpose. The Western liberal order was fundamentally a security community, but in its global configuration it has become widely seen as a framework for facilitating capitalist transactions. The progressive nationalist underpinnings of liberal internationalism have eroded.

—The liberal international project needs to be reimagined. It will have to acknowledge its limits and failures as well as its accomplishments. It will have to rewrite its own narrative—making it less triumphant and universal in its reach and appeal and more pragmatic in its vision. It will have to return to its roots—as a project to create a container within which liberal democracies can safely exist. Liberal internationalism has been most successful when it has supported and protected liberal democracy at home. It needs to find new ways to do this again. It will need to see itself less as a Whiggish theory of world-historical progress and more as a time-tested approach to coping with the problems and opportunities of modernity. In doing this, the liberal international project will need to focus in particular on the problems of mutual vulnerability and shared dangers that emerge along with rising economic and security interdependence. This is a bleaker face of liberalism: a liberalism of danger and insecurity. But for two centuries, this face of liberalism has always lurked within liberal internationalist thinking and action. The ultimate defense of liberal internationalism is that it is the only viable response to the collective dangers of the twenty-first century.

Liberal internationalism has its wellsprings in liberal democracy. Over the past two hundred years, the efforts of liberal democracies to cooperate and build order have been driven by shared values and common interests. But there is a deeper, almost existential motive that has led liberal democracies to make common cause: the mutual vulnerability that emerges from modernity itself. Woodrow Wilson may have had this in mind when he argued that the League of Nations was needed "if civilization is to escape the typhoon."[16] The architects of the post-1945 Western order may likewise have had it in mind when they proposed permanent multilateral institutions to manage the world's economic and security relations. Liberal internationalism, as a project for organizing and reforming international relations, is uniquely able to respond to the perils and opportunities of rising economic and security interdependence. This claim, as this book will develop, generates some confidence that liberal internationalism's days are not yet over. But it must present a more cautious vision, less enamored of a global march to some inevitable liberal democratic future and more focused on the necessity of building collective capacities and institutions to protect modern societies from themselves, from each other, and from the violent storms of modernity.

What Is Liberal Internationalism?

Liberal internationalism is one of the grand traditions in international relations. It is a family of ideas, theories, agendas, and orientations that seek to explain basic patterns and characteristics of how nations interact. It is a "tradition" in the sense that it has founding thinkers, classic texts, and a complex lineage of theories and debates that have been passed down and updated since the early modern era.[17] It is a tradition whose core ideas remain contested even as they evolve over the decades and centuries. Liberal internationalism comes with sweeping narratives. It identifies problems and dynamics that reappear across time and space. It is both a scholarly tradition, with theories, hypotheses, and empirical tests, and a set of political ideas and agendas—an ideology—used by actors in the real world.[18] It is a political project: among practitioners, there is a sense of inheritance, lineage, and genealogy, a shared belief in liberal internationalism as an ongoing intellectual and political enterprise.[19] In all these ways, liberal internationalism is a map, a compass, and a flag that scholars and political actors use both to explain international relations and to engage in political action.

Liberal internationalism arose in the eighteenth and early nineteenth centuries along with Western liberal democracy.[20] In Europe and North America, absolutist and monarchical states were yielding to mixed parliamentary regimes with early markings of constitutional democracy and republican rule. The American founding and the French Revolution were dramatic launching points of the liberal democratic age, as was Britain's evolving parliamentary system. Through the nineteenth century, Western liberal democracies slowly grew more numerous and more formidable. The result is what has been called the "liberal ascendancy." As Daniel Deudney writes: "For most of history, republics were confined to small city-states where they were insecure and vulnerable to conquest and internal usurpation, but over the last two centuries they have expanded to continental size through federal union and emerged victorious from the violent total conflicts of the twentieth century."[21] Liberal internationalism emerged from the ascendancy of Western liberal democracies as they made repeated efforts to build and organize Western and, later, global order.

Liberal internationalism thus offers a vision of order in which sovereign states—led by liberal democracies—cooperate for mutual gain and protection within a loosely rules-based international space. The threads of this vision can be traced from the eighteenth century to the present. Open trade, international law, multilateral cooperation, collective security, political rights and protections, and democratic solidarity are some of the elements of the liberal internationalist vision—or more precisely, the multiple visions that have appeared and been reworked over the past two centuries. Liberal

internationalism is not a fixed doctrine but a family of evolving—and often conflicting—ideas, doctrines, projects, and movements.[22]

Often, liberal internationalism is defined in contrast to its great theoretical rival, political realism. The two traditions offer alternative ways of framing the core problem of international relations.[23] For realists, the core issue of international relations is the problem of anarchy. The defining feature of international politics is the structural predicament that states find themselves in: a decentralized world without a central government to establish order. States cooperate, compete, and struggle for survival under conditions of anarchy. The great dramas of world politics—power balancing, security competition, hegemonic war, imperial rivalry—occur endlessly across the ancient and modern eras because of this deep unchanging reality. Anarchy and the inability of any state to be completely confident of any other state's intentions explain the limits and constraints on cooperation between states.[24]

Realists differ among themselves on the sources of international order. Some see it as the conscious or unconscious outcome of the balance of power among leading states, and others think it is created through the domination of a hegemonic state.[25] In both instances, international order is shaped by states' material capabilities—which are the ultimate source and arbiter of order. International order does not come from understanding and agreement, either tacit or expressed. It is a property that emerges from the power relations among states. Of course, realism is a rich and sprawling tradition, and realist thinkers disagree among themselves on the extent to which the conditions of anarchy control the shaping of international relations. Nonetheless, in the grand realist narratives, the defining moments of world politics—war and peace and the rise and fall of order—are played out in the shadow of anarchy. History moves in cycles, international order comes and goes, and progress is fleeting.[26]

While liberal internationalism also addresses the problem of anarchy, its greater preoccupation is with the problem of modernity. Modernity is understood broadly as the set of deep, worldwide transformations in domestic and international society unleashed by the forces of science, technology, and industrialism. It is, as Ernest Gellner puts it, a "tidal wave" that pushes and pulls societies in a common modernizing direction.[27] Beginning in the eighteenth century, Western societies were propelled forward by interconnected and unfolding developments: scientific and technological advancement, the industrial revolution, the rise of capitalist society, and the emergence of rational-bureaucratic states.[28] Several characteristics distinguish this world from the premodern world. First, societies are understood to be moving in stages and phases along developmental pathways. Traditional societies give way to modern ones that continue to grow, evolve, and advance. Liberal democracy, born in this modern age, has also pushed modernity forward. Second, modernity is a global phenomenon, pushing and pulling societies into a single, increasingly interconnected and interdependent world system. Third, modernity is not experienced evenly across the world—there are vanguards and laggards, creating new forms of hierarchy and domination. The unevenness of modernity's development led to the West's domination of the world in the nineteenth and twentieth centuries. But the world's motion has not stopped, and every society is modernizing in its own way. Hierarchies and formations of power are not static. International relations take place within this open-ended, unfolding world-historical process. Modernity both empowers states and makes them vulnerable.[29]

With these ideas as their starting point, liberal internationalists have debated a range of views about the character and implications of modernity. In some eras, they have argued that modernity tends to stack the deck in favor of liberal democracy. At least over the long term, the forces of modernity bias political development in this direction. This vision has waxed and waned over the past two centuries. The optimistic view of modernity held by Europeans during the belle epoque was radically different from the views held by their grandchildren as they surveyed the rubble of World War II. The most enduring view—embraced in the middle decades of the twentieth century and by many liberal internationalists today—is that modernity is a Jekyll-and-Hyde phenomenon that brings both extraordinary dangers and great opportunities. There is much to gain and much to lose.

This distinction between realism's focus on the problems of anarchy and liberalism's focus on the problems of modernity is not absolute. Leading mid-twentieth-century realists, such as E. H. Carr and Hans Morgenthau, saw anarchy and the struggle for power as the defining problem of interstate relations, but their arguments were full of insights about the ways in which modernity and industrial society were reshaping the character of states and power politics. Both Carr and Morgenthau appreciated the transformations wrought by the modernizing world. For Morgenthau, modernity's most important change was its impact on human nature and morality. For Carr, it was the crisis generated by the breakdown of laissez-faire capitalism, parliamentary democracy, and national self-determination as well as by humanity's increasing capacity for interstate violence.[30] By the same token, liberal internationalists acknowledge the dangers and insecurities that flow from anarchy. It was G. Lowes Dickinson, an early twentieth-century liberal internationalist, who coined the term *anarchy* and argued that the Great War resulted from an international structure of heavily armed, independent states operating "under the conditions of international anarchy."[31] But for liberal internationalists, it is the deeper forces of modernity that shape and reshape the character of states and the terms of economic and security interdependence. The character and consequences of anarchy are not immutable.[32] States—particularly liberal democracies—are able to use diplomacy and institutions to alter the way they define and pursue their interests.

Realists and liberal internationalists differ in their views on the underlying conditions within which international relations operate as well as on the sources of international order. For realists, international order is an emergent property: a manifestation of anarchy and the distribution of power. For balance-of-power realists, it is a dynamic equilibrium that results from the competitive checking of power. For hegemonic realists, it is the structure of relations shaped by the dominant state. For both balance-of-power realists and hegemonic realists, order embodies and reflects the realities of power. Liberal internationalists, by contrast, tend to see order as a constructed outcome that is shaped by organizational structures and agreements. To be sure, liberals differ on how far states can go to shape the setting in which international relations take place. But for liberal internationalists, international order has the characteristics of a contract. It is a product of human intent that reflects the efforts of states to construct the rules and institutions by which they will engage with each other.[33] Agreements, bargains, and institutions are the tools of liberal statecraft that allow states to shape the environment in which they cooperate and compete. The theory is normative: while liberal internationalists understand that a world ruled entirely by power is certainly possible, they argue that an international order governed by rules and institutions makes the world a better, more humane place—and safer for liberal democracy.

The task for liberal democracies, therefore, is to engage in "order building"—to work together to create rules and institutions across the international system to realize modernity's gains and guard against its dangers. Sovereign nation-states provide the foundation for the liberal internationalist agenda: the creation and development of a worldwide system of intergovernmental cooperation. The varieties of internationalism that they champion are possible only with at least a core of sovereign nation-states. In reconciling sovereignty and interdependence, liberal internationalists seek to preserve and strengthen their national systems of liberal democracy. Their orienting impulse is to organize international relations in ways that advance the security and well-being of liberal democratic societies. Given that the world is constantly modernizing, liberal internationalism can never be "finished." Opportunities and dangers are always emerging. This sense of liberal internationalism as an ongoing project is reinforced by its roots in late nineteenth-century reform liberalism and the twentieth-century American progressive tradition. Modernity constantly throws up new challenges, and the project of liberal internationalism is thus the permanent activity of internationally organized problem solving.

What the best liberal international order is and what it should accomplish are unsettled questions to which different groups of people have offered a wide range of answers.[34] But as I elaborate in chapter 2, throughout the nineteenth and twentieth centuries, a consistent set of ideas and convictions has emerged about how to organize international space.

—International openness. Trade and exchange are sources of mutual gains and stable peace. To varying degrees, in a liberal international order, states open their economies and societies to each other. The terms of openness can be managed and underpinned by principles and norms such as nondiscrimination and multilateral dispute settlement.

—Multilateralism and rules-based relations. International rules and institutions guide the ways states conduct their affairs, and they are integral to creating an international space in which liberal democracies can operate. Embedding interstate relations in a system of multilateral rules and institutions facilitates cooperation and gives the resulting order a measure of legitimacy.

—Democratic solidarity and cooperative security. Liberal democratic states may or may not tie themselves together in formal alliances, but they affiliate with each other in various ways to increase their security. Their shared values reinforce trust and solidarity and increase their ability and inclination to work together to generate security.

—Progressive social purposes. Liberal international order is expected to move its inhabitants and their societies—and the international order itself—in a progressive direction. Liberal internationalists tend to promote reform-driven advancements in the well-being of citizens, measured in terms of rights and protections associated with welfare, security, and social justice. The liberal international order is not static. Societies that are part of this order are constantly developing, advancing, and backsliding.

With these characteristics, liberal internationalism can be seen as a form of international order that can be manifest in various ways. Nonliberal international orders—those that are closed and not rules-based—might take various forms, including geopolitical blocs, spheres of influence, mercantilist zones, or imperial orders.[35] Liberal international order has successfully coexisted with other systems, and there is a lively debate about whether liberal internationalism, organized within the liberal democratic world, leads to and depends on imperialism and empire elsewhere. Does liberal order have illiberal foundations?

The idea of a "liberal" international order carries two meanings. In the first, the international order is liberal in that it has liberal characteristics—

openness, the rule of law, and principles of reciprocity and nondiscrimination. But the order may also be liberal in the sense that it is built around cooperation among liberal democracies, and the specific aspects of that cooperation may or may not be "liberal." The American-led postwar international order has been built on a system of bilateral and multilateral alliances, and this cooperative security does not itself have liberal properties. It is liberal only in the sense that it is an alliance of liberal democracies. Liberal international order may also be based on hierarchical relationships that cut against liberal norms of sovereign equality and rules-based relations. And liberal democracies may act in decidedly "illiberal" ways outside the boundaries of the liberal order, intervening in and dominating societies on their periphery. In all these ways, the entanglements between liberal and illiberal forms of order are inescapable, complex, and shifting.

Finally, the social purposes embedded in liberal international order have varied over time. In the nineteenth century and at various moments in the twentieth century, the vision of liberal internationalism was limited to building an open system that protected property rights and facilitated transactions and functional cooperation. Other eras have been more ambitious, in seeking to build a cooperative order that provided far-reaching social and economic rights and protections.[36] At no time were the debates about the social purposes of liberal internationalism considered settled. Liberal internationalism has been seen as a vehicle for realizing the great economic and social gains latent in a modernizing world, and as a desperate, last-chance bulwark against an impending global calamity. Liberal internationalism has differed in its vision of how universal it can be as an order. It has been conceived as a political formation variously encompassing Europe, the Atlantic Alliance, the West, the free world, and the world.

Contested Narratives and Grand Debates

Liberal internationalism embodies a contested set of ideas and agendas— contested from outside by rival ideologies and political projects, and from within the liberal tradition itself. Debates among liberal internationalists are inherent to the tradition. Liberalism itself has been understood and defined in so many ways that it is essentially impossible to identify and agree upon a fixed core. For two centuries it has lived a protean and contested life. For some, it is the Lockean idea of individual rights and limited government; for others, it is the doctrine of the modern welfare state. Liberalism means different things to Europeans and Americans and to the nineteenth and twentieth centuries. Some see it as an Anglo-American project, while others emphasize French and German thinkers writing in the wake of the French Revolution.[37] In the early decades of the nineteenth century, European and American thinkers tried to conjure "liberal principles" of politics—rule of law, civil equality, constitutionalism, and freedom of press and religion—that navigated the revolutionary and reactionary forces that the French Revolution unleashed. In the late nineteenth century, liberalism found itself competing with other grand ideologies such as socialism and conservatism. Only in the twentieth century, particularly as the United States rose to power after the world wars, did liberalism become a uniquely American creed of individualism and political rights. As Helena Rosenblatt argues, the term has been "Christianized, democratized, socialized, and politicized" on the way to taking on its multiple modern meanings.[38]

Liberal internationalism is equally contested and conceptually unstable. It is woven, for example, into late Victorian ideas about trade, civilization, race, empire, and religion, as well as mid- and late twentieth-century ideas about global governance and universal human rights.[39] Liberal internationalist thinking has both justified Western empire and imperialism and inspired opposition to it. It has been associated with ideologies of racial and cultural hierarchy and with universal principles of equality and the rule of law. Liberal internationalist thinking is infused with mutually contradictory theories about trade, democracy, institutions, society, and progress. As noted earlier, it is not one thing but consists of many evolving threads of thought and action that combine, fray, and recombine as the larger body of liberal thought and experience itself evolves. Because the character of liberal democracy and the problems and opportunities of modernity are continuously shifting, there are few settled questions within the liberal internationalist tradition. The conflicting values at its heart—liberty and equality, openness and social stability, sovereignty and interdependence—are an open-ended invitation to debate.

Outside the liberal tradition, two schools of thought have offered particularly searching critiques of liberal internationalism: political realism and the revisionist left. Both are long-standing traditions of thought and action, bringing to the debate their own clusters of theories, narratives, programs, and internal disagreements. Within the realist tradition, the most famous critique of liberal internationalism remains one of the first—E. H. Carr's classic account of the failure of the Versailles settlement. For Carr, who was a member of the British delegation at the Paris Peace Conference, Woodrow Wilson's liberal internationalism was a utopian project built on illusions. "After the first world war," Carr writes, "the liberal tradition was carried into international politics. Utopian writers from the English-speaking countries seriously believed that the establishment of the League of Nations meant the elimination of power from international relations, and the substitution of discussion for armies and navies."[40] Sooner or later, liberal internationalism falters before the stubborn and brutal realities of power politics.

Over the past century, realists have offered two major lines of critique. One is the Carr argument that the project of liberal internationalism will always fail because of the anarchic realities of world politics. Liberal internationalism will always be in crisis, institutions will be weak, and cooperation will be problematic. For realists, the competitive system of states is not a stable foundation for the political superstructure liberal internationalism seeks to build. At best, liberal international order might be a momentary outcome of the balance of power or of hegemonic forces. In this telling, the post-1945 Western liberal order is an outgrowth of Cold War bipolarity and American hegemony that will give way as American power declines.[41]

The other realist critique centers on the claim that liberalism, as an ideology and regime type, is inherently expansionist and self-destructive. As John Mearsheimer asserts, liberalism harbors a deep universalist impulse to remake the world in its image, and this leads liberal states—particularly powerful ones—to pursue interventionist policies. "The principal source of the problem," Mearsheimer argues, "is that liberalism has an activist mentality woven into its core. The belief that all humans have a set of inalienable rights, and that protecting these rights should override other concerns, creates a powerful incentive for liberal states to intervene."[42] Incapable of exercising restraint, liberal states—starting with the United States—undermine their own liberal principles abroad and are unable to maintain a stable global order based on the balance of power.[43]

Revisionist critiques of liberal internationalism see a failure of social justice. Deep and growing inequalities, corruptions, and iniquities embedded in liberal societies and the global capitalist system render the liberal internationalist project politically untenable and morally suspect.[44] This critique is rooted in the claim that liberal internationalism is deeply tied up with empire. Underneath the talk of openness and global rules and institutions are the deeper realities of Western power and imperial forms of order. The "progressive" orientation of liberal internationalism hides the fact that it offers a very modest vision of social justice that is careful not to disturb the global status quo. Samuel Moyn argues that liberal internationalism is a project for securing America's hegemonic dominance, which currently means trying to "figure out how to encode its values on the world order before the arrival of . . . the post-American era."[45] In the twentieth century, Mark Mazower argues, the iconic institutions of liberal internationalism—the League of Nations and the United Nations—were tools for reconstructing and legitimating European empire. The United Nations did eventually become a site for the decolonization movement, but this has "tended to obscure the awkward fact that like the League it was a product of empire and indeed, at least at the outset, regarded by those with colonies to keep as a more than adequate mechanism for its defense."[46] In the postwar period, liberal internationalism flourished only to the extent that it could be made to serve American hegemony by providing a platform for a new type of informal empire—call it "liberal imperialism." In short, liberal internationalism has provided the ideas and institutions for Europeans and Americans to project power, protect their interests, and legitimate their dominance.

Critiques of this sort differ in their bottom line. Some critics argue for a radical rethinking of world order based on new organizing principles. The norms and institutions of the Westphalian system need to be reconfigured to facilitate the global redistribution of power, wealth, and authority, a project for reordering the world based on egalitarian principles and cosmopolitan solidarities. Liberal internationalists gesture in the right direction—toward principles of justice, equality, and rights—but their programs are simply too modest.[47] For these critics, liberal internationalists lack the courage of their convictions. They advance lofty ideals but fail to embrace the far-reaching transformations in global structures of power and privilege that would be needed to fully realize human rights and global economic fairness. Others see more promise in reform. The problem is not in liberal internationalism's agenda, but in its corruption by powerful states, class interests, and privileged elites.[48] Here the task is to rebuild and expand political coalitions within and between states to push the liberal project forward.

Although realist and revisionist critics differ in their theories, they are often aligned in their politics. For both schools, liberal internationalism is deeply implicated in what they see as the American pursuit of global dominance, manifest as a US-centered world organized around liberal hegemony and military interventionism.[49] Both schools argue that reform must begin with a pullback or retrenchment of America's far-flung security commitments and military operations. For realists, American retrenchment will set the stage for a return to a multipolar order that is regulated by the balance of power. Revisionists, on the other hand, see an American pullback as a first step toward a more domestic-oriented focus on improving American society or toward a new foreign policy directed at building a more inclusive and socially just global order. In each case, American hegemony and liberal internationalism stand in the way.

For both realists and revisionist critics, liberal internationalism fails because it rests on deeper and precarious foundations—anarchy among states, market capitalism, hegemonic power, empire and imperialism—that ultimately undermine and distort it. In the chapters that follow, I both concede and dispute this claim. We confront a paradox. On the one hand, liberal internationalism offers a remarkably capacious vision of order and change in the modern world. Its intellectual horizons are vast. It makes sweeping claims about the developmental logic of modern society and international order. But on the other hand, as a political project it is remarkably thin and limited. It is not a self-contained political movement. The world will never march only to liberal internationalism's beat. It is a flag without an army. For better or worse, the liberal project needs partners. It needs to tie itself to great powers, capitalist systems, and hegemonic projects. This is both its strength and weakness.

Realist and revisionists both attack the failings of liberal internationalism— its impulse toward intervention and empire and its weak regard for social justice. Ultimately, however, the problem with this critique is that it attacks its own foundations. It makes sense only within a system of values defined by the liberal ideas of self-determination, individual rights, and the rule of law.

Liberal internationalism emerged during the heyday of European empire and it intertwined with the imperial agendas of Western states. But it became the dominant model for international order in the twentieth century precisely because its vision of intergovernmental cooperation offered an alternative to empire. This becomes clear when we consider why the United States and other liberal democratic states found it useful to invest in the construction of a liberal international order. Even Mazower acknowledges this puzzle. "Most Great Powers in history have not, of course, felt the need for anything like the League or the UN. . . . What really demands explanation is why first the British, at the height of their world power, and then the Americans should have invested time and political capital in building up international institutions at all."[50] Yet Mazower is no more able than other realist and revisionist critics to explain this discontinuity.

Liberal internationalism has moralist tendencies and activist impulses, but it is ultimately a reform-oriented and pragmatic endeavor. Modern liberals do not embrace democratic governments, market-based economic systems, and international institutions out of idealism or as tools of empire but as arrangements better suited to realizing human interests than the alternatives. Liberal internationalists hold that world politics requires institutional cooperation and political integration in response to relentlessly rising economic and security interdependence. Liberal internationalists across the past two centuries have considered a global architecture of rules and institutions necessary to protect liberal democracy and realize basic human interests. They have not always kept the best company, and their history is tainted by colonialism, imperialism, slavery, racism, and sexism. Yet liberals have also led the efforts to end these practices. If the long arc of history bends toward justice, it does so thanks to the activism and moral commitment of liberals and their allies.

TWO

Liberal Democracy and
International Relations

L iberal internationalism has been shaped and reshaped by the liberal ascendency. In the late eighteenth century, the American and French revolutions signaled the dramatic but precarious emergence of polities based on popular sovereignty and representative government. By 1835, Alexis de Tocqueville could write that "a great democratic revolution is going on among us." Most of the world was ruled by monarchs, autocrats, and imperial states, but over the next two centuries, liberal democracies moved from a position of weakness and vulnerability to global preeminence through eras of war and upheaval. The spread of liberal democracy came in waves, propelled by the collapse of empires and movements for self-determination. The leading liberal democracies—Great Britain in the nineteenth century and the United States in the twentieth century—established their leadership and built order in part by fostering close relations with other liberal democracies. The liberal democratic world experienced its most perilous moment during the 1930s and World War II, causing Arthur Schlesinger Jr. to observe years later, "Democracy has survived the twentieth century by the skin of its teeth."[1] Yet by the end of the twentieth century, democratic states—old and new, Western and non-Western, advanced and developing—found themselves at the center of the global system. This liberal ascendancy is one of the most consequential transformations of our time.

The great debates about world politics in the modern age hinge on questions about this liberal ascendancy's causes, character, and impacts. Why did

Western liberal democracies emerge and grow powerful across two centuries of great-power wars, economic upheavals, and struggles with rival types of states? What did liberal democracies seek to accomplish in the great struggles over international order? What ideas played out over the long arc of the liberal ascendancy? And looking back at these centuries, what was their impact on world order? What, for better or worse, have the liberal democracies wrought?

As they spread and grew powerful, liberal states set the goals of the order they wished to build: it would create tools and capacities for governments to manage sovereignty and interdependence, foster cooperation among states to realize mutual gains, and secure political rights and social protections for their societies. Along the way, liberal internationalist ideas and agendas affiliated and aligned themselves with the other great forces and movements—nationalism, empire, capitalism, great-power politics, and Anglo-American hegemony. Liberal internationalism was also shaped and reshaped by its encounters with fascism and totalitarianism, by the Cold War, and by the nuclear revolution. The powerful liberal states that pushed it into the world, led by Great Britain and the United States, were not simply "liberal" hegemonic states but also great powers, capitalist states, and Western societies. Great Britain ran the world's largest empire. Liberal internationalism is deeply intermingled with these many revolutions, transformations, and identities.

This chapter explores the core ideas, projects, and political foundations of liberal internationalism. I begin by identifying its intellectual starting points rooted in the discovery of modernity and liberal Enlightenment thinking, which shaped its ideas and projects across two centuries. These origins are reflected in liberal international assumptions and convictions: in the way liberal internationalists think about the possibilities of cooperation in international relations; in their conviction that the political conditions of peoples and societies can be improved through the pursuit of enlightened self-interest; and in their belief that institutions and political orders can be devised to protect and advance the liberal democratic way of life. Most important, these origins shape the way liberals frame the basic orientation of international relations—as coping with the problems of modernity. Liberal internationalists do not agree on all the causes and consequences of modernity—there are optimists and pessimists, and views have shifted across the centuries. But, broadly speaking, they all agree that the engines of modernity—science, technology, industry, and associated forces—shape and reshape societies, creating both dangers and opportunities. Liberal internationalism is the ongoing response of liberal democracies to this world-historical predicament.

Second, I identify the core ideas of liberal international order: trade and openness; multilateral rules and institutions; liberal democratic solidarity; cooperative security; and progressive change. From these orientations, it is possible to see the distinctive ways that liberal democracies have sought to shape and act within the international order. Rights, protections, rules, and openness are key elements of the distinctive liberal orientation toward international relations. Interdependence between modern societies is an inescapable—and growing—reality that requires cooperation if it is to be managed. Rules and institutions provide the bulwark for order among liberal democracies. Political solidarity among liberal democracies is a reflection of their shared values, interests, and vulnerabilities. From these starting points, the liberal international order has been manifested in various ways. Liberal internationalism represents a family of ideas and activities marked by intellectual and political inconsistencies, dilemmas, and debates. Indeed, the "project" of liberal internationalism is in part an ongoing debate about its own ends and means.

Finally, I identify the four key forces and movements in the modern era that have shaped and reshaped liberal international ideas and projects: the rise and spread of liberal democracy, the shift from a world of empires to a world of nation-states, cascades of economic and security interdependence, and the rise and decline of British and American hegemony. Each of these movements has provided dangers, dilemmas, and opportunities that have shaped the logic and character of liberal internationalism.

Modernity and the Origins of Liberal Internationalism

The late eighteenth and early nineteenth centuries saw the emergence in the West of a new way of looking at the world. The industrial revolution and its attendant social transformations were overturning old systems of economics, authority, and rule. New assumptions and understandings about the world were emerging from the discourses of the Enlightenment and the rise of the sciences. Something called *modern society* was coming into being and replacing feudal and ancient social structures with new ones. Thinkers of this era—Montesquieu, Smith, Condorcet, Hume, Kant, and others—were convinced that these transformations had a developmental logic that could be discovered and understood. With the Enlightenment came the "discovery" of modernity.

Liberal internationalism is rooted in this Enlightenment notion of modernity. The world is in motion. It is experiencing a global modernizing movement that humans can understand and help direct. "It is not Fortune who governs the world," Montesquieu wrote in 1734. "There are general causes, moral or physical . . . all that occurs is subject to these causes."[2] Modernity is being driven by industry, commerce, science, technology, and evolving social and political institutions. It is a double move: *outward*, toward greater interdependence, and *upward*, along a common modernizing pathway. Societies are increasingly part of a global order, their development and progress driven by deep forces of change, and they are all moving forward toward a common future. In 1830, the English poet Tennyson rode on the first train from Liverpool to Manchester, and thinking that the train's wheels ran in grooves, wrote: "Let the great world spin for ever down the ringing grooves of change."

At the core of the idea of modernity was a vision of the world as a single, evolving system. Modern society may appear in some places before it appears in others, and there may be vanguards and laggards, but the structures and setting of modernity have a universal logic. Whether on the top or the bottom, all societies struggle with the problems of modernity. As Bjorn Wittrock argues, "we may look upon modernity as an age when certain structuring principles have come to define a common global condition."[3] The nineteenth century embraced this sort of grand narrative of the world. To think of the world as a modernizing whole, Anthony Giddens argues, entailed the creation of an "overarching 'story line' by means of which we are placed in history as beings having a definite past and a predictable future."[4] This understanding that the world was embarked on a great modernizing movement became an integral part of the liberal internationalist vision.

This emerging vision can be found in the works of Kant, Smith, Bentham, and many others. In an essay written in 1784, Kant tried to define the Enlightenment. "If someone asks are we living in an enlightened age today? The answer would be, No." But, he continued, "we are living in an Age of Enlightenment." He seems to be saying that the Enlightenment is a frame of mind—a human capacity and ongoing endeavor—rather than a realized condition. He understood himself to be living in a time when humans had acquired the ideas and tools to remake their world. Kant anticipated a cosmopolitan global age in which states would give up some freedoms, bind themselves together with public law, and establish a peaceful international order that would eventually encompass the world. Rule of law among states was the essential ingredient. Kant saw European history as "a regular procession of improvements in constitutional government" that began with the Greeks and "will probably give laws to all other states eventually." The progress toward rule-based relations among states, he wrote, was "discernible only in its broadest outline, a feeling for it is rising in all member states." Yet he believed that "when one takes into account the general premise that the world is constituted as a system and considers what little has been observed one can say that the indications are sufficiently reliable to enable us to conclude that such a revolution is real."[5]

Adam Smith offered a sweeping political-economic vision of a modernizing world order driven by an expansive capitalist logic of trade, specialization, and interdependence. It was an easy step for Smith to see the world as a single system, with laws and logics that were pushing and pulling states and peoples toward continuous advancement and expanding political community. In *The Wealth of Nations*, he provided an account of the economic progress of humanity by identifying phases or stages in the historical evolution of society.[6] Behind Smith's theory of trade and commercial society was a more general understanding of humans as social and moral beings. The pursuit of self-interest was driven less by greed than by the "moral sentiments" that draw individuals together to bargain, exchange, and build community.[7] Jeremy Bentham, who shared Smith's enthusiasm for free trade, articulated more elaborate political notions of a functioning global order. In his view, the most advanced nations of the world already constituted "one society" or "family of nations." He captured this vision of a modernizing world in the opening lines of his *Fragment on Government*, written in 1776: "Ours is a busy age in which knowledge is rapidly advancing towards perfection. In the natural world, in particular, every thing teems with discovery and with improvement. The most distant and recondite regions of the earth traversed and explored . . . are striking evidences, were all others wanting, of this pleasing truth."[8] Enlightened states and enlightened self-interest were essential assumptions for these thinkers. They did not see the world moving toward some sort of "world government" but toward a more complex and decentralized system—a society of states sustained by the rule of law.[9] Out of this mix of ideas emerged the modern notion of international order.

These early internationalists shared a deep conviction that humans are capable of rational and enlightened pursuit of their interests and that modern societies can build institutions that variously empower, encourage, restrain, and orient human activities.[10] It is not that humans as a species are becoming more intrinsically moral, enlightened, or cooperative. It is that they are capable of gaining a better understanding of their circumstances and placing themselves in institutional settings that bias their actions in desired directions. This liberal modernist sensibility, as John Robertson argues, was rooted in "the commitment to understanding, and hence advancing, the causes and conditions of human betterment in the world."[11] Modernity is thus seen as both a deep structural force and a product of human agency and purposive action. "Men make their own history," Karl Marx wrote, "but they do not make it as they please." For liberal Enlightenment thinkers, this observation translates into the pragmatic conviction that, in modernity, societies face deep and disruptive forces of change, but they have the capacity to shape and advance their collective well-being. Modern societies, they believed, will move—slowly perhaps, and certainly in fits and starts—in a direction that reflects the liberal ideals of limited government, religious toleration, freedom of expression and commerce, and the rule of law.[12]

Some Enlightenment thinkers embedded their vision in first principles— God, nature, or reason. Locke's liberalism was grounded in natural law, and

Kant's notion of moral obligation was grounded in the rational requirements of human dignity. There were grand anticipations by some Enlightenment thinkers that history was moving inexorably in a progressive direction. They shared a belief in something called *progress*, which was rooted in unfolding forces of reason and human nature. But there was also a pragmatic side to the liberal modernist imagination. What Dennis Rasmussen calls the "pragmatic Enlightenment" can be seen in the ideas of people like Smith, Montesquieu, Hume, and Voltaire. These thinkers did not build their worldviews on abstract universalist ideas or the blind workings of reason and rationalism. They saw liberal modernity as a more modest and cautious movement forward and they emphasized context, reform, and the limits of human understanding.[13] Peter Gay, in his portrait of eighteenth-century Enlightenment thinkers—the philosophes—argues that they were not simply projecting an abstract vision or philosophy of history onto the world. Instead they took their ideas from "ordinary things." As Gay puts it, "they were not too fastidious to seek the laws of political economy, legal institutions, and human motivation" in the world around them.[14] They saw modernity as a grand drama but one that was manifest in the give and take of people struggling with the practical problems of modern society. Progress does not follow inevitably from the universal working out of reason, nature, or moral obligations. It emerges from organized and pragmatic efforts to bring reason and knowledge to the building and reform of human institutions.

The internationalist ideas of these Enlightenment thinkers reflected their efforts to grapple with the global-scale dimensions of modernity. International relations take place within this unfolding world-developmental process. The capabilities and characteristics of human societies and institutions are constantly changing as the world moves through phases and developmental passages. The dynamics of modernity are global phenomena, and the world as a whole thus has "system" characteristics. Despite the great disparities in the human condition across the world, societies are connected and are transforming as a global system. Liberal modernist thinkers disagree among themselves about how deterministic or even definable this worldwide process is. Some, like the 1950s-era Western modernization theorists and the post–Cold War "end of history" liberals, see all countries moving toward more representative and rule-based societies. Others do not see modernity pushing states toward a single destination but instead talk of different pathways and "multiple modernities."[15] They agree, however, that modernity is a continuous process, global in scope, which generates a stream of opportunities and dangers. In this modernizing world, the human condition can be improved through cooperation in the pursuit of enlightened interests.

Elements of Liberal International Order

Liberal internationalism took shape and evolved within this modernist intellectual setting. At its core, it offers a vision of an open, rules-based system in which states trade and cooperate to achieve mutual gains. Liberal internationalists believe that liberal democracies—and to some extent the wider world of peoples and states—have common interests in establishing a cooperative international order organized around principles of restraint, reciprocity, and sovereign equality. They assume that states—particularly liberal democracies—are able to overcome constraints and cooperate to solve security dilemmas, pursue collective action, and create economic and political stability. They also assume that powerful states—particularly liberal hegemonic states—have incentives to restrain their exercise of power and credibly convey commitments to other states. Liberal democracies are understood to have distinctive goals for international order as well as distinctive capacities to cooperate with other liberal states. Interdependence, a fundamental condition of modern society, calls forth liberal internationalist agendas for cooperation and prompts nations to create international institutions as tools for managing and reconciling sovereignty and interdependence. Liberal democracies cannot be secure or prosperous alone; they must create a larger world so as to survive and advance. On this basis, we can identify five sets of ideas that have shaped liberal visions of international order over the past two centuries.

① *Openness and Trade*

First there is the idea of openness. Trade and exchange are understood to be essential constituents of modern society and sources of stable growth and peace. In a liberal international order, states have access to each other's societies and economies. This is most explicit in the ideas of the free trade movement of the mid- and late nineteenth century, inaugurated by Britain's 1846 repeal of a set of trade restrictions known as the Corn Laws. The notions of "freedom of commerce" and "freedom of the seas" had emerged in early modern Europe, and ideas of free trade were later developed by Adam Smith, David Ricardo, and others. What openness means and how it would be organized in a rapidly modernizing world were widely debated, as they are today. But liberal internationalism has proceeded from a conviction that properly organized trade, investment, and exchange across borders generate mutual gains for those engaged in cross-border practices and more generalized benefits for the liberal democratic world. The idea of openness is, first of all, an economic argument about the mutual gains of trade, built on the logic of specialization and comparative advantage. But in a deeper sense, it is an idea about modernization and political development, which are understood to be advanced when societies are able to exchange knowledge, transfer technology, and work together. The alternatives to international openness are closed systems—regional blocs, spheres of influence, mercantilist zones, and imperial orders.[16]

The basic economic claims about openness can be traced back to the rise and spread of capitalism and commercial society. As Smith and generations of his followers argue, market systems have a deep logic that transforms political institutions and social relations. Commerce and industry gradually introduce "order and good government," Smith maintained, "and with them, the liberty and security of individuals, among the inhabitants of the country, who had before lived almost in a continual state of war with their neighbors and of servile dependency upon their superiors."[17] The impulse toward trade and specialization gives commercial societies an outward-looking orientation that is reinforced by the people within these societies—such as capitalists and skilled workers—who benefit from exchange. The advantages of trade and exchange create economic interdependence, which in turn creates constituencies that favor stable and continuous relations with other trading states.[18] Another argument of Smith focuses on the diffuse political effects of economic interdependence. As states become interdependent, they find themselves increasingly thinking about their relations in rational ways that give primacy to an assessment of costs and benefits. As Albert Hirschman famously put it, "passions" are replaced by "interests."[19] As countries become increasingly integrated into a complex worldwide economic system, they find it harder to pursue ideological goals that would disrupt the flow of benefits.

Rules and Institutions

The liberal international vision of order is at least loosely rules-based. The rules and principles of international order shape the ways states conduct their affairs, thereby fostering cooperation. This is what Jeremy Bentham had in mind when he introduced the term *international* in his *An Introduction to the Principles of Morals and Legislation.*[20] He argued that law within and between nations needed a new coherence and philosophical foundation to govern the "mutual transactions of sovereigns." The building of a system of rules and institutions has been driven by several different functional and political logics. The liberal democracies, industrializing within a wider global capitalist system, responded to their growing interdependence by creating rules and institutions to secure property rights, facilitate cooperation, and lay down the infrastructure for modern international order. International rules and institutions were seen to embody—more or less—a principled set of organizational arrangements around which sovereign states could operate.[21] In this sense, the rules and institutions—at least those that form the core of the order—are not simply reflections of the power and interests of particular states. This is what John Ruggie calls "multilateralism," an "architectural form" of international organization that coordinates relations among a group of states "on the basis of generalized principles of conduct."[22] The rules, and the principles they embody, have some impartiality and independent standing. They are not merely the exhortations of a powerful state but norms of conduct to which a group of states adhere, regardless of their specific power or circumstance.[23]

This vision has three aspects. First, rules and institutions are ubiquitous in the modern international system because they work. They facilitate cooperation among states, allowing them to enjoy the gains from trade and exchange that come from an open international order. As Robert Keohane argues, institutions—or regimes—are useful to states because they reduce transaction costs, overcome uncertainty, and establish channels for ongoing cooperation.[24] The greater the flow of trade and exchange among a group of states, the more useful it is to have established rules and institutions to manage interdependence. They address one of the core problems of international relations: how to manage the trade-off between sovereignty and interdependence. It is not just that rules and institutions facilitate greater levels of interdependence; they also help states regulate those flows to help themselves gain the benefits of interdependence while protecting against its downside.

Second, a "system" of multilateral rules and institutions has a wider and more diffuse attraction for states. Multilateralism, as a principle of organization, gives states a certain procedural and status legitimacy. As Ruggie argues, the rules and institutions in a multilateral system put relations among states on a principled basis. States are, in effect, equal before the law. This gives the resulting order a wider appeal and legitimacy. Rules and institutions have a normative value—a quality that should be appreciated most of all by liberal democratic polities that are themselves founded on a constitutional commitment to the rule of law. The normative value that liberal democracies attach to rules-based international relations is noted by John Rawls: "Altogether distinct from their self-concern for their security and the safety of their territory, this interest shows itself in a people's insisting on receiving from other peoples a proper respect and recognition of their equality. . . . It is, therefore, part of a people's being reasonable and rational that they are ready to offer to other peoples fair terms of political and social cooperation."[25]

Third, great powers that seek to establish hegemony over a region or the global system find rules and institutions useful for gaining the acquiescence and cooperation of weaker and secondary states. The leading state consents to operate within an agreed-upon set of multilateral rules and institutions and not to use the full measure of its power to coerce other states. Rules and institutions allow it to signal restraint and commitment to states that may fear its power. The leading state gives up some ability to get what it wants, but in return, it puts itself at the center of a more durable and legitimate order that gives it the long-term advantages of leadership.[26]

Liberal Democratic Solidarity

In the liberal vision, international order is undergirded by democratic solidarity. Over the past two centuries, liberal democracies have seen each other as part of a grouping of states whose interests are united by history, geography, and shared values. How this solidarity is manifest has varied. It can be seen in diplomatic groupings and in patterns of alignments in international conflict and cooperation. Liberal democracies might simply inhabit a "zone of peace" or cooperate in more far-reaching ways. This capacity of democracies to establish peaceful working relations among themselves was hinted at by Robert Lansing, Woodrow Wilson's secretary of state, during the Paris Peace Conference. Writing privately to a friend, Lansing argued: "The acceptance of the principle of democracy by all the chief powers of the world and the maintenance of genuine democratic governments would result in permanent peace. . . . If this view is correct, then the effort should be to make democracy universal. With that accomplished I do not care a rap whether there is a treaty to preserve the peace or not. I am willing to rely on the pacific spirit of democracies to accomplish the desirable relation between nations, and I do not believe that any League relying upon force or the menace of force can accomplish that purpose, at least for any length of time."[27] In the twentieth century, liberal democracies have formed deep and enduring security ties, embodied in formal alliances and other forms of cooperative security. The NATO alliance, the most successful example, is the most comprehensive and longest-lived security pact in modern history. The European Union offers yet another form of liberal democratic solidarity.[28]

The underlying claim is that, because of their common interests and shared values, liberal democracies find it easier to work with each other than with nondemocracies. They are more likely to trust each other and to see each other's interests and policies as legitimate. Liberal democracies have a level of transparency and shared experience with government that makes cooperation easier. In an elegant statement of this vision, Charles Lipson argues that what makes democracies special are their "contracting advantages."[29] Unlike autocratic states, democracies can make credible long-term agreements with other democracies, thereby overcoming the uncertainties and insecurities that breed conflict.[30] Lipson identifies some traits that give constitutional democracies this advantage: the openness to outside scrutiny, the continuity of regimes, the electoral incentives for leaders to keep promises, and the constitutional capacity to make enduring commitments. By stressing these deal-making advantages, Lipson is able to explain the broader trend toward institutionalized cooperative security and economic relations.[31]

From this starting point, liberal internationalists expect a variety of long-term outcomes. First, liberal democracies should be particularly capable of generating power and developing capacities to operate in the rules-based international system. This power advantage follows from their ability to work together as alliance partners—leveraging their individual power capacities. In the short term, autocratic and authoritarian states can often mobilize power more quickly than liberal democracies. But over the longer term, liberal democracies should have advantages over alternative regime types, including in the mobilization for war.[32] Second, liberal democracies as a group should be actively engaged with each other, pursuing various forms of economic and political cooperation. There is a "sociability," rooted in shared interests and common values, that unites the liberal democracies.[33] At any given moment, states in the international system are divided into a wide variety of groupings, alignments, and coalitions, but the divide between "democracies" and "non-democracies" remains one of the most prominent and enduring.[34] Third, the liberal international order that these states create will manifest advantages in economic growth, security, and other outcomes that derive from sustained cooperation. In effect, the liberal international order gives these states a wealth advantage that yields military and political power. In return, this should reinforce the liberal international order and make the states outside this order want to find ways to integrate into it.

Cooperative Security

There is also the related idea of cooperative security. Liberal democracies have cooperated for mutual economic gain, but they have also built ties in pursuit of mutual security protection. Across the nineteenth and twentieth centuries, liberal internationalists have offered ideas about cooperation among the liberal democracies to prevent war, deter threats, and build rules and institutions that advance peace and stability. Liberal democracies have a variety of motivations to engage in security cooperation. One is the Kantian motive—namely, that a "zone of peace" is needed if liberal democracies are to retain their limited-state, republican character. War puts liberal regime principles at risk. Beyond this, liberal democracies may simply be responding to threats to their security as realist theory tells us all states do—cooperating with other states in efforts to balance against or deter the aggression of others. They may ally with nondemocracies as well, but the common interests and values that liberal democracies share—and their unique capacities to cooperate—will tend to bring them frequently into alliance. As Michael Doyle notes, "when states are forced to decide . . . on which side of a world contest they will fight, liberal states wind up all on the same side, despite the real complexity of the historical, economic, and political factors that affect their foreign policies."[35] Liberal democracies might also be motivated by more ambitious system goals: establishing a stable international order that can sustain high levels of interdependence and cooperation that are needed across various realms. Security cooperation may be a foundation on which liberal internationalists build more expansive agendas.

Liberal democracies may engage in security cooperation in response to threats from outside the democratic world. But they may also do so to manage threats from within. As we shall see, Western liberal states have pioneered the practice of co-binding—that is, the attempt to tie each other down and together in mutually constraining institutions.[36] By locking themselves together in institutions—such as military alliances—liberal states are able to keep an eye on each other and manage their relations. The historian Paul Schroeder has argued that the alliance behind the Concert of Europe was an early manifestation of this co-binding logic—what he called *pacta de controhendo*, or pacts of restraint. The institution provided a setting and mechanisms for states to influence and restrain partners within the alliance. "Frequently the desire to exercise such control over an ally's policy, Schroeder argues, "was the main reason that one power, or both, entered into the alliance."[37] The post-1945 American-led alliances exhibited even more extensive co-binding features.[38]

Security cooperation has been envisaged and pursued in various ways. The most elemental is manifest in geopolitical alignments—liberal democracies finding themselves on the same side of international conflicts, while endeavoring to settle their own disputes without war. These alignments may not aggregate into a formal system of cooperation but may simply manifest themselves in the politics of war and diplomacy within the state system. Formal alliances are a more organized form of security cooperation, though they can be more or less binding. In the twentieth century, particularly in US security relations with Europe and East Asia, such alliances have turned into permanent organizations that engage in a wide array of activities. Security cooperation can also develop into what Karl Deutsch has called "security community," a deeper political community in which large-scale war essentially disappears as a possibility. This type of security order has been most fully realized among Western liberal democracies in the postwar era.[39] Beyond this, liberal democracies have repeatedly tried to build more inclusive global systems of security cooperation—what is called *collective security*. Here the ambition is to define and limit the legal bases of war and to organize rules and institutions for collective action in the face of state aggression. The League of Nations and the United Nations embody this vision.

Progressive Social Purposes

The liberal international order is not static. Societies that are part of it are constantly developing, advancing, adjusting, and responding to crises. Liberal internationalism aspires to move the world's inhabitants and its societies— and the international order itself—in a progressive direction. By "progressive," liberal internationalists tend to mean reform-driven advancements whose success is measured in terms of rising living standards, improved health, better security against violence, increased rights, and social justice. An open and loosely rules-based international order, by allowing and encouraging its member states to settle their differences short of war, is expected to generate expanding opportunities for societies to improve the lives of their citizens.

This notion of progressive change has three aspects. First, the liberal international order is understood to embody a set of social purposes. It is organized with the idea that its rules and arrangements will advance certain goals. This is what Hedley Bull argued when he said that all international orders have "purposes" and that every order reflects "an arrangement of social life such that it promotes certain goals or values."[40] The liberal international order's social purposes can vary from simple to complex. They can be quite limited—providing only rudimentary arrangements for trade and exchange between states. Or the international order might have a more complex and elaborate set of rules, institutions, and capacities to achieve more far-reaching goals. The nineteenth-century system of trade and cooperation had more limited social purposes than the post-1945 system of what John Ruggie has called "embedded liberalism."[41]

Second, there is an expectation that a functioning liberal order will constantly evolve. Liberal orders are transformative orders, an idea that is embodied in the workings of the open trading system. Trade generates ongoing, often unexpected, transformations within societies and economies. Industries and sectors rise and fall. Economic growth and the shifting forces of the world economy push and pull societies forward. States outside the liberal international order might see these dynamics as a threat. Illiberal states—autocratic and authoritarian regimes—might want to participate in the open, rules-based system but worry about its long-term effects on their ruling class and other entrenched interests.[42] Transformation is also embodied in the deeper liberal internationalist vision, rooted in the ideas of the Enlightenment and liberal modernity. Societies are constantly evolving as part of an ongoing world-developmental process. Modernity itself is changing, generating new dangers and opportunities. Because of this, liberal international order is also constantly evolving in response to these shifting circumstances.

Finally, embodied in these ideas is the conviction that the global order can be reformed. When Woodrow Wilson said that international society was "corrigible," that is, capable of being reformed, he was arguing that it could be made to serve the social purposes of liberal democracy. The conflict and violence of power politics cannot be extinguished, but they can, at least to a point, be tamed. E. H. Carr famously depicted Wilson and the liberal internationalists of 1919 as "utopians" blinded by illusions about banishing power from world politics. His critique traced the utopianism of the postwar moment back to Enlightenment beliefs about science, reason, and the ability of humans to determine "universally valid moral laws" to which individuals and societies would ultimately conform. It was these beliefs, Carr argued, that "under Wilson's inspiration, dominated the world after the first world war."[43] Enlightenment thinking is indeed at the core of liberal internationalism, but the prevailing view is much more modest concerning the ability of states to transform international society. The liberal agenda calls for reform, not revolution. States and international anarchy remain. There is a conviction, however, that states, often through trial and error, can devise institutions and relationships that bias the flow of human events in a more peaceful and progressive direction.[44] This reformist view—a belief that relations between states are corrigible—sets liberal internationalism apart from other traditions: political realists who are deeply skeptical of the possibility of progress in international relations, and cosmopolitans and globalists who believe progress is possible only through world government and an escape from anarchy.

US-NOT
AGENT FOR
SOCIAL
REFORM

Varieties of Order

Beyond these core ideas, the visions of liberal international order are wide-ranging. Across two centuries, liberal internationalist ideas and real-world orders have differed in how the components of order are put together—how sovereignty, rules and institutions, and openness are manifest within the international system. Liberal international order can be organized in many ways. The differences fall along several dimensions: participatory scope, sovereign independence, hierarchy and equality, rule of law, and policy breadth and depth.[45]

Scope refers to the size of the liberal order—whether the grouping is selective, defined by regional or other shared characteristics, or global, defined by universal principles. The wider the scope of the order, the more diverse the participating states. Presumably, the order's social purposes will also be influenced by its scope. In an exclusive grouping of Western democracies, the shared goals might be quite expansive. A global liberal international order might enshrine ideas of openness and rules-based relations but find less space for agreement on advancing liberal political values. As I argue in later chapters, the American-led liberal order of the postwar period was built within the larger bipolar Cold War system. At its core it was a grouping of Western liberal democracies with ties to other regions and states. With the end of the Cold War and the collapse of Soviet communism, this Western grouping expanded outward. The "inside order" became the "outside order," triggering transformations that altered the grouping's logic and character.

Sovereign independence refers to the degree to which liberal order entails legal-political restrictions on state sovereignty. Sovereignty in this sense refers to the state's exclusive claim to authority within its territory, manifest in the internationally recognized domestic right to issue commands and enforce obligations. States can possess full Westphalian legal sovereignty and interact with other states on this basis, or else submit to agreements and institutions that involve some abridgment of their sovereignty.[46]

Hierarchy refers to the degree of differentiation of rights and authority within the international system. Liberal order can be organized around the sovereign equality of states, a horizontal ordering based on principles of equal access, rights, and participation. Or it can be hierarchical, with one or more states possessing special rights and authority. An order marked by sovereign equality generally has very little differentiation of roles and responsibilities. States enter into agreements and cooperate as more or less equal parties. In a hierarchical order, the roles and responsibilities will be differentiated and states will be organized, formally or informally, into superordinate and subordinate relationships.[47] One state may have the primary responsibility of protecting the others militarily, for instance, and for that reason have the dominant voice on questions of mutual security.

Rule of law refers to the degree to which agreed-upon rules determine the operation of the order. This degree can vary. The interaction of states may be informed by highly articulated sets of rules and institutions that prescribe and proscribe actions, or states may adhere to more ad hoc and bargained relations. Even ad hoc relations are informed by some minimal sense of rules—if only by the notion of reciprocity. Hierarchical order, which accords unequal privileges and authority to the most powerful state or states, can also be more or less rules-based.

Furthermore, liberal international orders can vary in the breadth and depth of their policy domains. They can be organized to deal with only a narrow policy domain, such as international security challenges. Or they can deal with a more expansive set of social, economic, and human rights issues. The more expansive the policy domains, the more the international community is likely to intervene, control, regulate, and protect politics and society within and across states.

These dimensions let us discern "types" of international order. In the midnineteenth century, under British sway, it was a trade order organized around a small core of Western liberal democratic states and relatively circumscribed in scope and social purpose. The order advocated by Woodrow Wilson after World War I was more expansive in scope, rules, and breadth of policy domains. Wilson envisioned an international order organized around a global collective security body through which sovereign states would act together to uphold territorial peace. Open trade and a belief in progressive global change also undergirded the Wilsonian worldview, even as it was also infused with assumptions of racial hierarchy and Western superiority. The liberal international order after World War II emerged as a Western-centered, multilayered, deeply institutionalized system organized and directed by the United States. In both security and economic realms, the United States found itself steadily taking on new commitments and functional roles, and its own economic and political system became a central component of the liberal hegemonic order. This version was more hierarchical and was infused with more expansive social purposes than earlier versions of liberal international order. As we shall see, this order expanded outward after the end of the Cold War, triggering a far-reaching shift in its logic and character that led to today's crisis of liberal internationalism.

Revolutions and Transformations in Global Order

From its liberal Enlightenment foundations, liberal internationalism provides a moral frame of reference with which to make sense of and respond to political and economic change. Its core ideas of openness, rules-based relations, cooperative security, and progressive social purposes have appeared in many combinations over the past two centuries. In that time, four major transformations have shaped the way liberal internationalism has evolved over the modern period. The rise and spread of liberal democracy, the shift from a world of empires to a world of nation-states, the advance of economic and security interdependence, and the rise and decline of British and American hegemony—separately and together are the forces and dynamics that have provided the problems, dilemmas, dangers, and opportunities around which liberal internationalism has generated its ideas and agendas.

TIME FRAME NOT PAST WW II

The Rise and Spread of Liberal Democracy

If the eighteenth century saw the glimmerings of modern society, liberal democracies soon became its vanguard. As the nineteenth century began, liberal democracy was still a new and fragile political experiment, a peculiarity within a largely premodern world of monarchy, autocracy, and empire. Two hundred years later, as the twentieth century ended, liberal democracy commanded the vast majority of the world's power and wealth, including roughly 80 percent of global gross domestic product (GDP). Across these two centuries, the industrial revolution unfolded, capitalism expanded its frontiers, Europeans built far-flung empires, the modern nation-state took root, and great powers made war and peace. The world also witnessed the rise, spread, and growing power of liberal democracies. The ideas and agendas of liberal internationalism were shaped in this environment.

The two main features that distinguished the emerging nineteenth-century liberal democracies are captured in the term *liberal democracy*. First, they are ruled by the people—what the Greeks called the *demos*.[48] This rule may be direct, as in ancient Athens, or indirect, through representative electoral institutions. In either case, there is an underlying notion that government is based on the consent of the governed. Second, they are *liberal* in the sense that they enshrine individual rights and civil liberties through the rule of law and a constitutional framework designed to limit state power.[49] These ideas date back to ancient Rome, and they were expressed in the early modern era by a long lineage of "republican" political thinkers.[50] With the American founding and movements toward representative democracy in

Europe, the ideas of constitutionalism and rule of law gave rise to a new form of government.[51]

From this starting point, we can identify five ideal features that give liberal democracy its distinct form. First, citizens in a liberal democracy possess civil rights and equality before the law. Freedom of religion, speech, and the press are integral to these rights and protections. Second, the government is a representative democracy that derives its authority from the consent of the governed. Third, it has institutions—or constitutional laws—that limit the power of the state through means such as the separation of powers, checks and balances, and an independent judiciary.[52] Fourth, the economy is based on private property. Various mixed economies are consistent with liberal democracy, ranging from laissez-faire to social democratic systems.[53] Finally, something called civil society exists within the society. This is a realm of life that is "outside the state" and to some extent outside politics. In *Democracy in America*, Alexis de Tocqueville identifies civil society as the realm of independent groups and associations that provide a social infrastructure for political organization and cooperation.[54] All liberal democracies, despite their many differences, share these core features. But who "the people" are, how their rights are represented, what the inclusiveness of citizenship and the franchise are, and what the larger social purposes of liberal democracy are have always remained contested and evolving.

The American founding and the French Revolution marked a new era in the struggle over the character of the modern state. The American struggle for independence legitimized the idea that the just powers of government must emerge from the consent of the governed. Thomas Paine called this "the representative system" and contrasted it with Europe's "corrupt systems of Monarchy and Aristocracy."[55] Consent of the governed became the banner unfurled by the American colonists in their rebellion against King George III and, together with the protection of property, political rights, and republican governance, it informed the crafting of the American constitution.[56] The French Revolution was a complicated struggle that lurched through phases of reform, dictatorship, monarchy, and constitutional republic, but it too began as a reform movement aimed at making the ancien régime more responsive to the people. Born out of these revolutionary upheavals was a liberal democratic imagination that continues to inspire political struggles in the West and around the world.[57]

The struggle over democratic rights ebbed and flowed across the nineteenth century. The peace settlement that ended the Napoleonic Wars in 1815 was negotiated by European statesmen who were frightened of revolution and eager to reaffirm the authority and legitimacy of monarchical rule. Yet liberal democratic aspirations reappeared in the 1830s and later in the popular uprisings across Europe in 1848–49—the so-called springtime of the peoples—that included revolutionary movements seeking to create national republics in Germany and Italy. These populist uprisings, inspired by both liberal reformist and socialist revolutionary ideas, largely failed—at least at first. Great Britain followed a more gradual path of expanding the franchise through the Reform Bill of 1832 and later steps leading to full male voting rights. Later in the nineteenth century, Italy was unified under a constitutional monarchy, while Germany, led by Count Otto von Bismarck, established a new imperial constitution. As the ideals of popular government spread across Europe, the historian William McNeill writes, "liberal and democratic principles suffered drastic dilution by admixture with elements of the Old Regime."[58] This was particularly the case in eastern and central Europe, where parliamentary controls were weak or nonexistent in the face of bureaucratic and autocratic power.

The nineteenth century nonetheless saw a shift in the way Western polities were understood, constituted, and legitimated. The American Declaration of Independence became a model for claims of independence based on ideals of popular sovereignty and individual rights that were taken up by political movements in the West and on the periphery of the European imperial system. In one sense, the American declaration was a conservative claim—that the American colonies were a people who sought sovereign independence within the wider system of sovereign states. They were not seeking to overthrow the Westphalian order but to join it on the same terms as Europeans. But in another sense, the claim of sovereign independence was based on a conception of "the people" as the rightful body to give consent to govern. As David Armitage argues, this American conception of "popular sovereignty" spread to other independence-seeking peoples, including in

Latin America, and elevated principles of constitutionalism and republican governance.[59] The principle of democratic rule was built on popular sovereignty but was more contested. The French Revolution dramatically introduced the idea of direct democracy, which exploded on the scene as a powerful political force but quickly failed as a stable political order. The American founders, led by James Madison and the Federalists, saw dangers in direct rule and established a constitutional system based on republican principles of representative and divided government. By the end of the nineteenth century, popular sovereignty and representative democracy had become tied together as the defining normative ideals of Western politics.[60]

Through the nineteenth and early twentieth centuries, these ideas of popular sovereignty and democratic rule spread outward into international society, which led to a struggle between alternative legitimating principles of the state. The notion of liberal democracy as a standard of legitimacy challenged the principles of monarchical rule embedded in the European ancien régime. The famous German historian Leopold von Ranke identified this struggle in his private lectures for King Maximilian II in 1848. The colonists of the American Revolution, he argued, "introduced a new force in the world," the idea that "the nation should govern itself" and "power should come from below." This new idea clashed with the older European notion of the king who "ruled by the grace of God had been the center around which everything turned." The struggle between these two principles, Ranke predicted, would shape "the course of the modern world."[61] In Germany, the older view persisted into the twentieth century, as reflected in Kaiser Wilhelm II's claim in 1907 that he would continue to rule by "appeal to only God and my sharp sword."[62] But as the polities in the industrializing world struggled over the principles and institutions of the modern state, the idea of liberal democracy gained ground. World War I was a major turning point: at its end, amid the rubble of collapsed empires, Woodrow Wilson elevated liberal democracy as a normative ideal. Democratic values became, as James Mayall argues, "a kind of ideological equivalent to the coin of the realm."[63] The statesmen meeting in Versailles in 1919 were working with a different— or at least an evolved—normative framework from the one that informed the diplomats in Vienna a century earlier. Liberal democracy had supplanted monarchy as the dominant basis for legitimating the modern state.[64]

The actual rise and spread of democracy has unfolded across several historical periods, depicted by scholars as a sequence of waves.[65] The first democratic transitions developed slowly and were inspired by nineteenth-century American and European political movements. In all, twenty-nine countries joined the democratic world during the nineteenth and early twentieth centuries. This phase ended with Benito Mussolini's rise to power in Italy in 1922, and the upheavals of the interwar years reduced the number of democracies to twelve. The second wave of democratic transitions began after World War II and peaked in the 1960s with thirty-six recognized democracies. This upsurge in democracy was a product of the postwar decolonization movement, which led to a rapid expansion of independent states. The third wave began in the late 1970s, as countries in Latin America, East Asia, and Southern Europe made democratic transitions. With the end of the Cold War and the collapse of the Soviet order, countries in Eastern Europe and the former Soviet Union followed a similar path. By the end of the twentieth century, democracies around the world numbered about eighty-five (out of 192 countries).[66] The rise of the democratic world—both in size and capacities— can be seen in its changing share of global GDP, which reaches a peak of approximately 80 percent of the world total by the end of the twentieth century (see figure 2.1).

As these patterns suggest, liberal democracy has emerged in clusters tied to shifts in the global configuration of power. Some international and regional settings have been more favorable to democratic transitions than others. As Carles Boix has shown, over the past two centuries, the probability of successful democratic transitions has been greatest when the leading great powers have been liberal democracies—in the late nineteenth century, after World War I, and again after the Cold War.[67] In these eras, the leading democratic states were in a position to pursue policies that favored democratizing societies—extending trade and aid, offering access to international and regional institutions, and diffusing democratic ideas and models. Other periods have been less hospitable to democratic transitions. In the early

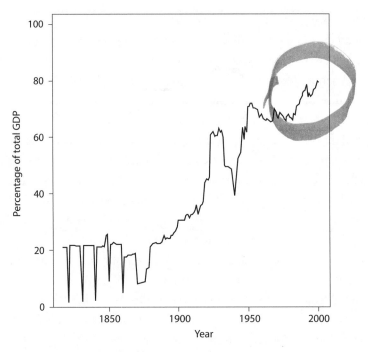

Figure 2.1. Gross domestic product of democracies as share of world total.

decades of the nineteenth century, the Holy Alliance actively suppressed democratic revolutions in continental Europe. During the Cold War, decolonization led to some democratic transitions, but the Soviet Union also rolled back democracy in Eastern Europe and.exported communism to the Third World, while the United States supported authoritarian regimes in Africa, Latin America, and Asia. In contrast, following the collapse of the Central Powers after 1918, democracy briefly flourished in Europe, and seventy years later, after the collapse of the Berlin Wall, another wave of democratization occurred in Europe and around the world.[68]

During these times of liberal ascendancy, liberal democracies have made repeated efforts to organize their wider world. Of course, not everything they did reflected their regime characteristics. Liberal states have pursued a wide range of foreign policies—realist, idealist, nationalist, militarist, imperialist, and liberal internationalist. But the rise and spread of liberal democracy did—and continues to—generate problems and opportunities that motivate and orient the liberal international project. We can identify three distinctive issues.

First, liberal democracies, generally speaking, have wanted to see their regimes survive—to safeguard their way of life—and the character of the international order bears on this prospect. They have sought to create a congenial international environment in which liberal democracy can survive and flourish. This means, at a minimum, a relatively stable and cooperative international order. More specifically, liberal regime principles—popular sovereignty and republican institutions—can succumb to illiberal forces in times of national danger. This worry has followed republican theorists from Roman times into the modern era—republics are fragile and vulnerable to demagogues and the wartime usurpation of state power. This threat led Kant to expect that republican polities would align with each other and build a "zone of peace" to protect liberties and the rule of law. Liberal democracies are not billiard balls reacting to events in simple, predictable ways, as some realists suggest. They are fragile political entities. The ideal international order for a liberal democracy is not a pool table but an elaborate system of protective institutions and relations orchestrated by cooperation among liberal states.[69]

Second, liberal democracies have found it easier to work with each other than with most other types of states. As noted earlier, this capacity for cooperation comes from their common interests, shared values, and institutional characteristics. Liberal democracies are more likely to trust each other and to see their interests and policies as legitimate. They have a level of transparency and shared experience with government that makes cooperation easier.[70] As Barry Buzan argues, "pluralist democratic states are those most attracted to high levels of international society, and in such states openness can only be sustained if societies themselves have converged [in regime type] to a significant degree."[71] In this sense, the rise of a group of liberal democracies creates opportunities for cooperation. This capacity of democracies to engage in deal making with each other creates opportunities for international order building that would not exist in the absence of liberal states. Beyond this, states with a strong domestic tradition of rule of law can create a normative expectation of rule of law in international relations as well. It is harder for a liberal democracy to violate this expectation than it is for an autocracy or an illiberal democracy—though of course it is far from impossible—because such behavior creates internal resistance that may acquire electoral force.

Finally, liberal democracies are modernizing societies, and this aspect creates its own challenges and opportunities. The ascendancy of liberal democracies over the past two centuries has involved building modern nation-states at home as well as expanding and intensifying interdependence abroad. Modern liberal democracy took root and expanded in nation-states, and it is in this context that these societies have experienced the expansion of political participation, the guarantee of rights and protections, and growth in the government's role in providing for economic and social well-being. These domestic pursuits are deeply intertwined with—and increasingly dependent upon—a well-ordered and congenial international system.[72] As a result, international relations in this rising and shifting liberal democratic world have involved the struggle to reconcile sovereignty with interdependence.[73] The challenge has not been to overcome nationalism and the nation-state, it has been to organize international relations in a way that allows liberal democracies to make good on their expanding roles and expectations. In these ways, liberal democracies have distinctive goals for international order and distinctive capacities to cooperate with each other.

From Empires to Nation-States

The global system has also been transformed by its movement from a world of empires to a world of nation-states. For millennia, empire was the world's dominant form of political organization. Even at the end of the nineteenth century, a majority of the world's people lived in imperial units. Yet, by the end of the twentieth century, empires had disappeared and given way to a global system of nearly two hundred nation-states, each claiming sovereignty, a seat at the United Nations, and a right to rule its own people. The extinction of empire in the face of the global spread of the Westphalian state system is, as David Armitage observes, "the most momentous but least understood development in modern history."[74] It was a revolution not just in the characteristics of politics and polities but in the underlying logic and principles of world order.

Liberal internationalism came of age as it grappled with this great transformation. Intellectually and politically, liberal internationalism had a complicated relationship with empire and imperialism. At some moments, it affiliated itself with European empire—particularly the British—or operated as a realm of order existing alongside empire. At other moments—particularly in the twentieth century—it has explicitly served as a countermovement against empire. This is seen most clearly in the aftermath of the two world wars, when many of the world's empires collapsed or were broken apart. In his famous Fourteen Points speech, Wilson argued that the principle of self-determination should be embedded in the postwar international order. After World War II, the principle was enshrined in the United Nations. As the global struggle for self-determination unfolded across the twentieth century, the leading liberal democracies often embraced nationalist movements half-heartedly and inconsistently. This pattern of movement from a world of empires to a system of nation-states carried forward by decolonization and statehood is captured in figure 2.2. But by the second half of the twentieth century, the liberal international project had tied itself to the world of nation-states—an order based on the Westphalian state system, sovereignty, and intergovernmental cooperation.[75]

Throughout the nineteenth century, European empire was the primary internationalizing force that organized and divided up the world and it provided the foundation for global order. This was seen as early as 1494, when Spain and Portugal signed the Treaty of Tordesillas, which divided their claims to all newly discovered lands outside of Europe. Four centuries later, the European imperial powers convened the Berlin Conference of 1884–85 to organize their scramble for Africa. "From the 1820s to the 1880s," Cemil Aydin notes, "regional orders were gradually subsumed under a Euro-centric imperial world order." Aydin calls this the "globalization of international order based on inter-imperial relations" under the "principle of inter-imperiality."[76] For centuries, empire—its power and ideas—had given the world an ordering logic and its social and political organization.[77] From the classical era to early modern times, as Jane Burbank and Frederick Cooper argue, "empires

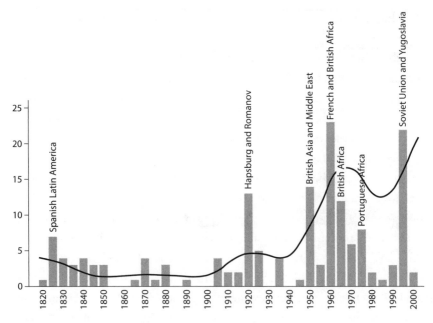

Figure 2.2. The growth of the Westphalian state system.

and their interactions shaped the context in which people gauged their political possibilities, pursued their ambitions, and envisioned their societies."[78] The breakdown of empire in the twentieth century was thus a crisis of the world's organizing logic. It was in this context that the Westphalian order of states built in Europe emerged as an alternative foundation for global order.

The rise and fall of these two ordering logics played out over centuries. For most of human history, world politics took place within geographical regions.[79] Empires and imperial civilizations eventually took root in most of these regions. A patchwork of empires, not a system of states, dominated the world. But within this global pattern, the European political order was anomalous. Despite repeated efforts to consolidate Europe into one empire— what the Europeans called "universal monarchy"—the continent remained a plural, multistate political order. Geography, religion, war, and state building all worked against a European-wide empire.[80] After the Peace of Westphalia ended the Thirty Years' War, this plural system was sustained by a balance of power among its states and the weakness of the claimants of European empire—the Papacy and the Holy Roman Empire. The Westphalian system was based on a roughly equal distribution of power among its major states and sustained by balancing practices that thwarted a succession of regional European empire builders, as well as by an increasingly elaborate system of public international law and ideological justification.[81] While this system rested on a balance of power, it was juridically crystallized into a system of mutually recognized sovereigns.

Outside Europe, however, the European states, including those that most energetically prevented empire within Europe, were extraordinarily successful in conquering and colonizing vast areas across oceanic distances. The Europeans did not invent empire, but they perfected the art of empire building on a global scale, largely because of the imbalance of power that stemmed from European innovations in technology and organization. The Europeans conquered and dominated empires, states, and peoples in every loosely coupled or isolated regional system across the world. They also established numerous colonies of settlers, mainly in North America and South America, Oceania, and the southern tip of Africa.[82] States from the Western European core of the Westphalian system thus brought into existence a world-scale political system made up of vast multicontinental empires of conquered peoples and scattered settler communities.

European empire building reinforced the division of the world into the West and the non-West. As they pursued empire abroad, Europeans continuously warred against each other for dominance within Europe.[83] These struggles were fought on a global scale. The Seven Years' War—the first "world war"—occurred in the late eighteenth century as Britain sought to prevent French domination of Europe, with the battle lines spread across Europe, North America, South Asia, and the world's oceans. Europeans found it difficult to conquer each other but easy to expand their empires at the expense of non-Europeans. Through these struggles "two worlds" emerged—a Westphalian world of states within Europe, based on the balance of power, and a world system of European empire, based on the imbalance of power. In this dual world, the norms and institutions of sovereignty and the nation-state remained overwhelmingly a Western affair. The Europeans, Edward

Keene argues, distinguished between Europe and the outside world, "adopting one kind of relationship, equality and mutual independence, as the norm in their dealings with each other, and another, imperial paramountcy, as normal in their relations with non-Europeans."[84]

Meanwhile, the Westphalian state system had evolved as a set of principles and practices, and as empires declined and broke apart, the state system expanded from its European origins to encompass larger parts of the globe.[85] The founding principles of the Westphalian system—sovereignty, territorial integrity, and nonintervention—reflected an emerging consensus that states were the rightful political units of legitimate rule.[86] Norms and principles that emerged in the Westphalian system—such as self-determination and nondiscrimination—further reinforced the primacy of states and state authority. These norms and principles have served as the organizing logic for Westphalian order and provided the source of political authority within it. In the twentieth century, under the banner of sovereignty and self-determination, political movements for decolonization and independence took hold in the non-Western developing world. Along the way, even as they have often been violated and ignored, Westphalian norms have nonetheless become the widely accepted rules and principles of international order.

Liberal internationalism, with its vision of liberal modernity and the rise of modern society, ultimately cast its lot with nation-states. Yet some liberal internationalists saw the "empire project" as a progressive force, or at least as a part of the world-developmental movement of modernity.[87] This view allowed them to be simultaneously liberal internationalists, of a sort, and champions of empire. Others disagreed, and this tension in the liberal international tradition still casts a shadow on its ideas and debates. Nonetheless, the roots of liberal internationalism are planted in the Westphalian state system. As it emerged in the nineteenth century, liberal democracy—the taproot of liberal internationalism—depended on functioning sovereign nation-states, political entities that could summon up the will of the people. The violent upheavals of the twentieth century shattered the world of empire, but their disappearance left a large residue: unacknowledged empires, imperial nostalgia, and "national" boundaries destructively at odds with local ideas of nationhood. The transition from empire to nation-state created a new setting, including new constituencies and problems, for struggles over world order. In this transition, liberal internationalists clarified their vision: the European—and now global system—of sovereign nation-states was the political foundation on which their ideas and agendas would be built.

Rising Economic and Security Interdependence

The global system has also been transformed by the industrial revolution and the global spread of capitalism. Technological revolutions in energy, transportation, and communication in the late nineteenth century, and again in the twentieth century, provided the foundation for a rapid rise of Western power and wealth, which in turn intensified global integration. Rising economic interdependence was matched by the growth in war's destructive power. The world wars brought the horrifying spectacle of "total war"—with mobilized industrial societies and the weapons of war now capable of destruction on a vast scale. The Cold War nuclear arms race raised the stakes and intensified the vulnerabilities of security interdependence. Across the modern era, the liberal democracies found themselves both advantaged and imperiled by their growing interdependence. The liberal internationalist project took shape through its struggles with this multifaceted global phenomenon.[88]

The industrial revolution was the drama's opening act. Beginning in the mid-eighteenth century, first Europe and then North America embarked on a radical economic transformation. The earliest industrial advances began in Britain and were driven by technological innovations in the textile trade and steam power.[89] Over the next century, waves of technological change spread around the world, turning rural and agrarian societies into modern industrial countries. Trade expanded, capital accumulated, and new industries emerged. Industrial capitalism and the working class became defining features of Western societies. By the late nineteenth century, the rising industrial centers were connected by transportation, communication, and banking systems.[90] While its epicenter was in the West, the industrial revolution was a worldwide phenomenon in both its causes and consequences. As Barry Buzan and George Lawson observe, "the nineteenth century marketization of social relations fueled the growth of a global system of much more densely connected networks, governed through the price mechanism and structured via hierarchical core-periphery relations."[91] Capital was accumulated in part through global trade and investment, including colonial ventures and the slave and sugar trades. Wealth and industrial capacity also rose through war and military competition, and the Western states' advances in military and naval technologies could be used to protect long-distance trade and coerce closed markets—such as the Ottoman Empire, China, and South America—to open their doors.[92]

The industrial revolution moved through several phases. Until the 1870s, it was the age of coal and steam dominated by Great Britain and marked by innovations in factories and machinery. Trade, investment, and economic growth were driven by railroads and steamships. As Ian Morris evocatively puts it, industrial capitalism was led by "a new, steam-powered class of iron chieftains."[93] By the end of the nineteenth century, a new phase of the industrial revolution opened up with the development of new industries and technologies such as chemicals, electricity, the telegraph, and the automobile. Science and technological development became more systematic and professional with laboratories and scientific and engineering staffs tied closely to industry. In this new phase, Germany (after its unification in 1870) and the United States emerged as challengers to Britain. Japan also joined their ranks and embarked on rapid industrialization. As late as 1881, Britain still had a greater percentage of its workforce employed in industrial production than the others.[94] But Germany had a faster-growing industrial economy, for example, leading the world in chemicals and electrical technologies, and the United States was rapidly becoming the world's largest and most productive economy. The West enjoyed a massive power disparity with the rest of the world.

World trade increased tenfold between 1850 and 1913. By the beginning of the twentieth century, this system had generated unprecedented levels of economic interdependence within Europe, across the Atlantic, and between the industrial core of the world economy in Europe and North America and the relatively less developed periphery of Asia, Africa, and Latin America. At the same time, the older networks of global trading were replaced by more formal commercial agreements among states. The freeing of trade and the regulation of trade went together. Political and commercial elites in the Western industrial countries became more active in both opening and protecting their economies. As C. A. Bayly notes, "the old system of honorary consuls or consultation by local rulers with the headmen of 'guest' merchant communities was replaced by networks of commercial consulates and international economic treaties."[95] The growth of a complex, Western-dominated world economy was marked by increased state involvement in regulating the movement of trade and capital.

This open system collapsed with the coming of World War I and the economic depression of the 1930s. The United States led the way in reopening the world economy after World War II, sponsoring the Bretton Woods system of rules and institutions to manage the rebuilding of global capitalism. Cooperative international agreements facilitated the rebuilding of international trade and investment, trade tariffs were reduced, and currencies became convertible. Commerce and investment spread, first within the transatlantic world and gradually into other regions. A golden era of economic growth began. In the 1980s, East Asian countries became integrated into this expanding world economy. After the Cold War, many countries from the former communist world, most importantly China, pursued market reforms and joined the open world economy. Technological change led by innovations in computing and telecommunications opened up a new era of international economic integration. Economic crises continued to mark this long postwar growth—with the end of the Bretton Woods system in the 1970s and in the financial crises and economic downturns of the late 1990s and 2008.[96] These periodic crises of global capitalism illuminated the remarkable scope and intensity of world economic integration, as well as its many vulnerabilities.

The two-century rise of modern industrial societies has been accompanied by massive increases in military power and the destructiveness of war. The trajectory of great-power war from the Napoleonic era to the present day is defined by cascades of growth in its capability for violence. The twentieth-century world wars marked a new era of mass-casualty conflagrations. Rapid increase in the destructive power of weapons possessed by the great powers is a basic marker of rising security interdependence. Steve Biddle has traced this increase in firepower over the past two centuries—noting especially its great leaps during the two world wars and the Cold War.[97] Trevor Dupuy has also calculated the massive jumps in "weapon lethality" over the past century.[98] The trend is unmistakable: the ability of states to inflict harm has jumped dramatically from generation to generation throughout the modern era.

The cascades of rising economic and security interdependence that created the modern international system have been described by scholars using terms like *complex interdependence, interaction capacity,* and *dynamic density.*[99] These terms reflect efforts to capture the changing pattern of linkages and interactions between polities. As Buzan and Lawson argue, this increased "interaction capacity created a more intensely connected global economy and enabled the projection of military power around the world."[100] The general claim is that industrialization and the global expansion of capitalism have generated increasingly dense, complex forms of interdependence and brought the world of states and societies into ever closer contact. Along with the growth of interdependence have come increases in states' capabilities to harm each other.

At the heart of liberal internationalism is the search for ways to govern this evolving economic and security interdependence. Liberal internationalists have grappled with a variety of distinct problems and opportunities over the historical eras. First were what might be called the "functional" problems of interdependence.[101] These required building an international infrastructure of rules and institutions to facilitate and organize flows and transactions across borders. The standardization of time and space, international banking protocols, and units of account were the supporting frameworks for economic interdependence.[102]

Second, an open world economy was possible only with active cooperation between states to reduce barriers and regulate the flows of goods and capital. Governments want the benefits of open trade, but they worry about its impact on specific sectors or groups. In liberal democracies, the terms of openness to the outside world are generated by policy, which is an outcome of political struggles. Liberal internationalism has been preoccupied with finding international agreements that offer the benefits of openness while guarding against its downside.

Third, as countries become more open to the world system, they also become more exposed to various dangers that might be called "system vulnerabilities." Economic or political events in one country—such as bad economic policy, a pandemic, civil war and refugee flows, or the proliferation of lethal weapons—can generate instabilities and harms that ripple across the international system. International cooperation becomes essential if openness is to be reconciled with the safety and well-being of countries across the system. In a world of increasing interdependence, liberal democracies cannot be secure solely through their own actions. They must actively work with other liberal democracies and within the wider global system to reduce system vulnerabilities.

Finally, the rise of security interdependence has generated repeated efforts by liberal internationalists to regulate and restrain great-power war. The nineteenth-century peace movement in Europe and the United States was one reflection of this sensibility. Liberal internationalist ideas about arbitration, collective security, and congresses of nations proliferated in the late nineteenth century. The efforts in the twentieth century to found the League of Nations and United Nations follow in this tradition.

The Rise and Decline of British and American Hegemony

The global system passed through two eras of Anglo-American hegemonic leadership. Within the general pattern of the rise of Western dominance, Britain and then the United States emerged as the leading power of its day, with power, wealth, and unique opportunities to shape the terms of international order.[103] Along the way, power shifts and great-power wars created sharp breaks in the organization of international relations. In 1815 and again in 1919 and 1945, postwar moments opened up opportunities for Great Britain and the United States to assert leadership, build alignments, and promulgate global rules and institutions. These "hegemonic moments" became turning points for liberal internationalists to rethink and advance their ideas and agendas.

Emerging as the leading power in the aftermath of the Napoleonic Wars, Great Britain for the first time in its history exercised a commanding influence over European affairs. Its position rested on a combination of naval mastery, financial credit, commercial success, alliance diplomacy, and an expanding colonial empire. Its economy was the most advanced in Europe. Great Britain's actual GDP in 1815 was no bigger than the GDPs of France or Russia, but Britain was more technologically advanced and productive and it led the rest of Europe into a new phase of industrialization. As David Cannadine notes, "It was Britain's success in becoming the first industrial nation, combined with its corresponding success in becoming the world's pre-eminent financial nation, which propelled it to . . . global hegemony . . . by the middle of the nineteenth century."[104] Britain's position as an "off-shore" great power was integral to the ways it projected power. Its hegemonic leadership was manifest in a variety of roles: balancing great power rivalries on the continent, controlling the seas, fostering free trade, exporting capital, and presiding over a global empire.[105]

The United States emerged as the predominant world power in the twentieth century. Its ascendancy, like Britain's, was grounded in economic success. The United States passed Britain in economic size and productivity sometime in the late nineteenth century, and its lead increased in the century that followed.[106] By 1914, it already had an economy twice the size of Britain's, and after the war it was triple in size. As Paul Kennedy notes, "The United States seemed to have all the economic advantages which some of the other powers possessed in part, but none of their disadvantages."[107] This economic preeminence and its value to the allied war effort ensured a dominant American voice in the postwar settlement. Emerging from World War II, the United States took on an even more commanding position. While the other great powers—both America's allies and the defeated axis states—had been weakened by the war, the United States had used the conflict to build a massive industrial capacity. The American government was more centralized and capable, and the economy and military, unprecedented in their power, were still on an upward swing. The United States began the postwar era with roughly half of world economic production, a world-dominant military, leadership in advanced technologies, and surpluses of petroleum and food production. Its closest rivals—Great Britain and the Soviet Union—each had economies roughly one-fifth the size of America's.

There are important similarities between these two eras of dominance.[108] First, both hegemons were liberal democracies commanding the world's largest and most advanced economies. This was the source of their wealth and capabilities and the foundation for their outward orientation. Second, each was positioned—and grew powerful—on the edges of the great-power system. Britain was a European power but not a continental one. It was a maritime state that projected power and influence by maneuvering and tipping balances among the other great powers. The United States, separated from the other great powers by oceans, grew largely outside the traditional arenas of European and East Asian security competition. Third, the upheavals of great-power wars and power transitions created opportunities for both Britain and the United States to influence the postwar restructuring of international relations. The Napoleonic Wars and the two world wars destroyed the "old order," thus creating opportunities for Britain and the United States as rising global powers in their era to step forward and shape the new order.[109]

These eras of British and American dominance are central features of modern international relations. Realist scholars of hegemony see Pax Britannica and Pax Americana as long periods of order and relative peace established by the dominance of the leading state.[110] Hegemonic order reflects the efforts of the predominant state to use its economic and military capabilities to promulgate and underwrite a set of rules and institutions that add regularity and predictability for actors large and small. The leading state's role is distinct from the roles of the smaller states, which adds a degree of functional differentiation to international politics. A hegemonic order is not based solely on the power of the leading state but also on its capability and willingness to solve common problems that face all states in the system. The order gains durability and legitimacy as the leading state promulgates a model for organizing societies with wide application and appeal. Although hegemonic orders are based on concentrations of power, they fall short of being empires because the lesser powers retain their sovereignty as well as considerable maneuvering room and even influence on the leading state.[111]

Great Britain and the United States emerged as powerful states within a world of great powers. They were not simply liberal democracies but the leading states in a competitive global system. They were not merely seeking to build liberal international order. Realist hegemonic theory describes the variety of incentives, impulses, and strategic goals that rising hegemonic states might follow. In the nineteenth century, Great Britain's grand strategy had several components. It pursued a strategy of offshore balancing against the other European great powers, throwing its weight behind weaker states on the continent to thwart other powers' bids for dominance. Britain also tried to foster a European concert of powers, building on the framework of rules and diplomatic practices established by the Vienna settlement of the Napoleonic Wars, while it simultaneously pursued a strategy of empire building. In the past century, its empire had largely been a commercial enterprise, organized around a far-flung treaty port system. In the second half of the nineteenth century, empire building became a more explicit geopolitical undertaking.[112] Finally, Britain championed free trade and an open international economy across the Western capitalist world. The United States also pursued a variety of grand strategic impulses during its era of hegemonic leadership. For the half-century after World War II, it was engaged in a global Cold War with the Soviet Union built around strategies of balance, deterrence, and containment. Client states, alliances, and military interventionism all called for the United States to play different hegemonic roles.[113]

These two eras of Anglo-American hegemony provided the setting and opportunities for liberal internationalist ideas and agendas. Liberal internationalist ideas were inevitably tied to the foreign policies of powerful liberal democratic states, and these ideas in turn offered a vision of how rising states might seek to shape the international order. The great-power wars and postwar settlements demanded ideas and agendas for order building and thus provided audiences and constituencies for liberal internationalism. The fact that Britain and the United States, as the leading states of their era, were dominant presences in these postwar moments raised the potential salience of liberal international ideas and programs.[114]

Second, the substantive ideas of liberal internationalism—starting with notions of openness and rules-based order—were useful for liberal states seeking to build hegemonic order. As the leading capitalist states, Britain and the United States had much to gain from an open and loosely rules-based order. Trade and openness held intrinsic advantages for their economies. Politically, hegemonic order can be organized in many ways, some more "liberal" than others. But liberal internationalism across these two eras offered visions of how hegemonic order might be organized in ways that generated cooperation and legitimacy.

Finally, the British and American hegemonic eras also created dilemmas for and constraints on the liberal international project. Britain and the United States were driven by incentives and imperatives that took them away from, not closer to, liberal international visions of order. Liberal internationalism thus competed with other ideologies and visions, and liberal internationalists also found themselves building coalitions—intellectually and politically—with political actors who had different ideas and agendas. As a cluster of ideas and visions, liberal internationalism was sufficiently flexible to accommodate itself to others. As an intellectual tradition, it repeatedly found itself debating whether and in what ways to affiliate with other grand strategic projects—imperial, geopolitical, and otherwise.

Stepping back, liberal internationalism is intellectually and politically rooted in the Enlightenment and liberal visions of modernity. It is a loosely organized body of ideas and programs put forward by thinkers and political figures within the liberal democratic world—ideas and agendas that have evolved across the liberal ascendancy. At the core of its vision are ideas about and anticipations of modernity as a continuously unfolding world-historical drama. It is also a human project, driven forward by science, knowledge, and experience. Its fundamental conviction, constant across two centuries of liberal order building, is that the human condition can be advanced through the enlightened pursuit of interests and through the use of old and new institutions to shape the flow of events. Institutions are not just tools of the powerful or reflections of parochial interests. Humans can put themselves in institutional settings that shape, constrain, empower, and legitimize their actions. The owl of Minerva does not fly only at dusk. Societies can absorb their mistakes, learn new things, and organize themselves so as to better negotiate their circumstances. Progress is possible, though not guaranteed by God, reason, or nature. It has to be hard-won, and it is never finished.

THREE

The Nineteenth-Century Origins
of Internationalism

L iberal internationalism was born in the nineteenth century, and by the century's end it had begun to crystallize into a recognizable school of thought—a distinctive cluster of ideas and agendas for organizing international relations. The intellectual roots of this tradition trace back to the Enlightenment and the late eighteenth- and early nineteenth-century age of democratic revolution. Its political roots trace to the rise of "internationalism" in mid-nineteenth-century Europe, as articulated by diplomats, activists, thinkers, merchants, peace activists, jurists, and many others. An older idea of internationalism—defined as efforts to build rules, institutions, and relationships that connect polities and peoples across territorial divides— reaches back centuries. But in the nineteenth century, internationalism emerged as an increasingly distinct, self-conscious, and organized realm of activity, with the Western democratic world as its epicenter. States and societies were modernizing, growing powerful, and expanding their imperial and commercial frontiers. Modern internationalism was a product of this transforming moment.

Internationalism was in many ways the twin of nationalism, the ideology of the modern nation-state, which also emerged as a political movement in the nineteenth century. A "nation" or "people" came to be seen as the rightful foundation for political rule and the territorial state. In this sense, nationalism and internationalism were rivals—ideological alternatives and competitors for the political allegiance of peoples. Nationalism celebrated the division of peoples into ethnic, cultural, and geographic groupings, while internationalism celebrated the overcoming of these differences in cooperative pursuits. Yet, in a more profound sense, nationalism and internationalism were two sides of the same coin. "Whatever sense is given it, the meaning of internationalism logically depends on some prior conception of nationalism," Perry Anderson notes, "since it only has currency as a back-construction referring to its opposite."[1] But the relation between the two ideas is not so linear: they developed together. Modern nationalism emerged within the setting of the European state system. It defined identity and loyalty within a wider world of nations and peoples. Internationalism, in turn, emerged as a response to nationalism and the crystallizing world of nation-states. In all its varieties, internationalism entailed efforts to forge cooperative ties and bonds of solidarity across a world of peoples, nations, and states.

The rise of liberal democracy in the nineteenth century intensified the connections between nationalism and internationalism. Liberal democracy was both a national and an international project. The institutions of liberal democracy were national, established within the framework of the territorial nation-state. As thinkers such as John Stuart Mill and Giuseppe Mazzini argued, political rights and protections were to be secured within nations. Throughout the nineteenth century, struggles for liberal democracy were intimately bound up with nation building and movements for national self-rule. But liberal democracy, with its roots in the universalist aspirations of the Enlightenment, also had an international dimension. Its institutions and ideals were premised on an expanding world of trade, exchange, and community. Civil society—the backbone of liberal democracy—provided openings and connections to the outside world. Moreover, liberal democracy—its republican institutions and open society—were fragile creations whose vulnerability to geopolitical forces created an incentive to build a protective international order.

In the nineteenth century, internationalism became more than simply a diverse set of activities that cut across national borders. It became a realm of world politics manifest in organized activities bridging political units that set the stage for the grand projects of twentieth-century liberal internationalism. As Mark Mazower argues, by the mid-nineteenth century, internationalism had become an "ism," "a radical project closely connected to the rise of professions and the bourgeoisie, manufacturing and commerce, and to their ideological expressions in the form of powerful social philosophies that emerged for the first time in the post-Napoleonic restoration."[2] As an ideology and political activity, internationalism both rested upon and helped to create new projects and ambitions within international society. This world collapsed with the coming of world war in 1914. But the peacemaking and order building that followed, led by Woodrow Wilson and his Anglo-American and continental European contemporaries, built on the internationalist ideas and movements of the earlier era.[3]

It was out of these evolving strands of internationalism—commercial, legal, social, functional, and others—that liberal internationalism was woven together as a political project. This project made its debut with the peacemaking of Woodrow Wilson and others at Versailles after World War I. Ironically, it was in the aftermath of the most violent war ever seen—when a pacific world order seemed most out of reach—that liberal internationalism came of age.

This chapter makes three arguments. First, internationalism has come in many varieties, only some of which can be described as liberal. It is useful to distinguish between two other types: imperial internationalism and Westphalian internationalism. Each builds on two foundational forms of order in world politics: empire and the nation-state. Imperial internationalism can be defined as efforts by imperial states to build international rules, relations, and institutions to support their imperial projects. Internationalism is manifest in the activities of empires to institutionalize and perpetuate imperial order within the wider international system. In the nineteenth century, this type of imperial internationalism was manifest in the agreements between European imperial states to cooperate in stabilizing their global holdings. In the twentieth century, the League of Nations and the United Nations can be seen as efforts by European states—particularly Great Britain—to retrench and relegitimate their weakening empires.

Westphalian internationalism is cooperation between sovereign nation-states. It is manifest in foundational agreements about the norms and institutions of the sovereign state system and in more specific functional agreements in areas like security, economics, and the organization of the global commons. Various strands of nineteenth-century liberal internationalism built on and affiliated themselves with both of these foundational types of order. In the twentieth century, as European empires weakened and broke apart and the United States rose to global dominance, liberal internationalism increasingly tilted in the direction of building its projects on the foundation of an expanding Westphalian state system.

Second, the early strands of liberal internationalism emerged with the rise of Western liberal democracy. It was reflected in diverse, loosely connected ideas and movements aimed at building commercial, legal, social, and functional ties within the liberal democratic world. Some of these movements embodied classical liberal ideas about free trade and limited government, and others had more progressive social goals. Some internationalists saw their efforts as primarily "regulatory" in character, constructing rules and institutions to facilitate more peaceful and efficient transactions between states. Other internationalists held more "revisionist" goals for global order, seeking to build supranational institutions and promote progressive social and political changes within and between liberal states.[4] Some liberals sought to advance the cause of peace through international reforms in trade, law, and institutions, while others held to the view that a stable peace required change within societies, starting with the reconfiguration of liberal democracy itself. Free traders, the peace societies, and various legal and social internationalist movements advanced ideas for rules and institutional mechanisms to organize and govern a rapidly expanding and interdependent international society. These internationalist groups coexisted with other types of nineteenth-century international movements such as various radical socialist and workers' movements.

Finally, by the late nineteenth century, these diverse threads of internationalism increasingly combined into broader agendas for a reformed global order in which open commercial relations, arbitration mechanisms, representative and judicial bodies, and elaborate international rules and norms were all seen as essential elements. As Inis Claude puts it, the nineteenth century "brought about the combination of the continuing proliferation and solidification of states, particularly under the impact of growing nationalism, and the emergence of a pattern of technologically based contacts, unprece-dented in range and intensity, which made the world situation ready for in-ternational organization."[5] A world of modernizing liberal democracies and growing interdependence needed a new normative and institutional archi-tecture to guide relations. At century's end, international activists and think-ers could glimpse the outlines of an open and rules-based international order in which sovereign states would engage each other in multilateral forums to resolve disputes and tackle common problems.

Empire, Nation-States, and Liberal Internationalism

Liberal internationalism emerged in a shifting terrain of empire and nation-states. European empires dominated the world in the nineteenth century and, as they extended their global reach, they grew more powerful and com-petitive. At the same time, within Europe and the Western world, nation-states were gaining a political foothold and forming the core of the Westphalian state system. For the most part, the European great powers played both roles—consolidating a system of nation-states within the West while building empires outside it. As Edward Keene puts it, "within Europe, the leading purpose of international order was to promote peaceful coexis-tence in the multicultural world through the toleration of other political sys-tems, cultures and ways of life. . . . Beyond Europe, however, international order was dedicated to a quite different purpose: the promotion of civiliza-tion."[6] It is possible to imagine a world that is built entirely on one or the other deep foundation—a world of empires or a world of nation-states. But until the last decades of the twentieth century, both types of order—imperial hierarchy and Westphalian anarchy—coexisted in complex, hybrid political formations.[7]

Empire and nation-states embody alternative logics for organizing geopo-litical space. Empire, as an ideal type, exhibits a "hub-and-spoke" orga-nizational logic in which a metropole exercises control over weaker peoples and societies. It organizes international relations within more or less closed hierarchical spaces. Blocs, zones, and spheres of influence are the imperial order's spatial markers.[8] In contrast, a state system, as an ideal type, organizes international relations around the open and multilateral interaction of sovereign and formally equal units. This is the logic of the Westphalian order. It is built on the nation-state, described by Jürgen Osterhammel as a "special kind of state organization, which first emerged in the nineteenth-century and began to spread hesitantly and unevenly around the world."[9]

Of course, both forms of order vary widely from their ideal type. Empires have been more or less formal and more or less rigidly hierarchical. Their centers use different techniques and exert different degrees of coercive control. Informal empire has been manifest in commercial and financial domination with little overt hierarchy.[10] Systems of states have also varied in the degree to which rules and shared understandings have guided the interaction of units.[11] Westphalian orders are marked by different degrees of hierarchy. Where there are great power disparities among sovereign states—such as in the American-dominated liberal democratic world after World War II—the order has been more hegemonic.[12] While informal empire and hegemonic formations are harder to distinguish than the ideal types to which they belong, the key distinction between them is their openness to third parties. That is, what separates order built around empire from order built around a Westphalian system of states is "preclusion"—the imperial state's ability to deny outside states or empires access to the peoples and societies within the empire.[13]

How does liberal internationalism relate to these two foundational logics of order? The connections are as intimate as they are complex. Liberal internationalism is a cluster of activities pursued by Western liberal democratic states that—throughout the long nineteenth century—were simultaneously building empires and building the Westphalian system. It is useful to think of empire, nation-states, and liberal internationalism as three varieties of international order, each with its own ideas and agendas. Liberal internationalism embodies a "project"—or cluster of projects—for organizing international relations, but empires and nation-states do the same. Empire and the Westphalian system embody the basic units or building blocks of international relations, and liberal internationalism has pursued its activities on both these foundations. As a result it has taken a variety of mixed or hybrid forms.

Each form of ordering embodies a type of internationalism. Internationalism can be understood as activity pursued by agents of each of these types of order—empires, nation-states, and liberal democracies—to build institutions and cooperative relations to strengthen these entities' position or standing.[14] If, as Woodrow Wilson famously said, liberal internationalism is the project to make the world safe for democracy—meaning to build an international order in ways that strengthen the prospects and standing of liberal democracies—something similar can be said of "imperial internationalism": it is a project to make the world safe for empire. "Westphalian internationalism" is the project to make the world safe for the Westphalian state system. Each of these internationalisms is a "self-strengthening" activity, pursued through international rule making and institution building.[15]

Imperial order, Westphalian order, and liberal international order all carry ideas and projects for creating international rules, institutions, and arrangements to support their distinctive organizational forms. In some times and places, liberal internationalism has built on or accommodated itself to empire, manifesting itself as imperial internationalism. In other times and places, it has built on or accommodated itself to Westphalian order, manifesting itself as Westphalian internationalism.

The liberal international project began its life navigating this shifting world of empires and nation-states, and it accommodated itself to both logics. Well into the twentieth century, it had one foot in each world. The two centuries of liberal internationalism can be seen as a long struggle over whether and in what way the project would tie itself to each of these foundational forms. Through the world wars and the accompanying global power transitions, this struggle played out in the Anglo-American world as a contest between Great Britain, which sought to preserve its empire, and the United States, which sought to establish its dominance by organizing international space on the ruins of the crumbling European imperial order. The issue of "preclusive control" was at the heart of this contest.[16] By the second half of the twentieth century, liberal internationalism had come to rest squarely on the foundational logic of the Westphalian state system. Liberal internationalism took its modern form as it offered ideas and programs for a postimperial global system organized around the sovereign state, intergovernmentalism, and the management of complex interdependence.

Imperial Internationalism

Across the centuries, empires have been ruthless globalizers. As the metropolitan centers of empires have tried to preserve and advance their colonial and imperial enterprises, they have engaged in aggressive conquest and other coercive forms of order building. Histories of modern empire provide rich accounts of the many ways European empires ordered and internationalized the global system. In the nineteenth century, the European transoceanic empire provided the impetus for what it often thought of as the first age of globalization—the construction of a global infrastructure via railroad, telegraph, and steamship. The corners of the world were connected as commercial and imperial agents built a global capacity for transformation and communication. The standardization of time, space, and measurement around the world was an artifact of European imperial globalization.[17]

Imperial internationalism also promoted international norms and law. European states built on a long tradition of Westphalian norms and institutions of state sovereignty within the Western world and also used international law to define the terms of political hierarchy and division between the West and the outside world. The "community of nations" and "civilization" became boundary markers between the Westphalian and imperial realms. As Jennifer Pitts argues, "international law, together with the structures of international governance, is in important respects a product of the history of European imperial expansion."[18] Eighteenth-century discourses on the "law of nations" provided legal and normative frameworks for nineteenth-century European commercial and imperial expansion.

More generally, European states sought to protect and legitimate their colonial holdings as the old imperial world weakened and began to give way. Late nineteenth-century British thinkers, worried about imperial competition and the disquiet generated by democracy, debated various schemes for recasting the British Empire into a federal system that connected colonial and white settler communities in new forms of hierarchical union.[19] In the early twentieth century, Great Britain and other European states used the normative and institutional architecture of the League of Nations—and later the United Nations—to reorganize and legitimate their imperial relations with colonies making their transitions to independence. We can see this sort of imperial internationalism in the independent representation given to India and British Dominions in the Assembly of the League of Nations, even while they remained within the British Empire; and in the creation of supervisory international bodies like the League of Nations Permanent Mandates Commission that could interact directly with colonial peripheries.[20] It was also embodied in the functional interdependence between sovereign states and colonial peripheries.

Imperial internationalism can be seen as either a project to reconstruct and legitimate British Empire and the European imperial order or as a project to find transitional forms of international architecture for a world moving away from empire. Mazower emphasizes that key British and Commonwealth leaders understood the League of Nations as a tool for reworking and preserving British Empire, which he calls the "internationalist reinforcement of empire."[21] In this view, both the Commonwealth and the league reflected the fusion of empire and liberal internationalism, thus providing new institutional forms for reestablishing and securing British imperial control. Other scholars emphasize the transitional nature of imperial internationalism—seeing it as a reworking of imperial hierarchies to facilitate their integration into Westphalian and liberal international institutions. Susan Pedersen finds this logic in the league's mandate system. "The mandate system . . . was a vehicle for what we might call 'internationalization'—the process by which certain political issues and functions are displaced from the national or imperial, and into the international realm. Not administration but rather the work of legitimation moved to Geneva, as imperial powers strove to defend—and others to challenge—their authority. . . . In the history of the mandates system we thus recover the role of the League of Nations as an agent of geopolitical transformation."[22]

Obviously, state officials and other actors had varying intentions as they sought to bring empire into the world of multilateral rules and institutions. Some sought to re-create and preserve hierarchy and imperial control. Others hoped to usher in a postimperial international order, even if they had to do so through gradual institutional steps. Whatever the actors' intentions, the outcomes follow their own, often unintended pathways. Imperial internationalist moves to embed empire in international rules and institutions created platforms and vehicles for activists, reformers, intellectuals, and political groups to push their own agendas. Institutions are not just tools of the powerful. They are shields for the powerless as well as scaffolding upon which political struggles unfold. In the long run, imperial internationalism became the midwife of a slowly emerging twentieth-century postimperial international order.[23]

Westphalian Internationalism

The lineages of the nation-state reach back into the early modern European past. The origin of the modern state system is typically traced to 1648 and the Westphalian peace agreements that settled the Thirty Years' War. In the evocative words of Leo Gross, Westphalia was the "majestic portal" that led "from the old world into the new world."[24] But it was only in the nineteenth century that the modern system of nation-states made its appearance. "In the nineteenth century it is possible to speak for the first time of an international politics that sets aside dynastic considerations and obeys an abstract concept of raison d'état," Osterhammel argues. "It presupposes that the normal unit of political and military action is not a princely ruler's arbitrary patrimonium but a state that defines and defends its own borders, with an institutional existence not dependent on any particular leadership personnel."[25] This is when Europe became a system of sovereign nation-states. Westphalian internationalism can be seen as the efforts by these nation-states to build and reinforce the normative and institutional architecture of the Westphalian state system.

Westphalian internationalism has been manifest in efforts over the centuries to deepen and extend the norms and institutions of the sovereign state system. As noted in chapter 2, the original Westphalian notions of sovereignty and mutual recognition have been expanded to include a wider set of norms, including nonintervention and nondiscrimination. These efforts can be understood, as Daniel Philpott argues, as an unfolding revolution in international relations, building the "constitution" of international society.[26] At this constitutional level, Westphalian norms and architecture were built, rebuilt, and expanded through the modern era's upheavals of great-power war and postwar peace settlements.[27]

Westphalian internationalism was at work in the European great powers' rule making and institution building in the aftermath of the Napoleonic Wars. Groupings of great powers had emerged in Europe centuries earlier, but the Vienna Settlement of 1815 created a newly sophisticated framework for managing their relations. As Jennifer Mitzen notes, the Concert of Europe is "widely acknowledged as the first modern international security institution and thus a precursor to international governance as we know it today."[28]

The concert was a new way to organize great-power relations, reflecting, as Paul Schroeder argues, a "network of ideas" that European elites came to share about the sources of stable political order. It was a set of norms, practices, and institutional arrangements put in place to regulate conflict between major states.[29] The Concert of Europe was a club of great powers, self-appointed as the guardians of European community. The leading powers of Europe held sway over weaker and peripheral states, establishing a practice of "diplomacy by conference" as the centerpiece for the multilateral management of order. The concert system turned the major states of Europe into "a board of directors," but in doing so, as Inis Claude notes, "it also implied the existence of a corporation."[30] The idea of "great powers" became a more concrete reality, but so too did the idea of "Europe," which became the embodiment and carrier of Westphalian internationalism.

The working relations of the concert system were revealed, for example, at the Berlin Congress of 1878. Following political insurrections in the Balkans, the six leading European great powers came together with representatives from the Ottoman Empire and the Balkan states to end the conflict and determine the territories of the states on the Balkan Peninsula. The leading powers sought to mediate the dispute and even resolved to send an international police force to the region to restore order. Earlier, with the Treaty of San Stefano in the summer of 1878, the Russian government intervened to impose its own settlement, which enhanced its position in the Balkans. Seeing the treaty as a violation of the idea of the collective settlement of territorial disputes, the other great powers, led by Great Britain, intervened to substitute an international settlement at Berlin. The London *Times* hailed the Berlin Congress as a high-water mark of concert diplomacy, "the first instance of a real Parliament of the Great Powers."[31]

Behind the concert were older and evolving ideas of sovereignty, state authority, and international law. What was new was the crystallization of a set of institutions that reinforced the centrality of the European great powers. These conservative, monarchical states feared revolution, and the congress system provided a framework by which they could affirm each other's status and cooperate to keep destabilizing social and political forces at bay. Ironically, however, this great-power stability created conditions for other types of internationalism to emerge and spread. The global institutions built in the twentieth century—the League of Nations and the United Nations—were heirs to this Westphalian internationalism, which enshrined state sovereignty and illuminated a pathway for cooperation among nation-states.

The most prosaic form of Westphalian internationalism is intergovernmental cooperation. This is internationalism pursued to solve problems of sovereign states, regardless of whether they are liberal democratic, autocratic, or communist.[32] All have participated in this kind of Westphalian internationalism. Entry into this sort of internationalist activity does not depend on the character of your polity but on your capacity to keep commitments.[33] In the nineteenth century, Westphalian internationalism took the form of efforts by modernizing states to build diplomatic, commercial, and political rules and arrangements to facilitate their expanding global activities. In the twentieth century, the many forms of intergovernmental cooperation carried out under the auspices of the League of Nations and the United Nations followed this same logic. Westphalian internationalism was at work in the arms control agreements pursued by the United States and the Soviet Union during the Cold War. Countries of many types worked together to combat health pandemics in the post-1945 era, succeeding, for example, in a global campaign to eradicate smallpox. Another form of Westphalian internationalism, international cooperation to protect the global commons and combat climate change, has involved states from across regions and of diverse political orientation.[34]

Liberal internationalism has been built on this Westphalian logic of order in two respects. First, in its most straightforward sense, liberal internationalism is manifest as cooperation among liberal democracies, a project that rests comfortably on a Westphalian foundation. This is essentially intergovernmentalism pursued by sovereign states that happen to be liberal democracies, and it presupposes and depends on an orderly and well-functioning Westphalian system. Liberal democratic cooperation occurs within a wider system of nation-states, which itself may be global or may share space with empires or other non-Westphalian political formations. Second, as a project to protect and advance the prospects of liberal democracy, liberal internationalism can be pursued more directly by promoting the wider development and consolidation of the Westphalian system. A stable and expanding Westphalian system provides liberal democracies various benefits: it provides a more stable global order in which the liberal democratic subsystem can operate, and it provides rules and institutions that facilitate cooperation with nonliberal states.

Varieties of Nineteenth-Century Internationalism

A variety of internationalisms flourished in early and mid-nineteenth-century Europe and the United States, providing ideas, constituencies, and political space for cooperation among the emerging liberal democracies. The term *international* itself was coined as a way of describing the explosion of societies and activities devoted to international issues. "The terminology of the international was applied particularly to law but also to copyright, language, weights and measures, postage as well as to a wide range of voluntary bodies," notes Anthony Howe. "At this point 'international' seems to supersede the discourse of the 'universal'—a term applied to history, religion, peace and geography, appealing to the brotherhood of man, not to the citizens of different nations."[35] In this way, the rise of internationalism is tied to the rise of nationalism. Cooperation and community were built on a foundation of modernizing nation-states.[36]

Not all internationalisms were proto-liberal or reform-oriented. International movements spanned the ideological and political spectrum and they varied as well in their reformist and revolutionary ambitions. In 1864, Karl Marx raised the voice of organized labor for the first time in the First International. Nationalism itself emerged as an internationalist movement in the mid- and late nineteenth century.[37] As Glenda Sluga argues, "the political and institutional spaces that opened up around the idea of 'the international' crossed with the multiple strands of democratic, liberal, socialist, feminist, nationalist, imperialist, capitalist, federalist, and anticolonial aspirations."[38] Within this setting, nineteenth-century internationalism was an important carrier of liberal reformist ideas. By midcentury, a cluster of international movements and campaigns had become a prominent feature of the Western world and beyond. It was focused on trade and commerce, peacemaking, law and arbitration, social causes, and functional cooperation. These strands of internationalism were ultimately woven together in the early twentieth century as components of the liberal internationalist project.

Commercial Internationalism

An important strand of nineteenth-century internationalism was commercial or market internationalism, which had its roots in the free trade movement in Great Britain. The industrial revolution began in Britain and then spread to the continent and across the Atlantic. In the 1840s, British merchants and commercial groups won a landmark parliamentary victory with the repeal of the Corn Laws, which opened up an era of free trade—a watershed moment in the rethinking of the country's position in the world economy. Other countries followed Britain's lead, and free trade and protectionist coalitions in Europe, the United States, and other emerging industrial societies struggled over commercial policy and negotiated reductions in tariffs and the terms of trade in the decades that followed. The precursors to free trade can be traced back to the late eighteenth century, when European governments periodically loosened restrictions on imported grain, and trade agreements began to be used as a tool of commercial diplomacy. Adam Smith's ideas about trade and commercial society appeared in these decades, and the French Physiocrats promulgated their doctrine of laissez-faire, laissez-passer. Decades later, with Britain's repeal of its Corn Laws, free trade was transformed into an international movement.

Older mercantilist and colonial policies and ideas did not disappear. But new societal interests—the urban working class and commercial and financial interests—found ways to push Britain in the direction of freer trade and increased market internationalism. "The triumph of Free Trade in England," the historian Herbert Fisher writes, "was a victory of town over country, of the new manufacturing over the old landlord interests, of a middle class which while furthering its own material advantage incidentally promoted the interests of the poor."[39] In Parliament, Richard Cobden and John Bright emerged as leading advocates for free trade, linking trade liberalization to the building of a more peaceful international order. "The more any nation traffics abroad upon free and honest principles, the less it will be in a danger of wars," argued Cobden. "I defy you to show me how any Government or people on the Continent can strengthen themselves, even if they chose to carry on a war of conquest."[40] Peace and prosperity were seen as intrinsically linked. Free trade generates widely shared gains within and between countries. Reciprocity and the benefits that flow from the elimination of barriers to commercial exchange put the political relations among states on a more principled basis and undercut the constituencies for war.

The consolidation of the nation-state was seen as a precondition for free trade to emerge as a mechanism for building a system of international relations—a sort of consortium of nations. Commercial treaties would weave together nation-states and provide a way of reconciling sovereignty and interdependence. In the view of Cobden and other internationalists, trade agreements were a new type of international institution that would unite Europe in a pacific order based on rising prosperity. "Commercial treaties provided a new form of 'international compact,'" Anthony Howe argues, "with the potential to unite the peoples of Europe. . . . In this sense it was free trade which now made 'inter-nationalism' possible for the first time in world history."[41] Older visions of universal law gave way to a vision of order organized around consumers, citizens, and intergovernmental cooperation.

Economic interests, party politics, and ideological ideas shaped the outcome. In her study of the repeal of the Corn Laws, Cheryl Schonhardt-Bailey finds that economic interests—and the shifting balance of organized class interests—were the driving forces behind the decision, but it was also bound up in a larger spirit of reform and in ideological struggles over Britain's future within a rapidly modernizing global world.[42] Free trade was part of a larger democratic movement in Britain that included campaigns for parliamentary reform and the expansion of male suffrage. Politicians were responding to pressures to modernize the state and make it more representative of a society in which farmers and landowners were losing political ground to industrial workers and capitalists. This shift was reflected in the Reform Act of 1832, which doubled the size of the electorate and redistributed seats away from rural constituencies. The intellectual proponents of free trade found themselves making common cause with labor and manufacturing interests as well as the government reform lobby.[43]

The free trade movement included a variety of views about open markets. For moderate advocates, free trade was primarily an instrument for reorienting Britain's economic relations, promoting prosperity, and strengthening political ties with other countries. Others championed free trade in the pursuit of more ambitious goals: eliminating the sources of war or putting an end to empire. For the most ambitious, free trade was the leading edge of a global transformation, presaging, as Anthony Howe argues, "the dissolution of empire, the ending of territorial annexation and the abandonment of aristocratic militarism."[44] Controversial at first, by the second half of the nineteenth century, free trade was a core doctrine of British global policy. It had become, as David Cannadine notes, an "article of faith among most Victorian politicians, bankers, businessmen and manufacturers, and would remain so until the end of the nineteenth century—and in some quarters well beyond."[45]

This spreading set of ideas and interests culminated in various tariff reduction treaties with other Western industrializing countries, although economic downturns and panics periodically reversed the direction of policies. In 1860, Britain and France signed the Cobden-Chevalier Treaty, greatly reducing tariffs between the two leading European powers. These tariff concessions were later extended to other countries. Western industrializing countries signed more than sixty trade treaties. Technological revolutions in communication and transport along with economic specialization continued to develop across the world economy, thus providing impetus to this form of internationalism. Trade liberalization within the industrializing world continued even as European powers extended their imperial sway across the globe. In his classic study, Charles Kindleberger concludes that the rise of free trade in nineteenth-century Western Europe was driven by expanding coalitions of business and societal interests, but also by the ideology of free trade economics, the "intellectual triumph of the political economists" in Britain and the Continent.[46]

War itself also played a role in the growth of international trade. At the beginning of the century, the Napoleonic Wars led to the raising of tariffs across Europe and, indeed, the Corn Laws were enacted in Britain in 1812 through the efforts of a protectionist coalition of farmers and landowners. But Napoleon's invasion of Spain and Portugal in 1808 set in motion a wave of rebellions and independence movements across Latin America that led to the formation of new republics in the Caribbean, Mexico, and South America. These new states, once free of mercantilist restrictions, could join the open trading system. Second, the industrial revolution that began in Britain spread across Europe and the Atlantic world, bringing technological breakthroughs in production, transportation, and communication that were a boon to international trade. The steam engine, for example, had a profound impact on the integration of international commodity markets. The sharp drop in shipping costs created opportunities for import and export in a growing range of goods. These circumstances laid the groundwork for the opening of national economies and the integration of the world economy.[47]

The free trade movement enjoyed its broadest support in the middle decades of the century when free trade ideology was most closely tied to the Anglo-American peace movement. Cobden was the most influential internationalist of the moment. But by 1880 or so, these circumstances had begun to change. European imperial competition intensified and ideas of social Darwinism cast doubt upon the older liberal vision of natural, if latent, harmony among nations. In the hands of a new generation of European political leaders, nationalism and free trade were no longer seen as inevitably linked. The global economic downturn of 1873 contributed to backlash against commercial internationalism. In addition, growing demands of European governments for revenues, mostly to fund wars, made tariffs useful again.[48] For internationalists still seeking to build a community of peaceful liberal democratic nations, free trade remained a part of the vision. But other tools—legal and institutional—gained ground within the wider liberal internationalist movement.

Throughout the nineteenth century, the campaign for free trade was part of a larger effort to reform industrial society and build a more peaceful international order. Free trade was an instrument for strengthening representative democracy, reinforcing liberal rights, and generating a prosperous middle class, which was the vanguard of political and social progress. Richard Cobden and Victorian-era internationalists held firm in their belief that free trade would be part of a more general advance of modern democratic societies, pushed forward by enlightened self-interest. In the Cobdenite worldview, writes John Hobson, "the removal of trade barriers . . . came to have the value of an actually constructive policy, liberating as it did the forces of social harmony to weave their own pattern of human cooperation."[49]

The International Peace Movement

At the same time that British reformers were promoting free trade, antiwar societies were emerging in Britain and the United States, and later in continental Europe, advancing various schemes to promote peace. Early nineteenth-century business leaders in Britain and France took up the cause of peace and allied themselves with various religious groups. In Britain and the United States, Quaker-led peace societies advocated Jeremy Bentham's project of international dialogue and law. Richard Cobden and John Bright (himself a Quaker) built ties between the free trade and peace movements. Factions within the peace movement took on the related causes of anti-imperialism and abolitionism. Along the way, the social composition of the Anglo-American peace movement expanded beyond its roots in Protestantism to wider secular, radical, and internationalist groups. While much of this activity took place in Europe and the United States, peace movement activists could also be found in Latin America, Africa, and Japan. Throughout the nineteenth century, the peace movement helped advance international legal norms and create a constituency for treaties in the areas of arbitration, humanitarianism, and arms control.[50]

The first peace societies were founded in the United States and Great Britain after the Napoleonic Wars. In the United States, several existing peace groups combined in 1827 to become the American Peace Society under the leadership of William Ladd. In Britain, the London Peace Society was founded by William Allen in 1816. These societies, largely composed of nonconformist Protestants and led by Quakers, tended to use Christian arguments in their advocacy. The groups emerged independently in the two countries but eventually learned of each other's existence and began to exchange ideas. The aim of these early groups, as one member put it, was "to effect a change in public opinion on the subject of war, and to persuade men to examine it by the light of the Gospel." They spent most of their efforts debating and disseminating ideas about the peaceful organization of the world, building ties with like-minded activists in other countries, and eschewing party politics in favor of direct societal appeals.[51]

The Anglo-American peace groups' early debates focused on the extent of their opposition to war. Some opposed all war, an ethical stand that emerged from pacifist Christian beliefs. Others opposed war more selectively, reflecting more secular international convictions rooted in beliefs about progress and reform. What they tended to agree on was the importance of opposing and transcending the "custom of war." They jointly called on nations to renounce wars of aggression and embrace international institutions and legal norms for conflict resolution. "We hope," Ladd argued soon after the founding of the American Peace Society, "to increase and promote the practice already begun of submitting national differences to amicable discussion and arbitration; and finally of settling all national controversies by an appeal to reason, as becomes rational creatures . . . and that shall be done by a Congress of Nations, whose decrees shall be enforced by public opinion that rules the world. . . . Then wars shall cease."[52] This statement of aims, advanced nearly a hundred years before Woodrow Wilson's arrival in Paris, reflected a body of ideas about war, law, arbitration, and public opinion that would persist well into the twentieth century.

By the 1840s, the peace movement had spread to continental Europe, most notably France and Switzerland, and contained an increasing diversity of factions and coalitions. A radical peace movement arose in the 1830s as part of a wider social activism. New struggles for social and economic justice arose, led by the abolitionist movement in the United States and labor organizing in both Great Britain and the United States. William Lloyd Garrison's New England Non-Resistance Society, founded in 1838, made efforts in Britain to recruit working-class Chartists to their cause. In 1846, Elihu Burritt founded the League of Human Brotherhood as an international organization seeking to attract working-class members.[53] These groups represented the beginning of a long tradition of labor and progressive groups seeking to bring together the causes of social justice, human rights, and peace.

The peace societies also became connected to the free trade movement. Richard Cobden, who emerged in Great Britain after 1840 as the leader of both movements, spoke of free trade and peace as "one and the same cause."[54] Free exchange and nonintervention were seen as going hand in hand. "If governments would keep their hands off and allow the mutual interests of free commercial intercourse to weave bonds of union between people," as John Hobson summarizes Cobden's thinking, "peace on earth and good-will among nations would be secured, the waste and provocation of armaments would disappear, and the material and moral resources of every nation would be available for the improvement of the national life and for the enrichment of humanity."[55] This belief that peace—between states and social classes— could be achieved through the progress and prosperity generated by trade and exchange became an increasingly prominent theme within the peace community, particularly after the repeal of the Corn Laws. As Cecelia Lynch argues, this combining of free trade and peace agendas effectively co-opted British "working-class radicalism by the concern with prosperity through tariff reduction, which in turn affected the course of peace activity by diverting demands for peace based on economic equality to peace based on the promise of future prosperity."[56]

Beginning in the 1840s, peace groups on both sides of the Atlantic began to convene in international peace congresses. The purpose of these gatherings was to build support for the movement, particularly in continental Europe, and promote their evolving ideas and proposals. They provided a forum for debating plans for international institutions organized to develop norms of arbitration, adjudication, and the peaceful settlements of disputes.

At the first International Peace Conference held in London in 1843, participants agreed on resolutions advocating arbitration mechanisms as the means of settling international disputes and a "high court of nations" to keep the peace in Europe. The Brussels Congress of 1848 and the Paris Congress of 1849 also supported arbitration and the creation of an international court.[57] Furthermore, they passed resolutions for the improvement of communications between nations and against the raising of loans and taxes for "wars of ambition and conquest."[58] In Brussels, the delegates debated (but did not pass) a proposal by Elihu Burritt for a Congress of Nations, inspired by William Ladd's ideas from the 1820s. Beginning in 1843, the congresses also passed resolutions calling for the reduction of armaments expenditures and the creation of a system of international disarmament. But various factions differed on the rationale and purposes of disarmament. Some emphasized pacifist and Christian principles, while others, following Richard Cobden, argued on the basis of expense and taxation. Generally, the language of resolutions tended to favor internationalists—secular and pragmatic—over pacifists.

The peace congresses represented a high-water mark that the peace movement would not reach again until the early twentieth century. The peace coalition remained a mixture of pacifists and religious groups, labor activists, free traders, and establishment internationalists. The work of the congresses was directed at influencing both public opinion and, perhaps more directly, parliamentarians on both sides of the Atlantic. The most widely embraced proposals were those supporting arbitration and international legal mechanisms of dispute resolution. In 1848, resolutions were introduced in the French Chamber and the US House of Representatives for "stipulated arbitration" in future treaties, but these were defeated in both houses. More famously, Richard Cobden introduced a resolution in the House of Commons for the British government to enter into communications with foreign governments for the establishment of a worldwide system of arbitration. The advocates resisted making claims based on Christianity in favor of more practical arguments. As Cobden said, "I merely wish to bind [nations] to do before a war what nations virtually always do after war." The resolution was defeated, Palmerston arguing that arbitration was not applicable to the states of Europe and would undercut Britain's geopolitical position.

By the 1850s, the ideas of trade and social reform led peace groups toward internationalism that was reform-oriented rather than radical. Cobden, skeptical of the revolutionary upheaval of 1848, worried that it would fragment states into smaller units, worsen nationalism, and undermine free trade. But others saw upheaval as an opportunity. The Italian nationalist Giuseppe Mazzini argued that "countries are the workshops of humanity" and that democratic and nationalist revolutions would produce a world of large nations in which "all excuse of war would disappear, and in its place [would] arise a spirit of brotherhood and peaceful emulation on the road of progress."[59] In the coming decades, the peace movement increasingly focused on promoting international legal and institutional mechanisms to ensure peace.

In the second half of the nineteenth century, the peace movement began to weaken. When the Crimean War broke out in 1853, Britain found itself in its first major war in forty years. The upsurge in patriotic and nationalist sentiment drained away some of the peace movement's constituency. Richard Cobden and John Bright, the leaders of the trade and peace movements in Britain, lost their seats in Parliament in 1857. In the United States, the American Civil War had a similar effect, which led to the curtailment of peace activity and opened up divisions between American and British peace societies over support and opposition to the war. With the struggle over slavery, new groups focused on abolition and social justice emerged and the salience of the peace movement declined.

It reemerged in the last decades of the nineteenth century with its ideas and activities less rooted in Christian values and appeals to public opinion and more focused on shaping international norms and institutions. New reform moments, part of an era of political activism and progressivism, pushed for a wide agenda of economic regulation, social legislation, and political enfranchisement. Many of these groups joined forces with older peace groups in working for arbitration, disarmament, and the creation of international institutions. By the end of the nineteenth century, these progressive and peace movement groups had joined with international legal experts and groups seeking to strengthen international law and institutionalize norms of the peaceful settlement of disputes through arbitration and the building of an organization of nations with wide participation and authority over matters of peace and security.[60]

Legal Internationalism

Another variety of nineteenth-century European internationalism was what might be called legal internationalism. This is what Jeremy Bentham had in mind when he introduced the term *international* in his *Introduction to the Principles of Morals and Legislation,* in which he argued that law within nations and between them needed a new coherence and philosophical foundation to govern the "mutual transactions of sovereigns."[61] In the mid-nineteenth century, legal theorists and governments engaged in various efforts to identify and agree on the legal foundations of sovereignty, empire, and the colonial order. International law, the realm of law among states and nations, emerged as both a scholarly discipline and a diplomatic practice combining new visions of internationalism with the realities of modern nation-states.[62]

Nineteenth-century legal internationalism spoke the language of the "law of nations." This was a double-edged discourse that provided legal justifications for European imperial expansion and unequal and discriminatory treatment of peoples outside the "civilized world," but it also provided concepts and legal tools that could be used to limit imperial conquest. The early modern ideas of international law and their foundational statements in the work of Hugo Grotius and Emerich Vattel were brought forward and reworked. Vattel had conceived of the Society of Nations as a natural fact and thought that it functioned according to laws that could be discovered and codified. As Jennifer Pitts argues, "accounts of the law of nations came to be structured by an idea of nations as moral communities equal in status with, and independent of, one another."[63] In the late eighteenth century and into the nineteenth century, concepts, narratives, and legal principles produced by internationally oriented jurists gave increasing coherence to a vision of nation-states existing within an international legal community. The European state system, the law of nations, and emerging ideas about the "international" evolved together. By the turn of the nineteenth century, Pitts notes, "the European state system and its public law were coming to be seen as standing in for the international as a whole, representing a proto-international community or the germ of a global community."[64]

By the middle of the nineteenth century, this legal internationalism emerged in Europe as a bulwark for the management of state relations. Networks of international lawyers made efforts during these decades to institutionalize their discipline and construct the architecture of a global legal order that would regulate relations among nations and across the global imperial order. One visible manifestation of this legal internationalism was the 1851 Universal Peace Congress in London. "Over the following decades a new transnational elite emerged that shared the pacifists' view that the salvation of the world depended on transforming the conservative order created at the Congress of Vienna and challenging the authority of diplomats," notes Mazower. "But this elite's goal was codification and the professionalization of international legal practice, and their instrument was not mass mobilization but the formation of a new discipline with its own institutions, worldview, and sense of history."[65]

The expansion of European international law shadowed the dual character of the nineteenth-century global order. For European states, jurists elaborated the principles and terms of an international order underpinned by law that emerged through agreements of separate sovereign polities. Outside the West, international law functioned, as Cemil Aydin argues, "as an instrument of internationalism for European empires."[66] Europe exported international law to the non-Western world on terms that included the denial of sovereignty and the imposition of extraterritoriality. Japan, China, and the Ottoman Empire, for example, gained entry to the European-led international community by meeting "standards of civilization" set by European powers, yet they continued to struggle for equal status within the global legal order. By the end of the century, international lawyers in these non-Western sovereign entities had begun to push back against European legal hegemony, critiquing discriminatory applications of law and defending the interests of their nations or empires through the language of international law.[67] Japan became the first non-European and non-Christian state to gain legal recognition of its equal standing among imperial powers, but only after its defeat of China and Russia.[68]

In the 1870s, academics and legal experts in the United States and Europe began to elaborate legal codes to cover various fields of international relations. In Europe, scholarly law societies were created to fashion these codes. The first society of international law, the Institute for International Law, founded in Ghent in 1873, was intended to foster the development and codification of international law as an "organization of the world's conscience."[69] A society founded in Brussels, known as the Association for the Reform and Codification of the Law of Nations, worked broadly on the promulgation of public international law; in 1895 it became the International Law Society, a leading gathering of continental jurists. Russian jurists founded an International Law Association in St. Petersburg in 1880, and the first American society, the American Society for International Law, was founded in 1906. Similar societies emerged across continental Europe, all focused on developing codes of international law.[70] At the same time, diplomatic staffs and foreign ministries in Europe and the Americas increasingly included people with legal training. By the end of the nineteenth century, a law degree was a common credential for the diplomatic service. Legal norms and procedures came to influence the ways states defined problems and pursued the resolution of interstate conflict.

Compared to generals and politicians, international lawyers spoke and thought differently about international conflict, and their increasing influence had implications for the agreements that states were able to achieve. Martha Finnemore argues, for example, that Latin American governments transformed disputes over sovereign debt with the United States and European powers into legal disputes that could be settled through arbitration rather than military intervention. For centuries, states had used military means to enforce legally binding contracts. "After 1902 Latin American states began fighting back on this same legal turf," Finnemore notes. "Appealing to international law, they argued that sovereign equality of states was the foundational principle of international law and, indeed, of international order."[71] Latin American countries, reframing the sovereign debt issue in terms of legal principles of sovereignty, were able to persuade the "emerging community of international legal scholars of the rightness of their view and, through them, persuade creditor states to sign an international treaty at The Hague in 1907 barring the practice [of using military force to enforce contracts]."[72]

More generally, the rise of international law and lawyers as a profession affected the arbitration movement and the rise of multilateral institutions. International law offered a new terrain on which states could argue and seek agreement.[73] Lawyers arguing with other lawyers could agree more easily than could other interlocutors having similar discussions. Legal principles like sovereign equality provided a tool for weaker states to engage more powerful states and created new constituencies for multilateral mechanisms of dispute resolution.[74] While the first Hague Conference, in 1899, was dominated by traditional politicians and military officials, the second one, in 1907, was primarily a gathering of international lawyers.[75] A leading figure at the 1907 conference was US secretary of state Elihu Root, who had been the first president of the American Society of International Law and was an active participant in the arbitration movement. Several of the leading figures at the Hague Conference, including Root, had written extensively about the virtues of arbitration and the elaboration of international legal norms for the peaceful settlement of disputes.[76] The differences in the outcome of the two conferences—the second one was more ambitious and more successful in forging consensus on the blueprints for international governance—largely reflected the rising role of international lawyers and their framing of issues.

The second Hague Conference established international law as a means of building stable peace among nations, and thus as a leading form of internationalism. As Glenda Sluga argues, "by the turn of the twentieth century, international law was widely considered a crucial facilitator of the political ideals and administrative practices that had putatively made internationalism real."[77] The momentum legal internationalism gained through the last decades of the nineteenth century showed up in the elaboration of international law and the establishment of international courts for arbitration. The growing presence of international lawyers at diplomatic conferences altered the framing of issues and created new voices in favor of multilateral rules and institutions.

Social Internationalism

There was also a rise of social internationalism. Organized to promote the reform of liberal society, societal, religious, and public interest groups established myriad international networks and connections. This form of internationalism was expressed in many ways, always rooted in the causes that emerged out of liberal democracy. These groups sought to advance political rights, economic well-being, and social justice; struggled to expand the franchise and liberal education; mounted domestic reform campaigns; and supported the labor movement. The industrial economies emerging on both sides of the Atlantic were generating new social problems, class alignments, and political programs for reform. By 1900, the older antislavery and working-class groups had been joined by a new generation of progressive activists seeking to reform domestic economic and political institutions. While they focused on the reform of domestic society, they tended to frame theses societal problems not as distinctively national ones but as emerging across the industrializing world—and so they reached out into international society.[78]

In the second half of the nineteenth century, two new internationalist movements emerged on the scene—one based on class interests and the other focused on social and humanitarian issues. Beginning in the 1860s, the international labor movement became increasingly active across the industrial world. The founding movement was the First International, a meeting of a federation of working groups held in London in September 1864. Organized by the leaders of British and French trade unions, this group came to take the shape of a centralized party based on individual members organized in local groups and national federations. It met as a congress each year, led by a general council elected by the congress and located in London. Karl Marx's intellectual presence loomed over this organization, although from its early moments, the First International was divided among competing ideological factions.[79]

Various groups across the Atlantic promoted social and humanitarian causes, both within industrial societies and in the emerging world. Some of this humanitarian activity emerged as a response to the human devastation of the Crimean War and the US Civil War. It sought to make the conduct of war more humane and to protect noncombatants through international codes of conduct. In 1864, the Red Cross Convention was established in Geneva to treat soldiers wounded in war; it later evolved into a more general-purpose humanitarian organization. In the 1880s and into the new century, new groups emerged under the banner of progressivism and social reform— abolitionists, labor groups, settlement-house workers, and suffragists. Jane Addams's settlement-house movement was inspired by a similar movement in Great Britain. These reform groups had various domestic political goals and offered a range of critiques of laissez-faire economic policies. But they also saw reforms in international society as intimately connected to the re- form of domestic society. The Women's International League for Peace and Freedom, for example, expressed solidarity with the international peace movement and its campaigns for disarmament and the peaceful settlement of disputes.[80]

These various forms of social internationalism reflected the growth and evolution of liberal and capitalist society. As Akira Iriye argues, "the late nineteenth century saw the creation of many . . . organizations aiming at the exchange of scientists, artists, musicians, and others across national boundaries, thereby establishing what today would be called 'epistemic communities'—groups of individuals sharing ideas and interests."[81] These in- ternational associations moved forward on the tide of economic growth, trade, and the rise of middle-class society across the capitalist world. Iriye argues that these nongovernmental organizations and associations were car- riers of liberal ideas such as individual rights, the rule of law, limitations on state power, and civil society—aspects of liberalism that were enshrined in the worldviews of entrepreneurs, activists, and societal groups as they moved across borders. "Liberalism in the age of global capitalism," he writes, "was becoming internationalized."[82]

Functional Internationalism

The nineteenth century also saw the rise of what might be called "functional internationalism," or what Martin Geyer and Johannes Paulmann call the "mechanics" of internationalism. By this they mean the proliferation of international agreements, conventions, and organizations established to facilitate and regulate travel, communication, and commercial standards.[83] As Iriye writes, this is when Western nations agreed "to standardize weights and measures, to adopt uniform postal and telegraphic rates, and to cope with the danger of communicable diseases"—in effect, to lay down the infrastructure for global cooperation.[84] The result, Jürgen Osterhammel notes, was "a historically unparalleled norm setting in countless areas of technology, communications, and cross-border trade."[85]

This form of internationalism, a response to states' increasing recognition of their mutual interdependence, was expressed in new types of intergovernmental meetings and international conferences. It involved, as Inis Claude observes, the "establishment of a profusion of agencies whose terms of reference touched upon such diverse fields as health, agriculture, tariffs, railroads, standards of weight and measurement, patents and copyrights, narcotic drugs, and prison conditions."[86] Craig Murphy provides a rich account of the rise of these institutional bodies, tracing their role as tools of regulation and standard setting in the globalizing world of industrial capitalism and interimperial relations. They were functional responses to the pressures involved in expanding markets of the capitalist system, reducing transaction costs, and providing common standards for the movement of people, goods, and capital.[87]

One type of functional internationalism was what Cornelia Navari calls "administrative internationalism." As the Western states' bureaucratic and administrative tasks expanded, they acquired a parallel international dimension. "Each branch of government," Navari writes, "came to be shadowed in some of its functions by an international organization of some sort which

duplicated or supplemented its administrative tasks. Posts, health, and the European railways timetable union were the earliest examples of this form of administrative internationalism."[88] These "externalized bureaucracies" developed in two ways. In some instances, the most advanced industrial states established an agency or service, which was followed by the creation of an international body to facilitate coordination, and led in turn to efforts at the international level to get less advanced countries to follow suit. The International Postal Union (IPU), created in the 1850s, was an example of this developmental logic. The establishment of domestic postal services in Western Europe and the United States in the late eighteenth century led to the founding of the IPU, which began with twenty-two states that pledged to submit to arbitration all disputes concerning postal matters. The same process occurred with the establishment of European central banks, which began coordinating their activities in the 1930s and urged other states to follow their lead. In other instances, international coordination came first, and this spurred the development of domestic state agencies. For example, the outbreak of plague in the 1850s led to international efforts to contain the problem, and this in turn spurred the building of domestic state capacities to fight the disease through public health measures.

The evolution of these domestic and international bureaus followed the evolution of the liberal democratic state. "The first . . . international administrations, including posts and international health co-ordination, were a creation of nineteenth-century 'traditional' liberalism and conformed to its views of public purpose," Navari writes. "As the 'social question' began to concern governments, a second generation of 'new' liberal institutions began to be established, notably an international labour organization, established in 1919 to equalise conditions of labour."[89] It was a type of internationalism that created tools and capacities for modernizing liberal states. International agreements and agencies, as Inis Claude notes, "served as collection points and clearing houses for information, centers for discussion of common problems by governments, instruments for achieving the coordination by agreement of national policies and practices, and agencies for promoting the formulation and acceptance of uniform or minimum standards in the fields of concern."[90] The founding of the League of Nations, and later the United

Nations, continued this ratchet-like logic of state-intergovernmental institutional development. These international bodies took on an expanding array of tasks, many of them aimed at giving developmental assistance to emerging states.

These many types of nineteenth-century internationalism were all propelled forward by their affiliation with other major forces of change. Free trade internationalism was tied to the rise of industrial capitalism and the expansion of world markets. Legal internationalism was put at the service of empire and colonialism. Even though international law was not explicitly at odds with European imperial understandings of international society, the international law movement also sought to codify legal-institutional mechanisms for the peaceful settlement of disputes between sovereign states. Functional internationalism was most directly a response to the pressures and demands of modern global capitalism. Liberalism itself—as it arose in Europe in the nineteenth century—became tightly connected to the rise of nationalism and the consolidation of modern nation-states. As Martin Bailey argues, "even when conferences and congresses claimed to represent universal principles, they were now structured increasingly by the participation of nation-states."[91] What made these international projects "liberal" was their combined weight in moving the world toward a more open, loosely rules-based, progressively oriented form of order. The spread of liberal democracy was essential for liberal-oriented internationalism to gain momentum. But liberal internationalism rode its way into the twentieth century on the backs of empire, imperialism, nationalism, civilizational discourse, and industrial capitalism.

The strengthening of international law and institutions within a modernizing international society became the centerpiece of European and American internationalism. The ideas were not new—early nineteenth-century peace societies had championed a Congress of Nations, an international court, a system of arbitration, and the codification of international law. But by the early twentieth century, the groups and constituencies championing legal and institutional order building had changed and expanded. Among internationalists and activist groups, there was a general agreement that modern international order needed a Congress of Nations with as wide a membership as possible (though excluding "barbarous states") and an International Court, both operating through a code of international law.

Over the decades, the thinking behind legal and institutional internationalism had evolved from focusing on public opinion to focusing on relations between governments. The Anglo-American peace movement that began after 1815 originally sought to inspire public opinion, which would in turn prevail on governments. Agitating among the people, it was thought, would spur them to demand that governments commit to peace and create new international laws and institutions. Governments, in effect, were regarded as "instruments of the public will." The midcentury peace congresses held in London and Paris showed a shift toward addressing both constituencies—seeking to broaden the peace movement's appeal outside religious and trade groups while also fashioning proposals that could be directly taken up by legislatures. By the end of the century, international groups increasingly pursued their visions through professional elites and governmental circles.[92]

The growth of interest in arbitration treaties was a result of these changing constituencies and coalitions, but it also tracked the changes in the evolution of states and societies. As Arthur Beales writes, "the general acceptance of arbitration developed parallel with the growth of democracy."[93] This is true in two respects. First, the push for arbitration agreements—and for a more general international legal and institutional architecture—was a deeply political process unfolding within a nineteenth-century liberal democratic world whose civil societies were a fertile seedbed for internationalist ideas and movements. Political movements, peace groups, trade associations, learned societies, interparliamentary unions—these were the actors and agents of the new internationalism. Their struggles played out in parliaments and foreign ministries. Second, the idea of arbitration backed by international judicial and parliamentary organizations was in many ways an extension of liberal democratic ideas into international society. Rule of law and the peaceful settlement of disputes were at the heart of liberal democracy, so it is not surprising that groups and movements within these societies would seek to extend these ideas to the international system.[94] That liberal democracies in fact pursued arbitration agreements and treaties further suggests the particular affinity that seemed to exist between these states and nineteenth-century legal and institutional internationalism.

By the end of the nineteenth century, the threads that would coalesce into liberal internationalism were fully visible and loosely intertwined. The political and intellectual strands of this new internationalism tended to converge on a set of core ideas: open commercial relations, institutional mechanisms for dispute settlement, and rudimentary norms of human rights and humanitarianism. Internationalist movements and coalitions had expanded beyond the mid-nineteenth-century religious and commercial societies until, by the last decades of the century, the varieties of internationalism were increasingly dominated by secular and professional elites and progressive reform groups articulating proposals aimed directly at parliaments and foreign ministries. Growing interdependence among industrial societies and arms competition among the great powers provided the shifting setting for new efforts at government reform and the building of an international order.

Nationalism and Internationalism

The origins of liberal internationalism can be found in a nineteenth-century internationalism that was embodied in the kaleidoscopic activities of people and groups working across the emerging liberal democratic world—diplomats, merchants, peace activists, workers, intellectuals, lawyers, and many others. Internationalism was itself intimately connected to the rise and spread of nationalism and the nation-state. In one sense, internationalism and nationalism were rival movements, offering divergent logics for the organization of political space. But in a more profound sense, they were two halves of the emerging modern world order. Nationalism and the nation-state provided the framework of political order and identity among the Western democracies. Internationalism was visible in the multifaceted ways in which people and groups within these societies reached across borders to build relationships, institutions, and bonds of solidarity—and to pursue common projects. Liberal democracy emerged in the nineteenth century and anchored itself within the Western system of nation-states. This provided the expanding geopolitical space in which internationalism emerged.

The varieties of internationalism that flourished in the nineteenth century reflected citizens' growing consciousness that they lived in a modernizing and globalizing world. The peace movement, free traders, the international labor movement, and societies of jurists all recognized that interdependence was a moral and material fact that generated both dangers and opportunities. The past was receding and new forms of politics and society were emerging. Connections, affiliations, causes, identities, and political organization all gained a new internationality. The global interconnectedness of industrial societies and great powers was the central feature of nineteenth-century modernity. "The word *international* was beginning to connote a reality," Beales argues. "Common bonds among governments and interests which cut across frontiers were slowly coming to receive more than mere lip-service."[95] Internationalists were exploring new ways of organizing international space. These new global imaginaries and activities involved, simultaneously, notions of both the nation-state and international society.

Not all these internationalisms were liberal. But it was out of these multiple strands that liberal internationalism ultimately took shape as a relatively coherent, if multifaceted and shifting, political project. Liberal internationalism as a body of ideas and practices was less a unified set of beliefs than a "family" of ideas, many of which were in tension with each other. Liberalism, as it emerged in Europe in the mid-nineteenth century, had its own tensions: values such as liberty, equality, private property, and social justice often conflicted with each other. Liberal internationalism was a collection of ideas and projects built on a vision that the world was organizing itself into sovereign nation-states, led by Western liberal industrial societies, but various strands of which continued to make common cause with European empire and colonialism. The postimperial norms of self-determination, racial and political equality, and universal rights were not yet at liberal internationalism's core. The state—increasingly the nation-state—was seen as the source and seat of sovereign authority, but liberal internationalism also anticipated a growth in shared forms of collective governance. These tensions would remain at its heart.

FOUR

Wilsonian Internationalism

The first half of the twentieth century was cruel to liberal international-ism. The world wars, the Great Depression, and the rise of fascist and totalitarian great powers triggered repeated crises in the liberal internation-alist project. The belle epoque—the decades spanning the turn of the century, which Europeans would later look back on nostalgically as a time of opti-mism, prosperity, scientific advance, cultural achievement, and peace—revealed only one face of modernity. The industrialism that brought wealth, power, and social advancement to Western countries had a lurking dark side. The violent upheaval and geopolitical catastrophe of the Great War marked a turning point not just for world politics but for liberal internationalism—and so too would the wars, depressions, and political crises that followed. In the twentieth century, liberal internationalism endured a sequence of alter-nating golden eras and global calamities. The notion that modernity was leading a steady advance of societies and international order was abruptly and repeatedly dispelled by war, social upheaval, and resurgent illiberalism. The long arc of liberal internationalism came to be seen as an ongoing and in-creasingly world-weary encounter with the Jekyll-and-Hyde character of modernity.

The two most important moments occurred in 1919 and 1945. Liberal in-ternationalists were forced to pick up the intellectual and political pieces after unimaginably destructive world wars that left them debating the na-ture of "the global" and the deep logic of the modernizing world. But these wars also had the effect of collapsing the "old order," creating historical openings for the leaders of the major states to step forward with proposals to rebuild the international order on a new foundation. In the face of world events that seemed to directly discredit their assumptions and programs, liberal internationalists did not walk away from their project. Instead they tended to rethink and reimagine it. They argued, in effect, that war, depression, and illiberal challengers to liberal democracy all required more liberal internationalism, not less.

Woodrow Wilson is identified with liberal internationalism more than any other leader or thinker. "It would be the irony of fate if my administration had to deal chiefly with foreign affairs," he remarked to a Princeton friend a few days before he left for Washington in 1913 to begin his presidency.[1] Yet it was during his eight years in office that liberal internationalism as a tradition in international relations came of age. He accomplished this mainly in speeches—and in the peacemaking in Paris. His key ideas were articulated in his famous Fourteen Points speech, a statement of American war aims delivered to a joint session of Congress in 1918. The United States would seek a world of "open covenants of peace, openly arrived at," a world with "absolute freedom of the seas" where "economic barriers" were eliminated. To ensure the peace in this new postwar order, an international organization would be established for the purpose of settling disputes on the basis of "mutual guarantees of political independence and territorial integrity to great and small states alike."[2] Wilson's vision of postwar order is often seen as bold and original—the first stirring of the liberal international imagination. But, in fact, he was giving voice to ideas that had been debated in Europe and the Americas for decades. His contribution was less intellectual than political: it crystallized liberal internationalism as a political project.

World War I and the peacemaking of Woodrow Wilson and his contemporaries brought liberal internationalism into the twentieth century. It was only in the wake of the violence and upheaval that the old world of rival imperial domains could begin to recede and efforts could be made to unify and reorganize international relations in a liberal image. Liberal internationalism became a political project—a theory, ideology, and agenda for international reform. Wilson's vision was both progressive and conservative. It embodied a sweeping plan for reshaping international order, organized around free trade, collective security, and international law. But Wilson-era liberal internationalism was conservative in the sense that it did not frontally challenge European empire, racial or cultural hierarchies, or ultimately, the prevailing terms of state sovereignty. Wilson sought to initiate a political and moral project that would not transcend the Westphalian international order but bring independent, self-governing states and peoples together through the evolution of intergovernmental norms and political relations.

In this chapter, I make four arguments. First, World War I forced Woodrow Wilson and other liberal internationalists to step forward with explicit and comprehensive proposals for reforming the international order. The vision of undirected and incremental progressive advance in international society was shattered. "The facts of the world have changed," Wilson observed in 1919. The war had made clear the need for an active, institutionalized system of cooperation and mutual protection. But he and his contemporaries did not yet see the dangers to peace and liberal democracy rooted in modernity itself. The problem, as they saw it, was the failure of states to be sufficiently modern. Modernity had not yet fully done its work. Wilson placed Germany at the center of this critique: it was Germany's atavistic social and political features—the autocratic state, militaristic culture, and Junker class—that had caused the war. Thus the war itself was turned into an instrument of progressive change. "The object of the war," Wilson argued in September 1919, "was to destroy autocratic power; that is to say, to make it impossible that there should be anywhere, as there was on Wilhelmstrasse, in Berlin, a little group of military men who could brush aside the bankers, brush aside the merchants, brush aside the manufacturers, brush aside the Emperor himself, and say: 'We have perfected a machine with which we can conquer the world.'"[3] The solution was to build international order so as to allow modernity to envelop more of the world, including Germany. This was possible, Wilson believed, because the world was still on a modernizing path; liberal democracy was still in the ascendancy. Democratic societies and the world public opinion that democracy unleashed could provide the governing mechanism for international order.

Second, the core ideas that informed the postwar order were not new. They had been debated for most of the past century and were reflected in the various strands of nineteenth-century internationalism. At the heart of this order was a vision of a community of nations organized and led by the Western liberal democracies and featuring open commerce, international law, and mechanisms for conflict resolution. Sovereign and independent states would establish a permanent system of international institutions—judicial, legislative, and executive—with an assembly or congress of nations at its center. Permanent machinery for cooperation would be established, guided by the ongoing elaboration of international law and principles for the arbitration of disputes. Cooperation and commitments would be self-enforcing, based ultimately on enlightened self-interest and the power of international public opinion. These ideas predated Wilson and were not uniquely American.

Third, Wilson's specific vision of international order was an evolving synthesis of ideas built on a series of assumptions about modernity, liberal democracy, institutions, and progressive change. It was premised on the assumptions that liberal democracy was ascendant and that "civilization," a deep and evolving feature of the modern world, would push and pull international society forward. Wilson believed deeply in the diffuse and evolutionary impact of international law as it is embodied in the rules and norms of the community of sovereign states. He considered the League of Nations the absolutely essential first step in fostering a stable system of peace. Operating within this new governance system, state leaders would be progressively socialized into its rules and norms, and international public opinion would provide a diffuse enforcement mechanism. It was this faith in the socializing and evolutionary logic of international order that allowed Wilson to yield to European leaders on questions of reparations, sovereignty, and empire. He thought he could give ground on the details because his vision would ultimately triumph.

Finally, Wilsonian internationalism failed. The United States refused to join the League of Nations, and in the decades that followed, the Versailles settlement ended in depression and war. The project of an international order manifest as the "reign of law, based on the consent of the governed and sustained by the organized opinion of mankind," as Wilson proclaimed on 4 July 1918, was left in ruins. The causes and consequences of this failure have been debated for a century. In one sense, he simply blew it. The US Senate was willing to pass the treaty with clarifying resolutions, and the American political mainstream was not isolationist, but Wilson refused to compromise. In a deeper sense, the Wilsonian version of liberal internationalism was simply unsustainable when the West itself was not on a stable geopolitical foundation. Yet the Wilsonian moment did lay down the markers for later efforts at building a liberal international order. The League of Nations did come to life, and even though it failed to secure peace, it became a vehicle for multilateral cooperation and provided a normative and institutional pathway for the dismantlement of empire. Later generations of liberal internationalists applied the lessons and legacies of this era.

World War, Modernity, and International Order

The Great War was a global catastrophe, the most violent and destructive war the world had yet seen. It was the first major war of the industrial age, a bloodbath that left ten million soldiers dead and millions more injured and maimed for life. Europe marched off to war in the summer of 1914 confident that the boys would make it home for Christmas. They did not. An entire generation of young men was wiped out. Chemical weapons, trench warfare, mass killing, the battles of Verdun and the Somme, Gallipoli, the Waste Land—it was a horrific spectacle whose violence left few Europeans untouched. "Now the catastrophe has come," Wilson noted in a speech. "Blood has been spilt in rivers, the flower of the European nations has been destroyed . . . the old order is gone."[4] The war staggered the imagination. Contemporaries called it the Great War because of its epic scale, but also because of its profound impact on the ways people thought about war, peace, and the human condition.[5]

Most immediately, the war transformed the distribution of world power. The old empires of Eurasia—tsarist, Habsburg, and Ottoman—were ruined. New nation-states were created and independence movements flickered to life in Europe's colonies. The British Empire survived, but the European powers as a whole were greatly weakened. It was a power transition with multiple facets. The European great powers had spent the nineteenth century industrializing and extending their empires, establishing ever greater dominance over the world. Britain had been at the center of this global expansion of power, its empire was the greatest the world had seen, and it provided a sort of imperial architecture that other European states sought to emulate. The Great War brought all this to an end. The European great powers lost their hold over the international order, and empire lost its centrality as the order's organizing logic.[6]

The great beneficiary of the war was the United States. Its power, already on the rise for decades, received a big push. Its wartime economy continued to expand while the other great powers faltered. Almost overnight, the United States overtook Great Britain as the world's leading financial power.[7] A central drama in this global power transition was the Anglo-American relationship. "Since the beginning of the nineteenth century the British Empire had been the largest economic unit in the world," notes Adam Tooze. "Sometime in 1916, the year of Verdun and the Somme, the combined output of the British Empire was overtaken by that of the United States of America. Henceforth, down to the beginning of the twenty-first century, American economic might would be the decisive factor in the shaping of the world order."[8] In one sense, this was a passing of the mantle of leadership from the dominant liberal state of the nineteenth century to its twentieth-century successor. But the United States also represented a different type of great power—one that emerged outside the European state system. America's shores faced both Europe and Asia. America had acquired pieces of an empire in the aftermath of the Spanish-American War, but its territorial expansion had been largely limited to extending its federal system across the North American continent. The United States was rising in a world dominated by far-flung empires, and its own complex, conflicted, and ultimately antagonistic relationship with empire—both with specific empires and with empire as an organizational logic of order—would play out across the twentieth century.[9] The power transition was in part a hegemonic succession, but it was also, and more profoundly, a transition from British leadership of an imperial order to American leadership over a protracted global struggle for a postimperial world order.[10]

The Great War also created new opportunities for order building. The old order was destroyed by the war in several ways. Most obviously, the war left the great powers and their political relationships in ruins. The rules and institutions of international order had broken down and the option of operating in the existing international order had suddenly disappeared. In strictly practical terms, a new order had to be established. Beyond this, the war and the struggles surrounding it had delegitimated the old order's rules and institutions. The war itself was evidence of this failure. The war had also ushered in a new distribution of power, which created new asymmetries between powerful and weak states. Like a powerful storm, the war had cleared away the old rules and institutional structures and wiped the slate clean. With the old constraints at least temporarily thrown off, a newly powerful group of states had the opportunity to step forward to rethink and rebuild international order. The end of the Great War was a moment not unlike those in 1648, 1713, and 1815—and what would again appear in 1945. Newly powerful actors had their chance to shape world politics. In the chaotic aftermath of war, the leaders of the United States and other states found themselves in a position to put forward new rules and principles of international relations.[11]

The Great War also ushered in a new global ideological struggle. In the spring of 1917, the United States entered the war as the champion of liberal internationalism and a "new diplomacy." Wilson sought to use the war as an instrument of progressive change. In his address to a joint session of Congress on 2 April 1917, he depicted the war as a struggle of "free and self-governed peoples" against "selfish and autocratic power."[12] That fall, the Russian Revolution brought the Bolsheviks to power under the banner of communist internationalism and the dictatorship of the proletariat. For Vladimir Lenin, as for Wilson, the Great War was the backdrop for the world-historical change he sought to lead. In his famous April Theses, delivered at the Finland Station in Petrograd, Lenin depicted the war as a "predatory imperialist" conflict driven by "the capitalist nature" of Western bourgeois governments. He foresaw that the war would lead to more revolutions and the establishment of "a new International" of workers and peasant democracies.

In their competing visions of a new world order, Wilson and Lenin each put forward sweeping narratives about the causes of the world crisis—of the war, militarism, and the upheavals of industrial society. Each saw the war as a conflagration out of which would emerge a "new order of things." Each saw Europe as the embodiment of a retrograde past, and his own country as the beacon of an enlightened age to come. Each wielded a grand ideology and saw himself as the leader of an international movement. These competing internationalist ideologies would outlast the war, outlast the Versailles settlement, outlast Lenin and Wilson, and inhabit the decades to follow.[13]

The new importance of ideology in great-power relations was partly driven by a new divergence in types of regimes, embodied in Wilson's America and Lenin's Russia. But the ideological struggles also reflected the new saliency on the world stage of public opinion and democratic politics. The "stage" on which the diplomacy of order building was to take place had been transformed. Democracy and public opinion were now integral to international relations in two respects. Most obviously, the actual diplomacy was a more public affair—presidents and prime ministers had to build coalitions and persuade larger segments of their populations than they once did. This was partly a product of the war itself, which had mobilized and expanded the citizenry and soldiery of the great powers. In a speech two weeks after the armistice, British prime minister David Lloyd George proclaimed that the task at hand was "to make Britain a fit country for heroes to live in."[14] Great sacrifices had been made, and they gave what happened after the war—war aims and peace visions—a new urgency. Wilson's triumphant tour of Europe in advance of the Paris Peace Conference had all the flourishes of this new public diplomacy. But the century-long advance of Western liberal democracy also mattered in a deeper sense. The principles of international order now needed to be more tightly linked to the principles and aspirations of liberal democracies. The definition of a legitimate international order had shifted, and leaders now had to pay more attention to democratic sensibilities when building rules and institutions. This was reflected in Wilson's critique of the corruption and backroom deals of old European geopolitics and his call for open treaties and rules-based relations. It was also reflected in the new language of self-determination. The cause of a liberal postwar order would ultimately hinge on how well it advanced the principles of liberal democracy.

In these ways, the Great War generated demands and opportunities for the reorganization of international order. It did so precisely because the war itself was so shocking: shocking, of course, in its violence and destruction, but also in its revelations about the nature of modernity and Western understanding of progress, reason, and the interdependence of societies. The war shook the political and intellectual foundations of the Western old order. Famously, a leading British internationalist, Norman Angell, had published *The Great Illusion* in 1910, arguing that the European states had become so financially and commercially linked that war had become deeply irrational. "War in advanced capitalist countries," he argued, "would be unprofitable and therefore unthinkable."[15] In later decades, Angell would be ridiculed for his naive conviction that interdependence and the rational calculation of interests could put an end to war. His argument, however, had not been that rationality would prevail, but that if it did not, Western societies would pay a grievous price—which they did.[16] Along the way, the states of the Western world also found themselves increasingly imperiled by the growing capacities of armaments to inflict damage. The new technologies of war had dramatically increased the killing power of modern militaries. These new circumstances, ominously revealed by the war, weighed on the debates that followed the leading states to the peace table.

Lineages of Liberal Internationalism

Woodrow Wilson is remembered as the great prophet of liberal internationalism who brought forth new ideas for the rebuilding of a war-ravaged world. He wanted international arbitration, freedom of the seas, and a system of nondiscriminatory trade. He wanted codified international law that would embody the norms and principles of this open and rules-based order. And he wanted a league of nations as the order's symbolic and political capstone. But the main lines of these liberal internationalist proposals were already circulating decades before the war. As we saw, the nineteenth century was a seedbed of internationalism, liberal and otherwise. In the aftermath of the

Napoleonic Wars, as parliaments and elected politicians gained prominence in Europe and the United States, peace societies and reform movements put forward and debated the core ideas that Wilson would later champion as the liberal vision for international order. Wilson's influence was important for synthesizing these ideas, giving them voice, and linking them to America's rise to global power.

Trade, Arbitration, and International Organization

The first strand was the free trade movement. In the decades after Britain repealed the Corn Laws in 1846, tariff reduction efforts had ebbed and flowed with the growth of the world economy and the European push for empire. Britain remained committed to free trade, unilaterally lowering tariffs even when other countries raised theirs. "We stand to-day at the parting of the ways," Prime Minister Balfour said in 1904 in London to a crowd of thousands who had assembled to support free trade and open doors. "One road—a broad and easy one—leads to Protection, to conscription, to the reducing of free institutions to a mere name. . . . And the other road leads to the consolidation of liberty at home, and to treaties of arbitration and amity, with their natural sequences in the arrest and ultimate reduction of armaments."[17]

This claim that free trade was an instrument of peace along with other echoes of Richard Cobden could still be heard in Western capitals. But as European imperial competition intensified, the debate on trade began to shift from tariff reduction to the multilateral principles of trade, such as nondiscrimination and most-favored-nation status.[18] This emphasis was signaled in 1899 when US secretary of state John Hay announced the McKinley administration's Open Door policy toward China. The European imperial powers were actively carving up China, creating trading ports and imperial zones. The United States put itself in opposition to the European powers' scramble to establish exclusive trade privileges in China. It affirmed the principle of equal access for all traders and supported China's territorial and administrative integrity. Its policy was actually a restatement of Britain's original trade agreement with China from the 1840s, which took the shape of a most-favored-nation trade treaty that guaranteed equal trade rights to all parties. The Sino-Japanese War of 1895 had undermined open trade relations, as Japan maneuvered to gain special territorial and port privileges. Similar efforts by Russia, France, and Germany followed, and the scramble for "concessions" was on. In 1898, Britain asked the United States to join it in urging the other major states to maintain a policy of equal commercial access. The McKinley administration decided not to engage in a joint action, but in 1899 and again in 1900, Secretary of State Hay issued circular notes to the other great powers, laying out the Open Door policy.[19]

The Open Door policy said less about America's commitment to free trade than about its eagerness to ensure access in East Asia. As a congressman, William McKinley had been a protectionist, and during his presidency, the United States remained one of the most protectionist of the large economies. Nor was the Open Door an explicit attack on imperialism. The McKinley administration was acting aggressively to subdue revolts in the Philippines. The goal of Open Door was both to safeguard American trade interests in the region and to uphold the rights of the Chinese against foreign encroachments. The policy signaled that the United States was now ready to champion a principle that went to the heart of the organization of international order—the principle of equal access for goods and capital.[20] It was a policy directed against exclusionary zones and aimed at the protection of America's expanding economic interests but it was also an attempt to associate the United States with a broadly open and nondiscriminatory international order. Two decades later, Wilson and the internationalists around him would seek to embed this principle in the postwar settlement.

The international arbitration movement was also active before Wilson took office. Initially championed by peace societies in the last decades of the nineteenth century, arbitration became a reform agenda pursued by international lawyers and diplomats. The United States and Britain had resorted to arbitration to negotiate the Jay Treaty of 1784 and the Treaty of Ghent in 1814. During the nineteenth century, over two hundred international controversies had been settled by arbitration, including more than sixty between 1890 and 1900. Britain and the United States were the most active in using arbitration. The cases involved all sort of issues, including territorial disputes, seizure of ships, and interference with commerce.[21] Arbitration became a tool of states that increasingly had to settle complex commercial, financial, territorial, and imperial disputes.

The arbitration movement's most ambitious goal was to bring this dispute-settlement mechanism into the high politics of interstate relations. As noted in the preceding chapter, by the last decades of the nineteenth century, legal societies and other groups had begun to publish formal plans for an international system of arbitration. A milestone was reached in 1872 when the United States and Great Britain agreed to arbitration—with formal proceedings held in Geneva—to settle a set of legal disputes over the rights of neutrals. This was the most important use yet of arbitration by the great powers. Over the next two decades, internationalists in all the leading Western countries repeatedly put arbitration resolutions before their parliaments.

In 1887, the United States and Britain began negotiating a permanent arbitration treaty, an effort that bore fruit a decade later in the 1897 Anglo-American Treaty of Arbitration. This was both the most ambitious attempt yet to build an intergovernmental mechanism for the settlement of disputes and a moment that revealed the mechanism's limits. The parties agreed "to submit to arbitration, in accordance with the provisions and subject to the limitations of the Treaty, all questions of difference between them which may fail to adjust themselves by diplomatic negotiations." But each side made significant reservations—Britain would not submit disputes involving its "national honour or integrity," and the United States would not agree to settlements without Senate approval.[22] Even with these debilitating limitations, the treaty was rejected by the US Senate and never came into force.

In the first decade of the twentieth century, the arbitration movement was bolstered by the leadership of US secretary of state Elihu Root, who had a long history of activism in arbitration affairs. A lawyer by training and the first president of the American Society of International Law, over the years he had repeatedly voiced his support for expanding the role of arbitration to resolve international disputes. As secretary of state from 1905 to 1909, he also sought to improve relations with Latin America. In 1890, the United

States had organized the First International Conference of American States, creating what would be called the Pan-American Union. Although the United States and the seventeen Latin American states failed to establish a trade association, they did conclude a treaty of compulsory arbitration for the settlement of inter-American disputes. None of the states subsequently ratified the treaty, but its principles were incorporated in various diplomatic agreements. As secretary of state, Root sought to build on these efforts, looking specifically for a way to expand the role of arbitration in the settlement of disputes over sovereign debt.[23]

While some internationalists focused on arbitration and other mechanisms for dispute resolution, others championed a more general political association of states. The idea of a congress or league of nations can be traced back to Europe's distant past. In the eighteenth century, Kant envisaged a "federation of free states." Many other eighteenth-century thinkers—Charles-Irene Castel, William Penn, Jeremy Bentham—proposed international bodies that would meet to settle disputes and govern international affairs. The calls for such an organization intensified in the nineteenth century. From its very beginning, the peace movement had seen a Congress of Nations—a sort of parliament of sovereign states—as its ultimate goal.[24]

Internationalist groups saw their own periodic assemblies as precursors of a congress or league of nations. Prominent among these assemblies was a series of World Peace Congresses held in the major European cities around midcentury. The congresses were convened to champion open trade, arbitration, disarmament, humanitarian relief, and international legal norms relating to war and peace. Interparliamentary groups, learned societies, and internationalists in Europe and the United States used these gatherings to set forth proposals. In his history of the nineteenth-century peace movement, Arthur Beales notes that between the Panama Congress of 1826 and the Hague Conference of 1899, over a thousand international congresses of all different sorts, including the Red Cross and the Postal Congresses, were held to promote various causes.[25]

These internationalist movements culminated in the two Hague Peace Conferences of 1899 and 1907. These gatherings, as Inis Claude observes, "marked a new peak in the development of collective activity for the purpose of general, permanent reform of the system of international relations, as distinguished from the purpose of dealing with specific, temporary situations."[26] The actual proposal for a conference was made by the Russian tsar Nicholas II in a circular letter sent to other heads of state, with an aim of fostering peace through defining the "laws of war" and negotiating limits on armaments. The conventions that emerged gave governments the right to mediation, a logical corollary of the mediation article of the Treaty of Paris of 1856. Most important, the Court of Arbitration was established at The Hague; it ultimately settled fourteen cases before August 1914.[27] At the second Hague Conference in 1907, the idea of a world court was put forward, based on a British proposal dating to 1895; the court was established in 1920.[28] Use of these dispute-settlement bodies remained optional, resting in the hands of the states themselves.

Multilateralism and Sovereign Equality

The agreements reached at the two Hague Peace Conferences were modest and certainly insufficient to thwart the European march to war. But they had an important impact on the evolving norms of international cooperation. The international conferences helped crystallize new ideas about multilateralism and sovereign equality that would become central to Wilson's liberal internationalism.

Multilateralism in modern diplomacy has its roots in the Westphalian state system and the Congress of Vienna of 1815, but it did not reach its modern form until the two Hague Conferences.[29] The Congress of Vienna was unique at the time, bringing together representatives of many governments to negotiate around the same table. This multilateral form allowed the European great powers to discuss and act collectively on questions of territory and political order across the continent. After Vienna, the congress met only intermittently when one of the great powers requested a meeting. Reflecting the political hierarchy of Europe, the congress system remained a great-power club, although toward the end of the century the congresses were occasionally expanded to include other states. Hierarchy and status, rather than sovereign equality, were the basis for inclusion.

Over the nineteenth century, however, multilateral meetings evolved. Participation expanded, voting was introduced, and the meetings themselves became regular. The first multilateral agreement open to all sovereign states for signature was the 1856 Paris Declaration Respecting Maritime Law put forward by Great Britain and France at the end of the Crimean War. Aimed at abolishing privateering and establishing rules to regulate the relationship between neutral and belligerent shipping on the high seas during war, the declaration was eventually ratified by fifty-five states.[30] Similarly, the mid-century congresses organized by the peace movement and other civil society groups invited participants from peace societies wherever they existed. The international peace congresses in London and Paris were dominated by Anglo-American delegates, but the meetings themselves were intended to expand the participation of continental European and non-Western societies. The 1863 Geneva Conference on the laws of war, also organized by civil society groups, had wide participation. Later in the century, the multilateral conferences held on functional issues—postal union, sanitation standards, and so forth—also involved self-selected participation. In peace conferences as well as functional meetings, inclusiveness was more important than hierarchy, either because it expanded the constituencies for peace agendas or because it brought into the functional agreement all the countries relevant to its operation.

With the Hague Conferences of 1899 and 1907, this evolving multilateralism was extended to intergovernmental conferences on peace and security. While the first Hague Conference continued the older tradition of inviting a select group of states, the second established the norm of universal participation.[31] Previous major European congresses had been organized to exchange views, but the Hague Conferences made decisions through voting: each state received one vote. The 1907 conference also departed from previous conferences by resolving to reconvene on a regular basis. It created a preparatory committee to handle business between conferences and managed itself through parliamentary procedures. The expanded participation in the second Hague Conference resulted from the inclusion of eighteen

Latin American states—and the adoption of the norms of participation that these states had developed during the Congress of Panama in 1826. Martha Finnemore and Michaelle Jurkovich argue that the norm of "sovereign equality," fervently embraced by postcolonial Latin American countries, gave normative force to the idea of universal participation. "Sovereigns, recognizing no higher authority, are juridically equal under international law," they write. "Because they [sovereign states] could not be bound without their consent, ergo, all needed to participate in any rule-making enterprise."[32] Multilateralism began to take its modern form.

A glimmering of Wilson's signature vision of liberal order building can be found in Secretary of State Elihu Root's instructions to the American delegates to the second Hague Conference. "The immediate results of such a Conference must always be limited to a small part of the field which the more sanguine have hoped to see covered; but each successive Conference will make the positions reached in the preceding Conference its point of departure, and will bring to the consideration of future advances toward international opinions affected by the acceptance and application of the previous agreements. Each Conference will inevitably make further progress and, by successive steps, results may be accomplished which have formerly appeared impossible. . . . You should keep always in mind the promotion of this continuous process through which the progressive development of international justice and peace may be carried on."[33]

By the beginning of the twentieth century, the broad outlines of the liberal internationalist orientation had come into view. The sovereign states of the civilized world, operating in an open and loosely rules-based international order, would need to establish legal and regulatory principles that guided states toward the peaceful settlement of disputes. As Inis Claude notes, the goal "was to create devices and agencies which would be permanently at the disposal of states."[34] Grievances between states would be dealt with through negotiation, arbitration, and international conferences.[35] The precedent was established for permanent international representative and judicial bodies that would provide the machinery for cooperation and the settlement of conflicts following norms of multilateralism and sovereign equality. The capstone would be a league or congress of nations.

Anglo-American Plans for Postwar Order

Soon after the war began, in the summer of 1914, governments began to think about the peace. The debate on the goals for postwar order was a sprawling public affair in which diplomats, politicians, scholars, public intellectuals, and activists all participated.[36] Planning in European capitals intensified as the scope of the war became clear, especially after the horrific battles of Verdun and the Somme in 1916. In Britain, the war was managed by a coalition government of three parties, and debates over the postwar order took a backseat to fighting on the continent. At first, the Wilson administration kept the United States neutral and sought to act as a mediator, speaking the "counsels of peace." But by 1917, the United States joined the war under the banner of Wilson's agenda for a "new diplomacy" and the "self-determination" of peoples. Soon, the Bolsheviks in Russia advanced their own vision of new diplomacy and revolution. The Great War's ending was not even in sight, but the debate about the order to be built in its aftermath was in full swing.

In Britain and the United States, the discussion drew internationalists from across the political spectrum. Out of this diversity, it is possible to identify two general camps of internationalism—conservative and progressive. Both factions were liberal, in the sense that they were committed to reform of the postwar order. The carnage on the battlefield demanded nothing less. They shared the view that the centerpiece of the reform must be an international organization that would enshrine the principles of order and foster cooperation. But they differed in the depth of their critique of the old order. Conservative internationalists favored a postwar order that would rely on the great powers to keep the peace through a strengthened system of international law and diplomacy. Some advocated a sort of updated and expanded Congress of Vienna dominated by the great powers, while others emphasized strengthening international law and creating mechanisms for the adjudication of conflicts. Progressive internationalists tended to support a deeper reform of the global system. They sought to create an international order that would support progressive economic and social reform at home and abroad. New international rules and institutions were needed to manage the world's growing interdependence.[37]

On the British side, the first group to deliberate over postwar plans was the so-called Bryce Group, led by Viscount Bryce, a historian, jurist, and former British ambassador to Washington, along with members of the liberal foreign policy establishment such as G. Lowes Dickinson and Gilbert Murray. Bryce and his colleagues favored a postwar grouping of the Allied states, including the United States, that would operate within a league of nations organization to maintain peace. The group's most important work was its "Proposals for the Avoidance of War" in March 1915, which provided various ideas for a league constitution.[38] Bryce and his group also urged the development of compulsory arbitration to prevent conflicts from escalating into armed violence. Signatory states were to pledge to refer defined disputes to the Hague Court of Arbitration or some other tribunal for settlement. The plan was not to prohibit war as such, but to seek its delay by channeling disputes to an impartial body. The Bryce proposal did not suggest automatic sanctions if a state refused to accept the arbitration decision, or establish a means for the body to enforce international law. It simply "hoped and expected" that the Hague Conference would become a permanent forum for the codification and development of international law.[39] These ideas reflected the group's moderate liberal orientation. The Bryce Group was influential in fashioning a case for a league of nations grounded in mainstream thinking about security and great-power politics.[40] It developed strong links with American internationalists within Republican political circles, and its ideas were later picked up by Lord Robert Cecil, one of the leading architects of British proposals for the League of Nations put forward at the Paris Peace Conference.

To the left of the Bryce Group was the Union for Democratic Control (UDC), a group of liberal and socialist politicians and intellectuals who advanced a more progressive postwar agenda. Led by figures such as Ramsey MacDonald, Norman Angell, and Arthur Henderson, the UDC sought initially to oppose the war and the old traditions of secret diplomacy and class politics that caused it. Emphasizing popular and parliamentary control of foreign policy, they pushed for a postwar settlement in which democratic states would collaborate in open international forums to keep the peace and advance progressive goals. In the place of the balance of power, the UDC proposed an international council whose deliberations and decisions would be public. The body's main activity would be to begin and manage arms reductions.

The UDC had little influence during the war, and many of its members joined ranks with the League of Nations Society (LNS), which was set up in early 1915. With a membership that included internationalist stalwarts like G. Lowes Dickinson and Leonard Woolf, this group focused its efforts on promoting a postwar league. When the United States finally entered the war in 1917, the LNS gained acceptability and was joined by political figures such as the former foreign secretary Lord Grey and General Jan Smuts, who was to become a leading planner in Paris. In June 1918, the LNS joined forces with the League of Free Nations Association, which included notables such as Gilbert Murray and H. G. Wells, to form a combined League of Nations Union. This organization papered over the differences between conservative and progressive internationalists and provided a united front on the eve of the Paris peace talks.[41]

Aside from Lord Cecil and a few others, the league had few champions within the British government during the war. A more realist view prevailed, with some embracing the concept of a league of nations as an extension of the nineteenth-century congress system. The main question was whether the United States would join whatever postwar arrangements were agreed upon. The British government became interested in the league primarily to ensure its leverage over the Wilson administration's postwar ideas.[42] This concern with American thinking led to wartime contacts between Wilson's chief confidant, Colonel Edward House, and the British government, culminating in the House–Grey Memorandum of May 1916, which affirmed the American intention of taking an active role in ending the war and negotiating the terms of peace.

In early 1918, the War Cabinet commissioned a study, chaired by Lord Phillimore, of the implications of a league of nations. Surveying earlier efforts to create a league or congress of nations and foreshadowing what would become a Wilsonian idea, the Phillimore report concluded that the league idea would work only with democratic states and that "although the spread of democratic nationalism seemed to have paved the way to success," militarist and autocratic states always emerged to thwart the best plans for peace through cooperation.[43] The question for the future, therefore, was whether democracy and the "constitutional principle" would take hold to an extent sufficient to support a liberal peace. The Phillimore report can be seen as a cautious statement of the need for reform. The war had shown the need for mechanisms to settle international disputes, but the report argued that such a system should be built on the nineteenth-century tradition of the congress system, preserving the great powers' authority to act to uphold order.[44]

On the American side, the internationalist movement was also divided between conservative and progressive wings. The most influential group, composed mostly of Republican internationalists, was the League to Enforce the Peace (LEP), led by William Howard Taft and Harvard University president Abbot Lawrence Lowell. Created in the summer of 1915 to mobilize support for a postwar international organization, the LEP had views that were similar to those of the Bryce Group, and during the war years the two groups coordinated their activities.[45] The LEP's platform, "Warrant from History," called for American participation in a postwar league in which all nations would meet periodically to promulgate international law. Member states would also be bound to submit "justiciable" disputes—those that pertained to treaty obligations and international law—to a judicial tribunal, and "nonjusticiable" disputes to a board of conciliation. The plan also required member states to use economic and military force against any state that made war on another member state before submitting its dispute to an agency of settlement.[46] By the end of 1916, the LEP had established itself as a formidable presence, having tens of thousands of members, sponsoring lectures, and publishing pamphlets.[47]

LEP leaders saw themselves reconciling "two supreme ideas"—the idea of a league and the idea of an armed and independent America. Some of the fellow travelers in conservative internationalist circles were legalists, such as Elihu Root and Nicholas Murray Butler, the president of Columbia University, who sought to reform world politics by fostering greater respect for international law. Root argued that conflict among great powers could best be ameliorated by international legal norms and dispute-settlement mechanisms overseen by a world court. Other conservative internationalists, such as William Howard Taft, supported the expanded use of arbitration but ultimately believed that order must be enforced by the great powers operating within a new international body.[48]

American progressives, like their British counterparts, argued for greater reform. This wing of the internationalist movement was populated by an assortment of liberals, pacifists, socialists, and social reformers. Thomas Knock argues that the American Left was "at once the advance guard of the so-called New Diplomacy and the impassioned [proponent] of an Americanized version of social democracy."[49] Some figures, such as the feminist and social activist Jane Addams, advanced long-standing ideas of the peace movement. Addams organized the Woman's Peace Party (WPP), which brought several thousand delegates together in Washington, DC, in January 1915, to articulate a "program for constructive peace." Its proposals resembled those put forward in Britain by the UDC. The WPP called for an immediate armistice, international agreements to limits armaments, open trade, freedom of the seas, democratic control of foreign policy, self-determination, mechanisms for arbitration, and a Concert of Nations. Like the LEP, the WPP built itself into a formidable organization with thousands of members, and Addams herself emerged as a prominent figure in international gatherings.[50]

Other liberal scholars and activists also organized during the war to advance progressive peacemaking principles. Charles Beard and James T. Shotwell at Columbia University joined journalists like Herbert Croly and social workers like Lillian Wald to form a Committee on American Policy in 1918. It supported Woodrow Wilson's ideas for a postwar system of open diplomacy, national self-determination, recognition of the rights of colonial peoples, and the Open Door. In October 1918, this group reorganized as the League for a Free Nation Association (LFNA) to promote a "universal and democratic" league of nations. Its 1918 Statement of Principles contained many of the leading ideas of the progressive wing of liberal internationalism. A peaceful postwar order would require a bold departure in world affairs and establish the commitments and institutions required for managing the growing yet fragile interdependence among industrial societies. Peace would be "the starting-point of international cooperation, the beginning of common responsibilities jointly assumed" in order to overcome the social and economic troubles that led to war. These pro-league liberals argued that the goal was not to overcome nationalism but to make it more progressive. The United States needed to be at the center of a league of nations that promoted a world order based on free trade and "cooperative nationalism."[51]

While the Addams-led peace movement opposed the war, liberal intellectual leaders like Croly and John Dewey saw the war as an instrument of a progressive agenda.[52] Eventually, Wilson did as well. Like their counterparts in Britain, the conservative and progressive factions came together at the end of the war to support the proposal for a league of nations. On the eve of Wilson's departure for Europe in November 1918, the LEP and the LFNA, which had maintained cordial relations during the war, agreed on a common "Victory Program," urging the creation of a league of nations for "the *liberty, progress, and fair economic opportunity* of all nations." The league would both foster the peaceful settlement of the controversies that cause war and act as a "potential force" that would constitute "a standing menace against any nation that seeks to upset the peace of the world."[53] Despite this formal show of unity, the differences remained. The LEP was more interested in the league as a way to enforce order, while the progressive wing saw its purposes as rectifying the socioeconomic conditions that caused war.

Wilson himself stayed aloof from these groups, even though by 1918 many of their ideas had found their way into his Fourteen Points speech. The LEP's emphasis on the arbitration of disputes and guarantees of territorial integrity and political independence essentially accorded with Wilson's views. His ideas on sanctions and the way in which collective security might work within the League of Nations were not dissimilar. Where Wilson seemed to diverge from the LEP was in his belief in a postwar international order that, as the progressive internationalists urged, would tackle the economic causes of war, and in his emphasis on disarmament and self-determination. Collective security and arbitration would work to secure long-term peace only if the underlying socioeconomic conditions, along with liberal democracy itself, evolved in a progressive direction.

The Wilsonian Vision

The United States came late to the war, but Woodrow Wilson put himself at the center of postwar peacemaking. Earlier in his career, he had embraced internationalist and progressive ideas such as free trade, political reform, and international law. He shared turn-of-the-century American beliefs about modernity and movement toward a liberal democratic future. But the war forced his generation of liberals to embrace a more activist, programmatic, and sweeping approach to world politics. Reform could not be left to the civilizing tides of history. Wilson proposed a reorganized world order anchored in free trade, collective security, international law, and the League of Nations. States would actively need to enforce the peace and establish a system of law and diplomacy that would protect liberal democracy and allow it to flourish.

Wilson laid out his vision of a reformed international order in a series of speeches. In an address to the League to Enforce the Peace in May 1916, he laid down his commitment (he called it a "creed") to the principle of self-determination, arguing that "every people has a right to choose the sovereignty under which they shall live," a principle that would apply to small as well as large states. Wars, he claimed, have their "origins in aggression and disregard of the rights of peoples and nations."[54] In his "Peace without Victory" speech of January 1917, he offered his vision of the institutional framework for the postwar peace: "There must be, not a balance of power, but a community of power; not organized rivalries, but an organized common peace." This system of collective or mutual security would be established in a world where nations are given an equality of rights, and governments are based on the consent of the governed. A year later, on 8 January, his Fourteen Points speech provided the overarching statement of his New Diplomacy.[55] A variety of ideas and claims lay behind this vision.

Modernity and Global Transformation

Wilson and other liberal internationalists had a particular view about modernity and the pathway being traveled by the United States and the other liberal democracies. The world was clearly transforming. The Great War was

generating upheaval, but the international system had also seen revolutionary eruptions—Mexico in 1910, China in 1911, Russia in 1917. These movements brought with them critiques of industrial capitalism and imperialism.
War and revolution exposed the modern era's deep inner workings: the old
order was giving way, reform and reactionary politics were gripping capitalist societies, and these dynamics and their repercussions were playing out
on a global stage. "We are living and shall live all our lives now in a revolutionary world," wrote Walter Lippmann, after Wilson, backed by Congress,
had made America's declaration of war. "This means among other things a
world of restless experiment."[56]

Wilson shared this sense of the world-historical moment. It was the global
experience of modernity. The world was "a single vicinage," he argued in
1900, where "each part had become neighbor to all the rest." In 1907, he wrote
that the world was embarked on a great civilizing trajectory; it was being
"drawn into a common market" in which "peace itself becomes a matter of
conference and international combination. Cooperation is the law of action
in the modern world."[57] For Wilson, the terms *modern world* and *civilization*
were essentially interchangeable, and rooted in the historical-cultural West.
Free trade and socioeconomic exchange would have a modernizing and civilizing effect on states, undercutting tyranny and oligopoly and strengthening the fabric of international society. This was a central tenet of liberal
internationalism handed down from the nineteenth century. The internationalism of the modernizing world system was transforming states and societies. As Lloyd Ambrosius argues, Wilson "continued to believe, as he had
affirmed in *The State* (1889), that history moved in a single direction toward
the triumph of democracy."[58] The modernizing world created new functional
demands for cooperation. Trade, exchange, and progressive change were facilitating the emergence of liberal democratic societies that were predisposed to be disciplined and cooperative global partners.

The Great War had put these beliefs in doubt. The crisis of world war
pushed Wilson and others to reframe their understanding of the global. But
rather than retreat from the liberal internationalist project, they doubled
down, expanding its scope and ambition. The war revealed to liberals the
growing interconnectedness of the world. A European war was now inevitably

a world war. Modernity, Wilson argued, had managed to "make a world that cannot be taken to pieces."[59] The war had refuted nineteenth-century liberal internationalist expectations that reform would happen of its own accord. Wilson turned this around and made the war—and peace settlement—an instrument of his progressive agenda.[60]

This move was seen in the way he framed the nature of the war and America's entry into it. For Wilson, the war revealed the incompleteness of modernity in Europe. He pointed specifically at illiberal, autocratic, militaristic Germany as a dangerous manifestation of premodern and old-world political formations. The United States and its allies were fighting "a vast military establishment" that "secretly planned to dominate the world."[61] Wilson began to make distinctions between the Old World and the New World, between the European ancien régime and American liberal democracy. "Whatever might be the immediate occasion of America's entry into the World War, for Wilson its ultimate aim was to save the world from domination by autocracy, militarism and plutocracy," writes E. M. Hugh-Jones. "From this point of view America's declaration of war is the climax of Wilson's Liberalism."[62]

The Move to Institutions

Wilson and his followers now saw that after the war, the world could not wait for liberal democracy to spring organically out of civilization's soil. This was the judgment about twentieth-century global political change that inspired Wilson's famous comment that the world needed to be made "safe" for democracy. A modernizing world would not automatically create an open and rules-based liberal global order. There had to be an organized system of diplomacy, formal institutions, and a shared commitment to collective security. As the war went on, Wilson began to articulate a sharper and more far-reaching agenda for the reform of world order. This was the Wilson era's "move to institutions."[63] The project of liberal internationalism was to be focused on building a functioning, actively managed international order.[64]

In his academic years, Wilson had seen the world as moving in a progressive direction. He believed that democracy was spreading largely through the workings of modernity itself, driven by the global enlightenment and political advancements emerging from the West. But the war called into question this notion of modernity as an emergent and progressive force. During the debates over war aims and the postwar settlement, Wilson came to the view that a league of nations—and more generally, international cooperation organized within permanent multilateral institutions—was essential to undergird the democratic world, provide for the defense of the community of liberal democracies, and nurture its expansion. The multilateral body would act as a sort of club of democracies and international bureaucracy, as Tony Smith argues, "dedicated to formulating and enforcing a nascent rule of law, as well as to the autonomous growth of an organic consciousness among the peoples of the world."[65]

For Wilson, it was not the binding terms or enforcement mechanisms of international bodies that were critical to keeping the world on a modernizing path; it was the norms and expectations these mechanisms enshrined. This is the basis for his case for the League of Nations. His first public call for a postwar system of collective security came in May 1916, in a speech to the League to Enforce the Peace. "Only when the great nations of the world have reached some sort of agreement as to what they hold to be fundamental to their common interest," he said, "and as to some feasible method of acting in concert when any nation or group of nations seeks to disturb those fundamental things, can we feel that civilization is at last in a way of justifying its existence and claiming to be finally established." Later in the speech, Wilson called for a "universal association of the nations to maintain the inviolate security of the highway of the seas for the common and unhindered use of all the nations of the world, and to prevent any war begun either contrary to treaty covenants or without warning and full submission of the causes to the opinion of the world—a virtual guarantee of territorial integrity and political independence."[66] During the peace conference in Paris, he would offer more-developed plans for a postwar peace organization but the underlying ideas were present years before. An international organization would be established, embodying legal and normative principles of sovereignty, territorial integrity, and peaceful settlement of disputes. The enforcement of these principles would come from a shared sense of moral duty and the pressures of world public opinion.

Progressivism and Internationalism

Wilson's internationalism was connected to progressive ideas and politics that emerged in turn-of-the-century Europe and the United States. Wilson had been elected president on a platform of government and social reform. Progressivism was not a unified tradition or movement but an orientation toward industrial society and modern democracy. Its adherents advocated building state capacities for tackling the problems of industrialism and modern society, thus seeking a middle way between laissez-faire liberalism and revolutionary socialism.[67] Wilson traveled in progressive political circles and drew upon their ideas.[68]

At the turn of the century, progressives were already counted among the ranks of various internationalist movements, including peace campaigns and the international law movement.[69] Their internationalism had several aspects. One was a focus on the socioeconomic causes of war. Across the world, the ancien régime was holding on to power, and the resulting failure of reform was generating economic dislocation and reactionary politics. The problems of industrial society were global, and so were its consequences—illiberalism and military aggression. The campaign for a peaceful postwar order had to include building international capacities to encourage economic reform and social advancement. Wilson shared this view and occasionally criticized his domestic allies, such as the League to Enforce the Peace, as insufficiently attentive to economic reform.[70] Progressives applauded him when he described liberalism as "the only thing that can save civilization from chaos—from a flood of ultra-radicalism that will swamp the world. . . . Liberalism must be more liberal than ever before, it must even be radical, if civilization is to escape the typhoon."[71] A stable postwar peace must be built on self-government, open diplomacy, free trade, and national self-determination.

Progressives also looked at the challenge from the outside in. The institutions and political community that resided within the postwar international order would need to be organized to support liberal democracy. This was the meaning of Wilson's famous call to "make the world safe for democracy." The international order would need to be made congenial for liberal democracy to achieve its reform goals. This was an argument not for spreading democracy but for creating the conditions in which it could survive. David Hunter Miller, Wilson's legal adviser at the Paris conference, hinted at this idea in arguing that, paradoxically, successful "internationalism can rest only on satisfied nationalism."[72] Their vision was of a sort of progressive nationalism. As the historian Charles DeBenedetti writes, Wilson and the progressive architects of the peace "aimed to develop a controllable international order by reattaching liberal purpose to modern nationalism."[73] In this sense, they were attempting to recover the political impulses of the mid-nineteenth century, when nationalism and democracy were closely aligned. The league would provide its members a vehicle for realizing their national ambitions and for linking those ambitions to the gains that come from continuing cooperation among nations.[74]

Wilson's progressivism was manifest in his conviction that the postwar order would be a vehicle for nations and peoples to deliberate on their common challenges and engage in collective problem solving. As Trygve Throntveit argues, progressivism placed public deliberation and political experience at the heart of liberal democracy. In an age of growing interdependence in which the fates of industrial societies were tightly linked, this vision of political community and cooperative problem solving would necessarily be international in scope.[75] Progressive nationalism and liberal internationalism went together. The League of Nations was the institutional centerpiece of a new global architecture for deliberation and problem solving.

International Law and Society

Wilson championed a world ordered by international law. For a peaceful and orderly world, states would need to abide by agreed-upon rules and norms, which for Wilson were crystallized in international law. As he put it, "the same law that applies to individuals applies to nations."[76] Yet he had a nineteenth-century view of international law. He did not see it primarily as formal, legally binding commitments that transferred sovereignty upward to international or supranational authorities. Instead it had more of a socializing dynamic, creating norms and expectations that states would slowly come to embrace.

Wilson articulated this view of international law in a series of lectures he gave at Princeton University. He argued that international law was "not made" but had an organic character: it was "a body of abstract principles founded upon long established custom."[77] There were "fundamental, vital principles of right" embedded in the world that he ultimately traced to God and human reason. It was these principles of right that offered the possibility for a community of nations. "Regardless of race or religion," if nations recognized and abided by these principles, they could join the international community. Within the contemporary international system, the objective was to eliminate "disorder and invasion of right which provoked war" and replace them with "ordered relationships and recognized obligations" that promoted a "sense of community among states."[78] The foundation for this community of states ordered by law, Wilson argued, was liberal democracy. Representative, rule-of-law polities were most likely to identify and respect principles of right. Liberal democracy thus contained the "imperative forces of popular thought and the concrete institutions of popular representation" that would bring to international relations "the rule of counsel, the catholic spirit of free debate . . . [and] the ascendency of reason over passion."[79]

In Wilson's view, international law was useful for reinforcing the social and moral bonds between peoples living in a modernizing world civilization. "Interests" alone were not sufficient glue to keep the international system together. As he said in a speech in Manchester, England, in December 1918: "Interest separates men. There is only one thing that can bind people together, and that is a common devotion to right." Moral bonds were necessary. He made the same point in a speech in Mobile, Alabama, in October 1913, when he said that "interest does not tie nations together; it sometimes separates them," and therefore "it is a spiritual union which we seek."[80] Laws, institutions, and the bonds of moral responsibility would become the sources of international order, disciplined by the opinions of the world's people.[81]

Wilson was operating within a worldview shared by others. As noted earlier, in the decades before 1914, international jurists and legal thinkers—inspired by the two Hague Peace Conferences—saw international law as an ordering force in world affairs. In his 1912 Nobel Peace Prize address, former secretary of state Elihu Root argued that the world was entering an age in which the international community would increasingly move toward shared beliefs on "right conduct." The world was entering an age of expanding constitutional government, in which public opinion would render "judgment . . . upon the just and unjust conduct of nations, as the public opinion of each community passes upon the just and unjust conduct of its individual members." Root asserted that peace would be maintained in the world not by the enforcement efforts of a great power or international police force but by "the praise and blame, the honor and shame, which follow observance or violation of the community's standards of right conduct." International law was the embodiment of "right conduct" within a world community of democratic states that obey the dictates of public opinion.[82] As he argued in 1907 in an address promoting the Pan American Union, "the progress . . . in American international relations, is a progress along the pathway that leads from the rule of force as the ultimate sanction of argument to the rule of public opinion, which enforces its decrees by an appeal to the desire for approbation among men."[83]

For Wilson, international law and the system of collective security anchored in the League of Nations would play a socializing role and gradually bring states into a "community of power." International law was not simply a contract between states based on their deduced interests, but a catalyst for the evolution of state behavior toward a stable peace. The League of Nations would foster the long-term shifts in consciousness required to bring rules-based international order into being. Wilson explained this way of thinking to his adviser, Colonel Edward House in March 1918: "My own conviction, as you know, is that the administrative constitution of the League must grow and not be made; that we must begin with solemn covenants, covering mutual guarantees of political independence and territorial integrity (if the first territorial agreements of the peace conference are fair and satisfactory and out to be perpetuated), but that the method of carrying those mutual pledges out should be left to develop of itself, case by case. Any attempt to begin by putting executive authority in the hands of any particular group of powers would be to sow a harvest of jealousy and distrust which would spring up at once and choke the whole thing."[84] Tony Smith summarized Wilson's view: "If the League could give popular consciousness the opportunity to mature in a way that favored democratic government, so too could participation in its institutions give rise to a body of international law that over time could constitute . . . a rule book for international behavior."[85] Participation in the League of Nations would cause political elites and their publics to evolve habits, values, and interests that accorded with right conduct as it is enshrined in international law and the moral bonds of the community of nations.[86]

Collective Security

Wilson famously put collective security at the center of his internationalist vision. In the postwar world, no nation would be permitted to acquire territory by conquest. Nations would be accorded equal rights and they would be bound together by international law within a moral community governed by the principle of collective security. In effect, states would extend to each other a mutual guarantee of political independence. Early in his first term, Wilson had been intrigued by the Latin American states' proposal for a system of such guarantees between the republican states of Latin America and the United States. Colonel House, in urging the idea on Wilson, had argued that it might serve as a "model for the European Nations when peace is at last brought about."[87]

Wilson likely had this model in mind when he argued in his January 1917 speech for a postwar settlement based on "not a balance of power, but a community of power." The principle that "no nation should extend its polity over any other nation or people" would be upheld by a regime of commitments and sanctions in a system of collective security.[88] Collective security would be manifest as a complex scheme of national commitments and international mechanisms designed, as Inis Claude puts it, "to prevent or suppress aggression by any state against another state, by presenting to potential aggressors the credible threat and to potential victims of aggression the reliable promise of effective collective measures, ranging from diplomatic boy-cott through economic pressure to military sanctions, to enforce the peace."[89]

In the debate over collective security during the war and at the Paris Peace Conference, the key questions were about the principle itself and its enforce-ment. One faction, led by Theodore Roosevelt, William Howard Taft, and other traditional and realist-oriented internationalists, many of whom were associated with the League to Enforce the Peace, argued that the League of Nations should provide a forum for the great powers to enforce order. Mem-ber states would agree to the peaceful settlement of disputes, and states that violated territorial independence would be threatened with both economic and military sanctions. It was also understood that members of the league would continue to expand and codify international law so as to clarify their shared understanding of territorial rights and the obligations of mutual de-fense. Wilson's conception was not that different, except that he saw the league doing much more. It would embody principles of mutual defense but it would also have mechanisms to encourage disarmament, arbitrate disputes, and produce coordinated responses to violations of the charter.

For Wilson, collective security followed from and depended upon the realization of his larger reform agenda. Self-determination, reduction of armaments, and free trade were equally important pieces of the postwar order—and if war was to be prevented, these other pieces would all need to play an active role. On the other hand, Wilson did not differ from others—including critics in the Senate who would ultimately offer reserva-tions about the treaty—when he argued that the League of Nations would not abridge the sovereign independence of governments to uphold the trea-ty's collective security provisions. This was the famous question over the meaning of article 10 of the Covenant of the League of Nations, which spelled out the enforcement mechanisms of the postwar system. Wilson thought for-mal legal obligations would not be necessary because territorial guarantees would be upheld through the actions of states that independently came to value the logic and moral imperative of collective security.

Wilson's view was articulated in a revealing moment in a March 1918 White House meeting with Taft and Lowell, the leaders of the League to Enforce the Peace. Taft records that Wilson thought the league's member nations would want to "guarantee to one another their integrity and territory, and that if any violations of these were threatened or occurred, special conferences might be called to consider the question." Wilson said that the guarantee would emerge slowly, in the same way that common law had developed. Ultimately, through a series of conferences, it would be possible to develop peacemaking machinery whose character would be dictated by "precedents" and "custom." Wilson also "gave it as his opinion that the Senate of the United States would be unwilling to enter into an agreement by which a majority of other nations could tell the United States when they must go to war." Lowell asked the president if he thought it might be better to go to the peace conference with a more definite agreement in mind, making reference to the experience of the architects of the United States Constitution. Wilson replied that "it was wise to [arrive at the conference with] a definite program even more comprehensive and detailed than would probably be adopted."[90] According to Taft, Wilson considered it "very necessary to look after the smaller countries and secure protection of their integrity and that any plan should have that in mind."[91] He did develop a detailed plan for the League of Nations, which was attacked in the way he had predicted.[92]

But Wilson's comments reflected his long-standing view about how international law and the principles of collective security could become credible. "The establishment of a league of nations," he told a Swiss expert on international organization in November 1917, "is in my view a matter of moral persuasion more than a problem of juridical organization."[93] In the same way, the postwar system of collective security was not established through a legal process involving the transfer of sovereignty. It was a political and moral project to alter how states and peoples thought about rights and obligations and the imperatives to uphold them.

American Exceptionalism

Finally, Wilson believed that the United States, being at the vanguard of this movement, had special responsibilities to lead, direct, and inspire the world due to its founding ideas, geopolitical position, and enlightened leadership (which Wilson thought he embodied). America was the great moral agent in history, the midwife of progressive change. Addressing the Senate in July 1919, Wilson argued for the importance of American leadership in the League of Nations. "America may be said to have just reached her majority as a world power. . . . Our isolation was ended twenty years ago. . . . There can be no question of our ceasing to be a world power. The only question is whether we can refuse the moral leadership that is offered us, whether we accept or reject the confidence of the world."[94]

Wilson was not advocating American hegemonic dominance of the global system. Indeed, he was directly rejecting the great powers' traditional geopolitical dominance over the international system. His vision of America leading the world to a better place is captured in one of his last speeches in support of the League of Nations, delivered in Pueblo, Colorado, on 25 September 1919. Concluding the address, Wilson said: "There is one thing that the American people always rise to and extend their hand to, and that is the truth of justice and of liberty and of peace. We have accepted that truth and we are going to be led by it, and it is going to lead us, and through us the world, out into quietness and peace such as the world never dreamed of before."[95]

Empire, Race, Democracy, and Liberal Progress

The Wilsonian vision of liberal internationalism was both breathtakingly ambitious and surprisingly limited—a strange mixture of enlightened principle and moral blindness. This is a paradox that has long shadowed scholarly reflections on Wilson and his ideas. He proclaimed seemingly universal principles about the rights and protections of nations and peoples, but he never questioned prevailing imperial and racial hierarchies. His notion of the self-determination of nations and peoples was, in practice, quite limited. At Versailles, only the peoples within the European parts of the collapsed Eurasian empires were granted national recognition. The others were consigned to "protectorates." This failure to question imperial and racial hierarchies is predictable, if regrettable, in light of Wilson's support of the American post–Civil War racial order. As a scholar, he had criticized the Reconstruction effort to grant equal civil and political rights to black citizens. As president, he presided over the segregation of the civil service and was, as one biographer puts it, "timid, cold, practically indifferent to questions of racial justice."[96]

The Wilsonian peace project had attracted support from the luminaries of the progressive movement, including W. E. B. Du Bois and other civil rights figures. They at first believed that joining Wilson's war for democracy abroad would advance, at least indirectly, the prospects for racial democracy at home, but they were disappointed time and again. Du Bois had supported Wilson's election in 1912 but, after the failures of Wilson's first term, declined to do so in 1916. Yet, remarkably, he and other civil rights leaders made the journey to the Paris Peace Conference—still thinking that Wilson might seize the moment with the entire world watching. Du Bois sought an audience with Wilson in Paris but did not receive one. He did meet with Colonel House and urged the American delegation to address the future of Africa and questions of racial equality, but it did not. Du Bois would later write, "Here as elsewhere my conception of Wilson as a scholar was disappointing. At Versailles he did not seem to understand Europe nor European politics, nor the world-wide problem of race."[97] At Paris, Wilson seemed unwilling to extend his principles of self-determination and equality of nations to non-white peoples.

While Wilson did not think kindly about the European empires, his vision of peace did not entail their elimination. His confrontation with European imperialism was circumscribed. Starting with the Open Door period and continuing under Wilson, the United States did seek to establish an open and multilateral system of trade and exchange and was opposed to a world divided into imperial spheres and closed blocks. In Wilson's view, these imperial formations were bad for American business and, as importantly, they were the breeding grounds for autocracy and militarism. The principles he laid down for the postwar peace—self-determination and equality of nations—were anti-imperial in the abstract. But at Paris, in the practical elaboration of his ideas, his opposition to empire was quickly negotiated away. In a particularly egregious case, the Chinese delegation, which came to the peace conference calling for the end of imperial institutions in China, was shocked to discover that Britain, France, and Italy had signed a secret treaty that transferred Germany's territorial holdings in China to Japan. China did not sign the Versailles agreement.[98]

Wilson "had no interest in unsettling the imperial racial hierarchy or the global colour-line," Adam Tooze argues. "What the American strategy was emphatically directed towards suppressing was imperialism, understood not as productive colonial expansion nor the racial rule of white over coloured people, but as the 'selfish' and violent rivalry of France, Britain, Germany, Italy, Russia and Japan that threatened to divide one world into segmented spheres of influence." Wilson had an "anti-imperialist and anti-militarist agenda," and the league was to be the tool for ending inter-imperial rivalry.[99]

In the same way, Wilson did not have a particularly broad vision of human rights and racial equality. The League Covenant did not mention either one. Wilson projected a vision of universalism in rights and values, but quickly compromised when it was expedient. Even at his most idealistic, he did not attack Western ideas about racial and civilizational hierarchy. At Versailles during the drafting of the covenant, the Japanese put forward a resolution on racial equality. Wilson had also been considering a resolution on religious freedom, and at one point thought about combining this with the Japanese resolution. In the end, for pragmatic reasons, he acted to strike down the racial equality resolution. Britain saw it as a threat, particularly in Australia. Fearing the loss of British support for the treaty, Wilson invoked the unanimity clause to ensure its defeat. Naioko Shimazu's account of this drama shows that Wilson's reason for resisting the racial equality proposal was not a concern over its implications for segregation in the United States, but "nor was he personally committed to racial equality as a universal principle."[100] He emphasized national self-determination over racial equality, and self-determination outside Europe was itself to be managed by the great powers through the mandate system.

The limits of Wilson's liberal anticolonialism were reflected in the quick rise and fall of the "Wilsonian moment" across the non-Western world. Countries such as China and India were initially inspired by the principles that Wilson articulated in Paris—multilateralism, open diplomacy, and self-determination—only to see their hopes dashed. As Erez Manela argues, "for colonized, marginalized, and stateless peoples from all over the world—Chinese and Koreans, Arabs and Jews, Armenians and Kurds, and many others—the conference appeared to present unprecedented opportunities to pursue the goal of self-determination."[101] But by the spring of 1919 it had become increasingly clear to these groups assembled in Paris that Wilson was not above colluding with British and French imperial interests and that the Western domination of their societies would not end. This disillusionment, as Manela recounts, marked the beginning of an era of anticolonial nationalism in which leaders in Asia and Africa rethought their strategies, galvanized domestic constituencies, and embarked on campaigns for self-determination.[102] Japan, which had not been a victim of colonialism, followed a different path as political leaders in Tokyo embraced internationalist ideals and participated in the major postwar initiatives—the League of Nations, the Washington and London Naval Conferences, the Five-Power Treaty, and the Kellogg-Briand Pact. Japan's Wilsonian Moment ended with the outbreak of hostilities in Manchuria in September 1931.[103] Japan's internationalism was directed at Wilson's idea of a "great power concert" and not for the principle of self-determination, which it ignored as it reasserted its imperial interests in China.

Two aspects of Wilson's postwar vision allowed him these moral and political failings. One was that he thought the League of Nations would provide a vehicle for correcting mistakes and overcoming the flaws in the peace settlement. The single most important goal, in his mind, was to get the League of Nations; everything else would follow. So he was willing to yield to his colleagues at the Paris conference if it paved the way to their participation in the postwar body. This is how he handled the Japanese resolution on racial equality. As Robert Cecil, who worked closely with Wilson on the final draft of the covenant, put it, "we are not seeking to produce for the world a building finished and complete in all respects." Wilson thought the agreement reached in Paris had accomplished his most basic goal, putting the great powers on a path of institutionalized cooperation. Any injustices in the treaty could be rectified in due course.[104]

This logic followed from his view of the league as an embryonic political community. Wilson's thinking about international relations was infused with his Christian beliefs. The League of Nations could be thought of as a church in a town. Wilson, as a leader in the church, would naturally think that the most important way to make the town stable, peaceful, and civilized is to get people to go to church. He knows that potential churchgoers do not necessarily yet behave in a Christian way. The town had gangs and brothels, gambling houses and drug dealers, and some of the church's leaders have their fingers in these dark activities. But Wilson has faith that the church will do its work. Even if the churchgoers of this generation do not reform, their children will, and the town will slowly be transformed. This, in essence, seems to be Wilson's view of the league. It would be a living thing, and its principles of rectitude and right would slowly enlighten those who inhabited its conference halls.

The second aspect of Wilson's vision that allowed him to overlook transgressions of liberal ideals was his belief in the steady progress of democracy. He set off to Europe in December 1918 thinking the world was in the midst of a gathering democratic revolution. The extraordinary public adulation he received during his triumphal visits to London, Paris, Rome, and Milan seemed to confirm this view. If there was a constituency for his New Diplomacy, it was the citizens of the Western nations and other aspiring democracies around the world. He was making a moral and ideological appeal directly to the people, over the heads of European leaders.[105] Liberal principles were gaining support in Europe throughout 1917 and 1918, partly as a result of the Russian Revolution, which energized leftist parties throughout Europe and caused intellectual ferment across the political spectrum. Radicals in Britain were also clamoring for a liberal postwar order.[106] In the run-up to the Paris Peace Conference, Wilson was optimistic that the rising tide of democratic politics in Europe would bring to power center-left and progressive governments that would support his proposals for postwar order. And over the longer term, he was sure, a worldwide democratic upsurge would put the League of Nations on firm footing, enlarge the constituencies for a liberal peace, and strengthen the role of public opinion as a mechanism to enforce the league's principles and agreements.

At a deeper level, Wilson saw global political change as a slow evolution. Law and politics reflected the gradual and organic workings of social progress. This made it easier for internationalists in his generation to reconcile their liberalism with Western imperialism. In the long term, they thought, empire would pass away, but it would require time as the developmental logic of modernity unfolded. "Democracy," Wilson wrote in 1885, "is wrongly conceived when treated as merely a body of doctrine. It is a stage of development. . . . It is built up by slow habit. Its process is experience, its basis old wont, its meaning national organic oneness and effectual life. It comes, like manhood, as maturity to it is vouchsafed the maturity of freedom and self-control, and no other."[107] Ironically, this progressive vision that the world was advancing toward a future of liberal democracy was what let him countenance racial and imperial hierarchies and delegate their elimination to the slow forces of history.

Wilsonian internationalism saw the domain of international cooperation in narrow terms. It was essentially a system of collective security and free trade bound together by rules and norms of multilateralism and international law. Wilson did not call upon the international community to promote expansive notions of human rights, social protections, or economic development. To be sure, there was an underlying assumption that the international system would do this on its own. But liberal internationalism during this period did not contain an explicit agenda of building international capacities to defend or advance ambitious social ends. As a blueprint for postwar order, the Versailles treaty has been widely criticized for showing little understanding of the economic and social underpinnings of progressive change.[108]

The Legacy of Failure

Wilson's liberal internationalism was a historical failure, and not simply because the US Senate would not ratify the Treaty of Versailles. The true failure was that the underlying conditions in which a collective security system could function were not created. The Wilsonian version of liberal internationalism was built around a thin set of institutional commitments. Its strength was expected to come from a thick set of norms and pressures—public opinion and the moral rectitude of statesmen—that would activate sanctions and enforce territorial peace when needed. Wilson got around the problem of sovereign autonomy, which the Senate would not give up, by emphasizing the informal norms that would bring countries together to maintain a stable peace. The sovereignty of states as it related to both legal independence and equality would not be compromised or transformed. States would just be expected to act better, which for Wilson meant that they would be socialized into a "community of power."

The interwar era did not see this vision realized. Instead, the United States pulled back from active involvement in peace and security. The internationalism of the 1920s and 1930s returned in many ways to nineteenth-century internationalism—a project of financiers, traders, and social groups. It once again became essentially a private internationalism of banks and commercial firms struggling to manage the impacts of a contracting world economy. Legal internationalism was revived in the Kellogg-Briand Pact, which sought to return to the nineteenth-century uses of arbitration treaties to settle international disputes.[109] This multilateral treaty, which gave governments an opportunity to renounce war against other treaty members except in self-defense or certain other circumstances, was even less of a formal security pact than the League of Nations. And it shared with Wilson's liberal internationalism the conviction that public opinion and moral suasion were the means to activate cooperation and collective security.

Although the United States did not join the League of Nations, the league did begin its operations in 1920. Although it did not succeed in settling security disputes, the league became the hub for an expanding variety of international activities that cut across economic, social, and educational realms. In this way, the league was important in giving embryonic shape to the intergovernmental and transnational character of modern international order. As Glenda Sluga argues, "the international order shaped in 1919 created unprecedented political spaces for representing the diverse interests of the world's population . . . populated by flows of delegates, bureaucrats, and NGOs [nongovernmental organizations], and subject to constant reinvention."[110]

Wilson emerges in this portrait as almost a Periclean figure: flawed, burdened by hubris and moral blindness in equal measure, but full of verve and inspiration. His observation that "only one thing can bind people together, and that is a common devotion to right" is almost a direct invocation of the great Athenian leader's funeral oration.[111] The Wilsonian vision of liberal internationalism sought to transform the old global system—based on the balance of power, spheres of influence, military rivalry, and alliances—into a unified liberal international order based on nation-states and the rule of law. Power and security competition would be replaced by a community of sovereign and equal nations. But Wilsonian internationalism did not involve deeply transformative political institutions. The liberal international order was to be constructed around the soft law of public opinion and moral suasion. According to Wilson, the League of Nations would "operate as the organizing moral force of men throughout the world" that would turn the "searching light of conscience" on wrongdoing around the world. "Just a little exposure," he optimistically asserted, "will settle most questions."[112] In retrospect, it is clear that Wilsonian security commitments were too thin, and the thick norms of compliance and collective action were not thick enough.

The Allied peacemakers at Versailles—Georges Clemenceau, David Lloyd George, and Woodrow Wilson—can never escape history's judgment that in ending one world war, they planted the seeds of the next. The settlement they reached disappointed almost everyone. World War I had set in motion vast forces that were almost too much for diplomats to manage: the collapse of four empires, the implosion of the European great-power order, the Anglo-American power transition, the rise of revolutionary Russia, and the spread of new ideas about self-determination. The victors' treatment of Germany—a harsh peace that destroyed that nation's fragile democracy—was disastrously foolish. But the League of Nations, even without the United States, opened up a new era of social and economic cooperation and laid the foundation for later efforts to reinvent the liberal international project.

FIVE

Rooseveltian Internationalism

The crises and upheavals cascading through the 1930s and 1940s struck at the heart of liberal democracy. The Great Depression, the rise of fascism and totalitarianism, and the return of world war raised grave doubts about the viability of Western capitalist states and their ability to establish a working international order. Franklin Roosevelt and his contemporaries were forced to shed many of the liberal internationalist assumptions that had attended Wilson-era peacemaking. Public opinion was a weak reed to support the global enforcement of peace. If the socializing effect of "civilization" was even a credible force in world politics, its effects came too slowly. Most important, modernity itself harbored existential dangers. The problem with fascist and totalitarian states was not that they were insufficiently modern but that they were all too modern. They had become powerful and threatening by harnessing the modernizing capacities of the industrial state. The violence and illiberalism that turned the world upside down in the mid-twentieth century had come from within the West. It was this new characterization of "the global" that forced liberal internationalists to rethink their ideas yet again.

The international order that emerged after 1919 had few champions. The United States failed to join the League of Nations, France did not get the security guarantees it sought, and Germany was left seething with grievances. Nationalist movements for self-determination in the non-Western world were thwarted. The Versailles settlement seemed deficient in both realism and idealism. It delivered neither security nor justice. Peace had been established, but it left very few parties satisfied. "We are at the dead season of our fortunes," wrote John Maynard Keynes in his famous polemic against the peace treaty. "Never in the lifetime of men now living has the universal element of the soul of man burnt so dimly."[1] The Vienna settlement that followed the Napoleonic Wars had lasted almost a century. The Versailles settlement would last less than two decades.

Still, a semblance of stability had been established across the Western world. The institutions of liberal democracy had survived the war. In some liberal states, the war itself had catalyzed democratic reforms that strengthened their capacities and expanded the franchise. Remarkably, as the 1920s began, the whole of Europe west of the Soviet Union consisted of representative parliamentary regimes. Liberal constitutional government was almost universal across the world's sixty-five or so independent states. The world outside the state system, of course, remained trapped in empire; a third of the world's population lived under colonial rule.[2] Economic growth and signs of political stability could be seen across the industrial world. A working diplomatic system reappeared among the Western powers.

But this sanguinity vanished under a succession of economic and geopolitical crises. The collapse of the world economy in the 1930s and the rise of fascism and totalitarianism triggered grim doubts about the future of liberal democracy. For liberal internationalists, the years after 1919 were filled with debates about the failings of Versailles, the League of Nations, and collective security. With the aggression of the Axis powers and the return of war, the stakes were raised. "The rumble of deep uncertainty, a sense of proceeding without a map, remained relentless and enveloping," writes Ira Katznelson in his portrait of the United States in the 1930s. "A climate of universal fear deeply affected political understandings and concerns. Nothing was sure."[3] Industrial and modern state power had shown their dark sides. Could liberal democracy regain its footing in this world?

From the late 1930s to the late 1940s, a grand shift occurred in liberal internationalist ideas: they acquired the marks of New Deal liberalism and emerging Cold War notions of national security. The agenda became more expansive and progressive, laced simultaneously with appeals to universal-style rights and protections and to the solidarity of the Western democratic world. It was a vision of order that would be implemented within a widening array of intergovernmental institutions and, after the coming of the Cold War, sustained by American hegemonic power. For Woodrow Wilson, the liberal democracies were the glue that would hold together the international order. For the liberal international thinkers of the late 1930s and 1940s, the reformed international order was the glue that would hold the liberal democracies together.

This chapter makes three arguments. First, the depression, war, and spreading illiberalism of the 1930s and 1940s forced a long debate over the viability of Western democracy and the character and trajectory of modern industrial society. The failings of the old liberal order caused a rethinking of the problem of modernity across the political spectrum. The rise of fascism and totalitarianism as grand ideological alternatives to Western liberalism intensified the stakes, and the ideological struggle between Western democratic capitalism and Soviet communism further shaped the debate. One could take many different positions: those who broadly subscribed to a liberal democratic worldview embraced ideas ranging from classical liberalism to social democracy. Despite these differences, there was wide agreement that the Versailles settlement had failed to establish a stable foundation for liberal capitalist democracy.

Second, during the interwar decades, liberal internationalist thinking shifted. Wilson-era liberals had seen modernity as a developmental force pushing and pulling the world toward liberal democracy. Out of the ravages of the 1930s and 1940s, liberals came increasingly to see modernity empowering both liberal and illiberal states, and generating an ever more complex set of dangers and opportunities on a global scale. The racial, religious, and civilizational hierarchies implicit (or explicit) in earlier internationalist visions gave way to universal conceptions of rights and freedoms. During the 1930s and 1940s, liberal internationalist thinking became both more "globalist" and more "realist." It was globalist in the sense that the international order would need to do more to stabilize and protect liberal democracies. It would need to be more multifaceted in its scope and purposes. But it also became more realist in the sense that it would need to be more deeply embedded in a stable, ideally cooperative, great-power order led by the United States and the other industrial democracies. If the Western liberal democracies were to survive, they would need to build and operate in a new type of international order. The debates about postwar order among liberal internationalists were driven by this shared conviction.

Finally, Roosevelt, his contemporaries, and successors crystallized this new thinking. New Deal and Cold War liberalism reshaped the connections between liberal democracy and international order. At the heart of this new thinking was a more comprehensive vision of the liberal order's logic and functions. The liberal democratic state—its purposes and capacities—had evolved, and it followed that the international order that would support and protect modern liberal societies also had to evolve. As the notions of both national and social security expanded, modern liberalism would require a more activist agenda for organizing and governing the international order. Where Wilson's liberal internationalism was built around international law and enforced by public opinion and moral sanction, the liberal internationalism that emerged from the 1930s and 1940s incorporated new conceptions of political rights and social protections. If liberal democracy was to survive, it would need a "container," suited to the growing complexities and vulnerabilities of economic and security interdependence. An open, rules-based international order would need to be a more managed affair. Openness would be "embedded" in rules and institutions that would ensure stability and protect citizens' and workers' well-being. As the Cold War emerged, this liberal order became more hegemonic, organized around the leadership of the world's most powerful state.

The Twenty Years' Crisis

Despite the failures of Versailles, the Western states in the 1920s did work closely to manage economic and political instabilities and to establish the rudiments of a working postwar order. The League of Nations began operations in 1920 with forty-two founding members, mostly European, the first intergovernmental organization dedicated to the maintenance of world peace.[4] Under the league's auspices, governments cooperated to advance global health, resettle refugees, advance labor rights, and protect ethnic minorities. Germany was invited to join in 1926. Naval agreements negotiated by the maritime powers opened up a new era of diplomacy and arms control. European and American banks and financial institutions reestablished operations and, working with their governments, renegotiated debt and reparations.[5] Industrial production in Europe doubled between 1913 and 1929, spurred by growing consumer demand for automobiles and other modern products. In the mid-1920s, the American economy grew at around 7 percent a year and unemployment dropped below 2 percent. In his inaugural address in March 1929, US president Herbert Hoover seemed to speak for all the liberal democracies when he argued, "We have reached a higher degree of comfort and security than ever existed in the history of the world."[6]

Yet in a mere decade, this postwar order was shattered by sudden, escalating economic and political crises. The coalition of liberal states that had formed to manage the post-Versailles system fell apart. "Layer by layer, piece by piece, issue by issue," writes Adam Tooze, "this great democratic alliance . . . disintegrated."[7] The fragile foundations of world order were torn apart in a relentless process that would end in global war. The mounting crises that unfolded—economic collapse, the rise of fascism and authoritarianism, security competition, and war—were like nothing the Western capitalist democracies had seen before. Coming after a long and unprecedented speculative boom, the Great Depression brought mass unemployment to the industrial countries. As governments struggled to cope, international cooperation was the first casualty. Protectionism spread as countries scrambled to protect jobs and markets. Once the door was opened by economic crisis, reactionary and authoritarian movements walked in. Germany, Japan, and the Soviet Union embarked on massive rearmament programs. The collapse of the world economy discredited the ideas of free markets and classical economic liberalism that had been passed down from the nineteenth century. As the fascist and totalitarian states grew powerful, the deeper values and institutions of liberal democracy, which historian Eric Hobsbawm calls "liberal civilization," were called into question.[8]

The economic crisis had deep roots, but it made a sudden appearance with the October 1929 stock market crash on Wall Street and the ensuing worldwide business panic, which set the stage for the worst economic slump of the century. The international financial system ground to a halt and world trade collapsed. Governments raised tariffs in a scramble to protect dwindling market shares. In the United States, the Smoot–Hawley Tariff Act of 1930 imposed severe restrictions on imports from countries desperate to sell into the American market to pay off their dollar debts. This sparked a round of competitive protectionism. Germany and France subjected trade to direct controls. At the British Empire Economic Conference in Ottawa in 1932, Britain and its partners established a system of imperial preferences that discriminated against non-Empire producers of agricultural and industrial goods. The rush to tariff protection fragmented and closed off the world economy. Joblessness and poverty were the most graphic signs of the crisis. In the United States, one in four workers was unemployed in 1932. In Germany, two of every five were out of work. The absence in most industrial countries, including the United States, of public provisions for social security and unemployment assistance made the economic downturn even more traumatic.

The political crisis caused a weakening of liberal democracy and the rise of fascist and totalitarian challengers. In 1920, most of Europe was democratic. By the end of the 1930s, as world war approached, most European states were ruled by authoritarian leaders and single-party regimes. Britain, France, the small northern European states, the United States, and Britain's settler domains were the last remaining democracies. States took many pathways to dictatorship and authoritarian rule. Russia's brief experiment with constitutional democracy gave way after 1917 to the Bolshevik Revolution, and by the mid-1930s, Stalin had ousted his last opponents in the Communist Party and consolidated a brutal dictatorship. Elsewhere in Europe, authoritarian rule began with a move to the political right, followed by the capture of power by fascist or quasi-fascist parties led by popular civilian dictators, or else a return to power by military or royalist rulers. In Italy, Benito Mussolini, head of the Italian Fascist Party, was elected prime minister in 1922, which set the stage for one-party rule in 1926 and one-man dictatorship in the 1930s. Spain followed Italy in 1923, when a general seized control of a weak parliamentary regime. After a brief return to republican rule, Spain

broke down in civil war, and by 1939, Francisco Franco had established himself as supreme leader. In Poland, the military leader Józef Piłsudski gained
control of the government in 1926, and in the 1930s, the country became a
one-party state under military domination.[9] In Japan, the liberal government
was overturned by a national-militarist regime in 1931.[10]

Europe's turn away from parliamentary democracy took its most fateful
step in Germany with Hitler's rise to power in 1933. Like Mussolini, Hitler
and the National Socialist Party took office with the support of conservatives,
who joined them in a coalition government. The Nazis quickly destroyed
the power-sharing arrangements and consolidated their rule by outlawing
other political parties. The following year, Hitler combined the offices of
chancellor and president and became formally the German Führer. In 1936,
Heinrich Himmler, the head of Hitler's security guard, took control of all
the police and security forces in Germany. By this point, Hitler's dictatorship was firmly established. With this triumph in Germany, fascism became
an international movement.[11] Early in his rule, Hitler had announced that
"the boundaries of the year 1914 mean nothing at all for the German future."[12]
Now these words echoed across Europe.

As the liberal democratic world retreated, the geopolitical crises intensified. During the 1920s, Great Britain and France were strong enough to enforce the Versailles treaty and lead the League of Nations. They retained
their empires and used the league's mandate system to maintain their reach
into colonial areas. In 1925, Britain, France, Germany, Italy, and Belgium
signed the Locarno Treaty, guaranteeing their territorial frontiers. Several
years later, the French foreign minister Aristide Briand proposed to the United
States that the pact be made universal. In August 1929, he met in Paris with
the American secretary of state Frank Kellogg to sign the Kellogg-Briand
Pact, outlawing the resort to war except in self-defense.[13] Sixty-five countries
eventually signed the declaration. But rather than opening a new era of internationalism, the Kellogg-Briand Pact was its high-water mark. In the following years, the collapsing world economy, nationalist and antidemocratic
political movements, and the expansive geopolitical ambitions of Germany,
Japan, and Italy made repeated assaults on the international order. The
League of Nations stood helpless, its leaders preoccupied with their own

economic and political difficulties, in the face of Japan's conquest of Manchuria in 1931 and Italy's invasion of Ethiopia in 1935. Also in 1935, Hitler defied the Versailles Treaty and announced plans for rearmament. In March 1936, at the height of the Ethiopian crisis, he ordered German troops to reoccupy the Rhineland. In March 1938, Germany absorbed Austria.[14] When the leaders of Britain, France, Italy, and Germany met in Munich in September 1938, they stood amid the ruins of Versailles.

As crisis descended on the liberal democratic world, political leaders and intellectuals struggled to understand their increasingly dire circumstances. The future of capitalism, democracy, liberalism, and modernity came under sharp debate. The survival of liberal democracy was widely seen to be at risk, and the crisis deepened as the decade unfolded. In 1931, the historian Arnold Toynbee, writing in his annual survey of international affairs, observed that people across the world were beginning to realize "that the Western system of society might break down and cease to work." Eight years later, in May 1939, he delivered the annual Hobhouse lecture at the London School of Economics titled "The Downfall of Civilizations." Although no inexorable law led civilizations to collapse, Toynbee argued, given the evidence of history and the current moment, "the modern Western Civilization, in its turn is likely, on the showing of all precedents . . . to break down and disintegrate and finally dissolve."[15]

A related debate focused on the crisis of capitalism. Economists offered conflicting theories about the causes and nature of the Great Depression and what the best policy responses were. A great divide existed between those defending classical liberalism and those advancing social democratic alternatives. Here the grand ideas of Friedrich von Hayek and John Maynard Keynes crystallized a dispute that continues today. Hayek, an Austrian economist who moved to Britain in 1931, made the case for free markets, arguing that the depression was a result of underinvestment and overexpansion of credit. The proper response was to increase savings and stabilize economies at lower levels of prices and wages. Keynes, the Cambridge economist and public intellectual who had been a member of the British delegation at Versailles, argued that the crisis was caused by insufficient demand. Elaborating his ideas in his 1936 masterwork, *The General Theory of Employment,*

Interest and Money, Keynes argued that the freeing of markets would not, as Hayek claimed, cure the depression.[16] Market society had no automatic forces to produce a recovery. State spending was needed to reemploy workers and create sufficient demand to move toward full employment. While Hayek argued for a higher rate of savings, Keynes noted the "paradox of thrift": under conditions of uncertainty, higher savings would lead to stagnation and slow growth.[17]

The debate between Hayek and Keynes went beyond economic policy. Their ideas reflected divergent understandings of modern transformations in capitalism and the future of industrial society.[18] Hayek saw the modern state as a despotic force that threatened political liberty and economic freedom. In his 1944 book *The Road to Serfdom,* he framed his defense of laissez-faire economics in moral as well as economic terms.[19] Keynes sought to articulate a middle ground between unfettered capitalism and the statist economies emerging in the Soviet Union and Europe. "The outstanding faults of the economic society in which we live," he argued, "are its failure to provide for full employment and its arbitrary and inequitable distribution of wealth and incomes."[20] Keynes's ideas were in the ascendancy in the war years and the early postwar decades—all the more so because he was actively involved in negotiations over the rules and institutions of the postwar world economy. Hayek's ideas would lie dormant until the 1970s, when the Keynesian consensus across the advanced industrial world began to break down. Hayek provided the intellectual foundations for what would become neoliberalism. His ideas would inspire later generations of conservative economists and politicians who argued for a sharply circumscribed role of government in the economy. In the late twentieth century, some neoliberal views would also inform the policies of centrist governments on both sides of the Atlantic. It is important to note that Hayek's ideas were not simply arguments for the state's withdrawal from the economy. They were not advancing an argument for a "night watchman" government. The twin developments of liberal democracy and the modern state meant that a return to nineteenth-century market society was impossible. Instead, Hayek argued that the conditions underlying unfettered markets must be established and managed. As Quinn Slobodian argues, Hayek and his followers were not seeking to "liberate" markets so much as to embed them in social and legal institutions.[21] The ideas of Hayek and Keynes were both ultimately tied to expansive political projects.

Other thinkers offered sweeping arguments about the deep forces that were undermining the old international order and putting liberal democracy in crisis. The Hungarian-American economist Karl Polanyi went further than Keynes in offering a grand narrative of the breakdown of the world market system. In *The Great Transformation,* published in 1944, Polanyi argued that laissez-faire policies were themselves to blame for the crisis: "The origins of the cataclysm lay in the utopian endeavor of economic liberalism to set up a self-regulated market system."[22] The rise of market society, which reached its zenith in the nineteenth century and was destroyed by the Great War, began with the emergence of powerful states in early modern Europe that actively reorganized systems of labor, land, and markets. The "self-regulating" market did not emerge, Polanyi argued, but was built and embedded within an international system of geopolitical power and social order; thus it was neither natural nor truly self-regulating. Instead it was "submerged in [man's] social relationships."[23] The crisis of the interwar years was a consequence of the breakdown of this complex embedded system. If market society was to be rebuilt after World War II, Polanyi maintained, it would need to be a social democratic project of rebuilding institutions of social protection and political solidarity within a wider collaborative international order.

On the eve of war in 1939, the historian E. H. Carr published *The Twenty Years' Crisis, 1919–1939,* a portrait of the past two decades' political and economic instability. Carr argued that Wilson and the liberal peacemakers in Versailles sowed the seeds of crisis by trying to build a postwar order on utopian visions rather than power realities. The liberal peacemakers had brought to their work a shared—but mistaken—belief in the harmony of interests. Their fatal mistake was to think that international cooperation could be perpetuated through the establishment of institutions for resolving conflicts within a world society of liberal states possessing common interests and sympathies.[24] The nineteenth-century political order that was destroyed by the Great War did not rest on universal rational principles or ethical standards. It was built on a configuration of power, a balance of forces peculiar "to the economic development of the period and the countries concerned."[25] The "visionary hopes" of the 1920s had ignored this deep reality of power politics. Carr contended that liberals in the nineteenth century and again at Versailles thought that their international projects succeeded—and would again—because of the deep forces of rationalism and the harmony of interests. But this was an illusion. They were actually built on a foundation of hegemonic power and liberal ideology.

In Carr's view, stable international order must rest on a preponderance of power and the leadership of a hegemonic state. This was the role played by Great Britain in the nineteenth century, and it led to a "golden age of continuously expanding territories and markets, of a world policed by the self-assured and not too onerous British hegemony, of a coherent 'Western' civilization whose conflicts could be harmonised by a progressive extension of the area of common development and exploration, of the easy assumptions that what was good for one was good for all and that what was economic right could not be morally wrong."[26] Hegemonic states create international order, and their power gives them authority to do so. But stable international order also requires some degree of consensus—or at least the acquiescence of weaker states—and this favors hegemonic states that are "tolerant and unoppressive," or in any case more so than other would-be hegemons. For Carr, the twenty years' crisis was in the first instance caused by the decline of Great Britain, which had eroded the power on which the nineteenth-century order was based; this was a failure made worse because a new hegemonic power—presumably the United States—had yet to emerge.[27] It was also a moral crisis in that the "revolution against laissez-faire" had undermined the notion of public virtue manifest in the enlightened pursuit of self-interest, but no new public morality suitable for an era of mass politics and modern liberal democracy had been devised.[28]

In November 1941, a month before Pearl Harbor, Vera Dean, the head of the Foreign Policy Association in New York, published *The Struggle for World Order*, calling for a new set of principles—or "philosophy of life"—to guide the reconstruction of international order. Dean argued that World War II was a violent ratification of the failure of the Versailles peace settlement. But this failure was less one of diplomacy than of political imagination. The

Western democracies had simply not adapted to the social and economic transformations ushered in by the industrial revolution. Industrial modernity had left the masses in Western societies impoverished and disenfranchised, which was undermining liberal capitalism and creating openings for Nazi and communist movements. For Dean, the "real task" for the democracies was to reinvent themselves, both domestically and internationally: to define "the democratic concept of the postwar order in such a way as to convince people throughout the world that a victory of the Western powers would be, not the closing act of the drama, but the curtain raiser for a period of expanded and invigorated democracy."[29]

The democratic world would need to build a "new social order" that promoted the "welfare of the common man" and protected basic rights and freedoms. The old nineteenth-century institutions of democracy and laissez-faire capitalism had to give way to a political economic order that reconciled individualism with community. This project of rebuilding democratic capitalism involved both the reform of political institutions and the elaboration of a new ideology—or "spirit"—of liberal modernity. "Between the two extremes of untrammeled individual initiative and untrammeled state action lies a vast middle ground for fruitful cooperative living," Dean argued, "both on the national and on the international plane."[30] Winning the war against Nazism was the first step. The more momentous task for the Western powers was to develop a new vision of their common existence, which Dean called a "new horizon of democracy."[31]

Thus the debates of the late 1930s and 1940s centered on contending claims about the nature of the crisis and the sources of international order. Despite their differences, these public thinkers generally agreed that the crisis was not simply the result of the inability of leaders in the liberal states to pursue the right policies or settle their differences and cooperate. Deeper forces were transforming the world. The nineteenth-century international order that had brought the West into the modern era had broken down and could not be reconstructed. As Carr argued, "a twentieth-century malady cannot be cured by nineteenth-century specifics."[32] Economic, technological, political, and social forces had undermined the old order, and the Great War had finally destroyed it. The foundations for a new global order had yet to be built.

Rethinking Liberal Internationalism

During the calamitous 1930s and wartime years, liberal internationalists were forced to rethink their ideas. Many of these internationalists had been involved in the peacemaking at Versailles, shared Wilson's vision, and championed the League of Nations. Wilsonian internationalism had been premised on the assumption of a stable and expanding liberal democratic world. Modernity, it was thought, was unleashing economic, technological, and political forces that were encouraging the world to move in a liberal democratic direction. The liberal internationalists of Wilson's generation were not the utopians described by E. H. Carr.[33] The League of Nations was needed precisely because there was *not* a natural or inevitable "harmony of interests." They did, however, believe that some rudimentary shared interests did exist, and the league could cultivate them. Their conviction was that the post-1919 liberal democracies could devise a working system of trade and collective security that would bind them together in a stable and progressively oriented international order. The liberal internationalists who lived through the 1930s and World War II—including Franklin Roosevelt and his circle of advisers—continued to embrace the broad outlines of this vision. But their horizon of experience was radically different from what it had been for liberals in 1919, and this was reflected in their evolving ideas.

As the 1930s collapsed into depression and war, internationalists on both sides of the Atlantic debated ideas about how to govern the world. The academic discipline of international relations was itself slowly taking shape during the interwar years. The failure and unpopularity of diplomats after World War I opened space for academics to act as experts in foreign policy.[34] Institutions such as the Council on Foreign Relations in New York and the Royal Institute of International Affairs (Chatham House) in London were established to provide expertise and advice to governments, and other research centers were founded in Germany, France, Austria, and Switzerland. The League of Nations also became a site for internationalist thinking. Philanthropic organizations, led by the Rockefeller Foundation and the Carnegie Endowment for International Peace, funded university programs in peace studies and international affairs. Professional associations and

annual scholarly meetings also added to the growing intellectual and institutional infrastructure for internationalist research and debate.[35] In this setting, intellectuals and practitioners inside and outside the West grappled with what Arnold Toynbee called the "master-problem" of the time, which was to reestablish a stable system of international relations in an era when the older foundations of world order were giving way. The internationalism that had informed the postwar Versailles settlement had clearly failed. In circumstances even more dire than 1919, liberal internationalists searched for new ideas and visions.[36]

The internationalist debates of the 1930s and 1940s ranged widely, focusing on topics as diverse as anarchy and national sovereignty, technology and commerce, and international organization and world federalism.[37] But at the heart of liberal international rethinking was a changing view of modernity. Industrialism and technological change did not work simply to the advantage of liberal democracy. Indeed, the crises and instabilities unleashed in the 1930s were forcing liberal democracies to fight for their lives. The failures of Versailles could not be remedied merely by changes in the institutional design of the League of Nations. In this sense, the realist critique of Wilsonianism missed the point. It was the deeper transformations in industrial society that were endangering the liberal international project. The rise of powerful fascist and totalitarian states demonstrated the frightening ways that modernity could be harnessed to illiberal purposes. The fact that dictatorships and authoritarian states seemed to respond more quickly to the economic crisis of the 1930s, or found ways to avoid its severest consequences, only reinforced the point.[38] At the same time, the forces of modernity were generating a world that was so complex and interlinked that old ways of managing global space were no longer viable. In 1933, Philip Kerr, the British politician who served as Lloyd George's private secretary and championed the League of Nations, reflected on the spreading crisis of liberal democracy. The crisis was not a "failure of free institutions," he argued, "but the fact that they are becoming increasingly impossible to work owing to international anarchy in a world rapidly shrinking in terms of time and space."[39] The liberal international goal was still to organize the world so as to make liberal democracies safe, but the global conditions for doing so had changed.

This changing understanding of "the global" drove the debates about world order. The upheavals of depression and war had illuminated a new and dangerous world. Surveying midcentury Anglo-American political debates about world order, Or Rosenboim argues that internationalist thinkers were struggling to make sense of "the new political space of the global." They were looking at the world with a new appreciation of the political significance of the global as "a unitary whole made of interconnected, diverse political units."[40] These thinkers conceived of this global space in different ways, invoking transnational, cosmopolitan, and international ideas. Some schemes for ordering the global space entailed the rebuilding of Westphalian intergovernmental institutions, while others called for new types of political community and world government. What these internationalist thinkers shared, according to Rosenboim, was a belief that modern world order could no longer rest on a foundation of European power and empire. The search was for principles and an architecture that could give shape to a postimperial world order. This search for new conceptions of world order was also driven by a concern for the future of liberal democracy. The domestic and international threats to democracy loomed large both during and after the war. Liberal democracy would need to be reformed, but this could be done only within a reorganized international democratic order.[41]

In this context, British and American internationalists who had championed Wilsonianism and the League of Nations found themselves reconsidering their project. Broadly speaking, these thinkers became both more globalist and realist. A rebuilt world order would need to "do more work." It would need to be more ambitious in its efforts to support and protect the liberal democracies. The liberal democratic world—threatened in 1939 in a way it had not been in 1919—would need to organize itself in more thoroughgoing ways. At the same time, Wilson-era internationalists also gave more thought to the geopolitical foundations of liberal international order. A stable great-power order was necessary, and ideally this would involve the United States cooperating with the other great powers to uphold the order.

On the British side, Norman Angell had famously argued in *The Great Illusion*, published under the title of *Europe's Optical Illusion* in 1909, that under conditions of rising economic interdependence, modern industrial societies would recognize the futility of war and conquest.[42] The outbreak of war in 1914 forced Angell to rethink his views, and so too did the breakdown of order in the 1930s. Through the interwar years, Angell remained a champion of the League of Nations, and for these efforts he was awarded the Nobel Peace Prize in 1933. He continued to hold to the view that modern societies had more to lose than gain from great-power war, but he acknowledged that economic nationalism and the pursuit of power could overwhelm what he saw as the rational bases of peace.[43] Angell's expectation had been that the spread of knowledge and public education would slowly alter the way societies—manifest in enlightened public opinion—calculated their interests. By the 1930s, Angell no longer believed this was enough. In a 1933 reflection on his earlier thinking, he argued that security had to be provided through collective defense. The leading states would need to pool their power and work together to maintain international rules and institutions. Force had to be used by collective agreement to uphold global order. "The practical political conclusion . . . is not to insist that the world make suddenly one huge jump from armed anarchy to a world without force or arms at all, but that as a first stage, a stepping-stone or bridge, the force be transferred to the law, be organized as an instrument of community; and that the obligation be based upon clear political and diplomatic obligation."[44] Angell offered various ideas about how nations might constitute themselves as an organized society for the common defense, but the Western liberal democracies would form the core of this society.

In his indictment of Wilsonianism, E. H. Carr singled out Alfred Zimmern, an Oxford classicist who had played a leading role in shaping British proposals for the League of Nations. Zimmern moved in liberal political circles, and during the war he was recruited by Walter Lippmann to write for *The New Republic*, a progressive magazine then edited by Herbert Croly. Zimmern articulated mainstream liberal internationalist ideas even as he remained firmly committed to the British Empire. He shared the Wilson-era critique of the balance of power and secret diplomacy, was critical of the laissez-faire liberalism of the prewar era, and recognized the growing importance of the state in managing industrial societies. He agreed with the view of many liberals that nationalism was a cause of war, but he was skeptical of internationalist calls for world government.[45] Instead, Zimmern championed a sort of "liberal nationalism"—or as he put it, "Mazzinism" that is "brought up to date to fit the scale of our large scale civilization."[46] From the beginning, Zimmern supported the League of Nations as a vehicle for the prevention of future war. He based this view less on a belief in the idea of collective security than on the conviction that the league would foster a concert of powers, which in turn would act collectively to uphold the postwar order. "The League of Nations is, in fact, an instrument of cooperation," Zimmern argued:

> It is a standing agency facilitating common action by states animated by the co-operative spirit. In so far as they are desirous of co-operation, the League is available for their use. When this temper of sociability, this sense of solidarity, this team-spirit, are present in full measure, the League organisation functions with a minimum of friction and the League itself becomes almost—but never quite—a Confederation. But whenever this spirit wanes and competition and jealousy resume their sway, the League's activity dies down. . . . At such times the true League has ceased to exist. The machinery exists, but the spirit has departed from it. . . . It cannot function by its own effort nor survive indefinitely by its own momentum—a momentum originally supplied from the outside. . . . It is their [member states'] will and their will alone which can make the League a living reality.[47]

During the 1930s, Zimmern came to have doubts that the league could muster sufficient solidarity to become an effective treaty-based organization. In the face of the league's failure to respond to the Manchurian and Abyssinian crises, Zimmern urged Britain and France to "raise a hue and cry." He came to see the world divided into two blocs—the "welfare states," the liberal democracies with governments that "think in terms of responsibility," and "power states," revisionist states that think "in terms of force."[48] A stable international order could not be established by bridging the divide between them. The "power states" would have to be confronted. As the world of the

1930s crumbled, Zimmern argued that international order must be based on "co-operation between welfare states." He still affirmed his belief in the possibilities of progress in world politics and he thought that, over the long term, the rule of law could guide the relations of states. But by the late 1930s, he was convinced that such an order would need to be organized within the liberal democratic world.[49]

Robert Cecil, a leading architect of proposals for a league of nations within the wartime British government, remained a champion of the league in the interwar years. From 1923 to 1945, he served as president of the League of Nations Union, the leading pro-league political group in Great Britain, and he held positions in Geneva within the league itself.[50] In 1938, he received the Nobel Peace Prize for his efforts, and in his acceptance speech he reflected on the return of militarism and territorial aggression and the failure of the league. He saw a return to the "old ideas"—doctrines of reactionary nationalism and militarism—that had brought the world to war in 1914. Like other liberal internationalists, in the wake of Japanese, Italian, and German aggressions in the early 1930s, Cecil abandoned his belief in the power of public opinion and shifted to advocating military sanctions organized and authorized by broadly inclusive global institutions.[51] But his internationalism remained undimmed. The interdependence of nations was an inherent feature of the modern world, and the "principle of international cooperation" thus served the interests of all states. In the way of this principle were not the people but their governments. Cecil argued that "free governments" were uniquely capable of promoting the individual development and welfare of the people. Reform of the international system was still possible. After all, he argued, British constitutional progress took centuries to be realized.[52] Like Zimmern, Cecil placed his greatest hope on the grouping of Western democratic states, which, as the world contracted into reactionary and militarist blocs, would need to cooperate to keep the League of Nation ideals alive.[53] In Western Europe, Cecil argued, such a grouping of states might take the form of a "constitutional union of independent states, inside the general framework of the League."[54] In this rethinking, he was joining other internationalists in seeking to identify new ways in which liberal democratic states could organize themselves to uphold a wider system of rules and institutions.

On the American side, the failure of the United States to join the League of Nations was the defining event of the interwar period. During these years, liberal internationalists debated the failure of Versailles, the conundrum of American isolationism, and the future of internationalism.[55] Walter Lippmann, who had contributed to Wilson's peace proposals as a member of the Inquiry, the study group organized to prepare for the peace negotiations, and who traveled with the American delegation to Paris, reflected many observers' disillusionment with Wilsonianism.[56] His dissatisfaction came even before the Senate rejected Wilson's treaty: the peace settlement, he wrote, had been too punitive and failed to embody progressive ideals. Over the next two decades, his critique deepened. He argued that Wilson's great error was his overestimation of the ability of people and their leaders to pursue their enlightened self-interest. "We are mere mortals with limited power and little universal wisdom."[57] Yet Lippmann remained a committed internationalist who supported naval disarmament, cooperation with the World Court, and the struggle of the League of Nations to keep the peace. What he was searching for was a more pragmatic internationalism. For Lippmann, the key to a stable international order was to organize it around arms reduction and the international arbitration of disputes.[58] In the early 1930s, even after Germany and Japan embarked on aggression, Lippmann still did not call for an American alliance with the European democracies, hoping instead that the world could operate collectively to push back the revisionist great powers through an "international conscience and channeling international law."

By the time the United States joined the war against Germany and Japan at the end of 1941, Lippmann's earlier views had become a "shattered dream," and he began to offer more far-reaching arguments for a postwar order organized around American-led cooperation among the Western democracies.[59] These post-Wilsonian views were developed in his 1943 book *U.S. Foreign Policy: Shield of the Republic*. "If there is to be peace in our time," Lippmann asserted, "it will have to be a peace among sovereign national states."[60] Security among these states would come from a new type of political order among the liberal states that was backed up by American power and a system of alliances. Lippmann had lost his faith in the Wilsonian vision of collective security. Writing to Quincy Wright, a leading international relations scholar, Lippmann argued that a new postwar league based on collective security would inevitably break down into rival geopolitical alignments. "The great object of international organization in the next generation is to hold together the alliance and to hold it together at almost any cost," he maintained. "I want to find ways of binding together the Allies which are sure to bind them, and I do not believe they will be successfully bound together by any general covenant."[61] Lippmann was searching for an internationalism that distanced itself from both American proponents of isolationism and the "one world" or "universalist" vision of postwar order.

Other internationalists did not break fully with Wilsonianism but offered pragmatic arguments for building postwar order around American leadership, global institutions, and progressive goals. James Shotwell, a Columbia University historian and prominent internationalist, followed this path. Like Lippmann, he had been a member of the Inquiry and attended the Paris Peace Conference, and he later played an important role in founding the International Labor Organization. During World War II, he was part of a working group that prepared plans for a new international organization to replace the League of Nations, and he later helped draft the Charter of the United Nations. Across these decades, Shotwell remained committed to a progressive and reform-oriented internationalist agenda. He was one of the architects of the Kellogg-Briand Pact, which declared war to be illegal. Shotwell hoped that the pact would be followed by a sanctions regime as an enforcement tool that would provide an opportunity for the United States to finally participate in a system of collective security.[62] Later, as the world economy collapsed, he encouraged American participation in the World Economic Conference, held in London in the summer of 1933 under the auspices of the League of Nations. The conference, concerned primarily with stabilizing European monetary and financial relations, largely failed, in part because of the unwillingness of Franklin Delano Roosevelt's unwillingness to work with the Europeans on the international settlement of war debt. Shotwell thought FDR had not fully understood the "ominous rise of militant nationalism," symbolized by Hitler's coming to power the previous January, and therefore had not offered sufficient support to "the forces of liberalism in Europe."[63]

Despite the breakdown of order in the 1930s, or perhaps because of it, Shotwell remained convinced that the United States needed to find a way to tie itself to the League of Nations. In this sense, his critique was less about the limits of Wilsonianism than about the United States' failure to support it. As conditions deteriorated in Europe in the mid-1930s, Shotwell floated a proposal for revision of the league to create "graded responsibilities" and "associated membership" roles. Only countries with specific interests in a region would offer guarantees of peace and security in that region. Under this scheme, the United States could play a more limited role in upholding the peace process.[64]

With the outbreak of world war, Shotwell's ideas continued to evolve. Some sort of collective security system would be needed after the war, but its success would ultimately depend on cooperation among the great powers. At the end of the war, he argued that a stable postwar order hinged less on a working system of collective security than on creating conditions for economic stability and social progress. He hoped the Soviet Union would join a reorganized postwar order, but the core of this order would need to be built around the liberal democratic states. If there was to be a "revolution" in relations among nation-states, it would occur first in Europe and the Atlantic world. Shotwell continued to believe in the universal principles enshrined in the United Nations, but he argued that they would have to be defended by the community of Western democracies. By the 1940s, he had tied his internationalism to the liberal democratic world and programs of economic and social advancement. "There is . . . another and stronger defense of peace by the United Nations than police action or the threat of reprisals for aggression," he argued. "It is the upbuilding of common interests in welfare."[65] This meant building the postwar order around a core grouping of like-minded countries that would cooperate in the pursuit of security and progressive goals. Shotwell believed the forces of modernity—science, technology, industrialism—would continue to bring gradual improvement of societies, but that, like the emergence of parliamentary democracy and the rule of law, it would evolve slowly, through gradual shifts in cultural and human understanding. In the meantime, the Atlantic liberal democracies would have to form the nucleus of the emergent global order.

Sumner Welles, another leading liberal internationalist, held senior diplomatic positions throughout the Roosevelt administration. He began his diplomatic career during World War I and was inspired by Woodrow Wilson to embrace core internationalist ideals of free trade, collective security, and self-determination. In the 1920s, Welles remained committed to these causes, operating inside the State Department to support the strengthening of multilateral economic and political ties with Europe and Latin America. A close friend and adviser to FDR, he became one of the new administration's most vocal advocates of American-led internationalism. During the 1930s, he made speeches calling for the United States to lead the world in rebuilding an open world economy and putting an end to economic nationalism and colonialism.[66] He saw Latin America as an especially promising region for his internationalist agenda. In policy papers written for FDR, he advocated a new pact of cooperation between the United States and South American republics, based on principles of sovereign equality, nonintervention, and increased trade. Welles called this the "American System": the United States and countries within the region would establish themselves as a political community with a permanent regional body to resolve hemispheric disputes.[67] Some of these ideas found their way into FDR's Good Neighbor Policy, and in numerous hemispheric conferences during the 1930s, American and Latin American delegates gathered to debate the terms of pan-American unity. For Welles, even though Wilsonianism had failed as a global order, the Western hemisphere offered a promising political space for liberal internationalist ideas.

In the early 1940s, as the Roosevelt administration turned to postwar planning, Welles brought his evolving liberal international ideas to the debate. He was a champion of the United Nations, but he argued that it should rest on regional foundations. "Most of us, I think, never believed that world peace could be maintained unless some international organization could be created which was universal in its scope," he wrote in 1946. "But most of us also believed that this organization should be fashioned in such a way as to leave to the nations in the several geographical regions of the world, namely, the Western Hemisphere, Europe, the Far East, and the Near East, the utmost responsibility for maintaining peace, and for furthering social and economic progress within their respective areas."[68] In a sense, Welles was offering a model of international order based on an updated version of the League of Nations and the Good Neighbor policy. The global organization would provide a framework of international laws and enshrine principles of economic openness and human rights, but the real work of creating order and pursuing economic advancement would be carried on within regional groupings led by the great powers.[69] Within this postwar order, the United States would step forward as a hegemonic leader. American interests would be protected, ensuring worldwide access to resources and markets. But Welles saw a deeper normative basis for this vision of order, rooted in its principles of sovereign equality and self-determination and a moral commitment to economic and social advancement.

On both sides of the Atlantic, internationalists who had supported the liberal peacemaking aims at Versailles were forced during the 1930s and 1940s to rethink their ideas and agendas. The collapse of the post-1919 international order, the rise of the fascist powers, and the return of world war raised existential questions about the future of liberal democracy. The forces of modernity that seemed in earlier generations to favor liberal democracy now threatened the latter's existence. In the face of these grim developments, interwar internationalists did not abandon their commitment to the cooperative reorganization of global order. If anything, they saw their ideas as more rather than less relevant for a world being torn apart by mercantile nationalism, illiberalism, and revisionist great powers.[70] But it was clear to both European and American internationalists that if the liberal democratic world was to survive, it would have to be rebuilt on a new, more substantial foundation. The liberal internationalist debates of the interwar era ranged widely, but they were ultimately focused on the search for a new way of organizing the liberal democratic order. Wilsonian internationalism was premised on the rise and spread of liberal democracy as a reliable foundation for open

trade, collective security, and the League of Nations. By the 1930s and 1940s, this thinking had reversed itself: liberal democracy was now threatened and a new international order was needed to ensure its survival.

Broadly speaking, this search for a new liberal international order moved in two complementary directions. In one sense, this new thinking was more global. Liberal internationalists saw the modernizing world as more complex than the nineteenth-century world, larger in scope, and fraught with danger. As a result, the international order would need to be more comprehensive so as to facilitate the management of more problems. An international order would not just keep the peace. It would foster collective action and capacities in the liberal societies' pursuit of economic and social advancement. This new thinking was also more realist in that it was more focused on the great-power foundations of liberal internationalism. The liberal project would need to rest on a stable geopolitical foundation. For some, such as Welles, this meant holding out the possibility of stable postwar relations with the Soviet Union and the building of regional orders organized under the auspices of the United Nations. But other liberal internationalists, such as Angell, thought the geopolitical foundation for liberal order was seen as necessarily and inevitably tied to a coalition—or alliance—of Western liberal democracies. Liberal international principles had a "one world" logic, but a stable and effective international order had to rest on the solidarity of the liberal capitalist democracies.

The Roosevelt Revolution

At the root of liberal rethinking in the 1930s was the crisis of liberal democracy. Paradoxically, the modern democratic state was now seen to be both more fragile and more integral to the security and well-being of societies. The upheavals of this period had exposed the fragilities and incapacities of liberal democratic institutions. This was seen in the struggle of the liberal democracies to understand and respond to economic crisis; in their weakness in confronting the reactionary politics that economic crisis unleashed; and in their new sense of vulnerability to chaos beyond their borders. Only a few constitutional democracies were left standing on the eve of World War II, yet the modern democratic state was taking on new roles and responsibilities. Citizens increasingly looked to the state for the provision of welfare and security. The legitimacy of the modern state—and certainly the electoral fate of its leaders—was tied more than ever before to its ability to deliver employment and opportunity.[71] The relationship between state and citizen in a liberal democracy was increasingly organized around the politics of rights and protections.

Roosevelt's twelve years as president were defined by these transformations.[73] In 1936, he argued that the United States was waging "not alone a war against want and destitution and economic demoralization" but a "war for the survival of democracy."[74] The American state was called upon to expand its capacities to solve new and unprecedented economic and social problems, which would require the national political order itself to be transformed and the president to oversee the building of a new progressive domestic coalition. The Democratic Party, labor, social movements, and political interest groups were all drawn into the reworking of American liberalism. As David Plotke argues, the new political vision "fused democratic and modernizing themes in a progressive liberalism that advocated government action to achieve economic stability, enhance social security, and expand political participation."[75] The crisis of industrial society had generated demands for reform and mobilized the citizenry to seek greater security and opportunity. With the New Deal, Roosevelt had committed the government to providing socioeconomic security to the American people. "Among our objectives I place the security of the men, women, and children of the Nation first," he told Congress in the summer of 1934. His duty as president was to ensure "security against several of the great disturbing factors in life—especially those which relate to unemployment and old age."[76]

In 1930s Britain, a similar coalition of labor, social groups, and progressive reformers took shape and pushed for far-reaching political and social reforms. Britain emerged from the war with a government exercising greater centralized control over the economy and society than ever before. In 1943, a coalition government of Conservative and Labour Parties accepted the recommendations of a commission led by Sir William Beveridge for a new system of universal social security. This was followed by expanded opportunities for free secondary education. The growing hopes for social reform during these dark years led to a Labour Party victory in July 1945, setting the stage for a decade of progressive actions, including the introduction of a national health service. As the historian James Joll observes, the British people's "experiences of bombing, of universal military and civil defence service as well as the sense of dangers survived in common, all contributed to a desire for social reform and for a new society which might embody some of the ideals of equality and social justice which had been discussed during the war."[77] On the continent, countries like France and Sweden also pursued social reform and the expansion of liberal democracy.[78]

Across the industrial world, liberal democracies were forced to find new ways to operate, and thus to survive. What it meant to "govern" in a liberal democracy was becoming bigger and more complicated. "The twentieth century multiplied the occasions when it became essential for governments to govern," Eric Hobsbawm notes. "The kind of state which confined itself to providing the ground rules for business and civil society . . . became as obsolete as the 'nightwatchmen' who inspired the metaphor."[79] The modern democratic state was increasingly defined by its role in managing the instabilities and insecurities of industrial capitalism.

The transformation of the modern liberal state had profound international dimensions. To put liberal democracies on solid footing, a new type of international order was needed. The Great Depression and world war had expanded the constituencies that had a stake in the postwar order. The international order would need to do more things for more people. Even the very idea of the term *international order*—or *world order*—was just then emerging as a familiar term, indicating something whose multifaceted institutions and social purposes had to be built and managed and whose features were deeply connected to the ability of governments to accomplish their expanding goals at home.[80] This liberal rethinking had several aspects.

First, in the 1930s, liberals increasingly argued that international order should be put in the service of advancing economic security and social well-being. The goal of international order was not simply to prevent war but to facilitate the pursuit of human betterment in modern industrial society. Progressive ideas taking root in liberal democracies were being brought to debates about reforming the international system. While the New Deal in the United States set the example, countries such as Great Britain, France, Australia, Sweden, Norway, and Mexico were also experimenting with stronger employment and welfare programs. The 1930s were years of policy experimentation as governments searched for solutions to their growing economic and social problems. Experts across the liberal democratic world studied each other's policies.[81] They also looked on warily as the Soviet Union and authoritarian regimes pursued their more statist and centrally planned responses to crisis.[82] The Great Depression coincided with the Soviet regime's first Five-Year Plan, and many intellectuals on the Left in the United States and Europe had come to see Soviet communism as the vanguard of a new civilization. Socialists such as Beatrice and Sidney Webb and Harold Laski were inspired by the Soviet experiment, while liberals such as Keynes were more skeptical but also recognized its political potential and historical significance.[83] Keynes also thought Hjalmar Schacht had done a good job in Germany in the 1930s in reducing unemployment by non–laissez-faire means. In this global moment of economic crisis, political experimentation, ideological competition, and world war, liberals came to see a reformed and progressively oriented international order as integral to their vision.

In the United States, this new thinking centered on the advancement of political rights and social protections. Roosevelt's 1941 State of the Union Address to Congress was a landmark statement. After the "new order of tyranny" is defeated, he proclaimed, the world must affirm four "essential human freedoms": freedom of speech, freedom of religion, freedom from want, and freedom from fear.[84] When he and Churchill met off the coast of Newfoundland, they took these ideas a step further and drafted the Atlantic Charter, a general statement of liberal principles to guide the postwar settlement. They promised to seek a postwar order that would promote full employment, social well-being, and a new solidarity among nations. Their governments would seek "no aggrandizement, territorial or other" and would respect "the right of all peoples to choose the form of government under which they will live." In a new era of economic cooperation, all countries would have free access to the raw materials of the world. The charter was deliberately vague about postwar security cooperation, saying only that there would be a "wider and permanent system of general security."[85]

With this statement, the British and American leaders announced their visions of postwar order—even before the United States had formally entered the war. Interestingly, the draft that Roosevelt and Churchill agreed on turned out to be incomplete. As they prepared to depart, Churchill received a message from his war cabinet, led by the Labour leader, Clement Attlee, saying that the cabinet endorsed the principles but proposed an additional one. This became the charter's fifth point: a commitment to economic advancement and social security. As the historian Theodore Wilson notes, "The new paragraph received Roosevelt's enthusiastic approval, because it embodied one of his four freedoms."[86] After the meeting, Roosevelt sent the Atlantic Charter to Congress, and in his covering letter he added a corollary. Noting that the declaration self-evidently included "the world need for freedom of religion and freedom of information," he argued that "no society of the world organized under the announced principles could survive without these freedoms, which are a part of the whole freedom for which we strive."[87]

The Atlantic Charter message to the British and American people was: "If you fight and win this war, we will build a better world on the other side." In a radio broadcast six days after the meeting, Churchill emphasized that the charter contained "distinct and marked differences" from the postwar vision of the Allies after World War I. In particular, he said, "Instead of trying to ruin German trade by all kinds of additional trade barriers and hindrances, as was the mood in 1917, we have definitely adopted the view that it is not in interests of the world" that any "nation should be unprosperous or shut out from the means of making a decent living for itself and its peoples by industry and enterprise."[88] For Roosevelt, the domestic New Deal was to lead to a "New Deal for the world."[89] Dumbarton Oaks, Bretton Woods, and San Francisco were stops along the way. The stabilization and reform of the domestic economy and the creation of a competent and active government were of a piece with building a wider world of stable and well-functioning liberal democracies. "Atlantic Charter and Four Freedoms rhetoric envisioned an international order that internationalized the qualities of what political theorists call a 'decent' society," argues Elizabeth Borgwardt. "It transformed the domestic New Deal into an Allied fighting faith."[90]

Second, liberal internationalists saw new vulnerabilities generated by rising economic and security interdependence. This interdependence was understood to be rooted in the deep forces of modernity—and hence difficult if not impossible to escape. Americans in particular were finding it increasingly hard to hide from the rest of the world. Modern industrial societies were more and more vulnerable to the ill-advised policies of other states. Financial crises, protectionism, arms buildups—they could spread like a contagion. Liberal internationalists also saw the upside of interdependence. Trade and exchange generated gains and, over the long term, propelled great human advances. The postwar international order would need to realize these benefits while warding off the dangers.

For the United States, the problems of interdependence were embodied in the one-two punch of world economic collapse and Axis aggression. The country was protected by vast oceans, but technology and the deep interconnections of industrial societies made isolation less viable. In 1940, Arthur Vandenberg, a Republican senator who opposed the New Deal in the 1930s but turned into a staunch internationalist after World War II, argued for a policy of "insulation." "Isolation," he acknowledged, was probably impossible "in this present foreshortened world when one can cross the Atlantic Ocean in 36 hours. . . . But probably the best we can hope for from now on is 'insulation.' I should say that an 'insulationist' is one who wants to preserve all the isolation which modern circumstances will permit."[91] American political leaders and policy experts debated the character and implications of these "modern circumstances" until the attack on Pearl Harbor.

Roosevelt's internationalism during these years was increasingly defined by his appreciation of the vulnerabilities of modern economic and security interdependence.[92] He frequently spoke of the "contagion" effects that accompanied modern international relations. In his famous Quarantine Speech of 1937, he spoke of how war could spread as a contagion until it engulfed "states and people remote from the original scene of hostilities."[93] In January 1939, he told senators that the United States could no longer remain safe behind the two oceans as it had during the age of sea power. The new age of air power meant that the nation would need to establish its first line of defense in Europe and the Pacific Islands. In a public address the same month, he went further: "We have learned that God-fearing democracies of the world that observe the sanctity of treaties and good faith in their dealings with other nations cannot safely be indifferent to international lawlessness anywhere. They cannot forever let pass, without effective protest, acts of aggression against sister nations—acts which automatically undermine all of us."[94] The historian David Reynolds argues that this speech contained the "embryo of a new foreign policy." For reasons of both security and ideology, the United States needed to care about events thousands of miles away.[95] Roosevelt made the more general point the following December in a letter to Pope Pius XII: "Because the people of this nation have come to the realization that time and distance no longer exist in the older sense, they understand that which harms one segment of humanity harms all the rest."[96] He echoed this view in January 1941 in a letter to the US ambassador to Tokyo: "The problems we face are now so vast and so interrelated that any attempts even to state them compels one to think of five continents and seven seas."[97] This global modernist sentiment increasingly lay at the center of the liberal internationalist vision. The United States and the other liberal democracies had to find ways to mitigate the dangers of interdependence.

Third, there was a new emphasis on building permanent multilateral governance institutions. The idea of institutionalized cooperation among states was not new. Since the nineteenth century, liberal internationalists had championed peace congresses, arbitration councils, and intergovernmental unions. The League of Nations was a forerunner as well. But the agenda for multilateral cooperation that emerged out of the 1930s was more ambitious. International institutions and functional agencies—what Roosevelt called "a workable kit of tools"—would be at the heart of an international order configured to strengthen the liberal states' capacities to manage their modern-era vulnerabilities and responsibilities.

In his welcome speech to the Bretton Woods conference in 1944, Roosevelt placed the growing vulnerability of the modernizing world economy at the heart of the postwar agenda for multilateral economic governance. "Economic diseases are highly communicable," he said. "It follows, therefore, that the economic health of every country is a proper matter of concern to all its neighbors, near and distant." The "things that needed to be done must be done—can only be done—in concert."[98] This idea that new intergovernmental organizations could facilitate economic stability and growth was given a boost by Keynesian thinking. Jacob Viner, a leading American economist of the day, argued that any country by itself would find it hard to cope with business cycles and depressions, but with international cooperation "the business cycle and mass unemployment can be largely solved."[99] In asking Congress to approve the Bretton Woods agreements, Roosevelt argued that organizations such as the International Monetary Fund and the International Bank for Reconstruction and Development were to be the "cornerstones" for postwar economic cooperation. It was through these institutions that national states would get "more goods produced, more jobs, more trade, and a higher standard of living for us all."[100] In areas such as food and agriculture, aviation, and finance and monetary relations, agencies and organizations would provide a framework for international collaboration, equipping governments to deal with postwar social and economic problems as well as with problems of security.

The League of Nations provided an important body of experience to these Roosevelt-era ambitions for expanded institutional cooperation. The league had not been able to stop territorial aggression in Asia and Africa, but it did quietly establish itself as a site for a variety of social and economic undertakings in areas such as finance and trade, humanitarian relief, and decolonization. Susan Pedersen argues that although the league failed at peacekeeping, it performed two other functions: in the great transition from a world of empire to nation-states, it helped stabilize new states and managed the minorities and mandates system; and it facilitated the regulation of a wide variety of cross-border flows.[101] In both these respects, the league was a harbinger of the multilateralism that emerged after World War II.

Fourth, the linchpin of Wilson-era liberal internationalism was "public opinion." Wilson believed that this diffuse and informal enforcement mechanism would make the post-1919 order stable and peaceful. World opinion would pressure states to hew to accepted international norms and standards. But during the 1930s, liberal internationalists slowly abandoned this assumption. Totalitarian states were suppressing outside news sources while subjecting their people to heavy doses of propaganda. Roosevelt made this point to William E. Dodd, his Wilsonian ambassador to Germany, in January 1936: "The theory of Woodrow Wilson that one can appeal to the citizens over the head of the government is no longer tenable, for the reason that the dissemination of news—real news . . . is no longer possible."[102] The liberal internationalist project could not rest on world opinion and the promulgation of norms. The new authoritarian states hardly cared what the liberal democracies thought, and they could simply suppress the spread of news among their populations.[103] Roosevelt and other liberals still believed that underneath the nationalism and illiberalism of the 1930s lurked a more solidarist and cooperative international society. But bringing it to the surface would require a more developed and managed international order, anchored by formidable alignments of power.

If the international order could not rely on public opinion for the enforcement of norms, it had to rest on a deeper foundation of geopolitical alignments, great-power cooperation, and shared social purposes. International law could not be enforced as such. States would have to be disciplined by their desire to be part of a well-ordered, secure, and prosperous grouping of states. Participation in this club came with tangible rewards, but also with conditions. Liberal democracies that contributed to the club's security needs and played by the rules were allowed in. The liberal internationalists had to be ambitious about the order they sought to create, precisely because the incentives for orderly and cooperative behavior had to come from economic and security gains for states on the inside.

Fifth, there was a nascent universalism in these ideas. Global economic upheaval and war were occurring on a much greater scale than in Wilson's era. The continuing shrinkage of time and space meant that more of the world mattered and more of it was in play. The ideas themselves—the Four Freedoms and the Atlantic Charter—were wartime propaganda in a sense, an effort to rally support in the West and elevate the struggle in which Great Britain and the United States found themselves. But it was significant that the ideas themselves were uttered. They were hard to take back or narrowly circumscribe. Roosevelt famously dictated his Four Freedoms speech to his speechwriters in one continuous monologue. When Harry Hopkins heard the phrase "everywhere in the world," he spoke up: "That covers an awful lot of territory, Mr. President. I don't know how interested Americans are going to be in the people of Java." Roosevelt replied, "I'm afraid they'll have to be some day, Harry. . . . The world is getting so small that even the people of Java are getting to be our neighbors."[104] Even if one doubts Roosevelt's sincerity in espousing universal rights and protections, his words had an impact on subsequent struggles for human rights and global norms.[105]

This universalizing of liberal international ideas was also prompted by the ideological competition that Roosevelt and other liberal democratic leaders felt from rising fascist and totalitarian rivals. As war approached and Roosevelt made the case for American involvement, he argued that stakes were not just the nation's security but its values and way of life. If Wilson's Fourteen Points were in part a response to Lenin and the Russian Revolution, Roosevelt's Four Freedoms were a response to the demands of mobilizing the American people to face an even more dangerous set of threats—and a more dangerous rival ideology. His introduction of universal values had a practical purpose, but it also had a long-lasting influence on liberal internationalism.

Reinforcing this universalism was a change in thinking about the relationship between the West and the non-Western world. To be sure, Europeans and Americans held on to many of the deep assumptions about civilizational and racial hierarchies that informed the internationalists of Wilson's era. But they had a more sober view about the dangers of Western modernity itself. The modernizing world enabled the rise of powerful illiberal states that increasingly threatened to divide the world into blocs and imperial zones. Autocracies and dictatorships could harness modernity for their own aggressive purposes. This marked an important shift from the Wilsonian view, which regarded Germany's aggression as a premodern atavism. The West itself—not the "less civilized" non-West—was where the real threats lay. The liberal democracies would therefore need to be reorganized and brought under more progressive governance. State power had to be bound and restrained—and, if necessary, balanced.

Finally and most generally, there was a gradual shift in the way Western liberal democracies understood "security." In the United States, the depression and New Deal brought into existence the notion of "social security," and the violence and destruction of the world war brought into existence the notion of "national security." Both were more than terms of art. They reflected new conceptions of the state's role in ensuring the health, welfare, and safety of the people. "Social security" signaled the government's growing responsibility for stabilizing the economy and maintaining high employment. This responsibility was reflected in a long string of acts and measures, ranging from Wilson-era progressive legislation to the Social Security Act of 1935 and the Full Employment Act of 1946.[106] Likewise, in earlier decades, the most common term describing the military's overall purpose was *national defense,* which referred to the protection of US territory against traditional military attacks. The term *national security* was coined during World War II to express the new vision of an activist and permanently mobilized state protecting its interests across economic, political, and military realms.[107] "National security" required the United States to actively shape its external environment—coordinating agencies, generating resources, making plans, and building alliances. The National Security Act of 1947, which reorganized the agencies and departments for the conduct of the Cold War, embodied this new vision.[108]

The new language of security reflected a redefinition and expansion of the state's role in protecting its citizens, institutions, and way of life. National governments would need to do more things in more places to accomplish more purposes—both at home and abroad. In the years between 1914 and 1931, the phrase *national security* was uttered only four times, by two American presidents.[109] By the mid-1930s, FDR was using the term regularly in defining his administration's goals. "You and I agree that security is our greatest need," FDR told his audience in a Fireside Chat in April 1938. "Therefore, I am determined to do all in my power to help you attain that security."[110] During the war, FDR repeatedly returned to this theme. In a Fireside Chat in January 1944, he offered his vision: "The one supreme objective for the future, which we discussed for each nation individually and for the United Nations can be summed up in one word: security. And that means not only physical security which provides safety from attacks by aggressors. It means also economic security, social security, moral security—in a family of nations."[111] The upheavals in the center of the modern world—the Great Depression and the rise of fascist aggression—had generated a new and far-reaching condition of insecurity in the United States and across the democratic world. The task of the modern liberal state, therefore, would be to generate security.[112] In a world of cascading economic and security interdependence, a country's security depended increasingly on developments beyond its borders—and so the search for security was increasingly tied to a wide-ranging internationalist agenda. For Roosevelt, as the country moved toward war, this meant building and supporting the liberal democratic world. "Until FDR," the historian Andrew Preston argues, "no American statesman had presented security as having two equal parts—physical and normative, territorial and ideological—forming an integrated, indivisible whole that applied the world over."[113] This doctrine of national security laid the foundation for the United States to organize and lead a new postwar world order.

The Rooseveltian revolution is best understood as the culmination of the transformation of the way in which liberal internationalists thought about international order. The crises of the era had empowered modern liberal states to make their societies safe and secure, and this could only be done if the liberal democratic world itself was organized to solve the problems of modern industrial society. This would require building permanent intergovernmental institutions to manage the terms of interdependence. Markets would be open but they would be embedded in national and institutional institutions that gave government tools to manage instabilities and protect jobs. This Rooseveltian vision was both deeply Western and universalistic. FDR's Four Freedoms were in part a wartime effort to counter the ideological campaigns of Nazi Germany's "new order" and inspire American internationalism, but they also made claims about the universal character of rights and protections. The ideological contest between liberal democracy and its rising illiberal challengers reinforced the way Roosevelt and others framed the challenges that beset the liberal democratic world. Yet, at the same time, Roosevelt's liberal internationalism was also tied tightly to an alliance among the Western liberal democracies. To solve the problems of liberal industrial society, the advanced Western democracies would need to work together in new ways. They would need to operate as a grouping or club of democracies and the United States would be their "arsenal." How precisely the United States and its partners would actually build a new container for the liberal democracies had to wait until after the war ended.

Also part of the emerging consensus was that an open, well-functioning international economy was a critical component of a stable peace: the road to World War II had been paved with protectionism, trade blocs, and currency unions. But open markets needed governments to regulate and manage them or they would end in calamity. At the international level, this meant putting in place regulatory and public goods mechanisms to guard against economic dysfunction or failure, which could easily spread. Governments were now obligated to ensure employment, economic well-being, and social security—and the United States needed to create a more facilitating international environment to make good on its economic security obligations. The progressive notions embedded in New Deal liberalism became part of America's vision of an international order.[114] With the rise of the Cold War, the Truman administration and later presidents built a "liberal hegemonic" order that incorporated Roosevelt-era liberal internationalism into a wider project of American hegemonic leadership. The United States took the lead in fashioning a world of regimes, alliances, partnerships, client states, and regional orders—and put itself at the center of it all.

SIX

The Rise of Liberal Hegemony

World War II was the most violent and destructive armed conflict in human history. When it ended in the summer of 1945, the United States was left standing as the world's most powerful nation. While other great powers—both the Axis and Allied states—had been weakened or destroyed by the war, the United States had grown stronger. Its gross national product increased by 60 percent during the war, and by the end the United States had become the leading military power, producing more arms than the Axis states combined and almost three times the amount generated by the Soviet Union. America was everywhere, a global power with troops and outposts spread across the world. It occupied Japan and parts of Germany. The European-centered international order was in ruins. "A world war is like a furnace," writes Edward Mortimer, "it melts the world down and makes it malleable."[1] World War II was a blast furnace, and in its wake the United States found itself with an ability unlike any that existed before to shape a new world order.

American leaders understood the opportunities presented by this global rupture. "The United States is growing enormously in strength and power; the other nations are rapidly exhausting themselves; the disproportion between their resources and America's is constantly widening," noted a September 1941 Council on Foreign Relations planning document. "In looking into the future, it is clear that it is America's policy which give the first answer to what kind of world is to come out of the war."[2] By the end of the war, it was obvious that the United States would have an opportunity to shape and dominate the postwar system. The real question was: in what ways would it do so and toward what ends? What kind of international order would the United States seek to build and lead? The answers were not obvious. After all, the United States and the other liberal democracies had just come as close to extinction as they ever had. Militarist great powers had brought the modern world to its knees again—for the second time in thirty years. But the world war was as much consequence as cause. The collapse of the world economy, the rise of fascism and totalitarianism, and the fragility and retreat of liberal democracy were all part of the long and chaotic road to war. In the United States and Europe, the world war was widely seen as part of a deeper failure— dating back to Versailles or even earlier—to establish a stable foundation for modern liberal capitalist society.[3]

In the years between 1944 and 1951, the United States and its partners engaged in the most far-reaching international order building ever attempted. Order was built around new forms of economic, political, and security cooperation. Large multilateral institutions were established: the United Nations, the Bretton Woods institutions, the General Agreement on Tariffs and Trade, the World Health Organization, and an array of regional organizations. In 1948, the United States launched the massive Marshall Plan multilateral aid program to help rebuild Western European economies and prevent the spread of communism. Six European countries organized a Coal and Steel Community to regulate production in heavy industries, laying the groundwork for the European Economic Community. The United States built security alliances with European and East Asian partners, culminating in the signing of the North Atlantic Treaty in the spring of 1949. The year before, the United Nations General Assembly adopted the Universal Declaration of Human Rights proclaiming the inherent dignity and rights of "all members of the human family." This multifaceted order building took place as the distribution of power and great-power relations was rapidly shifting. It began with the United States and the Soviet Union working as allies to defeat Germany and Japan. It ended with the United States working with Germany and Japan to balance and contain the Soviet Union.

In the shadow of the Cold War, the United States and its partners built a distinctive type of order. This order has acquired various labels—Pax Americana, the Free World, Pax Democratica, the Philadelphian system, the Western order, American liberal hegemony.[4] These various terms reflect attempts to capture the logic and features of the Western postwar system. It is easier to say what this order was not. It was not simply an artifact of the Cold War balance of power.[5] The ideas and impulses behind the order predated the post-1945 struggle between the United States and the Soviet Union. Nor was it simply an American-style empire. The United States did dominate the order, and it engaged in various sorts of crude imperial behavior by intervening and coercing weaker regimes in Latin America, the Middle East, and other regions. But other features of openness, including consensual rule making, and diffuse reciprocity, particularly among the Western liberal democracies, cut against the logic of empire. What is distinctive about this order is that it embodied efforts by the Western liberal democracies to cooperate in reorganizing the international space within which liberal democracies could survive and prosper. The United States, as the most powerful state in the system, used its power to advance its interests. As the world moved from world war to Cold War, those American interests pointed in the direction of a postwar order that was relatively open, stable, and friendly.

In 1919, liberal internationalism was given voice by Woodrow Wilson and British internationalists and it entered the order-building process at the Versailles peace conference. In 1945, order building was more diffuse and protracted. There was no single moment—a peace settlement signed in the Hall of Mirrors—when the design of the postwar order was laid down. Even within the United States, there were many visions of order: realist, liberal, isolationist, idealist, and others. Choice, circumstance, uncertainty, and improvisation all played roles in shaping policy outcomes. American thinking about the world fused old and new ideas about liberal democracy, internationalism, great-power relations, and national security. The core impulse that drove the United States in its postwar order building was its recognition that, given its unrivaled power, it had an opportunity to shape the international environment and set the rules in which it and other states operated—and it could do this with an eye to the long term. An ordering moment had arrived and, faced with both great threats and opportunities, the United States was in a unique and perhaps fleeting position to do the ordering. Within this complex and shifting process, liberal international ideas and agendas, which had been rethought and reargued in the 1930s and wartime years, helped shape how the United States defined its interests and order-building goals. Ironically, although it began as a less coherent ordering project than its 1919 precursor, the post-1945 American-led order was ultimately more durable and functional, thus generating a deeper sense of shared commitment and social purpose among its core members.

In this chapter I make four arguments. First, the American-led postwar order was not a "single order," nor was it simply a "liberal order." It was not created at a specific moment but was cobbled together in a rolling process over the years and decades. It had many projects and moving parts and evolved through adaptation, trial and error, and problem solving. It contained various organizational logics—balance of power, hierarchy, and consensual cooperation among like-minded liberal states. The character of this evolving postwar system was shaped by two order-building projects. One was the Western project to reorganize and strengthen the foundations for liberal democracy within the advanced industrial world. This project grew out of the crises of the interwar decades and reflected the liberal international ideas and debates that circulated during the 1930s and New Deal era. The other was the Cold War project, oriented toward building political partnerships and alliances in the struggle with the Soviet Union. The Cold War was not the cause of the revolution in relations among the Western democracies, but it shaped the ways in which this project was pursued. Both projects pointed in the same direction, putting American power to work to create an open, institutionalized, and cooperative environment within which the liberal democracies could be secure.

Second, these postwar projects ultimately generated a functioning political order—what can be called a liberal hegemonic order. It was an order that emerged within the Western pole of the Cold War bipolar system. The "one world" vision of liberal internationalism articulated by Franklin Delano Roosevelt gave way to a "free world" vision under the shadow of the Cold War.

The universal postwar institutions—the United Nations and the Bretton Woods institutions—did not disappear. But under the conditions of Cold War bipolarity, the United States increasingly stepped forward to organize and run an American hegemonic order built around its economy and alliance system. This hegemonic order had both liberal and imperial characteristics. It was hierarchical but also organized around rules-based and reciprocal relations among the advanced liberal democracies. It was built on political and security bargains between the United States, Western Europe, and Japan. It provided a platform of functional institutions and political stability for elites and political parties across the advanced industrial world to pursue their agendas. Modern liberal democracy involves the balancing of various competing values—liberty and equality, individual and collective rights, openness and social protection, popular sovereignty and constitutionalism. The postwar Western system involved the creation of an institutionalized political order within which these trade-offs could be made.

Third, this liberal hegemonic order provided a relatively stable foundation for cooperation and shared social purposes. Built within one half of the global bipolar system, it was at its core a grouping of like-minded liberal states. The order had a "club" quality to it: to be on the inside was to have access to a shared system of trade and security. The order provided institutional capacities to governments to manage the problems of economic interdependence. Trade generated economic gains, and the vulnerabilities that came with openness were regulated. To be inside the order was to be inside a security community in the broadest sense. But membership also entailed expectations and responsibilities: to cooperate with other members, and to bandwagon rather than balance against the United States. The United States was the most powerful state, and the hegemonic order provided ways to harness its power for mutual gains while creating institutions and norms that offered at least a glimmer of protection against the coercive and indiscriminate exercise of American power. But the hegemonic order was not just an American order. Particularly in the 1970s and after, the liberal hegemonic order built mechanisms for shared governance leadership and opportunities for states undergoing economic and political liberalization to join and integrate within its widening parameters. Measured in terms of legitimacy, collective action, and institutionalized cooperation, the postwar liberal order was remarkably successful. More countries wanted in than wanted out. It is important to note that the multilateral foundations of this order provided a platform for wider efforts to build cooperation across economic, political, security, and environmental and global commons areas.

Finally, this American-led postwar order was built on contradictions that mostly remained submerged during the Cold War. One tension was between the universalism of its ideals and ideology and the particularism of its Western political foundation. FDR and succeeding generations spoke of universal rights and protections, but the liberal order itself was built as a trade and security pact between the United States, Europe, and Japan. There was also a tension between its hierarchical logic—seen by observers as either liberal hegemony or informal empire—and its principles of openness, multilateralism, and reciprocity. The United States accepted only minimal restraints on its own use of power. It sought to tie other states down to agreed-upon rules and institutions and leave itself as aloof as possible from such constraints. The United States had incentives to operate according to shared rules and norms to the extent that these provided legitimating cover for its power and encouraged weaker states to cooperate with, rather than resist, the American hegemon. These tensions reflected a more fundamental contradiction between serving both as a club or community of democracies and as a platform for organizing the wider world—an issue that would come more fully into view after the end of the Cold War.

American Power and Postwar Order Building

The destruction of World War II left no possibility of returning to the old international order. The war and the struggles surrounding it had ratified that order's failings and discredited its rules and institutions. They had also created a new distribution of power with new asymmetries between strong and weak states. The old European-centered world order had collapsed and the great powers on its periphery—the United States and the Soviet Union—emerged newly powerful.[6] The unprecedented violence of the war—sixty million deaths, the depravity of the Holocaust, the violent spectacle of Hiroshima and Nagasaki—dwarfed that of World War I. "At the end of the first world war it had been possible to contemplate going back to business as usual," Margaret MacMillan argues. "However, 1945 was different, so different that it has been called Year Zero."[7]

The United States had not just become stronger during the war. Its conceptions of its national and strategic interests also expanded. The war itself left American troops spread out over Europe and Asia. As Paul Kennedy notes, they were "over there" and everywhere.[8] So too were American postwar interests. Policy officials and strategic thinkers in and across the Roosevelt and Truman administrations disagreed on many things, but they generally shared a basic conviction: it was necessary to use American power to reshape the foundations of international order. They were not interested in simply securing specific interests or negotiating ad hoc deals. They certainly did not want the country to turn inward. Rather, they wanted to structure the international setting in which the United States operated to rebuild international order in a way that was congenial with America's long-term security and interests. A new infrastructure of international institutions and relationships would be put in place, creating a durable environment in which the United States could be prosperous and secure.[9]

Order building did not take place in one fell swoop or adhere to a unified vision. In this sense, 1945 was different from 1919. There was no identifiable moment when the issues of postwar order were settled. Nor did the United States have a specific plan of the sort that Woodrow Wilson brought to Paris. Order building after World War II was a rolling process. Decisions and agreements were made and revised as the world lurched from world war to reconstruction to Cold War. Roosevelt died before the war ended, and the world he envisaged at the Atlantic Charter meeting in August 1941 or at the Yalta Conference in February 1945 was not the world that Harry Truman, Clement Attlee, and other leaders encountered. The range of issues to settle was much greater than what confronted the peacemakers at Versailles, and many more voices and constituencies sought to influence the outcomes.[10]

From the moment it began to plan for peace, the Roosevelt administration aspired to build a postwar system of open trade and great-power cooperation. "The United States did not enter the war to reshape the world," the historian Warren Kimball argues, "but once in the war, that conception of world reform was the assumption that guided Roosevelt's actions."[11] In the reformed "one world" global order, the great powers would operate together in the background to provide collective security within a new global organization. They and the international governance institutions would have more authority than what Wilson had proposed, and Roosevelt's "family circle" of states—namely, the four postwar great powers—would manage openness and stability.[12] The Atlantic Charter had provided the glimmerings of this vision, and the wartime conferences at Bretton Woods, Dumbarton Oaks, and elsewhere provided the architectural plans.

The circumstances that confronted American and European officials after the war made Roosevelt's "family circle" impossible and drove American policy in new directions. The problems of rebuilding Western Europe and organizing a response to the encroachments of Soviet power triggered a more protracted and elaborate order-building process, which in turn altered the bargains, institutions, and commitments the United States undertook. Along the way, the management of the world economy moved from the Bretton Woods vision to one built around the American dollar and American domestic markets. Security cooperation moved from the United Nations Security Council to NATO and the other US-led alliances. As the Cold War broke the world into two blocs, Roosevelt's "one world" economic and security system became a Western system, and the order itself became in many ways an international extension of the United States.

Looking back, the postwar order was shaped by two interconnected projects—each with its own political vision and intellectual rationales. The first project aimed at reorganizing relations among the liberal democracies, and it is what drove Roosevelt and the liberal internationalists starting in the late 1930s. The goal was to unite the capitalist democracies in an open, cooperative system, to establish a stable foundation for Western order that had been missing since Versailles. The major industrial democracies would take it upon themselves to "domesticate" their dealings through a dense web of multilateral institutions, intergovernmental relations, and joint management of the Western and world political economies. Security and stability in the West were seen as intrinsically tied to an array of institutions—the United Nations and its agencies and the General Agreement on Tariffs and Trade (GATT), among others—that bound the democracies together, constrained conflict, and facilitated political community. The United States, Western Europe, and later Japan built the postwar order on a foundation of common liberal democratic values and interlocking multilateral institutions.

President Truman spoke in support of this project in March 1947, in an address at Baylor University in which he argued that the world needed to learn from the previous decade's disasters. "As each battle of the economic war of the Thirties was fought," he noted, "the inevitable tragic result became more and more apparent. From the tariff policy of Hawley and Smoot, the world went on to Ottawa and the system of imperial preferences, from Ottawa to the kind of elaborate and detailed restrictions adopted by Nazi Germany." He reaffirmed America's commitment to "economic peace," which would involve tariff reductions and rules and institutions to govern trade and investment. When economic differences arose, "the interests of all will be considered, and a fair and just solution will be found." Conflicts would be captured and tamed in a cage of rules, standards, safeguards, and procedures. "This," Truman concluded, "was the way of a civilized community."[13]

The other project, a reaction to the deteriorating relations with the Soviet Union, led to the containment order, which was based on balance of power, nuclear deterrence, and political and ideological competition. This was the project of fighting the Cold War. Truman gave voice to it on 12 March 1947 in his celebrated speech before Congress announcing aid to Greece and Turkey, which he wrapped in an American commitment to support the cause of freedom worldwide. The declaration of the Truman Doctrine was a founding moment of the containment order that rallied Americans to a new great undertaking, this one against Soviet communism's quest for world domination. A "fateful hour" had struck, Truman said, and the people of the world "must choose between two alternate ways of life." The United States would need to lead the way in this struggle.[14]

With this call to action, liberal internationalism was brought into the decades-long Cold War. The realist logic of balance, deterrence, and containment became tied to American leadership of the "free world." Although the balance of power (backed by nuclear weapons) may have helped avoid great-power war, it left scope for deadly conflict. What followed was a series of military conflicts and military interventions, which can be called the "peripheral wars" of the Cold War era—in Korea, Vietnam, Afghanistan, Central America, and Africa (Angola and elsewhere). The impulse behind these wars varied; the intervention in Korea was different from the intervention in Vietnam. But, violent and costly, they left millions dead and millions displaced.[15] The Vietnam War took a particularly bloody toll—over three million people were killed, half of them Vietnamese civilians, and fifty-eight thousand American soldiers—and bitterly divided the United States. Nonetheless, over the Cold War period, a broad American foreign policy consensus existed in favor of deterring and containing the Soviet Union and defending the noncommunist world.[16] This consensus in part reflected a rough, yet decisive, alignment of US geopolitical interests with the promotion of liberal internationalism. Liberal internationalist policies supported realist ends. Realist means supported liberal international ends. This was the strength—and occasional horror—of American foreign policy during the Cold War.[17]

The centrality of American power to the post-1945 liberal international project made it easy to argue that any measures to maintain or expand that power might be justified. This was combined with the threat (both geopolitical and ideological) of communism. While this threat was often exaggerated, it was surely real. Thus, stopping the spread of communism was, quite logically, a key focus of liberal internationalists and realists alike. Given this goal, interventions—even in support of illiberal forces or using illiberal means—could be construed as supporting broader liberal international goals. Under this consequentialist calculus, supporting illiberal regimes as bulwarks against communist expansion or intervening militarily were features, not bugs, of American liberal internationalism during the Cold War. They were, for many US liberal internationalists, an unfortunate means to an essential end.[18]

In the early 1950s, the two projects of reorganizing and defending the liberal democratic world and containing Soviet power came together. The construction of security partnerships and open economic relations with Western Europe and East Asia were essential for fighting the Cold War, while the imperatives of the Cold War reinforced cooperation within the liberal democratic world and created domestic support for American leadership. The project of reconstructing relations among the liberal democracies within a "one world" order dovetailed with building a "free world" counterweight to Soviet communism. The Roosevelt-era goal of building an open, institutionalized order underwritten by American power survived the onset of the Cold War. What changed is that the project of building the liberal order took place in a divided world and was pursued "inside" the bipolar system. But the goal was still to create a new type of order that would protect the United States and the other liberal democracies. This was acknowledged by the authors of the famous National Security Council planning document NSC-68, which laid out the doctrine of containment. The United States, it argued, needed to "build a healthy international community," which "we would probably do even if there were no international threat." The objective was a "world environment in which the American system can survive and flourish."[19] In other words, old-fashioned geopolitics mapped closely onto the objectives of liberal internationalism.

These two projects determined the shape of the American-led postwar order. This order contained an amalgam of ordering logics that combined liberal ideas about free trade and multilateralism with realist principles of balance of power and hegemony. It was more Western-centered, multilayered, and deeply institutionalized than originally anticipated, and it brought the United States into direct political and economic management of the system. The Soviet threat fostered cohesion among the capitalist democracies and facilitated cooperation in the rebuilding of the world economy. The American military guarantee to Europe and Asia provided a national-security rationale for Japan and Western democracies to open their markets. Open trade helped cement the alliance, and the alliance in turn helped settle economic disputes.

In both the security and economic realms, the United States found itself taking on new commitments and functional roles. Its economic and political system became, in effect, a central component of the larger liberal hegemonic order. America's domestic market, the US dollar, and the Cold War alliances emerged as crucial mechanisms and institutions through which the

postwar order was founded and managed, to the point that America and the Western liberal order fused into one system. The United States had more direct power in running the postwar order but also found itself more tightly bound to other states within that order. It became a provider of public goods—upholding a set of rules and institutions that circumscribed how it could exercise its power and providing mechanisms for reciprocal political influence. In the late 1940s, security cooperation moved from the UN Security Council to NATO and the other US-led alliances. The global system of collective security managed by the great powers became a Western-oriented security community.[20] Likewise, the management of the world economy moved from the Bretton Woods vision of global multilateralism to an American-led dollar and market system.[21] A new type of international order took shape—one that fused strands of liberal internationalism, national security, Cold War liberalism, balance-of-power politics, and American hegemony.

The Logic of Liberal Hegemonic Order

American officials and planners during and after the war shared a central conviction that the United States, because of its power and interests, needed to underwrite a new postwar international order. In a formal sense, the United States was simply following in the footsteps of past rising great powers that emerged from wars to set the terms of order. As a rising state grows in wealth and power, its interests tend to expand outward. The world beyond its borders matters more. There is more to gain and more to lose. Its interests—and therefore its incentives—for organizing international rules and relations are expanding, as are its capacities for doing so. Along this pathway, a great-power war generates a sudden disjuncture that clarifies these interests and creates new ordering opportunities. This is the grand logic of the rise and fall of states and the periodic struggles to shape world order.[22] If a leading state has sufficient power and opportunity, it will want to shape the overall environment or milieu within which international relations take place. It will want to set in place the institutions and principles of order.[23] The impulse is not simply to dominate and gain advantage over specific states but to shape the wider organizational landscape on which states cooperate and compete.[24]

These motivations have always affected powerful states, regardless of their regime character or historical era. But as the United States acted on this impulse in the 1940s and after, it did so with distinctive ordering imperatives. Its goal was not just to establish its dominance over other states but to create a stable international order that would support and protect its domestic order and the wider system of Western liberal democracies. As I argued in chapter 5, notions of economic and national security were evolving during the 1930s and 1940s even as the underlying vulnerabilities of liberal democracy were becoming more acute. The United States and the other Western liberal states were promising their citizens new rights and protections, the advancement of which would require a new and more elaborate international order. The United States shared with past great powers the impulse to create order, but it brought a cluster of new visions and goals to the task.

Emerging from the war as the leading world power, the United States saw itself as possessing "profound new responsibilities in connection with practically all vital problems of world affairs," as the official history of the Roosevelt planning process reports. American security was understood to be tied to the wider organization of great-power order, which the United States would orchestrate and lead. It was necessary, American planners believed, "to consider our own future security policy not only in terms of the American position alone but in terms with the world's requirements for peace. With these our own requirements were merging."[25] In an address at Yale University in November 1939, Dean Acheson argued that the United States needed to step into the role previously played by Great Britain: "The economic and political system of the Nineteenth Century, which throughout the world produced an amazing increase in the production of wealth and population," had rested on British financial and naval power. With Britain's decline, it was now necessary for the United States to take on "some responsibility for making possible a world of order."[26] Eight years later, Secretary of State George C. Marshall told the graduating class at Princeton University that among the "great 'musts' for your generation" were "the development of a sense of responsibility for world order and security, the development of a sense of [the] overwhelming importance of this country's acts, the failure to act, in relation to world order and security."[27] Because of its dominant global position and the ways in which the outside world impinged on its interests and security, the United States would have the primary responsibility for the global system's requirements for peace. "Increasingly," Stewart Patrick observes, "the concepts of national security and world order would conflate into one and the same."[28] The United States equated its own security with the stability and security relations prevailing worldwide. This conviction was the leading edge of the most consequential American idea that emerged during the war—that the United States would underwrite the world order.

The international order that in fact emerged reflected an amalgam of ideas and projects. Liberal internationalism, itself evolving, competed and combined with other agendas. This was true both within the American government as it made policy choices and in the negotiations that unfolded between the United States and other states. The United States used its formidable power in the 1940s and 1950s to build and lead a postwar order—and in so doing, it drew upon a variety of political ideas and organizational logics, some of which were liberal internationalist. Nonetheless, out of these various ideas and projects, a distinctive American-led order did take shape. It was both hierarchical and built around institutions. The order was "liberal hegemonic" in that it was marked by cross-cutting principles of hierarchy—based on America's superordinate position—and by the solidarity and sovereign equality that emerged from its core grouping of liberal democratic states.

This postwar hegemonic order had a variety of components, or logics. First was the logic of economic openness, a liberal internationalist idea that has persisted through the nineteenth and twentieth centuries. This deeply rooted conviction about how to organize the global system brought together economic, ideological, and geopolitical strands of thinking among American and European policymakers. One such group was composed of the free traders in the State Department, led by Secretary Cordell Hull. He and his colleagues made the classic argument for economic interdependence as an essential condition for peace and prosperity. In a November 1938 speech, Hull argued: "I know that without expansion of international trade, based upon fair dealing and equal treatment for all, there can be no stability and security either within or among nations. . . . I know that the withdrawal by a nation from orderly trade relations with the rest of the world inevitably leads to regimentation of all phases of national life, to the suppression of human rights, and all too frequently to preparations for war and a provocative attitude toward other nations."[29] His emphasis was less on free trade than on nondiscrimination and equal commercial opportunity. Open trade, according to American officials, had a double dividend. It would ensure the United States access to markets and raw materials around the world, a goal it had pursued since the Open Door policies at the turn of the century; and it would contribute to economic growth and interdependence, creating shared interests in a peaceful international order.[30]

Another group supporting open markets was made up of strategic planners and security thinkers in and out of government. The United States rose up as a global power in a world of empires, blocs, and spheres of influence. The world had long been dominated by large continental and maritime empires. In the 1930s and during the war, as Germany, Japan, and the Soviet Union built regional spheres, and Great Britain established its imperial preference system, it was possible to envisage a global order built around closed imperial blocs. American planners and scholars debated whether the United States could remain viable as a major state if it were isolated within its own hemisphere. Economists explored this question in planning studies that the Council on Foreign Relations conducted for the State Department, using the concept of the "grand area."[31] How large would the "grand area" need to be for the United States to prosper as a great power? The economists concluded that it had to encompass the entire world. The United States could not maintain its position as a leading and productive economy without access to trade and resources from Asia and Europe. "The United States can best defend itself—from an economic point of view—in an area comprising most of the non-German world," the group reported. "This has been called the 'Grand Area.' It includes the Western Hemisphere, the United Kingdom, the remainder of the British Commonwealth and Empire, the Dutch East Indies, China, and Japan."[32] Postwar Japan and Great Britain also would need access to trade and resources outside their regional systems. If the United States was to remain the leading industrial power and put itself in a position to build cooperative alignments with other great powers after the war, the world economic system would need to be open. As the historian Carlo Santoro summarizes the grand area experts' message, "the only area sufficiently large was the one equivalent to the world economy as a whole and driven by the United States."[33] The United States saw its interests tied to the breakdown of imperial blocs and spheres and the construction of an open postwar order.

Other defense planners and strategic thinkers shared this view, arguing that American postwar security would depend on openness and access to Europe and Asia. An influential figure in these debates was Nicholas Spykman, the Yale geopolitical theorist. In his 1942 study *America's Strategy in World Politics*, Spykman argued the United States could not be secure—in economic or security terms—within the Western Hemisphere.[34] Its position as a major world power depended on the maintenance of an open and balanced system of great-power relations across Eurasia. It was important to have access to the markets and resources of Europe and Asia, and this meant fostering alliances with friendly great powers and generating capacities to project power into these regions. This view was shared by strategists and planners during and after the war.[35] The great threat to postwar America was a world in which Eurasia was dominated by hostile great powers building closed systems of blocs and spheres. The United States would need to be actively involved in these regions to prevent this outcome. To the extent that the threats to openness and access were political and economic, more than military, the United States would need to support the reconstruction of these regions. The prevailing view in defense circles, as Melvyn Leffler notes, was that "American prosperity required open markets, unhindered access to raw materials, and the rehabilitation of much—if not all—of Eurasia along liberal capitalist lines."[36]

Second, there was the logic of institutional cooperation. For some in the Roosevelt administration, this view echoed the older Wilsonian sentiment about creating a world built around international law and collective security. Secretary of State Cordell Hull, for instance, argued in 1943 that America after the war should aim to replace "the anarchy of unbridled and discordant nationalisms, economic and political," with international "rules of morality, law, and justice."[37] The idea, which drew on an American tradition of constitutionalism dating back to the nineteenth century, was to build institutions at the global level that would embody the principles and norms woven into the American polity: rule of law, equal treatment, transparency and openness, reciprocal obligations, checks and balances, and compromise in decision making.[38] A more recent inspiration was the Roosevelt administration's efforts under the New Deal to devise new types of institutional capacities to stabilize capitalist society. Now the United States sought to build new international institutions that would help interdependent nations manage their economic, social, and political problems. Institutions were a response to growing economic and security interdependence. This strand of thinking had less to do with spreading liberal values than with creating functional tools that would bring technocratic expertise and pragmatism to modern global challenges.[39]

A variety of motives and purposes lay behind the many institutions established during this period. If there was a unifying vision, it was of an American-led system of intergovernmental cooperation designed to strengthen postwar industrial societies by building their governance capacities and managing the terms of interdependence.[40] The United Nations enshrined principles of sovereign equality and the peaceful settlement of disputes. The new world organization also retained and expanded the economic and social activities of the League of Nations. The United Nations created institutional authority for great powers to employ force, but it also laid the foundation for cooperation in areas of human rights, education, science, and economic development.[41] Some institutions were simply frameworks for negotiations. The General Agreement on Tariffs and Trade built on the 1935 Reciprocal Tariffs Agreement, which created governmental authority to negotiate reciprocal reductions in tariff levels. After the war, the GATT provided a multilateral framework for the continuation of these efforts. Other institutions, such as the International Monetary Fund (IMF), provided expertise and financial capacities that governments could draw on to address balance-of-payment problems and stabilize their currencies. The World Health Organization was also established to build scientific and governmental capacities to promote public health and fight epidemic disease. The US-led institutions were efforts to bind states together for mutual protection, thus providing mechanisms for establishing credible commitments and reassurance. They also provided institutional channels for bargaining and joint decision making, which in turn fostered support for an American-centered security order.[42]

The United States sought to build a postwar order that would be legitimate and durable. Institutions provided the order's tools and mechanisms. In building these institutions, the United States did not give up large amounts of formal policy autonomy. It agreed to work within these multilateral institutions but it retained substantial influence over their operations, at least those of the most important international bodies. The "overwhelming economic strength of the United States allowed it to determine the shape of the international organizations then on the drawing board," the historian Diane Kunz observes. "American goals became international reality; multilateralism often became unilateralism in disguise."[43] The "binding" character of these institutions was less formal and legal than political.[44] The United States and its partners agreed to create institutions that they both inhabited. After this, the binding was manifest in the ensuing political processes. In the simplest way, the institution provided a location for "pulling and hauling." The institution created a platform for interaction and mutual influence. Beyond this, the institutions established norms and expectations about cooperation in particular areas. If the operation of an institution actually generated benefits for those inside of it, this gave the institution value. To the extent that these postwar institutions muted or moderated the crude domination of the United States and other powerful states, they gave the order a measure of legitimacy—and legitimacy, even for powerful states, matters.[45]

Third, there was the logic of the social bargain, an effort to reconcile openness with social and economic security. Since the 1930s, the industrial democracies had been expanding the state's commitment to economic security and social well-being. Modern liberal democracy itself, as I noted earlier, was increasingly defined and legitimated by this effort. It was at the heart of the New Deal. It is not surprising, therefore, that democratic governments led by the United States and Great Britain sought to construct postwar rules and institutions that would support governments' efforts to make good on this commitment. It was tricky to do this while also supporting the building of

an open world economy because the two objectives were not fully complementary. Out of this dilemma emerged a political compromise—or social
bargain.[46] If the citizens of these countries would agree to live in a more open
world economy, their governments would take steps to stabilize and protect
their livelihoods through the instruments of the modern welfare state, such
as employment insurance, worker retraining, and retirement support. In this
way, the architects of the postwar system sought to build domestic support
and construct encompassing coalitions within countries around an international order that facilitated both economic openness and social protection.
John Ruggie has called this compromise "embedded liberalism"—a system
of managed openness.[47]

This effort to find a compromise between openness and security was reflected in the negotiations over the Bretton Woods system of institutions.
During the war, Britain had been skeptical of the relatively stark vision of an
open world economy advocated by Cordell Hull and the State Department.
John Maynard Keynes's famous trip to Washington in August 1941 to discuss
the terms of Lend-Lease aid to Britain brought these differences into sharp
relief. American officials wanted to reconstruct an open trading system after
the war, but the British wartime cabinet wanted to ensure full employment
and economic stability. In the months that followed, British and American
officials—led by Keynes and Harry Dexter White—negotiated the terms
of postwar monetary and financial relations. They agreed on rules and
institutional mechanisms that would establish convertible currencies and allow governments to manage exchange-rate imbalances while facilitating
growth-oriented means of adjustment. The Bretton Woods agreements, negotiated in 1944, reflected this consensus and established the implementing
rules and mechanisms.[48] The institutions of the postwar world economy were
designed to encourage industrial democracies to provide new levels of social support for their citizens.

These new attitudes, which contrasted sharply with the views of leaders
in earlier eras, were noted by the American economist Jacob Viner in 1942:
"There is wide agreement today that major depressions, mass unemployment,
are social evils, and that it is the obligation of governments . . . to prevent
them." Moreover, there is "wide agreement also that it is extraordinarily

difficult, if not outright impossible, for any country to cope alone with the problem of cyclical booms and depressions . . . while there is good prospect that with international cooperation . . . the problem of the business cycle and of mass unemployment can be largely solved."[49] What British and American experts agreed upon was that the postwar world economy would need a framework of cooperation. It would have to provide currency convertibility and stability of exchange rates, allow governments to address balance-of-payments deficits with expansionary policies rather than austerity, and establish new techniques of international economic management that would give governments the ability to reconcile movements of trade and capital with policies that promoted stable and full-employment economies.[50] Political leaders on both sides of the Atlantic embraced this compromise between open markets and social stability.

The fourth logic was cooperative security. Although not in Roosevelt's original vision, it soon became integral to the system. Cooperative security—or security binding—is the strategy in which states tie themselves together in economic and security institutions to foster cooperation and restraint. Security binding appeared throughout the postwar international order, most explicitly in the NATO alliance. It was manifest in the French decision to build binding ties with Germany through the Coal and Steel Community, which gave France some control over the terms of German economic integration. It was also manifest in the binding of Western European countries within a common economic community and the binding of the United States to Europe through the Atlantic Alliance. This strategy was a response to rising Cold War pressures to balance against Soviet power, but it was also part of the original liberal internationalist project of reorganizing relations among the Western democracies. Rather than balance against each other as potential security rivals, the Western nations agreed to embed themselves within layers of functional institutions—capped by a security alliance—that locked them into long-term cooperation and mutual restraint.[51]

For the United States, this strategy meant agreeing to remain closely allied with other democratic countries, especially through NATO and the US-Japan Alliance. This security system ensured that the democratic great powers would not revert to old patterns of strategic rivalry. The Atlantic

Alliance had multiple and evolving purposes. The United States was eager to see Germany integrated within a united postwar Europe, particularly as the Cold War intensified, and the British and French governments sought to bind the United States to Europe. The French insisted that Germany's rehabilitation would be acceptable only within a security framework that involved the United States. If the American-led alliance bound both Germany and the United States to an open and united Europe, it also reinforced British and French commitment to that goal. In an echo of Wilson's critique of Europe's "old politics" after the Great War, American officials after 1945 emphasized the need to reform nationalist and imperialist tendencies. In their view, integration would not only make Germany safe for Europe but would also make Europe safe for the world. The Marshall Plan reflected this American thinking, as did the Truman administration's support for the Brussels Pact, the European Defense Community, and the Schuman Plan. Negotiating the NATO treaty in 1948, US officials made clear to the Europeans that an American security commitment hinged on European integration.[52]

The elements of the Atlantic countries' institutional bargain—NATO, the Marshall Plan, and the postwar multilateral institutions—all fit together. As the historian Lloyd Gardner argues, "Each formed part of a whole. Together they were designed to 'mold the military character' of the Atlantic nations, prevent the balkanization of European defense systems, create an internal market large enough to sustain capitalism in Western Europe, and lock Germany on the Western side of the Iron Curtain."[53] The evolution of policy in Washington, from pushing for a postwar Europe that would be a unified and independent "third force" to accepting an ongoing security commitment within NATO, was marked by American reluctance and European persistence. At each turn, European leaders agreed to move toward greater integration only in exchange for corresponding assurances and commitments from the United States. The American security commitment embodied in NATO was a solution to multiple interlocking problems: worry about a return of German militarism, British ambivalence about European economic integration, the growing Soviet threat, and uncertainties about American power.[54] Although NATO was the capstone of postwar security binding, its logic can be seen across the postwar international order.

A fifth logic was democratic solidarity. The American and European architects of the postwar order felt a shared sense of community even before the Cold War divided the global system into two competing armed camps. To be sure, the general ordering principles espoused by postwar leaders were universal: openness, nondiscrimination, multilateralism, and so forth. But they sought to build this order on a core set of commitments and institutions anchored by the Western liberal democracies. They shared an authentic belief, which was felt in Washington and European capitals and later in Japan and East Asia, that the "free world" was not just a temporary alliance against the Soviet Union but a community of shared fate.[55] Secretary of State Dean Acheson, for example, emphasized this democratic solidarity when he introduced the NATO agreement to the American public. The bonds of the Atlantic Alliance were "fundamental"—the "strongest kind of ties, because they are based on moral conviction, on acceptance of the same values of life."[56] These states were affiliating with each other not just out of temporary expediency but on the basis of centuries-old shared bonds. As the historian Anne Deighton argues, NATO has been "the overarching organization that exemplifies what has been meant, in Europe, by the West."[57] The character of the order that emerged after the war reflected this sense that the United States, Europe, and the wider liberal democratic world formed a political community defined by a common fate and shared affinities of value and identity.

That this order was anchored in an alliance of Western liberal democracies was partly due to the failure of Roosevelt's "one world" vision and the inability of universal institutions like the Bretton Woods agreements to deal with the practical economic and security problems that emerged after the war. Rebuilding the European economies and constructing a security alliance required intense cooperation across the Atlantic. The sense that the United States and Europe faced a common threat strengthened Western solidarity. This shared identity had several layers. One layer invoked by Churchill and Roosevelt at the Atlantic Charter meeting was the Anglo-American bond. With the meeting taking place aboard the HMS *Prince of Wales* in Placentia Bay, Newfoundland, the two leaders may also have been eager to remind Nazi Germany that they still commanded the sea. It was a reminder as well, in the words of the *London Daily Telegraph*, that the

Atlantic Ocean was no longer an "abyss dividing us" but "a means and a bond of union."[58] At other times, the bond was defined in terms of a Western or Atlantic community or a community of liberal democracies—a "free world" unattached to geography or the West. But in all these forms, the vision was of a political, even moral community defined by common values and democratic governance, the existence of which created special opportunities to cooperate and build postwar institutions. This sense of community was important because it brought the expectation that dealings among the United States, Europe, and other liberal democracies would be based on political give-and-take, consensus building, and diffuse reciprocity, not on the imperial or patron-client exercise of American power.

The United States did occasionally resort to cruder power politics in Atlantic relations, most famously during the Suez Crisis, when the American president threatened severe damage to the British financial system if it did not call off its invasion of Egypt.[59] But this was more the exception than the rule. As John Lewis Gaddis notes about US policy during the early Cold War, "It was not that the Americans lacked the capacity to force their allies into line. . . . What is surprising is how rarely this happened; how much effort the United States put into persuading—quite often even deferring to—its NATO partners. . . . The history of NATO, therefore, is largely one of compromise despite the predominant position of the United States."[60]

Finally, the postwar order had a hegemonic logic. The United States put itself at the center, taking on the duties of leadership over the functioning of the system as well as the rights and privileges of "first citizen." American power loomed large in the postwar period. In the building of postwar order, this was both a problem and an opportunity. It was a problem in that weaker and secondary states had to worry about American coercion and domination. Why would these states seek to ally with the United States rather than balance against it? But the disparities of power were also an opportunity. The United States was so powerful relative to other states that it could make calculations about the long-term shape of international order. It did not need to bargain on every front to get its way. It could focus on creating institutions, setting the rules, and organizing the terms of hierarchy. In a sense, this was a much more profound act of power than imposing its will in day-to-day struggles to gain advantage over specific states. This long-term strategic calculation is what made liberal internationalism—and its ideas and projects for organizing international space around multilateral frameworks of cooperation—attractive to the architects of postwar order.

Bargains, Constituencies, and Platforms

During the Cold War decades, this amalgam of organizing ideas and logics took shape as a sort of rudimentary political system—a liberal hegemonic order. It had organizing principles, authority relations, functional roles, shared expectations, and settled practices through which states did business with each other. Led by the United States, it existed inside the larger Cold War bipolar order. It took on the characteristics of a relatively stable political community. It had layers of overlapping institutions—European, Atlantic, trilateral, and universal, or at least potentially universal. But at its core it was a political community dominated by the advanced liberal democracies. The Cold War ideological struggle with the Soviet Union sharpened the perception that this Western system was more than a temporary balancing coalition. It was a political community, a "free world" grouping of liberal democracies. In formal and informal ways, it had various markers of a working political system—across its many institutions and political groupings, it had political boundaries, members, rules, expectations, and a loosely shared political identity. The evolving dynamics of this American-led hegemonic order can be seen in its strategic bargains, constituencies, and political projects.

At the heart of the order were strategic understandings—some explicit and others tacit—between the United States and its European and East Asian partners, which constituted a sort of "hegemonic bargain." The United States would lead and manage the international order, providing security, supporting economic openness, and upholding its rules and institutions, while other countries would agree to operate in this order and accept American leadership.[61]

The liberal hegemonic order had two types of strategic bargains—a security bargain and a political bargain.[62] In the security bargain, the United

States agreed to provide military protection and access to American markets, technology, and resources in an open world economy. In return, America's allies agreed to be reliable partners and provide diplomatic, economic, and logistical support for the United States. This bargain was most explicitly embedded in America's security alliances with Europe and East Asia. America's nuclear umbrella and its doctrine of extended deterrence tied the security of the United States to that of its allies. Throughout the Cold War, the United States made security commitments, stationed troops, and maintained ongoing strategic partnerships. Alliance partners gained access to the American market, thus bolstering their growth and tying their governments more closely to the United States. Japan and West Germany in particular were highly dependent on American security protection and felt obligated to support Washington's trade and monetary leadership. As Carla Norrlof argues, American monetary hegemony fostered cooperation and provided benefits to other states, but it also allowed the United States to shift the costs of adjustments onto its allies, costs that, absent these "positional advantages," the United States would have had to bear on its own.[63] Countries acquiesced in this hegemonic system, which gave the United States special privileges to act unilaterally to promote its own interests. In return, the United States underwrote the rules and institutions of the order, allowing these states to promote their own economic prosperity and political agendas.[64]

The political bargain was focused on the uncertainties associated with America's preeminent position. No state had ever been as powerful relative to the rest of the world as the United States was at the end of World War II. The danger for allied states was American domination and abandonment. The United States might try to coercively impose itself on the world as an imperial superpower or unpredictably intervene in and withdraw from their regions. The political bargain was an effort to make American power more palatable—indeed useful—to states in Europe and East Asia, which in turn made these states more willing to work with the United States and support its hegemonic leadership. While the proliferating postwar international institutions bound the United States to other states, they also provided tools for governments to cooperate and engage in collective action, and provided a political framework within which states could do business with each other and engage in consensual decision making. As Michael Mastanduno has argued, "Multilateral decision making procedures may be less efficient, and powerful states are often tempted to act unilaterally. But multilateral procedures help to reassure other states that they are not simply being coerced or directed to follow the dictates of the dominant state."[65] In championing these postwar institutions and agreeing to operate within them, the United States was effectively agreeing to open itself up to political engagement with other countries, particularly the liberal democracies.

The character of this hegemonic order varied across regions, relationships, and functional realms, and it varied as the postwar era unfolded. In some parts of the order, hierarchy had liberal characteristics, particularly in relations between the United States and the other leading liberal democracies. These countries had "voice opportunities." The bipolar competition of the Cold War and the array of multilateral institutions reinforced patterns of compromise and reciprocity. The United States had incentives to build close relations with allies, integrate Japan and Germany into the order, share the gains from trade, and generally operate in ways that were seen as mutually acceptable. As Charles de Gaulle reluctantly noted, "Confronted with its present dangers, the free world could do nothing better, and nothing else, than adopt the 'leadership' of Washington."[66] In other parts of the order, America wielded its power in more traditional great-power or imperial ways. In its relations with Latin America and the Middle East, the United States engaged in more old-style coercion and domination.

This American-led hegemonic system had a distinctive architecture. The institutions and political bargains created a framework within which governments could pursue diverse political projects and reconcile commitments to economic openness with support and protection for stable domestic political order. "The industrial West rebuilt its political economies on the basis of compromise among nations, classes, parties, and groups," argues Jeffry Frieden. "Governments balanced international integration and national autonomy, global competition and national constituencies, free markets and social democracy. . . . Socialists and conservatives, Christian Democrats and secular liberals worked together to build modern welfare states."[67] Across the European continent a new generation of leaders made efforts to dampen old nationalist hatreds and build institutions and economic relations to bind their states together, including Jean Monnet and Robert Schuman in France, Paul-Henri Spaak in Belgium, Alcide De Gasperi in Italy, and Konrad Adenauer and Walter Hallstein in Germany.[68] In these various ways, the liberal hegemonic order brought together under one political roof a diverse array of constituencies and stakeholders.[69]

In Britain, Clement Attlee and the Labour Party defeated Churchill in the 1945 election, and for the next decade they pursued an agenda of welfare-state development and Atlantic-centered internationalism. "In many ways we still live in the world of Attlee's creation," argue John Bew and Michael Cox. "His government of 1945–51 was the most radical in history, and gave Britain the NHS [National Health Service], National Insurance, NATO, and the atomic bomb."[70] Attlee, who believed in the progressive potential of American power and saw the New Deal as charting a path forward for the liberal democracies, worked with Truman to shape the major postwar economic and security institutions. Like other Europeans who had lived through the 1930s, he saw the West in a world-historical struggle with the dark forces of totalitarianism. He and his foreign minister, Ernest Bevin, took a critical but friendly attitude toward the United States.[71] The Labour Party sought to build a new British nationalism around the welfare state and active government management of the economy. The Bretton Woods institutions, the Atlantic system of security partnership, and the ideological uniting of the Western democracies all fit Attlee's agenda. The $3 billion Britain received in Marshall Plan aid helped as well. Britain struggled with the United States over the disposition of its empire, but at the end of his career, the two things Attlee was most proud of were the 1946 National Insurance Act and the independence of India.[72]

After the war, West Germany was rebuilt within European and Atlantic institutions. Its postwar leaders found these multilateral frameworks useful in creating space and tools for Germany to reinvent itself and regain international standing.[73] By 1948, West Germany was reintegrated into the general plans for European economic recovery. Marshall Plan assistance and currency reform triggered a period of rapid economic recovery. The Social Democratic Party, initially as suspicious of the West as it was of the Soviet

Union, gradually broke with its Marxist past and became a counterpart to the British Labour Party, thus emphasizing reform within the liberal capitalist system. In the formative years of the West German state, the Christian Democratic Union, which was led by Konrad Adenauer until his retirement in 1963, largely brought Germany back to the West. The Cold War reinforced the process; as Adam Tooze notes, it "made Adenauer's *Westbindung* (attachment to the West) seem infinitely preferable to the Soviet alternative."[74] The return of growth during these years seemed to validate the free market and parliamentary government. Adenauer and the Christian Democrats used these growth years to fashion a distinctive economic vision that combined classical market capitalism and the social welfare state.

In foreign policy, Adenauer also took advantage of the Cold War's unifying pressures to define a new German role within the West. West Germany would regain its status and influence as a major European power by forging close ties with France and integrating with the wider regional economic and security institutions. In the early 1950s, Mary Hampton writes, Adenauer and West German policymakers were able to pursue their national goals "by linking Washington's concern with military security during this period of heightened international tension to the norms and principles codified within the 1949 North Atlantic Treaty."[75] In the face of French resistance to a rearmed West Germany, Adenauer persisted in invoking the principles of equal status and nondiscrimination among freely associating states as a requirement for a West German contribution to Western defense.[76] Five years after Washington insisted on total and permanent disarmament, it found itself urging West Germany to build up its army as a full partner.

Japan followed a similar path. Its first postwar prime minister, Shigeru Yoshida, led Japan to membership in the Western community by concluding the San Francisco Peace Treaty and the US-Japan Security Treaty in September 1951. These agreements enabled Japan to join the American alliance system and gain access to US markets and technology. Yoshida was a nationalist and a conservative who had escaped responsibility for the war because conflicts with the military leaders led to his reassignment as ambassador to Great Britain. Returning to Japan and assuming leadership of the dominant Liberal Democratic Party, he navigated a middle course between the more extreme nationalists and the political Left. The Treaty on Mutual Cooperation and Security, signed in 1960, established the United States as Japan's security patron. Japan's constitution forbade it to maintain "land, sea, and air forces" and renounced "the threat of force as a means of settling international disputes." Yoshida articulated a vision of Japan as a "commercial state" guided by liberal principles associated with the United States and the Western democracies. The nation would be dedicated to economic growth, integration into the Western free-market trading system, the nonuse of military power, and allegiance to the democratic principles of its constitution.[77]

Like West Germany, Japan was able to use the postwar alliance and multilateral institutions to fashion a distinctive great-power role. Under the leadership of Shigeru Yoshida, the prime minister from 1946 to 1954, it took on the identity of a "civilian" great power—gaining authority and status as a major state not through the possession of traditional power assets but as a stakeholder state upholding international rules and norms.[78] "It was Yoshida's gamble," writes the historian Kenneth Pyle, "that Japan could better achieve its interests by participating in the American system than by actively resisting it."[79] The alliance made Japan dependent on the United States for national defense, but this allowed it to concentrate on rebuilding its economy and reentering the international system as a trading nation. "The benefits turned out to be huge," Pyle argues. "Depending wholly on American bases for its security, Japan over succeeding decades was able to acquire economic aid, technology, and market access to a greater degree than any other state."[80] Along the way, several generations of postwar Japanese leaders embraced an internationalist agenda—antinuclearism, nonproliferation, and the United Nations. The postwar system of economic and security cooperation provided the framework for Japan's reemergence as a civilian great power. In the postwar debates about the country's role and identity, Japanese leaders navigated a middle path between right-wing nationalism and left-wing pacifism. As Richard Samuels argues, "The Left learned to live with the alliance and the Right with Article 9. Security policy would now aim to enhance autonomy but would center on trade and international cooperation. A new consensus would be achieved around a Japan that would be a 'non-nuclear, lightly armed, economic superpower.'"[81]

In the meantime, Japan was able to gain authority and standing in the international system through rapid growth and economic advancement rather than geopolitical mastery in East Asia. It became a major provider of foreign aid in Asia and across the wider developing world and a major supporter of the United Nations. It articulated various ideas about "human security" and "comprehensive security" and was in the vanguard of advanced energy and environmental technology. In all these ways, Japan pioneered a distinct identity and role by working within the United Nations system and the American-led liberal order. Under American sponsorship, it joined the IMF and the World Bank in 1952, the United Nations in 1956, the GATT trade system in 1956, the Organisation for Economic Co-operation and Development (OECD) in 1966, and the so-called G-7 system in 1976. Japan supported America's leadership role and, in return, it acquired voice and authority as an ally and leading state.[82] Japan found a way within the wider postwar system to regain its status as a leading East Asian power by tying itself to the United States and the institutions of the Western world economy.[83]

In the first postwar decades, this American-led hegemonic order provided the site for projects of economic and political advancement across the liberal democratic world. It was in the 1950s and 1960s that the Western states lived through their "golden years"—dramatic growth in their economies marked by rising GDP, full employment, falling mortality rates, technological change, and the internationalization of business. It was within the space created by the postwar order that the movement for European unity gathered momentum, and European colonial rule in Africa and Asia was also largely brought to an end. As the historian James Joll argues, the project of European integration provided a way of "asserting Europe's identity and of restoring Europe's place in the world" at a moment when European states were losing their empires and were no longer as powerful as the United States and the Soviet Union.[84] Across Europe, social democratic parties split off from radical-left groups and joined ruling government coalitions. These developments were supported by the wider community of advanced Western countries. The Marshall Plan and postwar organizations such as the OECD promoted centrist, integrative, and growth-oriented policies in Europe and across the Atlantic.[85] The United States and Canada joined the OECD in 1960 and Japan joined in 1964, and the body became a consultative forum on the problems of Western capitalism, promoting transparency and peer review of national economic policies. The influence of the OECD waned in the 1970s, but it continued to operate in the background to foster cooperation and expertise in what it described as the "problems of modern society."[86] With the convening of the World Economic Summit at Rambouillet in November 1975, annual leadership summits became a core part of multilateral economic diplomacy within the advanced democratic world. The United States used multilateral institutions such as NATO and the OECD to exercise leadership and draw other Western countries into favorable policy alignments.[87] It placed itself within these multilateral settings, opening its own policies to scrutiny and diplomatic give-and-take over the terms of economic growth and social progress.

The wider postwar system also provided a platform for a sprawling range of international cooperative efforts. Under the auspices of the United Nations, and building on the Universal Declaration of Human Rights, a series of human rights declarations and conventions affirmed a wide variety of political and social ideals and outlawed atrocities such as genocide and torture. During the 1960s and 1970s, the United States and the Soviet Union negotiated a series of nuclear and conventional arms control agreements. The Non-Proliferation Treaty—designed to prevent the spread of nuclear weapons and technology and promote the peaceful use of nuclear energy—went into force in 1970. In the 1980s, the United States and Soviet Union agreed to sweeping arms reductions treaties as part of the diplomatic settlement that later ended the Cold War. An array of agreements signed in the areas of the global commons and environment included the Outer Space Treaty, the Law of the Seas, and regimes to combat pollution of the oceans and stratospheric ozone depletion, protect endangered species and wildlife, and reduce emissions of gases that contribute to global warming. These various international agreements, institutions, and regimes are listed in box 1. Altogether, during the first fifty years of the postwar era the number of intergovernmental organizations more than quadrupled (see figure 6.1).

Box 1 Postwar Intergovernmental Cooperation

United Nations (San Francisco, 1945)

—Various functions of UN organizations and conferences

Trade and economic openness

—General Agreement on Tariffs and Trade and World Trade
  Organization
—Bretton Woods (International Monetary Fund and World Bank)
—Export-Import Bank
—Reciprocal Trade Agreements Act of 1934

Human rights

—Universal Declaration of 1947
—Nuremberg and Tokyo war crimes tribunals
—Outlawing of extreme human rights abuses, such as genocide
  and torture

International arms control

—Truman's Baruch Plan
—Eisenhower's Atoms for Peace and Open Skies
—US-Soviet nuclear arms control treaties of the Kennedy, Johnson,
  and Nixon years
—The Non-Proliferation Treaty
—Sweeping arms reduction treaties of Reagan and George H. W.
  Bush ending the Cold War

Global commons and environment

—Outer Space Treaty
—Law of Sea Treaty
—International regimes for telecommunications and air travel
—Regimes to combat pollution of the oceans and stratospheric
  ozone depletion, to protect endangered species and wildlife, and
  to abate gases contributing to global warming

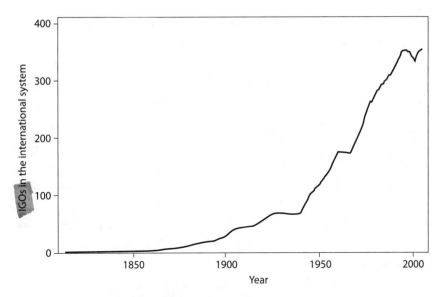

Figure 6.1. Number of intergovernmental organizations in the international system.

The effectiveness of these myriad agreements and treaties is widely debated. But it is striking how the Western postwar order and its architecture of multilateral institutions provided a platform for an explosion of new forms of cooperation across economic, political, environmental, and security realms.

The United States dominated this Western postwar order. It was an order built on asymmetries of power, but not a straightforward imperial system. It was a complex and multilayered political formation with liberal characteristics—openness and rules-based principles—that generated incentives and opportunities for other states to join and operate within it.[88] Across the postwar decades, states—not only liberal democracies but also other types of regimes—found pathways into its complex system of rules and institutions. Germany and Japan found roles and positions of authority in the postwar order, and since the Cold War, many states in Eastern Europe, East Asia, and elsewhere have joined its economic and security partnerships. The multilateral logic of the order made it relatively easy for states to join and to rise within it. It was built around institutions, and this provided opportunities for shifting and expanding coalitions of states to share leadership. The complexity and multilayered character of the order have provided a multiplicity of venues and forums for states to pursue their interests and exert leadership. These aspects of the postwar hegemonic order created incentives and opportunities for liberal democracies and other states to integrate into its core economic and political realms. Its pluralistic character allowed states to "work the system"—to join in, negotiate, and maneuver in ways that advanced their interests. This, in turn, created an order with expanding constituencies that had a stake in its continuation.

The postwar order merged the Roosevelt-era project of rebuilding the liberal democratic world with the project of fighting the Cold War. "One world" became the "free world" order, built inside the emerging bipolar system. It was here that liberal hegemony took root as a sort of container for liberal democracies to gain greater security and protection. To be inside the liberal hegemonic order was to be positioned inside a set of full-service economic, political, and security institutions. It was both a *Gesellschaft* (a "society," defined by rules, institutions, and governmental ties) and a *Gemeinschaft* (a "community," defined by shared values, beliefs, and expectations that was deeply tied to a global system of American power), but it was also manifest as a nascent political or security community. To be inside this order was to be more secure and prosperous. It was legitimated as a sort of moral community. But, unlike Wilson's vision, the system did not rely on moral rectitude and global public opinion for its discipline and restraint. These came from the rules and institutions of the order. They were the price to be paid for the benefits of security.

This American-led postwar order provided institutions and working relationships useful to liberal democracies. Modern liberal states are themselves built around various values that are in tension with each other—liberty and equality, individual and collective rights, openness and social stability, hierarchy and sovereign equality. The Western system provided a framework within which liberal states could manage these tensions and trade-offs. This was true in various ways. The postwar system of "embedded liberal" states provided mechanisms and capacities for these states to manage the terms of economic openness. Governments were given tools to reconcile and balance the benefits of open trade with demands for economic stability and social protections. The alliance system provided a basis for sharing the costs of security protection, allowing governments to manage the trade-offs between "guns and butter." The alliances—along with the wider system of multilateral institutions—provided a framework that allowed Germany and Japan to reemerge from the war as "civilian" great powers, facilitating greater solidarity and community among the Western liberal democracies. The bargains and institutions behind the hegemonic order also give these states the ability to balance hierarchy with sovereign equality. The United States used its preeminent position to underwrite and lead the order, but its binding institutional ties with other liberal states altered the terms of domination.

Yet the tensions and contradictions inherent in the American hegemonic order did not disappear. The United States remained a rule maker and privilege taker. The restraints on its power were less formal and legal than informal and political. It remained free to define its own interests, enlightened or not. The universalism of the ideals that were enshrined in the American postwar order—openness, nondiscrimination, reciprocity, rights and protections—remains only partly and unevenly realized in practice. Some multilateral institutions and principles of order were indeed global—such as the United Nations and the Universal Declaration of Human Rights. But the American security system was more exclusive. The Western order had a club character, and this is what gave it coherence and functionality. There were states inside and outside this liberal hegemonic order. Finally, the vision of a community of democracies was in some respects just that—a vision. The goal of fostering cooperation among the Western democracies did not eliminate old-style power politics, which continued to be practiced by the United States and other liberal states both inside and outside the Western system. The United States and the other liberal democracies built a postwar order—but it was an order with many layers and realms and with both liberal and illiberal characteristics.

SEVEN

Liberalism and Empire

For two centuries, liberal internationalism has been shaped by its entanglements with empire. Liberal democracies emerged in the late eighteenth and early nineteenth centuries in a world of empires. The United States began as a rebellion of thirteen colonies seeking to break free of empire. It went on to conquer and absorb vast continental territories. Liberal democracy took hold in Europe even as European great powers simultaneously built and expanded their empires. At the turn of the century, the United States began its own career of empire following the Spanish-American War. Just two decades later, during World War I, Woodrow Wilson argued that the principle of self-determination must be upheld in the postwar world. The following decades' efforts to discredit empire as a principle of governance would trace their lineage to this moment. Wilson's colleagues at Versailles, including leading British internationalists, championed the League of Nations precisely because it offered a way to put their empire on a more stable and legitimate footing. After World War II, the self-determination of subject peoples became an organizing goal of the United Nations. Yet even as formal empire waned, informal economic and institutional artifacts of empire remained. While to some observers, liberal internationalism offered a post-imperial vision for the postwar world, to others it was only a fig leaf to hide the deep continuities of imperial domination.

What is striking is the way liberal internationalism has been on both sides of the world-historical experience of empire, used to defend as well as to oppose empire. Through the nineteenth and early twentieth centuries, Britain and other European states simultaneously championed imperial and liberal principles of order. In the Victorian era, Britain continued to build its empire, as symbolized in 1876 when Queen Victoria crowned herself emperor of India, yet it also embraced free trade, arbitration, and multilateral cooperation among Western industrial societies. Individuals who played a critical role in building the League of Nations—including Robert Cecil and Jan Smuts—were simultaneously defenders of Britain's empire and committed liberal internationalists. At any moment, states have found it possible to be both liberal and imperial—as have many of their leaders.

The taint of empire has followed liberal internationalism across two centuries and into the current era of American global dominance. The debate over liberal internationalism follows two lines of critique, both of which have deep intellectual and political roots. One, coming from the political Left and revisionist historical scholarship, argues that liberal international ideas and programs have done little to alter the deep imperial character of the Western great powers, including the United States, and that the continuities between nineteenth- and early twentieth-century empires are more striking than the discontinuities.[1] The primary piece of evidence for this critique is often Woodrow Wilson, who articulated grand principles for a "new diplomacy," including self-determination, free trade, the rule of law, and collective security, but who, in the give-and-take of negotiating the Treaty of Versailles, largely capitulated to European imperial interests. Lurking behind Wilson's liberal internationalism, moreover, were deeply held beliefs about racial and cultural hierarchy.[2] The critics go on to argue that vestiges of this imperial thinking have survived into the current era, even as formal empire has not. The rules and institutions of liberal internationalism may mute and restrain the imperial impulses of Western capitalism and great-power dominance—but in the final analysis, they tend to legitimate these hierarchies of wealth, power, and privilege more than they fundamentally alter them.[3]

The other line of critique comes from within the realist tradition: some realists argue that liberalism has an activist impulse embedded in its core. America's liberal tradition has launched it on a century of misguided and dangerous foreign adventures. As the United States rose to power in the twentieth century, its interests and purposes have been shaped by its liberal ideology and institutions, which at the grandest level led generations of its leaders, starting with Wilson, to try to "remake the world" in its own image— to pursue military interventions and idealist crusades while ignoring sober calculations of the national interest.[4] The most recent version of this realist critique focuses on the United States in the decades after the Cold War, when the power-balancing disciplines of the bipolar world gave way to an era of American unipolarity. In these decades, the system of liberal hegemony that was built in the shadow of the Cold War became the foundation for an expansive project of American global activism and domination.[5] To these critics, the failed and costly Iraq War is the apotheosis of American liberal interventionism.

These realists sometimes make common cause with critics who advance classical republican worries about the corrupting influences of empire. This is a long tradition stretching back to the nineteenth-century peace movement, and it has been articulated by such diverse figures as William James, Mark Twain, Walter Lippmann, and J. William Fulbright. Stephen Kinzer locates the anti-imperial tradition in the United States in the aftermath of the Spanish-American War, and its ideas can be found today in libertarian critiques of Washington's open-ended military interventionism.[6] Unlike the realist analysis, this critique is rooted in the liberal tradition. David Hendrickson traces it to the liberal Enlightenment and the republican ideas of the American founders. Republics—or what we today call liberal democracies—are fragile entities that are vulnerable to illiberal forces generated by military power and war. The mobilization of military power has the effect of strengthening the state's executive power, threatening civil liberties, checks and balances, and the rule of law. With the rise of the American national security state in the postwar era, republican liberty has been put at risk. The pursuit of empire, including informal empire manifest as ongoing military interventionism around the world, is a danger for the same reason.[7] For these critics, the liberal tradition is the source of their anti-imperialism.

In this chapter, I use four arguments to explore these claims. First, I argue that liberal internationalism was brought into the twentieth century on the back of European empire. Liberal democracy accommodated itself to Western empire in several ways. Its Enlightenment roots and early visions of liberal modernity allowed liberals to reconcile their conceptions of hierarchy and civilization with their ideas of long-term world-historical progress. Liberal internationalism also accommodated—indeed, celebrated—the progressive logic of global capitalism. British hegemony in the nineteenth century and American hegemony in the twentieth century created important opportunities to tie liberal internationalism to the interests and ambitions of powerful liberal states. In all these ways, liberal internationalism has dirty hands. Its ideas and projects are implicated in the other great forces that have shaped the modern world: nationalism, capitalism, hegemony, and empire.

Second, I identify the sets of forces, working on multiple levels over long periods that have intervened to separate liberal internationalism from empire and imperialism. One force is geopolitical, manifest in the efforts by the United States to gain access to the various regions of the world in the aftermath of the two world wars, when anti-imperialism was an instrument of great-power politics. The shifting landscape of ideas and norms regarding international order also worked against imperialism. Roosevelt's Four Freedoms were the public and visible tip of the intellectual and normative transformations that occurred within liberal democracies during and after World War II, which created new constituencies for universal principles in an emerging international society. International institutions, starting with the League of Nations, also created platforms on which experts and activists could operate in the service of liberal multilateral projects. They operated as sites for a variety of constituencies and projects—imperial and nonimperial. Together, and often in ironic and unintended ways, liberal internationalists found themselves helping to usher out the Western imperial age.

Third, the underpinning of liberal internationalism shifted as the world itself moved from an empire-based order to the Westphalian state system—one of the grand transformations of the modern era. The decline of empire was a complex world-historical process in which changes in technology, economics, geopolitics, and normative ideas all played a part. It was driven in part by the "pull" of peoples and societies seeking independence and standing within a spreading Westphalian order. It was also driven by the "push" of leading states seeking to gain markets and political influence as the old imperial order crumbled. By the end of World War II, the political project of liberal internationalism was firmly grounded in the Westphalian state system and was offering a vision of a postimperial world organized around sovereign states linked by rules and institutions of multilateral and intergovernmental cooperation.

Finally, we are left with the problem of liberal interventionism. Are liberal states inherently revisionist? This is essentially the claim of restraint-oriented realists and critics on the Left. At some deep level, the answer seems to be yes. Liberal internationalism begins with the idea of modernity—that the world is relentlessly transforming itself through science, technology, and industrial innovation. The liberal capitalist system is being continuously reinvented. Trade and investment are inherent forces for economic and social change. If liberal internationalism has a core idea it is to foster an international order that makes liberal democracies prosperous and secure. It is not simply order based on the balance of power, but a working system of politics and economics that has integrative and expansive characteristics. But this does not mean that liberal internationalism is inherently imperial. Liberal states have ideas and institutions that can be used to restrain and resist imperialism—and the capacity to learn from its ugly consequences.

Liberalism and Empire

How is liberalism related to empire? At first glance, the two are political opposites. Empire is about domination, and liberalism is about resistance to domination. As types of order, they embody divergent organizing principles. Empire has many different meanings and manifestations, but in essence it can be understood as a hierarchical form of order in which a leading state exercises formal or informal political control over a weaker polity. It is a relationship, as Michael Doyle writes, "in which one state controls the effective political sovereignty of another political society."[8] Relations are organized vertically, often in a hub-and-spoke manner. Weaker peoples and societies

on the periphery are dependent on and coercively tied to the imperial center. They are the subjects of alien rule by a distant powerful state. In practice, however, empires have rarely been tight systems of coercive domination.
The European empires of the eighteenth and nineteenth centuries relied on
informal control and the co-option of local elites. The British Empire consisted of a wide range of hierarchical relations: formal colonial possessions,
informal governing arrangements, protectorates, and spheres of influence and
control.[9] Nonetheless, despite their diversity of political and authority relations, imperial orders are all ultimately enforced by the coercive power of
the leading state.

Liberalism, in contrast, is founded in the search for constitutional limits
on state power. Rooted in the ideas of John Locke, Montesquieu, the founders of the US constitution, and other thinkers, liberalism offers a vision of political order based on restraint of power; its principles include the rule of law,
separation of powers, protection of property rights, and guarantees of political rights and freedoms. In the same way, liberal internationalism offers
principles and projects for the postimperial organization of the world. In
the liberal international vision, order is established by independent self-
governing states—led by liberal democracies—that cooperate to uphold a
relatively open and rules-based international space. There will inevitably be
stronger and weaker states, but each exercises a measure of control of its own
domestic and foreign policies. In the international space created by liberal
democracies, imperial principles of order should be unwelcome.

Yet, despite these differences, liberalism and empire are intellectually and
politically entangled. In the nineteenth century, liberals were generally internationalist and defined by their support for open trade and international
law, but their liberal internationalism was widely understood to apply only
to "civilized" states. "Then, as now," argues Duncan Bell, "liberals remained
divided over the question of empire. Most supported it, but then so too did
most non-liberals, and liberal imperialists differed over the forms of empire
they defended, the intensity of support they offered, and perhaps most significantly, the justificatory arguments that they articulated."[10] Liberals'
commitment to equality and self-government made them suspicious of empire, at least within the world of modern liberal states. But other features of

liberalism have made it tolerant or even supportive of empire, including its developmental view of history and its suspicion of non-Western political and cultural institutions.[11]

It is easy to establish liberalism's complicity with empire and imperialism. But is this complicity inherent to liberalism, or contingent to it? Uday Mehta, in his influential study *Liberalism and Empire*, argues that the "urge" to empire is "internal" to liberalism.[12] Looking closely at the ideas of John Locke and John Stuart Mill, Mehta argues that nineteenth-century liberalism turned the Western political experience of recent centuries into an abstract universal theory of history. What it means to be civilized, advanced, and legitimate was defined in Eurocentric terms. The nineteenth-century liberal "urge" to empire springs from a developmental understanding of civilization and progress. Those who are "outside" modern civilization are lower in the global developmental hierarchy. Civilizational development was seen as moving through stages, but progression was not automatic, and so empire— defined as outside rule from a superior cultural power—offered a path forward. As John Stuart Mill argued in 1861, empire could carry less-developed societies forward, "clearing away obstacles to improvement which might have lasted indefinitely if the subject population had been left unassisted to its native tendencies and chances."[13] In Mehta's reading, nineteenth-century liberals tied Locke's rationalism to Mill's vision of civilization and historical progress, generating the "urge" for empire. Mehta finds the justifications for empire deeply encoded in the intellectual wellsprings of liberalism.[14]

But other accounts of early liberal ideas see more variety and contingency in their orientation toward empire. Sankar Muthu's study of eighteenth-century proto-liberal philosophers, including Kant, Diderot, and Herder, identifies powerful strands of anti-imperial argument. These thinkers were convinced of the basic moral equality of humans—the belief that all "deserve some modicum of moral and political respect" as a consequence of their shared humanity. In these philosophers, Muthu finds a rich appreciation of humans as cultural agents populating a world that should be and always will be diverse. Entire societies and peoples should not be judged superior or inferior based simply on comparisons to a European model. As Muthu argues, these Enlightenment arguments gave anti-imperialists grounds for defending non-European peoples' freedom to order their own societies.[15]

Jennifer Pitts also finds important liberal strands of anti-imperial thinking. Looking at the ideas of Edmund Burke, Jeremy Bentham, and Adam Smith, Pitts identifies an early counterpoint to John Stuart Mill's "imperial liberalism." In criticizing European imperialism, she argues, these thinkers drew on ideas such as "the rights of humanity and the injustices of foreign despotism, the economic wisdom of free trade and foolishness of conquest, the corruption of natural man by a degenerate civilization, the hypocrisy required for self-governing republics to rule over powerless and voiceless subjects, and the impossibility of sustaining freedom at home while exercising tyranny abroad."[16] Emerging from these depictions are multiple intellectual traditions giving rise to liberal "urges" both for and against empire.[17]

Throughout the Victorian era, liberals continued to hold a diversity of views about empire and imperialism. As Casper Sylvest notes, "The many basic differences within liberalism—the trenchant rationalism of Cobden, the blustering assertiveness of Palmerston, and the at once humble and far-reaching religiosity of Gladstone—could translate into a variety of views of imperial expansion."[18] Liberal views could be found along a whole internationalist spectrum, ranging from the radical anticolonial views of Cobdenites to those that advocate Palmerston's strategy of expanding the empire to encourage trade. John Bright, a leader of the Anti–Corn Law League, famously argued that the British Empire was "a gigantic system of out-door relief for the aristocracy."[19] Liberal support of or opposition to empire hinged in part on what precisely they meant by the term. British liberals were more inclined to support "white settler" colonies than other types of imperial possessions, and they often saw their own empire as more enlightened than the other European ventures.[20] If Victorian liberals did share a view, it was probably that of Gladstone, who claimed that "while we are opposed to imperialism, we are devoted to the empire."[21]

Several factors shaped the liberal "urge" for empire. First, liberal democracies emerged in the late eighteenth and early nineteenth centuries within a global system of empires. From their first moments, therefore, liberal states had to make choices about whether and how to build, oppose, accommodate, or work around Western and non-Western empires. As noted in chapter 3, nineteenth-century liberal internationalists often made common cause with "imperial internationalists" who were working to build the global infrastructure to support the expanding system of European empires. Bright lines between liberal and imperial internationalism did not yet exist either intellectually or politically—one could be both at the same time. The expansion of "the global," pushed forward by the industrial revolution and global capitalism, was a raging river on which everyone navigated. They were all internationalists with overlapping agendas, working with and accommodating themselves to European empire and imperialism.

This thinking can also be seen in the British liberal internationalists who championed the League of Nations during and after World War I. Most of them saw the league as a step toward building an open and rules-based international order, and simultaneously as a vehicle for putting the British Empire on stable footing. Taming the forces of anarchy and strengthening the British Empire went hand-in-hand. This was the view, for example, of prominent members of the Round Table movement, which was founded before the war to promote a confederal British Empire and Commonwealth. Three of its leading members—Lionel Curtis, Philip Kerr, and Robert Cecil—were also influential members of the British Empire delegation to the Paris Peace Conference. As members of the Round Table, they were concerned with the "imperial problem"—that is, with what they saw as the pressing need to give the British Empire a new institutional architecture that would be viable in an era of nationalism, democracy, and reform-oriented internationalism. These thinkers grappled with ideas such as "imperial union" and "imperial parliament" before ultimately advancing the idea of Commonwealth.[22] The empire would remain, but as a political community of shared traditions, laws, and commitments that, as Kerr wrote, embodied "Western ideas of self-government and liberalism."[23]

British officials brought both liberal and imperial agendas to the Paris Peace Conference and to their support for the League of Nations. This can be seen in the thinking of three influential figures—Jan Smuts, Alfred Zimmern, and Robert Cecil. Each wove a defense of the British Empire into his liberal internationalism. Smuts, a South African nationalist, was an early champion of the League of Nations and wrote an influential draft blueprint for the League Covenant. Envisioning the British Empire as a framework that would strengthen the political standing of the dominions, he described the Commonwealth as "a beacon of light to the peoples of the world in their gropings toward peaceful international government," and a model for the organization of global order.[24] The League of Nations, in turn, would strengthen the Commonwealth, giving it legitimacy while tying Great Britain and the United States together. Smuts argued in 1918 that the league would occupy the position "rendered vacant by so many of the Old European empires."[25] It would provide a framework for disposing of the territories of failed empires, creating stability in parts of the world not yet ready for sovereign statehood. The Commonwealth, meanwhile, would stand as a central pillar of the postwar world. For Smuts, the league embodied enlightened principles that would foster the spread of self-rule and international law while shoring up the British imperial system. Mark Mazower calls this the "internationalist reinforcement of empire."[26]

Another British internationalist who was influential in planning the League of Nations was the Oxford classicist Alfred Zimmern. A prominent member of the Round Table and a founder of the League of Nations Society, Zimmern worked for the Foreign Office and, as a member of the Phillimore Committee, he was involved in the drafting of detailed proposals for the league. Like Smuts, he was a campaigner for international peace and reconciliation who championed the league as the centerpiece of a reformed postwar international order.[27] Zimmern's strand of the liberal embrace of empire was rooted in moral arguments about the progressive role of Western civilization. The challenge of rebuilding peace in the postwar world was to make it "as interdependent in its spiritual relations just as it is in its economic relations."[28] Zimmern offered a vision of international society shaped and inspired by the ideals of Western civilization in which the principles embodied in the British Commonwealth would guide the organization of the postwar order. The league was not a replacement for the European imperial system but a framework that would stabilize the British Empire and establish a basis for British and American leadership. This leadership, in turn, would guide the world toward freedom and self-government.[29]

Robert Cecil, a conservative politician and diplomat, was also a leading architect and defender of the league. He helped build support for it in Britain and later served, along with Smuts, as a British member of the League of Nations Commission. Cecil was an ardent free-trade internationalist who shared the Cobdenite vision of a world ordered by commerce, international law, and the peaceful settlement of disputes. He championed the league as a way to advance this international vision and, as he put it, to "uproot the old jungle theory of international relations."[30] He also saw the league as a vehicle for reforming the British Empire. Less convinced than Smuts about the Commonwealth as a model for the wider postwar system, he instead hoped that the league would draw the United States into actively restraining the British and French temptations to expand their empires into the former Ottoman territories.[31] Nonetheless, Cecil had great respect for the British Empire as a bulwark of civilization. The league would reinvigorate the empire by putting the Commonwealth countries on a more equal footing in assembly debates, which would both strengthen their independence and reinforce their solidarity with Britain. As Cecil argued, "It is not too much to say that the system of the League is an almost ideal machinery for the preservation of the British Empire."[32]

On the American side, Woodrow Wilson gave rhetorical support to the self-determination and equality of nations. In a public speech in 1916 in which he announced his support for a postwar league, he acknowledged America's failure to fully honor these principles.[33] In this sense he was putting the United States in a position to oppose empire. But Wilson's critique of empire was limited; at Versailles, expediency ruled his decisions and kept his confrontation with European imperialism remarkably circumscribed. Adam Tooze argues that the United States, from the Open Door period to Wilson's presidency, "had no interest in unsettling the imperial racial hierarchy or the global colour-line. What the American strategy was emphatically directed towards suppressing was imperialism, understood not as productive colonial expansion nor the racial rule of white over coloured people, but as the 'selfish' and violent rivalry of France, Britain, Germany, Italy, Russia, and Japan that threatened to divide one world into segmented spheres of influence."[34] Wilson was a critic of empire, but in confronting European states he wielded an antimilitarist agenda, not an anti-imperial one. The league was to be a tool for ending interimperial rivalry, and only in the longer run would it slowly lead the world away from empire.

In all these ways, liberal internationalists accommodated and worked around the European imperial system. Liberal internationalists during this period offered far-reaching indictments of empire and imperialism. Leading figures in the Union of Democratic Control, John A. Hobson, Norman Angell, H. N. Brailsford, and Helena Swanwick, as well as thinkers such as Leonard Woolf, did champion the league as a framework for ending the imperial world order. But for most British liberal internationalists during the interwar period, the British Empire—if not European imperialism itself— was to be an integral part of the postwar order.[35] As the empire itself became reorganized as a Commonwealth, empire could be seen not simply as an illiberal realm of order outside the Western system but as a vehicle for spreading the rule of law and limited government. In the strong version of this British exceptionalist worldview, the empire was itself seen as liberal.[36]

Second, during the nineteenth century and well into the twentieth, liberal democracies were a small and distinct group of states. In the liberal imagination, it was natural for these states to see themselves as unique—a modern type of regime that had broken from the past to embrace more enlightened political principles. In the sweeping narratives of the liberal ascendancy, liberal democracies were vanguard states leading the world into a new political epoch. Liberal internationalists saw the world being reshaped by the forces of modernity: some states were leading the way and others were following. While these internationalists tended to see liberal democracies operating on a horizontal plane of sovereign equality, they also saw the wider world as a vertical landscape of advanced and backward states and societies. This vision of global hierarchy, rooted in the developmental logic of liberal modernity, made it easier to break the world into liberal and imperial spheres.

In seeking to build the world order, liberal states invariably differentiated this "inside" order from the world outside. Edward Keene has called this the "dualistic nature of order" in world politics. Relations among the liberal democracies were built on the foundation of the European state system. At the same time, the "outside" order built between these states and the world beyond Europe was based on European-led colonial and imperial systems. Each of these patterns of modern international order, Keene argues, "was dedicated to its own goal, and therefore possessed its own unique normative and institutional structure."[37] The European or Western order was dedicated to building relations based on mutual recognition, sovereign equality, and territorial independence. The extra-European order was dedicated to promoting a particular idea of civilization and transmitting its supposed benefits to the rest of the world. In this outside realm, relations were not established on the basis of reciprocal recognition of sovereign independence between states, but on the imperial enforcement of individual and property rights. As Keene notes, this bifurcated world vision was fully developed by the mid-nineteenth century, and it marked a division between the "family of civilized nations" and the "backward and uncivilized" world beyond.[38]

The development of modern international law reflects efforts to codify this division between the two worlds. International law is typically traced back to the rise of European states in the seventeenth and eighteenth centuries. In some versions of the history, legal principles were put in place to regulate relations among European states and later exported to the rest of the world.[39] Recent scholarship, however, has illuminated the complex ways in which international law was also an artifact of European empire and a system of thought for perpetuating Western domination. Jennifer Pitts traces the ideas embodied in eighteenth- and nineteenth-century legal and political treaties from Christian juridical thinking to secular universal conceptions of law inspired by Emer de Vattel's mid-eighteenth-century landmark *The Law of Nations*. She shows that these early writings on international law were often exercises in specifying universal ideals that would unite the "civilized world" as a moral community. But the notions of universalism and equal treatment in these writings tended to mask Eurocentric exclusionary thinking. The evolving "law of nations" was used to justify the actions of imperial states and their agents and provide a legal basis for the quest for territory, the seizure of other states' ships, and the imposition of discriminatory trade regimes.[40]

In the nineteenth century, international law became an ordering project aimed at defining realms of community among "civilized" states and establishing the legal bases of European imperialism. It was during this era that the legal and administrative trappings of Western colonialism were turned into a more formal and comprehensive system of what Lauren Benton calls "imperial constitutional law."[41] Colonial officials and international jurists elaborated legal concepts that codified imperial relationships. The search for a legal structure to define and regulate the terms of empire was driven by the politically indeterminate character of imperial dependencies. Subject peoples were certainly not sovereign, nor did they have legal status within the imperial state. The challenge was to establish international law in ways that defined gradations of rights and obligations within these subordinate polities.[42] For the British experience, India was the central preoccupation, as lawyers and colonial officials sought to clarify the authority of indigenous elites and their own imperial jurisdiction over internal affairs. By the end of the nineteenth century, these efforts to reconcile colonialism with international law took the shape of a distinctive imperial legal order.[43]

At the same time that international law was codifying the division between the civilized and the backward worlds, the international legal infrastructure also provided tools for the critique of empire. Liberals used the language of law to debate the civilizing mission of the West, the hierarchy of nations, and the rights and political standing of peoples. Andrew Fitzmaurice argues that nineteenth-century legal skeptics of empire were not motivated by idealism or humanitarianism but by worries about empire's corrupting effects on liberty. The modern revolutions in Britain, France, and the United States had won freedoms that empire threatened. As Fitzmaurice observes, empires "created a space in which arbitrary rule and absolutism could return and be repatriated to Europe."[44] The debate among jurists intensified during the late nineteenth-century scramble for Africa. Some liberal reformers saw international law as a tool to foster cooperation among imperial powers so that European imperial expansion could continue without jeopardizing the peace. This was the agenda of the Berlin Conference of 1885, a gathering of the European great powers presided over by German chancellor Otto von Bismarck, convened to map Africa's colonial borders (most of which remain in place today). International jurists were called upon to clarify the legal bases of sovereignty, property, and imperial rights. Liberal critics of empire, worried about the fragile rights and liberties within the liberal democratic world, used international law in their efforts to restrain Europe from entering a new era of imperial conquest.

These realms of international law were not invented by liberal internationalists. But liberals did build upon the ambiguous character of international order as a basis for their own political projects. The evolving international law of empire had dual implications for liberal internationalism. On the one hand, the fact that imperialism was increasingly brought within an international legal framework made it easier for liberal internationalists to reconcile empire (for the British, at least their own empire) with a vision of a world ordered by law and cooperation. But on the other hand, over the longer term, this imperial legal order also provided principles and institutions that jurists and political activists could use to oppose empire.

Third, the liberal internationalism of the Victorian era and the early twentieth century was interwoven with notions of racial and civilizational hierarchy, and these often unspoken normative assumptions lurked in the background in Western debates about liberalism and empire.[45] Ideas of racial and civilizational hierarchy had existed well before the appearance of liberalism. The ancient Greeks and Romans distinguished between civilized and barbarian worlds. These notions have existed wherever there has been conquest, subjugation, and exploitation across racial and cultural divides. It is not surprising that nineteenth-century Western thinkers brought ideas of racial and cultural superiority to their efforts to shape the global order— ideas that in turn were shaped by the actual European experience with empire and colonialism.[46] These ideas and images were woven into liberal internationalism.

The term *civilization* or *civilized world* has a long history and various meanings, but during the nineteenth century it became widely used by European thinkers to describe the character of Western society in relation to other peoples. It conveyed the idea that European society was distinct from other societies by its advanced institutions and culture. There was only loose agreement on which specific values distinguished civilized society from uncivilized societies. But it was a doctrine of recognition. To be civilized—as a people, nation, or state—was to be recognized as a member of the leading and most advanced political community. Those so recognized were entitled to be treated according to the rules and norms of this privileged grouping of nations.[47] The American colonies, for example, in breaking away from the British Empire, sought this recognition by attempting to demonstrate "a decent respect for the opinions of mankind."[48] In this sense, civilization marked the boundary between the inside and outside realms of global order. It divided the international society organized around sovereignty and the equality of nations from everybody else.

In the late nineteenth century, *civilization* increasingly became a legal principle, with specific markers for what Gerrit Gong has called the "standard of civilization." These markers include rights of liberty, property, and commerce, an organized and efficient political bureaucracy, adherence to international law, a domestic system of courts and laws, and the embrace of "civilized" social and cultural practices.[49] It was effectively a European standard, associated with the "civilizing mission" of European empire. At the Berlin Conference in 1885, the European imperial states used this civilizational discourse in defining relations between themselves and African and other colonial peoples. The signers of the Berlin Act agreed to "regulate conditions most favourable to the development of trade and civilization in certain regions of Africa," and to "bind themselves to watch over the preservation of native tribes, and to care for the improvement of the conditions of their moral and material well-being" with the aim of "instructing the natives and bringing them the blessings of civilization."[50]

The division of the world into "civilized" and "backward" peoples was an artifact of culture and race. Western images of a world organized according to race and civilization date at least as far back as the European age of discovery. Many of the early figures in the liberal tradition—beginning with John Locke and the American founders—all too easily reconciled their enlightened political principles with the deprivations of slavery and the ugly treatment of indigenous peoples. In the nineteenth century, with the arrival of Darwinian ideas of adaptation and natural selection, the conception of a world ordered by race became explicitly tied to ideas of progress and the division of the world into weak and strong societies. For Herbert Spencer, "the conquest of one people over another has been, in the main, the conquest of the social man over the anti-social man; or, strictly speaking, of the more adapted over the less adapted."[51] Western thinkers elaborated sophisticated ideas about the hierarchy of human progress as a justification for empire and the position of white Europeans at the top of the developmental hierarchy.[52] The civilizing mission of Western states became a project of white people instructing nonwhite people about how to organize their societies for social advancement. It is only a small step to Kipling's poem "The White Man's Burden."[53]

In the United States, Wilson's liberalism was also infused with ideas of civilizational and racial hierarchy. One way to try to reconcile Wilson's racism with his liberalism is to see them as divergent impulses. There is his racism, rooted in the American experience of slavery and the Civil War. This is the Wilson who resegregated the federal civil service and acquiesced in racial discrimination at home and abroad. Then there is Wilson the moral idealist, who championed liberal international principles of equality and self-determination. In his portrait of Wilson, Stephen Skowronek argues that Wilson's liberalism cannot be separated from his Southern attitudes toward race. Wilson's embrace of self-determination can be seen as an extension of his long-standing criticism of what he saw as the American federal government's overbearing involvement in reconstruction of the Southern states after the Civil War. "When Wilson envisioned 'every people free to determine its own polity, its own way of development, unhindered, unthreatened, unafraid, the little along with the great and the powerful,'" Skowronek writes, "he was, in effect, turning the southern voice into the voice of America on the world stage."[54] Wilson was critical of powerful states using force to extract loyalty and enforce their rule because he saw the world through the eyes of the South during Reconstruction. For the same reason, he shared Edmund Burke's opposition to British policy toward the colonies during the American Revolution: the subjects of power politics were "civilized" people. For less advanced peoples, their acceptance into the civilized world and their ability to benefit from self-determination and protection against imperial rule were contingent. In this way, Skowronek concludes, Wilson's vision was double-edged: he combined a critique of power politics with "his inbred sense of racial hierarchy," which both supported a tutelary role of leading states in advancing the prospects of weaker peoples and opposed the European states' pursuit of militarist policies as they competed with each other.[55]

Wilson and other American and European officials at Versailles did not have a particularly wide-gauged vision of human rights, let alone convictions about social and racial justice. The league did not mention human rights in its founding charter.[56] In speaking of "universal" rights and values, Wilson did not condemn Western ideas about race and civilization. During the drafting of the League of Nations Covenant, the Japanese put forward a resolution on racial equality. Count Makino Nobuaki, the Japanese delegate, argued that since the equality of nations was a fundamental idea on which the league was based, the covenant should explicitly affirm the principle of respect for all races and nationalities. Wilson had been considering a resolution on religious freedom, and at one point he thought of combining this with the Japanese resolution. In the end, however, he acted to strike down the resolution on racial equality, bending to the pressures of practical politics. Britain saw the resolution as a threat, particularly to Australia's "white policy" on immigration. Fearing the loss of British support for the treaty, Wilson invoked the unanimity clause to ensure its defeat. Naoko Shimazu's rich account of this drama shows that while Wilson did not resist the racial equality proposal because of its implications for segregation in the United States, "nor was he personally committed to racial equality as a universal principle."[57] The point is that he did not have an expansive liberal vision of world order. He emphasized national self-determination over racial equality, and self-determination was itself to be managed by the great powers through the mandate system. As for most other social purposes, he was willing to compromise or ignore them.

Finally, at the most basic level, liberal internationalists across the nineteenth and twentieth centuries have tended to view international relations as shaped by dynamic and progressive forces that are continuously reshaping the world. As noted earlier, this vision is rooted in liberalism's Enlightenment foundations. The deep forces of science, technology, discovery, and learning are constantly altering human society. The concept of modernity attempts to capture the logic and consequences of these unfolding dynamics. The idea of progress implies that the change inherent in modern life creates opportunities for societies to improve their circumstances. These concepts of modernity and progressive change are woven through the ideas and doctrines of liberal internationalism, which allowed liberals to see empire as a transitional artifact of world development.

This vision of modernity and advancement has several layers. One layer is simply a view of the dynamic movements of capitalism and market society. Western capitalism and the industrial system that ushered in the modern world are deeply expansive. Trade, investment, and exchange push societies outward. Unless it is stopped by the territorial state, capitalism is inherently transnational. Societies with the capital, technology, and capacities to project power dominate this process of expansion. It is expected that societies within a liberal international order that is open and interdependent will find themselves in a constant process of change. When countries trade with each other, industries and sectors will inevitably rise and fall, and businesses and workers must adapt. The instabilities and vulnerabilities of open societies will generate political forces for change. These capitalist dynamics do not necessarily lead to formal systems of empire, even though European imperialism was pushed forward by the expansionary logic of capitalism. But liberal internationalism contains deeply revisionist assumptions. Liberal internationalists expect the world built by liberal democracies to be continually disrupted, disturbed, intruded, and overturned.[58]

At another layer, some early twentieth-century liberal internationalists argued that capitalist and market forces were not inherently or permanently aligned with empire. Liberals in the Cobdenite tradition saw trade and economic interdependence as constitutive elements of a peaceful order organized around modern industrial societies. John Hobson argued that the imperial impulse came from oligarchic capitalism and thus could be avoided by more progressive economic polities. Norman Angell argued that the steady growth of economic interdependence among capitalist societies would make war increasingly irrational. Joseph Schumpeter argued that European imperialism was rooted in premodern social formations that would erode as modern capitalism spread. Empire did not show that capitalism had triumphed but that its dominance was incomplete, held back by the ancien régime and aristocratic, nationalist, and militarist forces.[59] In these theories, far from be-

ing inherently predisposed toward imperialism, the forces of market capitalism could work in the long term to end empire. Even if capitalism were not
inherently anti-imperial, it could be shaped and directed in ways that brought
an end to formal empire.[60]

At the deepest level, it was the belief in the modernizing logic and worldwide advance of liberal democracy that, ironically, opened the door to the
liberal urge for empire. Liberals' conviction that the forces of modernity were
moving societies forward along a liberal democratic pathway allowed them
to explain and defend the world's economic and political hierarchies as consequences of an incomplete revolution. Europe and the Western democracies at the front of this great march forward embodied what it meant to be
modern. Liberals like John Stuart Mill could call self-rule the highest form
of government yet argue that much of the world was not ready for it. In this
grand modernist vision, as Dipesh Chakrabarty aptly puts it, "Indians, Af-
ricans and other 'rude' nations" were consigned "to an imaginary waiting
room of history."[61]

Liberal Internationalism against Empire

If liberal internationalism had an urge for empire, it also had an urge to oppose it. In the late nineteenth century, liberal thinkers in the United States
and Europe added their voices to movements against empire and colonialism. After the world wars, many liberal internationalists, particularly in the
United States, championed the League of Nations and the United Nations
as institutions that enshrined principles of self-determination and sovereign
equality—and thus offered a path away from empire. As the twentieth century
unfolded, liberal internationalists grew increasingly committed to postimperial forms of order. These changes in orientation played out in the struggles between the United States and Britain during and after World War II
over imperial preferences and global spheres of influence. The shift away
from empire emerged as part of the general reimagining of liberal internationalism in the 1940s and during the Cold War, when the United States put
its weight behind a world organized around sovereign states as it pursued
its expanding geopolitical interests and built postwar order. In important

respects, however, it was not the West that turned liberal internationalism against empire and imperialism but the non-West, which seized upon ideas and principles—universal in character but often instrumental in origin and purpose—and applied them to struggles over sovereignty, rights, and rules.

Wilson-era liberal internationalism had offered global ideas, but it retained an old-style Western parochialism. The vision of liberal order put forward by Wilson and his peers was more "civilizational" than "universal." The League of Nations would be open to the wider world, but it was organized around the Western liberal democracies. States that were considered insufficiently mature to join the community of sovereign states would have to wait until they were ready. As Edward Keene argues, the League of Nations entailed the "internationalization" of civilization—so there were limits on the universal or global scope of membership and standing. "Although ideological concerns were beginning to become more important in defining the boundaries of the civilized world, racial discrimination was still a major element in deciding which peoples were entitled to membership in the new organization and thus to have their sovereign status recognized."[62]

With the rebuilding of order after World War II and the establishment of the United Nations, this civilizational view—the distinction between the "family of civilized nations" and the rest of the world—gave way to a more universalistic and inclusive conception. Keene argues, "Simply put: the United Nations was envisioned as, or quite rapidly became, an organization *of* all the world's peoples, with universal participation in the projects of preserving peace and developing global civilization, whereas the League had, above all, been an organization of civilized nations, working collectively *for* all the world's peoples." Postwar notions of states, peoples, sovereignty, and civilization were becoming less based on nineteenth-century notions of the social hierarchies of peoples. As Keene notes, "the development of the UN system reflected a much more inclusive attitude toward non-European peoples, in keeping with the recognition that they were no less civilized than their European counterparts."[63] What changed between 1919 and 1945 was the conception of how peoples and societies from different regions and civilizations related to each other as moral and legal entities, a move driven in part by a fuller acknowledgment of the universal reach of the notion of sovereign equality.[64] But it was also driven by the growing salience of the "rights of peoples"—the spread of the claim that all human beings, by virtue of being human, have fundamental and inalienable rights.

Behind this shift were changing views of modernity and civilization. Civilization itself was weakening as an intellectual construct, and modernity was not seen simply as something spreading outward from its Western center. The new divide was not the West versus the non-West—which had become untenable—but the liberal democratic world versus the illiberal world. Modernity empowered both sides of this political universe. In World War II, the great struggle on behalf of civilization had been against Nazi Germany, a European power that was itself employing scientific theories of race to legitimate its violence and aggression—ideas that had been used in the nineteenth century to defend European imperial domination over "backward" non-European peoples.[65] In this sense, the old civilizational justification for two world orders—a Western system of civilized states and a backward and uncivilized world beyond—did not fail because non-European peoples gradually joined the "family of civilized nations." It collapsed when civilized states—Germany, Japan, and Russia—joined the noncivilized world.[66]

As I noted in chapter 5, this shift in thinking occurred in the United States during the war years and continued during the Cold War. The rise of fascism and totalitarianism led Roosevelt and his contemporaries to let go of their notions of civilization, race, and nation and rethink the nature of liberalism and modernity. With threats to the liberal capitalist order now coming from inside the West, what it meant to be civilized could no longer be defined by race or culture or geography. This sentiment was captured by Leonard Woolf in a short book published in 1939, *Barbarians at the Gate*, in which he argued that civilization was not a geographical or even a cultural construction but a way of regulating individual behavior within human communities. Europe might have found a distinctive approach to restraining violence, tyranny, and predation, but civilization was distributed more widely around the world—and so too was the antithesis of civilization, or what Woolf called barbarism. Writing on the eve of World War II, Woolf argued that "the barbarian is, therefore, not only at the gates; he is always within the walls of our civilization, inside our minds and our hearts."[67] This new sense that the dangers to the liberal democratic world came from inside that world forced American and European internationalists to rethink their principles and projects.

American liberal internationalists began to make more serious efforts to separate their project from the legacies of European imperialism. This separation was driven by evolving ideas about sovereignty and self-determination, grand shifts in geopolitical interests, depression, and wartime politics within Western liberal democracies, as well as by more immediate struggles brought on by the war and the way it changed the Anglo-American relationship. The United States did not have the same attachments to empire as the British, and cracks opened up within the West on whether and how the world would transition away from empire.[68] This was seen most clearly at the Atlantic Charter meeting in 1941, where Roosevelt and Churchill disagreed over the future of the British imperial preference system and the principles of sovereign rights and self-determination.[69]

The Logic of Geopolitics

Four distinct forces in these decades were pushing the United States and the liberal international project away from empire. First, there was the straightforward role of geopolitical interests. The United States, as a rising global power, saw its long-term interests associated with the breakup of empires. Roosevelt and American officials viewed European colonialism as a declining and unstable form of order that would inevitably meet national resistance movements. Cautiously and selectively, the United States aligned itself with these movements so as to spread its influence and weaken that of the other great powers. This geopolitical calculation crystallized during the war, when the United States had an overriding interest in an open and stable postwar world system. It was a grand strategic "urge" with decidedly anti-imperial implications.

It was helped by geography and historical timing. In the 1930s, with the nation rising up in a global system dominated by empires and imperial zones and spheres of influence, American strategists began to debate whether the United States could be a great power and remain isolated within its own hemisphere. How large would its "grand area" need to be for the United States to be a viable great power? During the war, a loose consensus emerged: the grand area had to be global.[70] The United States would need access to markets and resources in most of the regions of the world. American officials—liberal internationalists and others—saw the nation's interests tied to breaking down imperial blocs and spheres of influences to construct an open global system. Rather than continue old-style imperial organizing ideas, the United States championed global rules and institutions that promoted the open door and self-determination—not for idealist reasons but to open up Europe, Asia, and other regions for trade, investment, and diplomacy. Its isolated location and late arrival as a great power motivated the American approach to organizing the global order. The United States was globally oriented because it needed to open up and link itself to the major regions of the world. This in turn gave it incentives to articulate anti-imperial principles such as openness, nondiscrimination, and self-determination. If the United States built the first "global empire," it did so by elevating universal principles and multilateral rules and institutions and turning the old organizational logic of empire on its head.

The unique geographical position of the United States also influenced the way it projected power. All the other major states in the twentieth century were on the Eurasian continent and thus were neighbors of rival great powers. The United States was alone, separated from Europe and Asia by vast oceans. This made it potentially useful to other states as an outside balancing state. States in postwar Europe and East Asia sought to draw the United States into playing economic and security roles within their regions. They looked for ways that an American military commitment could help solve regional security problems. France and Great Britain, for example, wanted an ongoing American security commitment as part of a wider regional system that would help integrate West Germany into Europe. Japan used its alliance with the United States to solve its security problems and find a path back to growth and modernization. These circumstances gave the United States hegemonic—rather than imperial—relations of power. America's distance from these regions made it less threatening, thus allowing Europe and East Asia to worry more about abandonment than domination. In turn, the

United States worried about the credibility of its commitment. At least for a select group of alliance partners, the upside of getting the United States to provide security was greater than the risk of domination and lost autonomy associated with being a junior partner or client state. It was not that American domination goes away, but that its character lended itself to negotiated bargains and the building of institutions that establish commitments and restraints.[71]

The same factors of geography and timing also reinforced America's incentives to support national movements toward statehood and self-rule as part of its anti-imperial order-building logic. If a great power cannot directly dominate a weaker state, its second best option is to support that state's sovereignty and independence so that it will not be dominated by a rival great power. Ian Chong, for example, argues that the United States championed sovereignty and self-determination in East Asia as a way to avoid being excluded. Great powers might prefer outright domination if they can get away with it, Chong argues, but in most of the world outside of the Western Hemisphere, this was not a realistic option for the United States. So in postwar states such as China, Indonesia, and Thailand, the United States put its weight behind movements toward national self-determination.[72] In Chong's view, the United States is not unique in pursuing this "second best" strategy. Great Britain and other European powers have promoted self-determination and sovereign independence in many parts of the developing world to undercut rival powers' bids for regional domination.[73] But geography and historical timing made this a dominant American impulse.

The way the United States rose and shaped the twentieth-century international order was unique. It grew powerful in relative isolation from the other major states and became a world power during the high tide of empire. It did not become a great power through conquest outside of its region, but instead stepped into vacuums and postwar moments to shape geopolitical settlements. In a sense, it was like Great Britain in the nineteenth century in trying to shape events as an offshore power without seeking to become a continental power. Its comparative advantage was in offering other countries security protection, undercutting bids for dominance by land powers in Asia and Europe.[74] Unlike Great Britain, the United States did this through a system of alliances and client states. It sought to build a global order by advancing expansive principles and multilateral rules and institutions.[75] These tools of domination tended to make the order more hegemonic than imperial, providing opportunities for liberal internationalists to articulate visions of post-imperial order.

Liberal Internationalist Ideas

A second force separating liberal internationalism and empire was the ideas themselves, filtered through political movements both in the liberal democracies and outside the Western world. Roosevelt's Four Freedoms and the Atlantic Charter, the most sweeping of these ideas, can be seen as efforts by wartime democratic leaders to mobilize their people for war. In this sense, they served an instrumental purpose. For Roosevelt, the Atlantic Charter was a way to legitimize for the American people their imminent entrance into the war. It was an effort to counter Nazi propaganda by offering subjugated nations and neutrals in Europe a sweeping liberal democratic vision of a better world to come. But even if universalist principles are uttered for instrumental reasons, once they enter into the discourse they become part of the contested ideological landscape upon which political struggles are waged.[76]

To be sure, some liberal internationalists were deeply committed to presiding over liberalism's separation from empire. Roosevelt's closest adviser on postwar planning, Sumner Welles—the driving force behind the Atlantic Charter and later the United Nations—earnestly sought to use wartime negotiations with the British to escort Britain's empire offstage. He and other Wilsonians had spent the 1930s reflecting on the failures of 1919, looking for new ways to build a cooperative global order that, as Welles put it, "implies the juridic equality of every nation and the acceptance of a moral order and of effective international law."[77] Welles sought to lay down principles that would weaken the political standing of empire in the postwar world.[78]

But it was the wider use of self-determination and sovereign equality that gave these principles impact. This struggle was waged on many fronts, driven by geopolitical and ideological clashes and movements within the West and between it and the non-West. It is not simply—or primarily—a story of the West "externalizing" its ideas and institutions to the rest of the world. Non-Western peoples and societies seized on the principles and institutions that the West had developed for itself and adapted them for their own purposes in their struggles for independence. Witnessing the decolonization movements in 1964, Rupert Emerson observed that when non-Western people "press for equality, democracy, and the right of self-determination, they are asking their present and erstwhile rulers to live up to the ideals which these same rulers have transmitted to them and proclaimed as their own. . . . The nationalism which developed in the imperial West in the nineteenth century, with its implied right of self-determination, can in this sense be seen as one of the key sources of anti-colonialism."[79] Westphalian and liberal internationalist ideas were both pushed and pulled into the rest of the world. The "reception and remolding of Western ideas" by peoples and societies in the non-West, C. A. Bayly argues, "set limits on the nature and extent of their domination by European power-holders."[80]

The formal and informal unraveling of empire and colonialism is one of the great dramas of the post-1945 era. From the 1950s to the early 1960s, the previous century's era of imperial expansion underwent a radical reversal. Robin Winks notes, "One after another, the colonized territories tried to establish their independence from European control. From Guinea to Somalia, from Morocco to India, the flags of France, Britain, Italy, Holland, Belgium, Spain, and Portugal came down. In their place were hoisted newly designed flags of the newly sovereign states. By the mid-1980s, no substantial area was under colonial rule, although the radically discriminatory regime prevailed in the Republic of Africa."[81] The predominant view in Europe at the end of the nineteenth century was that the imperial system would remain the core organizing logic of world order. Yet, in less than a hundred years, these empires—along with the Soviet Union—had disappeared.[82]

Political movements in the United States and the other liberal democracies also had a behind-the-scenes impact on their government's policies toward empire. In the nineteenth century, the British anti–slave trade movement pressed the Parliament to abolish the slave trade throughout the British Empire. During and after World War I, the women's suffrage movement in the United States and Britain became increasingly active in international affairs. The war itself affected the lives of women, galvanizing the suffragist movement and illuminating the role of war in modern society. Many in the movement made a direct connection between the right to vote and campaigns for peace and worldwide social justice.[83] During the war, women's groups on both sides of the Atlantic, led by figures such as Jane Addams and Emily Greene Balch, actively participated in debates on the postwar settlement.[84] Together, Addams and Balch became leaders of the Women's International League for Peace and Freedom, devoted to peace education, international dialogue, and socially progressive causes, for which they later received the Nobel Peace Prize.[85] This group and others explicitly linked the denial of women's rights and social justice in their societies to the pursuit of militarism and imperialism abroad.

During the 1940s, domestic political struggles—particularly over civil rights—and the continuing activities of progressive movements reinforced liberal internationalist efforts abroad. Americans struggling for civil rights explicitly linked their causes with anticolonial movements.[86] The linkage showed itself, for example, in June 1942, when Walter White, representing the National Association for the Advancement of Colored People, met with Sumner Welles and urged the Roosevelt administration to call a "Pacific Conference" devoted to ending colonial rule in Asia. White wanted FDR to meet with Indian leaders such as Nehru and Gandhi and the Chinese nationalist leader Chiang Kai-shek to announce America's support for Asian statehood and national self-rule. White also suggested that, with the "Pacific Charter" in hand, a delegation of Americans, led by Wendell Willkie and a "distinguished American Negro whose complexion unmistakably identifies him as being a colored man," should go to India and announce American support for the Indian struggle."[87] The idea did not have great support in the administration. Even those who took issue with the British Empire were unwilling to take steps that might weaken Britain's position in the struggle with Nazi Germany.

After World War II, the American civil rights movement and social justice campaigns drew connections between their struggles and the struggles of nationalist and anti-imperialists abroad. In 1947, W. E. B. Du Bois used the platform of the United Nations for "An Appeal to the World," describing the injustices of racial segregation and inequality in the United States and associating the struggles of African Americans with the victims of colonialism in Africa and elsewhere. "Our treatment is not merely an internal question for the United States," he argued, "it is a basic problem of humanity."[88] Not only did civil rights activists appeal to international audiences for support and solidarity, many US political leaders also saw progress on civil rights as integral to fighting the Cold War. During these decades, the American government's relationship to civil rights legislation was shaped by the sense that it was necessary to manage its international image. As the historian Mary Dudziak argues, "the need to address international criticism gave the federal government an incentive to promote social change at home."[89] The connections also ran in the other direction as the American civil rights movement, along with other social justice advocates, put pressure on the US government to support anticolonial causes abroad.[90]

Institutional Platforms and Capacities

Third, the international organizations established after the two world wars created platforms and capacities that experts and activists could use in their struggles against empire. While the League of Nations and, later, the United Nations helped Britain and other European states secure what remained of their imperial holdings, they also served as institutional sites for activism and repositories of universalistic norms and principles that opponents of empire could deploy in their struggles for self-rule. Both the league and the United Nations created institutional channels for groups that previously had little input into diplomacy or the shaping of international rules and practices to provide a counterweight to the old imperial order. These groups included women's organizations, international activists, and non-Western governments and peoples.[91]

As I have noted, the Great War did not quell the European appetite for empire, and the League of Nations was widely seen in Europe and Great Britain as an opportunity to strengthen the prestige and administration of imperial rule. But the league also played a role—if a conflicted and awkward one—in moving the world toward the end of empire and the spread of self-determination. "If one considers its work in stabilizing new states and running the minorities protection and mandates system," Susan Pedersen argues, "the League appears as a key agent in the transition from a world of formal empires to a world of formally sovereign states."[92] Pedersen looks specifically at the league's Permanent Mandates Commission, the system established in 1921 to manage the territories in Africa, the Middle East, and the Pacific that Germany, Austria-Hungary, and the Ottoman Empire had lost in the war. The mandates system did not directly alter the aims of the remaining imperial powers, which sought to preserve their colonies and continued to see empire as a civilizing mission. "What was new," Pedersen argues, "was the apparatus and the level of international diplomacy, publicity, and 'talk' that the system brought into being." The mandates system was a vehicle for "internationalization"—a process "by which certain political issues and functions are displaced from the national or imperial, and into the international realm."[93] Unintended by its architects, the mandates system became a vehicle by which those favoring self-determination and revision of the Versailles settlement could press their claims. It provided a platform for internationalists, humanitarians, nationalists, and others who sought to expose the dark side of imperial rule. The wider league complex of institutions had the same effect, drawing international commissions, organizations, lobbyists, and experts into a sprawling and ongoing debate about the future of European empire and the normative foundations of statehood.[94] It would take decades and another world war to bring about a global system of sovereign states. But the league pointed the way.

India took advantage of the League of Nations to gain rights and recognition before its independence in 1947. Great Britain, in an effort to strengthen its presence and voting share at Versailles, overcame the opposition of the other great powers to gain separate representation for its dominions, including India. Although still a British dependency, India—along with Australia, Canada, New Zealand, and South Africa—actively participated in the conference's deliberations and signed the peace treaty on the basis of "legal equality."[95] Because the Covenant of the League of Nations was part of the peace treaty, India acquired the right to become a founding member of the

league, the only state among the thirty-one original members that was not
legally self-governing. India's internal and external relations continued to rest
with the British government, but as one observer notes, "for the first time in
the modern period, [India] came into direct and formal contact with the
outside world."[96] Between 1919 and 1947, India's position within the international legal system remains anomalous. While formally not a sovereign
state, India exercised treaty-making power and participated in almost every
international conference after 1920. As a league member, India attended the
Washington Conference on Naval Armaments in 1921, signed the Washington treaty, and was admitted to the International Labour Organization, the
Permanent Court of International Justice, and other league-related organizations. It signed numerous multilateral treaties, including the Kellogg-
Briand Pact of 1928.[97] In 1945, India was invited to the San Francisco
Conference of the United Nations, and it became a founding member of
the new world organization. Over this period, India's self-governing status
remained limited and many Indian nationalist leaders saw their country's
presence in these international bodies as a capitulation to British imperialism. Nonetheless, India took advantage of the status it gained over these
decades to pave the way for independence, consolidating India as a diplomatic unit and giving its nationalist movement international recognition.[98]

The United Nations was even more explicit in facilitating the transition
away from empire. It formally enshrined the idea of universal membership
in a world of sovereign states and provided the legal and political framework
for the recognition and integration of new states into the postimperial Westphalian order. As decolonization accelerated, the United Nations rapidly expanded from 51 original members in 1945, to 100 in September 1961, and to
159 by the end of 1985. Ironically, the United Nations is widely seen as the
embodiment of internationalist ideas, but its greatest achievement may be
the global triumph of the sovereign state system. Adam Roberts notes the
United Nations' importance in providing a framework for decolonization:

> The UN sometimes assisted the process of decolonization through
> referenda, and also through General Assembly resolutions—most

notably the 1960 Declaration on the Granting of Independence to Colonial Countries and Peoples. But its most important contribution was in providing a framework for entry into international society of the numerous new and reconstituted states, many of which were intensely vulnerable. For them, the UN was not just the main means of securing diplomatic recognition, but also a world stage, a negotiating forum, a provider of well-paid jobs, and a source of symbolic protection. The UN embodies principles, including racial equality and the sovereign equality of states, that were vital to the decolonization process.[99]

Global Expansion of the Westphalian System

Finally, the deepest and most far-reaching force separating liberalism from empire has been the struggle over the global expansion of the Westphalian state system. A world of sovereign states was a precondition for the spread of liberal internationalism. Therefore, the struggle to extend sovereign rights of statehood to peoples and nations was the real bulwark against empire. By building on and reinforcing this grand shift from empire to the nation-state, liberal internationalism ultimately placed its "project" within the Westphalian system—it became, in a sense, the set of ideas for organizing the world once the world finally shed its imperial foundations. Empire had ordered the world for centuries, and when the twentieth century asked what would replace empire as the world's organizing logic, liberal internationalism stepped forward as the alternative.

How the Westphalian state system came to encompass the world is a question that still requires scholarly attention.[100] The sovereign state arrived quite late for most regions outside the West—essentially in the twentieth century, after the world wars. For most of the past five hundred years, European great powers were not eager to export or universalize the Westphalian order. They held on to empire and colonies until forced to give them up. In this sense, the spread of Westphalia is not a story of the imposition of a Western idea on the rest of the world, but of the failure of the European state system to sustain empire.[101] To pursue movements for independence and self-determination on their own, peoples and societies outside Europe took advantage of the cracks and clashes in the European imperial system.

As noted earlier, Edward Keene argues that great wars between liberal and totalitarian states discredited the old civilizational vision of sovereignty and imperial hierarchy. Christian Reus-Smit finds, in the universalization of norms of sovereignty and self-determination after two hundred years of struggles over individual rights, a story of the "evolution and transmission of the legitimating institutions that sustain sovereignty."[102] This surely is part of the explanation. But it remains to be explained why empires, as a form of global order, failed. John Darwin argues that empires have tended to fail for four reasons: "external defeat or geopolitical weakness; ideological contagion and the loss of legitimacy; domestic enfeeblement at the centre of empire—the loss of political will and economic capacity; and colonial revolt."[103] All of these triggers of imperial crisis seemed to be present in the twentieth century. Considered as wars of empire, the world wars decisively weakened and brought to an end the European system of empire.

In this drama, the United States played an important role in both undercutting empire and promoting the Westphalian state system. It did this first during the two world wars, by joining and later leading coalitions of allies that ultimately defeated states with expansive imperial projects. In World War I it was Imperial Germany, which had conquered a large area of Eastern Europe and seized much of the Russian Empire's western territories. This war resulted in the collapse of four long-established European empires: Romanov Russia, Habsburg Austria-Hungary, Hohenzollern Germany, and Ottoman Turkey. World War II effectively finished off the Japanese empire and severely weakened the British and French empires, though the latter two, because they were on the winning side, took a couple of decades to dissolve.

During the Cold War, the United States also engaged in balancing against the Soviet Union—seeking to contain the expansion of Soviet power and influence as well as thwarting communist coups and revolutions in many weak, independent states. At the same time, as noted earlier, the United States played a variety of roles in facilitating states' ability to survive as independent members of international society. It led efforts to institutionalize Westphalian norms of nonaggression and sovereign independence, first with the League of Nations and then with the United Nations Charter. In the second half of the twentieth century, the American-led international order institutionalized open trade and multilateral cooperation, providing the infrastructure for a global economic system, which in turn strengthened the smaller states' ability to sustain their sovereignty. Also in the second half of the twentieth century, the American system of military alliances dampened violent conflicts among allied states, particularly in Europe and East Asia, and this prevented the Westphalian system from falling back into violent conflict and empire building.[104] Thus the "American century" was also the century of the global spread of the nation-state. They were different political projects, but each helped the other gain ground.

Liberalism and Interventionism

The United States has presented many faces to the world. As the dominant power in the postwar era, it presided over the almost universal unraveling of empire and colonialism. The American-led postwar order was in fact sold to the world as a modern replacement for the old European imperial system. The global institutions that the United States championed—the United Nations and the array of postwar organizations and regimes—provided the framework for this grand shift in the organizing logic of global order. Yet during the same decades, the United States engaged in military interventions and covert actions around the world. As Chalmers Johnson puts it, the United States built an "empire of bases," projecting military power and putting itself at the center of regional orders in Europe, Asia, and the Middle East.[105] Fighting communism, protecting allies, defending freedom, promoting human rights, building nations, defeating terrorism—the official purposes of American actions have varied. But intervention—military and otherwise—has remained a consistent and controversial feature of American foreign policy.

How do we square these contradictory impulses? If liberal internationalism has offered a vision of a postimperial global order, is it also implicated in a pattern of liberal interventionism, or liberal imperialism? Some critics see liberal internationalism as a fig leaf with which elites disguise and legitimate more traditional great-power impulses. The problem with liberal internationalism is that it does not put a sufficient ideological or political brake on American interventionism. Other critics make an even stronger argument—that liberalism itself drives American interventionism. As ideologies and political projects, liberalism and liberal internationalism are inherently revisionist. It is American liberalism that leads the United States to intervene and seek to reshape other societies. For realist critics, the liberal sources of American interventionism look particularly striking since the end of the Cold War, when the United States emerged unrivaled and undisciplined by the bipolar balance of power. Equipped with unipolar power and liberal internationalist ideas, the United States found itself supporting the expansion of NATO and the European Union, engaging in humanitarian intervention, projecting itself into regional conflicts and civil wars, and pursuing violent regime change, most fatefully in the 2003 invasion of Iraq. The suggestion is that a more realist-oriented America would have pursued a more restrained vision of the national interest.[106]

The liberal tradition has certainly informed the conduct of American foreign policy. As I noted in chapter 6, during the Cold War, liberalism became a "fighting faith" that tied American power to a global struggle to protect the liberal democratic world when that world was under attack from powerful illiberal forces. A great contest between open societies and totalitarian challengers was an ideological struggle but also a military and geopolitical struggle. Leading liberal thinkers of the day, such as Arthur Schlesinger Jr., Isaiah Berlin, and Raymond Aron, considered the survival of the democratic way of life to be at extreme risk. Western liberal democracies had stumbled in the 1920s and 1930s by failing to respond to the instabilities and inequalities of capitalist society. In response, these Cold War liberals, as Jan-Werner Müller argues, sought to "craft a principled politics of freedom for the twentieth century."[107] Their view of the threats to liberal democracy focused on both the troubled internal politics of Western societies, where the political center was threatened by extremism on the Right and the Left, and the wider world-historical struggle then unfolding with the Soviet Union and international communism. Schlesinger's influential 1949 book *The Vital Center* epitomized this worldview. It offered a defense of pluralism and open societies and called for the continuation of New Deal–style reform by activist governments. But in response to the larger global challenge, Schlesinger urged collective action by the liberal democracies, led by the United States, to defend their institutions and the liberal international order from totalitarian rivals.[108] The challenge to liberal democracy was manifest in a worldwide struggle between alternative visions of modernity. Cold War liberalism offered a narrative that put liberal internationalism in the service of an activist American foreign policy.[109]

Is the American liberal tradition inherently interventionist? Do liberal principles predispose the United States to actively seek to impose democracy on other states? A long tradition of realist thinking has argued that they do. As Henry Kissinger maintains, "the idea that peace depends above all on promoting democratic institutions has remained a staple of American thought to the present day," and he traces this idea back to Woodrow Wilson.[110] The United States is often depicted as a "crusader state" seeking, under the sway of liberal ideas, to remake the world in its own image.[111] More recently, realist scholars have linked American liberalism to controversial American foreign policy actions in the wake of the September 11 terrorist attacks, such as the doctrine justifying preventive war and forcible regime change. John Mearsheimer argues that liberalism provides the impulse and legitimating rationale for repeated episodes of American military interventionism. Liberal ambitions spurred the United States to push Western institutions to the doorsteps of Russia and China and provided the rationale for the disastrous war in Iraq. Similarly, Michael Desch traces American interventionism to the founding ideas of liberal internationalism. He sees Kantian liberalism as providing the philosophical justification for military efforts to democratize illiberal sovereign states by force. In effect, the liberal tradition generates what David Hume called an "imprudent vehemence" toward illiberal regimes.[112]

These claims bring the debate back to the question of whether liberalism contains an "urge" to empire. Mearsheimer and Desch essentially take the view of liberalism that is elaborated by Uday Mehta in *Liberalism and Empire*. Here it is not empire but military interventionism that the leading liberal state uses to bring backward people and regimes into the modern world. Intervention and regime change are embedded in the assumptions that liberalism makes about the "state of nature" and the conditions for peace. Only when all states embrace representative government will liberal democracies be truly safe. But the urge to intervene to promote democracy is clearly contingent, not absolute. Most liberal internationalists would almost certainly agree that, all else being equal, liberal democracies would be safer in a world dominated by liberal democracies. But whether this justifies forcible regime change is another matter. Kant's view of intervention was surely more complicated—and contingent—than Desch admits. Kant did believe that a republican constitution is the ideal, he also acknowledged that even despotic states have a claim of legitimate authority that entitles them to nonintervention. Kant did argue that "perpetual peace" depends on all states developing republican forms of rule, but this does not generate a right by liberal states to bring about such a result by force.[113]

Michael Doyle has shown that liberalism is conflicted—even "congenitally confused"—on the question of intervention. Liberalism embraces principles that are in tension with each other. On one hand, liberal principles accord all states, including illiberal states, the right to noninterference, even when these states inflict harm on their own populations or violate their rights. On the other hand, liberalism also emphasizes that the rights of individuals in these societies must also be respected, and this opens the door—at least under extreme conditions—to intervention.[114] Doyle argues that Kant "made a strong case for respecting the right of non-intervention because it afforded a polity the necessary territorial space and political independence in which free and equal citizens could work out what their way of life would be."[115] But Kant could also imagine polities that so abused their people—committing massacres or genocide, for example—that the duty of nonintervention would not apply. This contingency, of course, raises the question of how liberal states should decide whether and how to respond.

Liberalism thus offers arguments for and against intervention. Georg Sørensen has described these alternative logics as the "liberalism of imposition" and the "liberalism of restraint."[116] The liberalism of imposition is manifest in the state's employment of power to expand liberal principles. John Stuart

Mill argues this position when he writes that noncivilized societies—which he calls "barbarous" nations—do not observe the rules and traditions of international morality, and therefore their independence does not merit full respect. Liberalism of restraint, Sørensen argues, stresses a different set of liberal values, such as "pluralism, non-intervention, respect for others, moderation, and peaceful cooperation on equal terms."[117] This is the vision that Gerry Simpson has called "charter liberalism," with its values embodied in the United Nations Charter. States are accorded equality of treatment, their sovereign independence is respected, and each state is allowed to determine how to establish its own rights and protections.[118] Restraint liberals recognize that some states will violate basic rights, but until some extreme line of violence and genocide is crossed diversity is tolerated, in the belief that over the long run, these societies will evolve toward universal standards of rights and decency.[119]

These debates within the liberal tradition burned fiercely during the years surrounding the Bush administration's invasion of Iraq. How much was liberal internationalism implicated in this decision? The Bush administration articulated a sweeping new doctrine of national security based on American global dominance, the preventive use of force, "coalitions of the willing," and the struggle between freedom and tyranny. In the spring of 2003, this doctrine provided the intellectual backdrop for the invasion of Iraq. As the invasion turned into a protracted war, the Bush administration increasingly invoked liberal internationalist ideas to justify its actions. In his now famous second inaugural address, George W. Bush stood on the steps of the US Capitol and proclaimed, "We are led, by events and common sense, to one conclusion: the survival of liberty in our land increasingly depends on the success of liberty in other lands."[120] The echoes of Woodrow Wilson and the Cold War liberal internationalism of Truman and Kennedy were unmistakable. But was Bush truly Wilson's heir? Liberal internationalists themselves debate this issue.[121] Some argue that Bush followed a "neoconservative" stand of liberal internationalism, focused on putting the full weight of American power behind bringing the "blessings of liberty" to oppressed people.[122] Others argue that this neoconservative turn in American foreign policy was a distortion of liberal internationalism and that the Bush grand strategy was more imperial than liberal. Multilateralism is at the heart of the liberal international vision, these people argue, but the Bush administration willfully put the United States above the rules and institutions of the liberal order. In the long run, liberal democracies will be safer and more secure in an international order undergirded by shared rules and norms, cooperative security, and mutual restraint—and the Bush administration was undermining such an order.[123] Liberal internationalists clearly differ on the importance of democracy promotion to their project, and on whether democracy is best promoted through force or example.[124]

But were the ideological origins of the Iraq War really traceable to liberal internationalism? The principal architects of this ill-fated venture were, by all accounts, Vice President Dick Cheney, Secretary of Defense Donald Rumsfeld, and Deputy Secretary of Defense Paul Wolfowitz.[125] It is difficult to describe the political ideology of any of these officials as liberal internationalism. For all three, the primary objective of the war was the preservation and extension of American primacy in a region important to American national interests. They saw Iraq as a regional revisionist state with a demonstrated record of chemical-weapons use and a long-standing ambition to acquire nuclear weapons, making it a military threat to American forces and allies in the region. The decisive defeat of Iraq was also meant to provide a worldwide demonstration of America's capacities and willingness to defend its global position against challengers such as North Korea and Iran and to dispel lingering doubts created during the Clinton years about America's willingness to use force. In the decade before the war, Cheney, Rumsfeld, and Wolfowitz had all been associated with efforts to enunciate a post–Cold War American grand strategy of preventing the emergence of a peer competitor.[126] All three had publicly urged the overthrow of the Saddam Hussein regime for more than a decade before the 2003 invasion. Their utterances betrayed no trace of liberal internationalism.

Put simply, the Bush administration's policy in Iraq was decidedly realist. Prominent academic realists opposed the war, offering eloquent critiques of American hubris and grand strategy.[127] But the case for war was also argued, at least initially, in realist terms. Democracy promotion was among the rolling rationales for the war offered by the Bush administration, but it is difficult to believe that this goal was the originating impulse for the war. It is more plausibly seen as the administration's public justification for the war and possibly a template for postwar Iraqi reconstruction. Democracy was not a core objective: it emerged later, as a program for making Iraq into a pillar of the hegemonic American order in the region.[128] Some liberal internationalists supported the war and others opposed it, but many of those supporters were less focused on democracy promotion than on the genuinely frightening threats that weapons of mass destruction posed and on the search for responses to this threat when deterrence and arms control were not effective. (It turned out, of course, that the reason Hussein could not be persuaded to give up his weapons of mass destruction was that he had nothing to give up, and he wanted to hide this fact from neighboring enemies like Iran.) Finding cooperative solutions to rising problems of security interdependence was at the top of the post–September 11 liberal internationalist agenda, but it tended to get lost in the controversies over the Iraq War.[129]

Even if one could disentangle American liberalism from power politics, it is not clear that a purely realist-oriented foreign policy would be more restrained or enlightened. There is no necessary link between liberal internationalism and coercive regime change. Liberalism may provide reasons to intervene abroad, but it also provides ideological and institutional mechanisms that restrain the exercise of military power. Realist critics think they can prevent another Iraq by removing liberal internationalist ideas from policymaking. But liberal internationalism also inspired the building of the wider system of postwar rules, institutions, and partnerships. Realists cannot assume that this system would have been built in a purely realist world of offshore balancing. If the goal is a "restrained" foreign policy, the postwar system of rules and institutions that ties the liberal democracies together under shared commitments and rules of conduct is surely part of the solution and not the problem.[130] A large part of the resistance to the Bush administration's war in Iraq was based on standards of conduct that the United States had championed. Western Europeans, for example, criticized the war as a transgression of liberal internationalist notions of sovereignty, multilateralism, and international law. Two scholars have called this "liberal anti-Americanism."[131] If military interventionism is not inherent in either liberalism or realism, the question comes down to the quality of political institutions and decision making. Does the United States learn from its mistakes? The lack of enthusiasm for new Iraqi-style interventions does suggest that foreign policy decision makers—liberal internationalists or not—do rethink their views.

The Revisionist Tradition

Liberal internationalism has been on each side of the global struggle—both for and against empire. The tradition's underlying ideas about the progress in human societies opened the door to liberal imperialism, an impulse also encouraged by Western notions of civilization and racial superiority. In the nineteenth century, the internationalist agenda of building an open, rules-based international order reconciled trade with colonial rule, international law with imperial order, and European dominance with universal-style claims of rights and property. Imperial internationalism and liberal internationalism were thus deeply entangled. But this urge for empire is contingent. Liberal internationalism rode into the twentieth century on the back of empire, but in that century it pushed empire off the global stage. Complicity with empire turned into complicity with political movements that championed self-determination, statehood, and universal rights of recognition and sovereignty.

In the twentieth century, liberal internationalism slowly—and then suddenly—planted its projects on the foundation of the Westphalian state system. The globalization of the Westphalian order was driven by many factors—normative, geopolitical, technological, and cultural. In this unfolding drama, the United States played a pivotal role as the most powerful state in the system and as the political and ideological embodiment of liberal modernity. Through two world wars, it acted to create a congenial international space for its way of life and expanding interests. But in doing this, it also undermined and defeated the great twentieth-century imperial projects— German, Japanese, and Soviet. Its pursuit of its hegemonic interests had system consequences, and formal empire was one of the casualties. The

United States may or may not have been more "enlightened" than the other great powers, but its geopolitical interests were different. It needed a "grand area" that was effectively global in scope, and empires in Asia and elsewhere stood in the way. In this sense, the United States was doing what other great powers did—trying to shape its international environment for self-interested reasons. But the global scale and reach of American power ultimately led it to oppose the imperial organization of the world. Liberal internationalism affiliated itself with this shift in the logic of global leadership.

Scholars who see continuities in imperial projects across the centuries might look at the United States as the first "global empire." But a global empire, simply by aspiring to span the world, is a fundamentally different sort of project from the classic empires of the past. Classic empires are based on efforts to carve out exclusive zones or blocs. A globe-spanning political order, by contrast, is premised by definition on breaking down and abolishing exclusive zones and blocs. Organizing and managing a global system requires a different set of rules and institutions from the set required in an imperial order. It needs universal rules and institutions. The task of building global order takes states down a road different from that taken by imperial projects of the past. In taking that road, the United States tied itself to the two great projects that were unfolding during this era—the Westphalian project and the liberal international project. The United States did not put these schemes in motion, but it harnessed them as it built the postwar order. They shaped the logic and character of the American-led order and undercut empire as the dominant political form.

Formal empire disappeared in the second half of the twentieth century, but American interventionism did not. Liberal internationalism is implicated in almost constant military interventions during the era of American global dominance. Trying to disentangle the American liberal tradition from realist and other logics of foreign policy demands that one rely on counterfactual claims: what foreign policy would the United States have pursued during the Cold War and post–Cold War decades if it were not a liberal great power, or if it were not seized by liberal internationalist ideas? What is clear is that the American liberal tradition cuts both ways. It has legitimated interventionism, but it has also inspired ideas and institutions that restrain interventionism. The most telling critique of liberal internationalism is not its urge for empire or tendency to pursue coercive regime change. It is the opposite: that liberal internationalism is too often weak and easily co-opted by other agendas.

EIGHT

The Crisis of the Post–Cold War Liberal Order

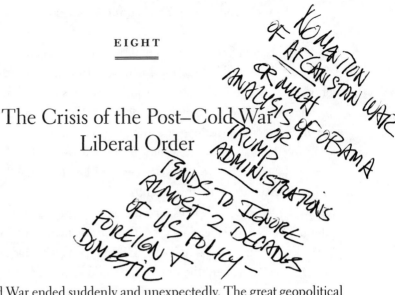

[Handwritten annotations: "No Mention of Afghanistan war or much analysis of Obama or Trump administrations. Tends to ignore almost 2 decades of US policy — foreign + domestic"]

The Cold War ended suddenly and unexpectedly. The great geopolitical struggle between the United States and the Soviet Union ceased. One era of great-power relations ended and another began. But it was a historical turning point unlike the postwar moments of 1815, 1919, and 1945. In 1991, the old bipolar order collapsed without a great-power war. The Cold War ended not with a military victory but with a political and ideological triumph: the collapse of the Soviet Union—and with it, the political and ideological collapse of communism. Moreover, unlike what had occurred at past post-war moments, the global system was not overturned. Quite the contrary—the world that the United States and its allies created after World War II remained intact. The end of the Cold War simply consolidated and expanded this order. The Soviet bloc, estranged from the West for half a century, collapsed and fitfully sought a place within the West, at least for a while.

What followed in the 1990s was the closest the world has come to a "liberal moment." The great contest between liberal democracy and communism seemed to be settled. The American-led order was left standing, and no rival geopolitical or ideological challengers were in view. "While the collapse of communism did not bring an end of history," David A. Bell writes, "it did, briefly, seem to establish a worldwide consensus." The wars and upheavals of the twentieth century appeared to have rendered a verdict as to which social and political system was superior. "That system was what could be called the liberal ideal, constructed around representative democracy,

[Handwritten annotation: "See p. 303"]

human rights, and free-market capitalism complemented by a strong social safety net."[1] The world of the 1930s had been turned on its head. The question was not whether liberal democracies would survive, but how to organize relations within an expanding world of liberal democracies, unchallenged by grand ideological rivalries or competing centers of power.

During the first decade after the Cold War, democracy and markets flourished worldwide. The progressive forces of history that liberal internationalists had invoked since the nineteenth century seemed alive and well, and were working to reshape and expand the liberal democratic core of the global system. The North American Free Trade Agreement (NAFTA), the Asia-Pacific Economic Cooperation (APEC), and the World Trade Organization (WTO) signaled a strengthening of the world economy's rules and institutions. The European Union opened its doors to new members and continued on its path of political and economic integration. NATO expanded eastward and the US-Japan alliance was renewed. Russia became a quasi-member of the West, joining the G-7 process to create a new G-8, and China became Washington's "strategic partner." President Clinton's policy of building post–Cold War order around expanding markets, democracy, and institutions was the seeming embodiment of the liberal vision of international order. By the end of the 1990s, American officials were describing the United States as the world's "indispensable nation," using its power, ideas, and inheritance of institutions and partnerships to underwrite global order. For the first time in the modern era, scholars could talk about a unipolar world order.

But this moment did not last. Just two decades after the "liberal ideal" swept the world, liberal democracy and liberal internationalism were in retreat. The dark forces that were supposedly banished from the West—illiberalism, autocracy, nationalism, protectionism, spheres of influence, territorial revisionism—reasserted themselves. China and Russia dashed all hopes that they would quickly transition to democracy and support the liberal world order. To the contrary, they strengthened their authoritarian systems at home and flouted liberal norms abroad. Even more stunning, the United States and Great Britain seemed to step back from their role as champions of liberal international order. For the first time since the 1930s, the United States, with the election of Donald Trump in 2016, has had a president who was actively hostile to liberal internationalism. Trade, alliances, international law, multilateralism, torture and human rights—on all these issues, the American president made statements and pursued policies that, if fully realized, would effectively end the country's role as leader of the liberal international order. Britain's vote to leave the European Union (EU), and myriad other troubles besetting Europe, appeared to mark an end to the long postwar project of building a greater union. Meanwhile, liberal democracy came under threat in all corners of the globe, as varieties of authoritarianism rose to new salience in Hungary, Poland, the Philippines, Turkey, Brazil, and elsewhere. Across the liberal democratic world, populist, nationalist, and xenophobic strands of backlash politics proliferated.[2]

This is where we stand today. The worldwide consensus on the liberal ideal, if it ever truly existed, has vanished. What explains this reversal in fortunes? If the liberal international order is in crisis, what sort of crisis is it and what are its sources?

It is important to recall that the postwar liberal order did not begin as a global order. It was built "inside" half of a bipolar system as part of a larger geopolitical project of waging a global Cold War. Its original bargains, institutions, and social purposes were tied to the West, American leadership, and the global struggle against Soviet communism. When the Cold War ended, this inside order became the outside order. As the Soviet Union collapsed, the great rival of liberal internationalism was swept away, and the American-led order expanded outward. Liberal internationalism was globalized. Although this was seen as a moment of triumph of Western liberal democracies, the globalization of the liberal order put in motion two shifts that later became sources of crisis. First, it upended the political foundations of the liberal order. As new states entered the system, the old bargains and institutions that provided stability and governance were overrun. A wider array of states—with more diverse ideologies and agendas—were now part of the order. This triggered a crisis of authority: new bargains, roles, and responsibilities were now required as precisely the moment when the United States and its old allies were no longer in a position to assign them. These struggles over governance and authority continue today. Second, the globalization of the liberal order weakened its capacity to function as a security community. This can be called a crisis of social purpose. In its Cold War configuration, the liberal order was a sort of full-service security community, enhancing the capacity of Western governments to pursue policies of economic and social protection and advancement. As liberal internationalism became the platform for the wider global order, this shared social purpose eroded.

Taking all these elements together, the crisis of liberal order can be understood as a crisis of success, in the sense that its troubles emerged from its post–Cold War expansion. Put differently, the troubles might be seen as a "Polanyi crisis"—turmoil and instability resulting from the rapid mobilization and spread of global capitalism, market society, and complex interdependence, all of which have overrun the political foundations that supported global capitalism's birth and development.[3] It is not, fundamentally, what might be called an "E. H. Carr crisis," in which liberal internationalism fails because of the return of great-power politics and the problems of anarchy.[4] Even though China and Russia are real and dangerous competitors, the troubles facing liberal internationalism are not primarily driven by a return of geopolitical conflict. The problems of liberal order are due less to the problems of anarchy and more to the problems of modernity—to the challenge of reestablishing stable foundations of liberal capitalist democracy.

I make this argument in four steps. First, I look at the restructuring of the international system after the Cold War and its implications for liberal order. Here the focus is on the globalization of liberal internationalism. The expansive nature of liberal order is rooted in its logic of multilateral and open relations. The American hegemonic political order in which liberal internationalism was embedded also contained a logic that facilitated the expansion of the order after the Cold War. Second, I offer an account of the sources of the liberal order's crisis, focusing on the erosion of its institutional and political foundations and the hollowing out of its social purposes. These are the twin crises of authority and community that have unfolded as liberal order has expanded. In effect, the liberal order has become wider but shallower. The erosion of domestic social supports within the Western liberal democracies—the system of embedded liberalism—is at the root of the breakdown. Third, I look at the ways in which China and Russia have responded to the post–Cold War globalization of liberal order. The bargains and partnerships that facilitated the integration of Germany and Japan into the postwar liberal hegemonic order could not be extended to China and Russia on terms that either state could accept. Fourth, I identify the sources of stability and resilience in the contemporary liberal international order. While the Cold War–era liberal order took the form of a relatively coherent, if loosely organized, political community, the expanded post–Cold War liberal order is fragmented into various international realms. It has become less a matter of being either "in" or "out." This has allowed states—particularly illiberal states such as China and Russia—to pick and choose their connections to it. The globalized liberal order contains many layers and realms of order, each with its own logic and operation within the wider system. On one hand, this fragmentation weakens the liberal order. But on the other hand it has also created a more diverse array of constituencies and interests that support an open, rules-based system.

The Globalization of Liberalism

The end of the Cold War was a tale of two orders, both forged in the 1940s. One of these was built in response to the threats and imperatives that emerged in the struggle with the Soviet Union. This was the bipolar order organized around deterrence, containment, and ideological struggle between the two superpowers, and it ended with the fall of the Soviet Union. The other was the U.S.-led international order built inside the bipolar system; this is the Western liberal order. It was reinforced by the Cold War but was constructed, as we have seen, as a distinct project dating back to the early decades of the twentieth century. Under the cover of the Cold War, a revolution in relations among Western great powers rebuilt this order around binding security ties, managed open markets, social protections, multilateral cooperation, and American hegemonic leadership. After the Cold War, this order provided the liberal logic for the wider international system.

The end of the Cold War was an "incredibly swift transition," Adam Roberts observes, "dramatic, decisive, and remarkably peaceful."[5] Earlier great wars had destroyed and discredited previous international orders and opened the way for sweeping negotiations over the basic rules and principles of a new order. But the American-led system not only survived the end of the Cold War but was widely seen as responsible for the West's triumph. The Cold War was a bipolar competition between two ways of organizing the modern world, and the collapse of the Soviet Union was seen to render a verdict. Western policy toward the Soviet Union was vindicated, as were the relations among the advanced industrial democracies. In this sense, the end of the Cold War was a conservative event. It entailed the peaceful capitulation of the Soviet Union—reluctant, to be sure, and not on the terms that Mikhail Gorbachev, the last Soviet premier, had hoped for. But the fall of the Soviet "pole" left in place the American "pole," and the American-led rules, institutions, and relationships that had been built during the Cold War became the core of the post–Cold War order.[6]

The end of the Cold War was felt most immediately and profoundly in West Germany, which saw the peaceful end of hostilities and the prospect of national reunification as a ratification of its western side's long postwar commitment to the European project and the Western rules-based order. The European Community and the Atlantic Alliance had provided the framework for West Germany to turn itself into a stable parliamentary democracy and pioneer its own distinctive social market society. They would now provide the framework for unifying Germany and integrating its eastern neighbors into a united Europe. In arguing for unification to a wary Europe and Russia in 1990, German foreign minister Hans-Dietrich Genscher quoted the novelist Thomas Mann: "What we seek is a European Germany, not a German Europe."[7] The Western liberal order and the European project within it allowed Germany and Europe to solve a geopolitical problem that had remained elusive since the 1870s: reconciling a powerful Germany with a stable European state system. The German people mostly welcomed this transition because it let them see their country in a new light. After a dark past, they were now on the right side of history, offering a model to Europe and the world. "The unification of Germany and the more gradual unification of the European continent were seen as a template of the future for all other regions of the world," argues Thomas Bagger, a German diplomat.

"It defined the prism through which Germans watched, analyzed and interpreted global events."[8]

America's first impulse after the Cold War was to build on the logic of this Western liberal order. President George H. W. Bush, who took office as the Soviet Union was breaking up, described the coming order in liberal internationalist terms. Its underpinnings would be democracy, open trade, and international law. "Great nations of the world are moving toward democracy through the door of freedom," Bush said in his 1989 inaugural address. "We know how to secure a more just and prosperous life for man on earth: through free markets, free speech, free elections, and the exercise of free will unhampered by the state."[9] In a speech later that year to the United Nations, he argued that democracy was on the march and commerce was a force for progress. In this "new world order," the United Nations and multilateral institutions were to play a critical role in "the central issue of our time," that "the nations of the world might come to agree that law, not force, shall govern."[10] The United States would stand at the center of this expanding world of liberal democracy and multilateral cooperation, in what Bush called a "widening circle of freedom." With the Cold War over, the United States invited the world into its Western liberal order.[11]

This liberal international vision was reflected in the work of the Bush administration, which sought to expand regional and global institutions in both security and economic cooperation. In relations toward Europe, State Department officials began a series of institutional steps: the evolution of NATO to include associate relations with countries to the east, the creation of more formal institutional relations with the European Community, and an expanded role for the Conference on Security Cooperation in Europe.[12] In the Western Hemisphere, the Bush administration pushed for the North American Free Trade Agreement and for closer ties with South America. In East Asia, it used the APEC forum to create more institutional links in the region, demonstrate American commitment, and ensure that Asian regionalism moved in a trans-Pacific direction. Bush's secretary of state, James Baker, later likened his administration's post–Cold War order-building strategy to the American strategy after 1945: "Men like Truman and Acheson were above all, though we sometimes forget it, institution builders. They fostered the economic institutions . . . that brought unparalleled prosperity. . . . At a time of similar opportunity and risk, I believed we should take a leaf from their book."[13]

This orientation toward expanding the Western liberal order continued under President Clinton, who tried to use multilateral institutions to stabilize and integrate the emerging market democracies into the advanced democratic world. Anthony Lake, Clinton's national security adviser, said the strategy was to "strengthen the community of market democracies" and "foster and consolidate new democracies and market economies where possible." The United States would help "democracy and market economies take root," which would in turn expand and strengthen the Western democratic order.[14] This strategy primarily targeted those parts of the world that were beginning the transition to market democracy: countries in Central and Eastern Europe and the Asia-Pacific region. Domestic reforms in these countries would be encouraged—and locked in if possible—through new trade pacts and security partnerships. In the formal statement of its strategy, the Clinton administration called for a multilateral approach to major foreign policy challenges like nuclear proliferation, regional instability, and unfair trade practices.[15] Multilateral cooperation would provide a foundation for an expanding liberal democratic world.[16]

By the end of the 1990s, the consolidation and expansion of the liberal international order appeared to be well under way. NATO was expanded eastward to include states that had previously been in the Warsaw Pact. This expansion was controversial, and caused leading American foreign policy figures to publicly warn that it could undermine fragile relations with Russia. But the Clinton administration wanted to show solidarity with countries making democratic transitions—and to institutionally embed these new entrants into the Western order.[17] Because they had no hostile intentions toward Russia, administration policymakers assumed Russia could be persuaded that NATO expansion was not a threat. NAFTA and APEC were also pursued as mechanisms to lock in the worldwide movement, begun in the 1980s, toward economic and trade liberalization. The creation of the World Trade Organization in 1995 was a further attempt to expand and strengthen the institutional foundations of liberal international order. Building on the old General Agreement on Tariffs and Trade, the WTO marked a major step in formalizing international trade law. An organization was established with an independent secretariat, a dispute-settlement mechanism, and an expanded framework for trade cooperation.[18] In an interview in 2006, Clinton made the point directly: "I was heavily influenced by the success of the post–World War II and cold war multilateral organizations. . . . I saw that they worked, and at the end of the Cold War, I saw an opportunity for the first time in history to globalize them in a way that the East-West division had prevented."[19] The postwar era was not so much a "unipolar moment" as a "multilateral moment," an opportunity for the United States to shape the world in a way that would outlast momentary power advantages.[20]

The Clinton administration's decision to invite China to join the WTO was perhaps the capstone of this liberal internationalist strategy. Clinton saw China's rise as part of a rapidly unfolding globalization of the world system. The United States would gain in this globalizing world, China would be transformed, and its integration into the world economic system would be a win-win proposition. China's involvement in the trade system would have liberalizing effects on its society, creating domestic constituencies for openness and political reform. Once it became enmeshed in the WTO's liberal rules and practices and began to realize the benefits of trade and economic growth, incentives would be generated to liberalize its domestic economy and institutions. This was not a naive expectation that China would turn into a Western-style democracy. The assumption was that economic openness would have a liberalizing effect on Chinese society and that this would lead to bottom-up demands for political change.[21] In May 2000, Congress voted to award China permanent normal trade relations, and effectively backed China's bid for WTO membership. Clinton emphasized the liberal logic of this move. "By joining the WTO, China is not simply agreeing to import more of our products; it is agreeing to import one of democracy's most cherished values: economic freedom."[22] China was growing rapidly and its impact on the world economy was unavoidable. WTO membership would bias its ascent in the direction of Western norms and practices. At this transitional moment, globalization was seen as a liberalizing force and, as one administration official put it, Clinton "bet his presidency on globalization."[23]

This American engagement strategy with China extended into the George W. Bush administration. China would grow both economically and militarily, but through the dynamics of interdependence it would also become more democratic at home and cooperative abroad. "Open trade is a force for freedom in China. . . . Free trade has introduced new technologies that offer Chinese people access to uncensored information and democratic ideas," President George W. Bush argued in May 2001. "When we open trade, we open minds."[24] Several years later, Deputy Secretary of State Robert Zoellick provided an explicit statement of this logic in a speech urging China to take on the role of a "responsible stakeholder." Zoellick maintained that China was a major beneficiary of the American-led international order, and the United States expected it to act responsibly. China would gain voice and leadership in exchange for supporting the existing international order—and its Western-defined values and priorities. Zoellick urged China to "adjust to the rules developed over the last century." If it did, it could expect to become a leading state within this order: "It would work with us to sustain the international system that has enabled its success."[25] The door to China's integration into the Western liberal order was open.

Meanwhile, economic and political liberalism spread worldwide. Having watched in the 1980s as the diverging economic fortunes of the Soviet system and export-oriented capitalist states became increasingly apparent, governments in the 1990s increasingly engaged in market-oriented economic reforms—liberalization of their foreign economic policies, privatization, and deregulation. Economic liberalism was manifest in a wide range of policies. The privatization of state enterprises, as Beth Simmons, Frank Dobbin, and Geoffrey Garrett observe, "went from an iconoclastic policy idea in Margaret Thatcher's 1979 British election manifesto to a major element of economic policy in both the developed and developing world over the course of twenty years."[26] During the same period, countries increasingly opened their economies to cross-border flows of capital and trade. Internationally, the World Bank, the International Monetary Fund (IMF), and other financial institutions embraced the Washington Consensus, proscribing market-oriented

policies for borrowing countries and governments pursuing economic reforms. IMF lending and world trade grew rapidly. By the turn of the century,
developing countries accounted for 47 percent of world gross national product and a third of world trade.[27] Countries everywhere began to integrate into
the world economy and operate within its expanding system of rules and
institutions.

The 1980s and 1990s were also a period of political liberalization when a
"third wave" of democratization and liberal constitutionalism spread around
the world.[28] In what Simmons, Dobbin, and Garrett call the "headline sta-
tistic of the late twentieth century," the proportion of democratic countries
more than doubled, rising from under 30 percent in the early 1980s to almost 60 percent in the first decade of the twenty-first century. (The number
of sovereign states in the world also doubled in these decades.)[29] Political transitions to democracy manifested different patterns across regions. Latin
American countries began to democratize in the 1970s, and East Asia and
the Pacific followed in the 1980s. The fall of the Berlin Wall and the collapse of communism in the former Soviet bloc triggered a wave of democratization across Eastern Europe.[30] The end of Cold War polarization also
undermined many military and one-party dictatorships that had previously
been backed by one of the superpowers. Not all the resulting regime changes
fully crossed the democratic threshold. Some authoritarian regimes used par-
tial liberalization as a way of holding on to autocratic rule.[31] Other regimes,
which did engage in more thoroughgoing democratic transitions, have since
reverted to authoritarianism. But as the 1990s ended, democracy appeared
to be on the march.[32]

The broad trends toward economic and political liberalism during the last
decades of the twentieth century are captured in figure 8.1, which tracks shifts
in three indicators of liberalization from 1980 to 2004. The first indicator
shows the percentage of government revenue that comes from the privatization of state ownership, which is an indicator of domestic economic liberalization. The second is a measure of the global average of financial
openness—or capital account openness—which shows the degree of foreign
economic liberalization. The third indicator shows the proportion of democratic countries in the world.

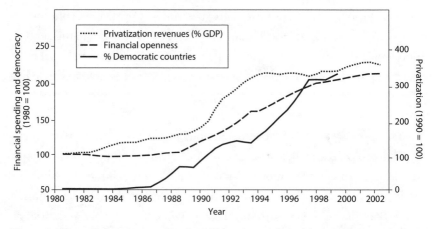

Figure 8.1. Spread of economic and political liberalism. Adapted from Beth Simmons, Frank Dobbin, and Geoffrey Garrett, "Introduction: The Diffusion of Liberalization," in Beth Simmons, Frank Dobbin, and Geoffrey Garrett, eds., *The Global Diffusion of Markets and Democracy* (New York: Cambridge University Press, 2008), p. 3.

The confluence of these trends shows that the shifts toward liberal democracy and an open world economy were simultaneous and reinforcing during the decades. The spread of economic and political liberalism was driven by a variety of forces, including, importantly, that capitalist democracies were increasingly outperforming countries in the Soviet bloc. This was true well before the end of the Cold War. With the collapse of the Soviet Union, communism disappeared as a grand alternative to liberal capitalist democracy. In the meantime, the United States and the other leading capitalist states increasingly seemed to provide the world with an attractive model for domestic and foreign economic reform. The IMF, World Bank, and other institutions provided the policy ideas and resources that reinforced this liberalization movement. The United States put its unrivaled geopolitical and ideological weight behind the movement, supporting the expansion of regional and global institutions that would facilitate and lock in liberal economic and political transitions.[33] The Western liberal subsystem of the Cold War bipolar world was spreading outward, providing the ideals and institutions for a one-world global order.

As the twentieth century ended, the United States found itself at the center of an expanding liberal international order. In one sense, the spread of political and economic liberalism reflected the shifting distribution of power. The collapse of the Soviet Union left the United States as the unipolar power. This one nation possessed such a disproportionate share of material capabilities that it was unambiguously in a class by itself. Given its unipolar position, the spread of economic and political liberalism is easy to explain. The character of the international order reflected the orientation of its most powerful state. The United States used its commanding position to push liberalism outward into the world. There were no alternative centers of power and no other games in town. But the causal arrows also flow in the opposite direction. In important respects, unipolarity was not the cause but the consequence of liberal order. Unipolarity was created by a distinctive material distribution of capabilities, but also by the absence of other states attempting to become poles. A pole is not only an aggregation of power but a hub of institutions and relationships that states use to connect to other states.[34] What made the United States unipolar was not only its unrivaled possession of hard power, denominated in military, technological, and economic assets; it was also that America was situated at the center of liberal international order that other states sought to join.[35] Power created order, but order also created power. Unipolarity emerged in the post–Cold War period because alternative poles, seen not just as projectors of power but as attractors of allegiance, fell away.[36]

Several features of the post–Cold War liberal order made it easier for states to join it rather than resist it or balance against it. First, the order was organized around multilateral rules and institutions. This made it relatively easy for states to make political and economic transitions and apply for membership. Multilateral economic organizations, starting with the Bretton Woods institutions, were designed to be expandable. The specific criteria for entry into regional and global institutions varied across the system. But the underlying logic of multilateralism was that states meeting the standards are welcome to join, which biased the post–Cold War transitional moment in favor of integration and expansion. Beyond this, the liberal order attracted transitioning states because it offered benefits and protections. In effect, it provided "goods and services" for states that affiliated with it. The most basic of these services was security protection. Other goods and services included access to markets, foreign aid, and technical assistance. To be inside the order was to gain favorable terms in an open system of trade and investment. Institutions like the IMF and the World Bank provided standby assistance when developing economies entered a crisis. In effect, the liberal order was an intergovernmental club in which membership had its privileges.[37] Third, to the extent that the United States and the other powerful states in the system also operated inside this order—respecting its rules and institutions—smaller states had some reassurance that these leading states would not simply coerce and dominate them. Obviously, the United States did sometimes employ coercion, intervention, and crude forms of power politics, but it was at least possible for states undergoing liberal transitions to see complexities and institutional restraints in the American exercise of hegemonic power. The institutional underpinnings of the liberal order made America's material power position both more durable and less threatening to other states. To join the liberal order was to gain voice opportunities and institutional access to the world's most powerful state.[38] In these ways, the liberal order biased the strategic direction of states toward integration and participation.

The world that emerged in the aftermath of the Cold War was both surprising and remarkable. It was surprising to many observers that the Western liberal order built during the Cold War survived the end of this bipolar struggle. Balance-of-power realists, in particular, predicted that NATO and the other Western institutions created in response to the Soviet threat would not remain in place—let alone expand—when that threat disappeared.[39] What these observers missed was that the Western liberal democracies' order-building project had begun before and had been pursued in the shadows of the Cold War. This was a product of the revolution in relations within postwar Europe and between Europe, the United States, and the wider world of liberal democracies. It was the project driven by the disasters of the 1930s and efforts to put the Western liberal capitalist countries on a more stable foundation. The order that undergirded the wider global system after the collapse of Soviet communism did not need to be constructed, unlike in 1815, 1919, and 1945, because it was already in place.

The Crisis of the Liberal Order

During the Cold War, the American-led liberal order was lodged and its foundation was laid within the Western side of the bipolar world system. After the collapse of the Soviet Union, as the nucleus of an expanding global system, this liberal order was freed from its Cold War foundations and became the platform for an expanding global system of liberal democracy, markets, and complex interdependence. A worldwide "liberal moment" had arrived. Yet at this very moment, the seeds of crisis were planted. The globalization of liberal order was more fraught than many liberal internationalists appreciated at the time. During the Cold War, the bipolar global system served to reinforce the roles, commitments, and community that were together manifest as the American-led international order. The Cold War-era Western order was not simply an alliance or a grouping of trading partners. It was a loosely functioning political order with institutions, bargains, and shared understandings of its social purposes. The crisis of liberal internationalism can be seen as a slow-motion reaction to the global expansion of this postwar Western order. The characteristics of the liberal order that made it stable and resilient during the Cold War, and thus attractive to transitioning states after the Cold War, were eroded as it globalized.

Specifically, the expansion of liberal internationalism weakened and undermined two facets of the postwar liberal order. One was the order's governance logic: its political bargains, institutional commitments, and authority relations. The other was its social purposes and embedded liberal protections. In both these dimensions, the underpinnings of the postwar liberal order have given way. The order has lost the shared understanding of itself as a "security community," a group of like-minded states cooperating for mutual protection and advancement.[40] And it has become weaker, thinner, and less connected to the political and economic well-being of the societies and constituencies at its core. We can look at these two facets in turn.

Governance and Authority Relations

The globalization of the liberal order created problems of governance and authority. During the Cold War, the Western-oriented liberal order was led by the United States, Europe, and Japan, and organized around a complex array of bargains, working relationships, and institutions. In the early postwar years, most of the core agreements about trade, finance, and monetary relations were hammered out between the United States and Britain. West Germany and Japan later became "junior partners" in a Western-oriented trilateral system. These countries did not agree on everything, but relative to the rest of the world, they were a small and homogeneous group of states. Their economies converged, their interests were aligned, and they generally trusted each other. They were also on the same side of the Cold War, and the American-led alliance system reinforced cooperation. This system of alliances made it easier for the United States and its partners to make commitments and bear burdens and for European and Asian states to accept American leadership. In this sense, the Cold War liberal order reinforced the belief that the liberal democracies were involved in a common political project.

At the heart of this order was a set of strategic bargains between the United States and its economic and security partners, especially West Germany and Japan. As the leading state, the United States provided them with security protection and maintained a relatively open domestic market to absorb their exports. In return, these partners held US dollars, allowing the United States to run balance-of-payments deficits without facing the adjustment requirements of other states.[41] This arrangement allowed the United States to be a generous provider of both security and markets. The United States underwrote the rules and institutions of the order while reserving the right to act unilaterally to protect its own national interests. Its partners enjoyed the benefits of these bargains. They gained access to the American market and raw materials and were protected by American military power. Alliance-based security protection also allowed these states to devote greater resources to domestic economic growth and competitiveness.[42] The United States, as the dominant power, placed itself within a complex of institutions that gave its partners regular channels of access to Washington policymaking.[43] The United States played the role of liberal hegemon, supporting openness and stability across the order. In return, its partners supported the United States in the Cold War.

But since the Cold War ended, the set of bargains that held this core grouping together has slowly weakened. To be sure, these states' overall orientation has remained remarkably stable. Japan and Western Europe, led by Germany, continued through the 1990s and into the current period to be committed to open trade relations and alliance ties with the United States. The United States remained committed to leading—indeed expanding—the liberal order. But as Michael Mastanduno argues, the key sources of American leverage behind the Cold War–era hegemonic bargains—the security dependence of its partners, the unique position of the dollar, and the indispensability of its market—have eroded.[44] The end of the Cold War eliminated the common threat that had made NATO and the US-Japan alliance necessary. After the September 11 terrorist attacks and the American invasion of Iraq, the security challenges that had united the leading liberal democracies were less fully aligned. The expansion of the world economy, led by the rise of China, meant that the American market was no longer the indispensable engine of global economic growth. Germany and Japan remain tied to the American market, but both are increasingly integrated into their own regional trading and production systems; and because of this, they have found it less necessary to finance US deficits, by holding dollars, or to play the role of junior partners. In these various ways, the old security and economic bargains between the United States and its key partners have eroded.

Even if the old trilateral partnerships endure, they are no longer at the center of all markets and exchanges. The rise of China, in particular, has altered the center of gravity of the world economy. In 2010, China passed Japan to become the world's second-largest economy in market-exchange terms, and it is closing in on the United States. Since it began its market reforms, China's foreign trade has expanded rapidly, from approximately $20 billion in 1978 to $500 billion in 2000 to $3 trillion in 2016. In the past two decades, China has become the hub of fast-growing regional economies linked together by trade and manufacturing networks. When the Cold War ended, the United States was the leading trade partner with Japan, South Korea, and most of the countries of Southeast Asia. Three decades later, China holds this position. In 2015, it also became America's largest trading partner.[45] As its economy has grown, China has also increased its military capabilities and expanded its geopolitical ambitions in East Asia and around the world. It is now both a major player in the world economy and a rival of American hegemony in East Asia and beyond.

These new circumstances complicated American governance of the liberal international order. It is now China—not Germany and Japan—that the United States must engage in managing the world economy. But the trilateral economic and security bargains that underlay the Cold War liberal order and its expansion in the 1990s are not easily re-created in US-China relations. As I noted earlier, the United States did offer a hegemonic bargain to China. Beginning with George H. W. Bush, each post–Cold War American president—until Donald Trump—tried to entice China into the role of "responsible stakeholder." In the 1990s, China seemed to agree to this bargain. It joined the WTO and accepted the market-opening commitments that came with developing-country membership. In the decade after it entered the WTO, China's imports and exports expanded rapidly. It did not actively challenge the American security position in East Asia and it agreed to hold large quantities of US Treasury securities. China articulated a grand strategy of "peaceful rise," it integrated into the world trade and financial systems, and enjoyed rapid economic growth.[46] Seen from Washington, China was growing rapidly and becoming powerful, but it was doing so, at least loosely, within a framework of Western-oriented rules and institutions that would bias its political development in an open and liberal direction.

Over the past decade, this liberal hegemonic bargain began to break down. China got what it expected—access to the world trading system and achievement of rapid economic growth—but it did not undertake the liberal reforms that Western governments expected in return. Under President Xi, China became more illiberal, more nationalistic, and more assertive. Its military buildup, expansive maritime claims, and assertive economic diplomacy were increasingly seen by Washington as direct challenges to America's hegemony in the region. As Mastanduno argues, "Xi's China has acted less like a rule taker, even less as a responsible stakeholder, and more as a nascent rule maker."[47] Starting with the Obama administration, the United States responded by looking for ways to counter China's emerging rule-making role in Asia and the world economy. President Obama announced a "pivot to

Asia," seeking to reassure allies of America's economic and security commitment to the region. At the center of this pivot was the Trans-Pacific Partnership (TPP), a framework for negotiating closer trade ties between the United States and its East Asian partners. While the TPP was expected to generate economic gains, Obama defended it as an initiative to help ensure that China would not "write the rules of the global economy."[48] It was also seen as a way to strengthen ties to allies and forge new ties with countries, which would be necessary to form a counterweight to growing Chinese power. By then, liberal anticipations that China would integrate itself into the liberal international order as a responsible stakeholder had all but disappeared.[49]

Given a pathway into the expanding post–Cold War liberal order, China achieved rapid and dramatic economic success. But this very success has undermined the hegemonic bargains holding the order together. As China has become an economic peer of the United States, it has been increasingly discontented with the role of a junior partner or rule taker. During the Cold War and the 1990s, the liberal international order was structured around bargains between the United States, Western Europe, and Japan, which were embedded in an alliance system that made it easier for these states to settle their differences. But China is growing powerful outside this alliance system, and its sheer size makes it a more independent player in the world economy. It thus sits both inside and outside the post–Cold War liberal international order. It is sufficiently large and integrated into the world economy to be critical to the stable functioning of this order. But it is also sufficiently outside it—and outside the liberal democratic world—to make agreements on the governance of the order very difficult.

The changing position of the United States has also unsettled the liberal order. American unipolarity after the Cold War did not trigger immediate efforts at great-power balancing in part because China and Russia were not yet in a position to challenge the United States. But the other powers also felt less need for balancing because the American-led order was built on a foundation of rules, institutions, and strategic bargains that shaped and restrained the way power was exercised. Nonetheless, the United States did not entirely escape reactions to its unrivaled power. As the world entered its unipolar moment, American power was increasingly an issue in world politics.

During the Cold War, American power had a functional role in the system: it served as a balance against Soviet power. With the sudden emergence of unipolarity, American power was both less constrained and less functional. New debates emerged about American hegemonic power. What would restrain it? How credible was America's commitment to an open, rules-based international order?[50] The American war in Iraq and the Global War on Terror exacerbated these worries. The 2008 financial crisis, which began in the United States, also raised questions about the American economic model and its commitment to manage the open world system. With the Trump administration, the global reaction to American power has taken a new and dramatic turn. It is no longer a question of whether the United States will exercise power outside of a preexisting system of rules and institutions, but of how fully it is bent upon undermining that order. The entrance of the Trump administration has caused the political crisis of the liberal order to crescendo.[51]

The globalization of economic and political liberalism, in short, put in motion forces that undermined the governance logic of the order. As increasingly diverse states entered the order with new visions and agendas, the democratic world became no longer primarily Anglo-American or even Western. The liberal democratic world was expanding, but expansion made it a less coherent political community. The post–Cold War era also brought into play new and complex global issues, such as climate change, terrorism, weapons proliferation, and the growing challenges of interdependence. It was particularly hard for states in different regions, with different political orientations and levels of development, to reach consensus over these issues that raise fundamental questions of authority and governance. Who pays, who adjusts, who leads? How would authority across the expanding liberal order be redistributed among rising non-Western states? The old coalition—led by the United States, Europe, and Japan—built a postwar order on layers of bargains, institutions, and working relationships. But this old trilateral core is no longer as central to the global system as it once was. The crisis of liberal order today is partly a problem of how to reorganize its governance. The old foundations have weakened, but new bargains and governance relationships have yet to be negotiated.[52]

NO 2 SENSE

Social Purpose and Embedded Liberalism

It is also a crisis of social purpose and embedded liberalism. During the Cold War, the core states that formed the Western liberal order had a shared sense that they lived inside a community of liberal democracies—a political order that generated security and economic well-being for those within it. For most people, to be inside this order was to be better off than those outside it. Liberal democracies were able to reconcile economic openness and social protections within an organized system of multilateral cooperation. Together, the Western-oriented liberal order had features of what could be called a security community—a sort of mutual-protection society. But in more recent decades, as the liberal order has globalized, these security-community functions have eroded. The liberal order's social purposes—mutual protection and social advancement within a community of democratic states—have thinned out. It has come to look less like a security community and more like a platform of rules and institutions for capitalist transactions.[53]

During the Cold War, the economic foundations of this security community were organized around what John Ruggie has called "embedded liberalism."[54] As noted in chapter 6, this was the idea that the leading liberal democracies would seek to organize the world economy so as to reconcile market openness with social protections. The collapse of world markets in the 1930s was disastrous for the Western industrial societies; a central goal of policymakers was to reorganize and reopen the world economy while giving national governments the tools to promote economic stability. "Unlike the economic nationalism of the thirties," Ruggie argues, "it would be multilateral in character; unlike the liberalism of the gold standard and free trade, its multilateralism would be predicated upon domestic interventionism."[55] The compromise of embedded liberalism was aimed at taming the disruptive effects of market openness without eliminating the efficiency and welfare gains that came from open trade. Liberal democracies worked together to create rules and institutions that allowed states to stabilize and manage market risks. "National societies," Rawi Abdelal and John Ruggie argue, "shared the risks through varieties of safeguards and insurance schemes that composed, in part, the European welfare state or, in the ever-exceptional

[handwritten margin notes:] CONTROL MARKET FOR SOC WELFARE GAINS

[handwritten note at bottom:] DETERIORATION OF SOCIAL PROTECTIONS, ACCORDING TO JI, CONTRIBUTES TO WEAKENING OR DISORDERING OF GLOBAL LIBERAL ORDER. HOW TO EXPLAIN SIMILAR WEALTH INEQUALITY 1890–1928 IN USA + WHAT FOLLOWED?

United States, the New Deal state."[56] This is why large segments of society across the liberal democratic world became constituencies for postwar liberal order.

The crisis of liberal order stems partly from the breakdown of this compromise. Beginning in the 1980s, the globalization of the liberal order entailed the liberalization of markets in both the advanced industrial and developing worlds. Policy elites in the United States and Europe championed the opening and deregulation markets—this was the so-called neoliberal policy agenda.[57] In trade, efforts at multilateral liberalization were extended to new areas, such as services, agriculture, international property rights, and regulatory harmonization. In the 1990s, the liberalization agenda was extended still further: the Clinton administration, in coordination with the IMF and the World Bank, tried to get developing countries to liberalize their closely guarded financial markets. Banking, stock, and bond markets were opened, and countries in Latin America, East Asia, and Central Europe moved from state-led economic growth strategies to reliance on market forces. In what became known as the Washington Consensus, the expansion of market society was widely seen by Western elites as the key to political liberalization and expansion as well as consolidation of the liberal world economy, thus opening up a new era of growth and social advancement.[58] Political and economic liberalism were seen as mutually reinforcing. But market expansion created new, sharp economic divides between winners and losers in Western societies, while weakening embedded liberal supports and protections. As Jeff Colgan and Robert Keohane argue, "the effects of a neoliberal economic agenda have eroded the social contract that had previously ensured crucial political support for the [liberal] order."[59]

The liberal order's social purposes have been undermined by rising economic insecurity and inequality across the advanced industrial world. Even before the 2008 financial crisis, the fortunes of workers and middle-class citizens in Europe and the United States had been stagnant for decades.[60] From the end of World War II to the 1970s, incomes grew rapidly in the United States for both lower- and upper-income classes, and the income gaps did not significantly widen. But this changed beginning in the 1970s. In the United States, almost all the growth in wealth since 1980 has gone to the top

20 percent of earners in society. Those without skills or a college education have increasingly fallen behind. Between 1974 and 2015, the real median household income for Americans without a college education declined by 24 percent, while median incomes for those with college degrees continued to gain. The concentration of income and wealth at the very top of society has risen to a level not seen since the 1920s.

Similar patterns played out at the global level. Branko Milanović has famously described the past two decades' differential gains across the global system as an "elephant curve." He finds that the vast bulk of gains in real per capita income have gone to two very different groups. One consists of workers in countries like China and India who have taken low-end manufacturing and service jobs at very low wage levels and have experienced dramatic gains—even if they remain at the lower end of the global income spectrum. Since 1990, more than a billion such people have moved out of extreme poverty—a remarkable shift in the life fortunes of a huge part of the global population.[61] This is the elephant's back. The other group is the top 1 percent—even top 0.01 percent—who have experienced massive increases in wealth. This is the elephant's trunk, extended upward.[62] Meanwhile, the middle and working classes in the advanced industrial countries have seen the fewest income gains. This stagnation in the economic fortunes of these middle segments of Western society has been reinforced by long-term shifts in technology, trade patterns, union organization, and manufacturing sites.[63] There have been great winners in the recent growth of the world economy—but the old constituencies of the Western liberal order are not among them.[64]

The security-community aspect of the liberal order has also been weakened by the simple expansion of the scope and diversity of the peoples and societies that make it up. The democratic world is now less Anglo-American, less Western. It includes most of the world—developed and developing, North and South, colonial and postcolonial, Asian and European. This too is a crisis born of success. But it brought an increasing divergence of views across the order about its members' place in the world and their historical legacies and grievances. The liberal world order now less resembled a community with a shared narrative of its past and future.[65] Expansion had weakened the shared identity—historical, geographic, and cultural—of the societies within it.

Taken together, the liberal order's social purposes are not what they once were. It is less obvious today that the liberal democratic world is a security community. What do citizens in Western democracies get from liberal internationalism? How does an open and loosely rules-based international order deliver physical and economic security to the great middle class? Throughout the twentieth century, liberal internationalism was tied to progressive and social democratic agendas within Western liberal democracies. It was not seen as the enemy of nationalism but as a tool permitting governments to pursue economic security and advancements at home. But in recent decades, this connection between social and economic advancement at home and liberal internationalism abroad has been broken.

The Limits and Durability of the Liberal Order

The expansion of the liberal order has revealed both its limits and its resiliency. The limits are most obvious in the order's increasingly fraught relations with China and Russia. Any hope that either country might become a "responsible stakeholder" in this order has been dashed. With Russia, the bargains between Washington and Moscow that ended the Cold War did not survive the 1990s. The expansion of NATO, disputes over energy pipelines, and the refusal to accommodate Russia's regional ambitions all helped break down relations.[66] The collapse of the Russian economy at the end of the Cold War left Russia weakened and resentful. The West's efforts to manage relations have also labored under the burden, centuries in the making, of antidemocratic and antiliberal Russian domestic politics. Russia's loss of empire and the West's encroachments on its traditional spheres of influence added to its grievances and rivalry.[67] The United States could have made more far-reaching concessions to Russia on security, such as forgoing NATO enlargement. But this would have meant ignoring the desires of Eastern European states to join the Western alliance and European Union and to create an institutional basis for their transitions to liberal democracy. In any event, it is not clear that a more generous post–Cold War settlement would have put Russia on a path to Western-style reform and integration.[68] That path disappeared with the failure of Russia's transition to democracy in the 1990s.

China's reversal of its experiments with economic and political reform is a more recent and surprising development. For the first two decades after the Cold War, American leaders looked for ways to integrate China into the existing order. China, in turn, pursued ambitious programs of economic liberalization, joined the established global multilateral bodies, and became deeply integrated in the global system. It took over Taiwan's permanent seat on the UN Security Council. It participates in the WTO and plays a role in the IMF, the World Bank, and the G-20.[69] In ideology and vision, it slowly moved away from earlier decades' calls for a "new international order" and began calling for incremental reforms to global rules and institutions. Its discourse became more about fairness and justice in the organization of the global order—which meant, fundamentally, giving China a greater voice in running the existing global institutions. It now seeks to make the international order "more reasonable" by giving China a larger role in the IMF and the World Bank, more voice in international leadership forums such as the G-20, and, over the long term, making the renminbi a world reserve currency. These reforms all suggest a Chinese movement toward the center of the international economic order.

Yet under President Xi's leadership, China has signaled that its embrace of reform has limits. It has redoubled its commitment to one-party authoritarian political rule and begun to pursue ambitious regional economic programs—such as the Belt and Road Initiative. Now neither fully inside nor fully outside the post–Cold War liberal international order, it is actively pursuing its interests inside most of the leading global institutions, while also trying to move the world toward a post-Western order that is less tied to liberal economic and political values.[70] China had its most successful decades of economic growth and rising living standards during the era of American unipolarity, and it is now using its rapidly acquired wealth and power to challenge and reorient this order.

These developments help illuminate the limits of the global spread of liberal internationalism. First, the failure of the hegemonic bargain offered it by a succession of American presidents shows that China has become too big to be integrated into a US-led liberal international order. Unlike Japan and Germany, China rose up (or as the Chinese would say, reemerged) outside the United States alliance system. The security and economic bargains that provided the foundation for the Cold War–era liberal order are not transferable to China, which is increasingly a peer great power. Second, liberal internationalists assumed that as China liberalized its economy and integrated into the world economy, growing domestic and international pressures would compel it to liberalize its political institutions. This did not happen. Unlike South Korea, Taiwan, and other East Asian countries, China was large enough to resist international pressures and, absent a democratic transition, its autocratic state elites have incentives to resist the rules and norms that privilege liberal democracy. Finally, globalization has fragmented the liberal order. It was an amalgam of institutions and policy realms even during the Cold War, when it was more delimited in geopolitical space and membership. But as this "inside" order became the "outside" order, what was once a loose political community became a sprawling and fragmented system of rules, institutions, and relationships. This shift in its character has made it easier for states—particularly those like China that are ambivalent about liberal order—to pick and choose which parts of the order they wish to join. China can get the benefits of participating in an open and loosely rules-based order, without committing to domestic regime change or strategic partnership with the leading liberal states.

The expansion of the liberal order has also illuminated the sources of its durability.[71] First, it clearly has integrative tendencies. States of many sizes and types have found paths into the club. Germany and Japan were the first major states to reconstitute themselves—initially through coercive occupation—and integrate into postwar security and economic institutions. Some states joined the order as client states or frontline allies during the Cold War. After the Cold War, many former Soviet client states and some of the former Soviet republics joined the European Union and NATO. Many countries integrated into the order by making political and economic transitions. One can see this in the steady expansion of the Organization for Economic Cooperation and Development, a club of the developed market economies, which has grown from twenty countries at its founding in 1960 to thirty-four today.[72] The point is that a wide range of states outside the West have sought to get into this order so as to enjoy its benefits. The order's institutions and ideology—hegemonic and liberal internationalist—seem to facilitate this integration.

A second source of durability is the liberal order's hierarchical authority relations. Hierarchical orders can differ in the extent to which they are dominated by a single state. A leading state can organize and dominate, standing above other states, or else the order might consist of a coalition of major states that cooperatively exert leadership. In the latter case, the order is organized around an array of great powers, junior partners, client states, and other stakeholders. In the economic realm, authority and decision making are shared. The formal multilateral institutions—the IMF, the World Bank, and the WTO—are organized this way, as are the informal leadership groups like the G-7 and G-20. They are hierarchical institutions inhabited by coalitions of leading states. The United States and Western Europe remain overrepresented in many of these institutions, but they are not based on a fixed membership.[73] Doors are open, and bargains are on the table. That the G-20 has joined the G-7 as an important leadership forum is a reflection of this capacity of governance mechanisms to evolve and expand beyond the old Western great powers.[74]

A third source of durability is the way economic gains are spread across the international order. Orders can differ in their distribution of economic and other material rewards. In traditional imperial orders, the profits and gains flowed overwhelmingly to the imperial core. In colonial and informal empires, they flowed disproportionately to the wealthy and powerful states, classes, and social groupings that organized and ran the order. But the American-led liberal order, with its system of open trade and investment, distributed economic gains more widely.[75] Trade and investment across the system allowed states near and far to grow and advance and, often, to outpace the United States and its Western partners.[76] States around the world have integrated themselves into the existing system in pursuit of trade and growth.

A fourth feature of international order is the degree to which it accommodates diverse models of capitalism and economic development. In practice if not in ideology, the postwar global order has been relatively open to these differences.[77] There have been three general types of capitalist models: the Anglo-American neoliberal or market-fundamentalist model that has dominated economic debates in Western capitals from the end of the Cold War until the 2008 global financial crisis; an older postwar model of "embedded liberalism," which has emphasized the social welfare state and "managed" openness; and the statist model that has been pursued throughout East Asia and the developing world.[78] These models have tended to coexist and wax and wane across the decades. A recent study of the "distribution of identity" relating to models of political economy across major Western and non-Western countries revealed a remarkable convergence of ideological preferences for some combination of economic liberalism and social democracy. In all the countries surveyed, there was great skepticism about neoliberalism but widespread support for social democratic and liberal approaches.[79]

What makes the liberal international order resilient are the many constituencies and interests tied to it. Its relatively open and integrative features have led to a steady expansion of stakeholders but also to fragmentation.[80] As the social purposes and embedded liberal protections have eroded, the order has overrun its political foundations and lost political support within Western industrial societies. It is now a more complex system of semi-independent international institutions and cooperative relations. While this fragmentation has weakened the coherence of the order, it has also reduced the incentives for outright opposition. Liberal order is less like a castle with a drawbridge and walls and more like a shopping mall. It is easy for states to enter and exist and it is easier for them to resist or avoid its rules and institutions. By the same token, the order provides both less opportunity and less need for outright opposition to it.

Many of the institutions and regimes that make up the liberal international order are not uniquely liberal. Rather, they are Westphalian, in that they are designed to solve problems of sovereign states, whether democratic or authoritarian—and many of the key participants are not liberal or democratic. Even during the Cold War, when the liberal order was primarily an arrangement among liberal democracies, the Soviet Union often worked with these countries to help build international institutions. Moscow's committed antiliberalism did not stop it from partnering with Washington to create arms-control agreements or cooperating with the World Health Organization to spearhead a global campaign to eradicate smallpox. More recently, countries across the democratic and authoritarian divide have crafted global rules to guard against environmental destruction. The signatories of the Paris climate agreement, for example, include autocracies such as China, Iran, and Russia. Westphalian approaches have also led to agreements governing the oceans, the atmosphere, outer space, and Antarctica. The 1987 Montreal Protocol, for example, which reversed the destruction of the ozone layer, was supported by both democracies and authoritarian states. Westphalian internationalism involves agreements that do not challenge the sovereignty of states but embody collective measures to solve problems that states cannot address on their own.[81]

Most institutions in the liberal order do not demand that their backers be liberal democracies. They simply need to be status quo states that are capable of fulfilling their commitments. These institutions do not challenge the Westphalian system; they codify it. The United Nations, for example, enshrines the principle of state sovereignty and, through the permanent members of the Security Council, the notion of great-power decision making. All these factors make the order more durable. Because much international cooperation has nothing to do with liberalism and democracy, regimes that are hostile to liberal democracy can still retain their international agendas and support the order's core institutions. The persistence of Westphalian institutions provides a lasting foundation on which distinctively liberal and democratic institutions can be erected and defended.

Finally, the durability of a loosely organized system of open and rules-based order rests on the deep political imperatives that spring from rising economic and security interdependence. Liberal international ideas and projects have remained alive and evolved over the past two centuries because liberal democracies—and other states—have struggled to cope with the complex challenges of interdependence. As long as interdependence—economic, security-related, and environmental—continues to grow, peoples and governments everywhere will be compelled to work together to solve problems or else to suffer grievous harm. Growing interdependence creates incentives for political cooperation at the heart of the liberal international project. Liberal democratic capitalist societies have thrived and expanded because they have found a way to reconcile sovereignty and interdependence—exploiting the gains that come from modernity while protecting themselves from its dangers.

This dynamic of constant change and ever-increasing interdependence is only accelerating. Global capitalism has drawn more people and countries into cross-border webs of exchange, making virtually the entire world population dependent on the competent management of international finance and trade. The alternatives to a functioning liberal international order are not very attractive; even China, the most powerful illiberal state in the world, has no grand alternative vision of order to offer. If it is not possible to radically reduce the conditions of economic and security interdependence, then the alternative to liberal international order is simply a more chaotic and dangerous interdependent world. International order does not rise spontaneously and liberal order is not self-generating. But the interests and constituencies that have a stake in some sort of updated and reformed liberal international order are growing—not shrinking. This is the ultimate source of the resiliency of liberal international order: more people stand to lose from its undoing than stand to win.

In short, the same forces of globalization that brought large parts of the world into the Western liberal order also made that order less like a club and more like a public utility—a system of functional institutions and regimes to which states could variously attach themselves. At the same time, the stagnation of incomes and rising inequality in Western industrial societies eroded the order's ability to fulfill its old social purposes of economic and social protection. This is why a major "outside" power like China is able to embed itself only partially within the order: accepting the whole package is no longer either as necessary or as attractive as it once was.

Yet, even as the postwar liberal order has overrun its foundations, overturned its borders, and undermined its social purposes, its deep logic of open and rules-based cooperation remains intact. Indeed, the crisis has illuminated it. Liberal democracies still exist, as they always have, within a wider world of increasing economic and security interdependence. The current political backlash to these global realities is both inevitable and doomed to fail. There is no escape. Liberal democracies will find themselves doing what they have always done in moments of crisis—searching for ways to reestablish and reinforce the political foundations for liberal capitalist democracy.

NINE

Mastering Modernity

L iberal internationalism has traveled across two centuries of crises and golden eras to arrive at today's troubled moment. Its ideas and projects have come in many guises. Under its banner, political thinkers, activists, and leaders have championed free trade and laissez-faire economics as well as social democracy and the welfare state, others have justified empire and military interventionism, and still others have promoted visions of global governance and the rule of law. Liberal internationalism has been used to defend racial and civilizational hierarchy and to inspire movements for self-determination and universal human rights. It has been conceived as a regional grouping of Western states and as a framework for a worldwide liberal order. Its ideas and projects have been shaped and reshaped as the liberal democratic world itself has moved through periods of war, depression, breakdown, growth, and renewal.

Liberal internationalism can be understood as a tradition of order building that emerged with the rise and spread of liberal states, and its ideas and agendas have been shaped and reshaped as these countries have grappled with the great forces of modernity. The essential goals of liberal order building have not changed: creating an environment—a sort of cooperative ecosystem—in which liberal democracies can operate by providing tools and capacities for their governments to manage economic and security interdependence, balance their often conflicting values and principles, and secure rights and protections for their societies. Liberal internationalism aims to foster international order in a way that protects and facilitates the security, welfare, and progress of liberal democracy. It is best understood as an ongoing project to make the world safe for democracy.

The open, loosely rules-based system that constitutes the liberal international order has a handful of key markers: openness, multilateralism, democratic solidarity, cooperative security, and progressive social purposes. Behind these markers lies a cluster of convictions. Trade and exchange generate mutual gains. Rules and institutions facilitate cooperation. Shared values reinforce trust and solidarity. Rising economic and security interdependence generates both opportunities and dangers—so gaining the benefits of interdependence while guarding against its dangers requires international cooperation. In the liberal internationalist vision, liberal democracies are the most advanced societies, but they are also uniquely vulnerable, precisely because they are relatively open societies operating in an open international system. Liberal democracies thus can be secure only together, but not alone. That is the elemental insight that drives liberal internationalism.

The great historical arc of modern internationalism has followed what I have called the liberal ascendancy. Liberal democracies rose from weakness and obscurity in the late eighteenth century to become the world's most powerful and wealthy states, propelling the West and the liberal capitalist system of economics and politics to world preeminence. This occurred amid world war, economic upheaval, and transformations in the scope and character of liberal democracy. At key points, when Western liberal states have had opportunities to shape international order, liberal international ideas and projects have found their way onto diplomatic and order-building agendas.

Today, liberal internationalism finds itself at an impasse. The international order—particularly those parts built in the postwar decades by the United States and its allies—is eroding. The United States and Great Britain, the old patrons of that order, have stepped back from leadership. Under the Trump administration, the United States has even sought to undermine the international order's institutions and relationships, at a time when liberal democracy itself seems to be under threat. Authoritarianism and populist nationalism have spread and the postwar political bargains, class compromises, and growth coalitions in the advanced industrial societies have weakened or unraveled. The rise of China and the resurgence of Russia as different kinds of revisionist powers have opened the door to rival political projects with illiberal ideologies. If China's "project of modernity" of building capitalism without liberalism or democracy succeeds and outperforms its Western rivals, the implications for liberalism will be profound. In the meantime, the post–Cold War era of the 1990s, marked by unipolar power and a global consensus around the "liberal ideal," has faded away. The rock on which the liberal project was built appears to be crumbling.

In this book, I have followed liberal internationalism's journey from the age of democratic revolutions to the present. That journey did not begin in 1991 or 1945. Seen from a two-century perspective, the project is as much a story of struggle as triumph. It is a drama marked by breakthroughs, near misses, and failures. More than once, liberal internationalists have had to pick up the pieces and rethink their project. Liberal internationalism exists in a world of political movement and countermovement, rising and declining great powers, and grand ideological contests. The liberal international order—however it is manifest—is built on and around other political projects and power formations. It is never a done deal, always a work in progress. It never extinguishes or completely tames the underlying forces of change that move modern societies forward or backward. In fact, it is precisely because these underlying forces—collectively called "modernity"—cannot be fully mastered that liberal internationalism is necessary. It offers ideas and projects for coping with the consequences of modernity. The liberal international order does not eliminate these consequences or settle modernity's problems; it creates institutions and relationships for coping with the unending series of dangers and opportunities thrown its way.

In this chapter, I look first at the logic and character of liberal internationalism as an unfolding political project. What forces have moved it forward and account for its accomplishments and failures? As I have argued, liberal internationalism is a project whose logic and character have unfolded over time. By looking at the forces that have shaped it, we can draw up a balance sheet of its strengths and weaknesses. Liberal internationalism is paradoxical. It offers expansive ideas about the organization of international order, enshrining universalist principles and articulating sweeping claims about the progressive advance of the modern world. It provides a rich vocabulary for thinking about shared interests, political community, and the moral foundations of international order. Yet it is also quite thin and limited as a political movement. Liberal internationalism was brought into the twentieth century in alliance with other movements—nationalism, imperialism, capitalism, great-power politics, and British and American hegemony. Its shape-shifting character has allowed it to affiliate with other grand forces, and this has amplified its impact. But it has also made the liberal international project dependent on the calculations and agendas of other actors and movements. Liberal internationalism has always needed partners, and this has been both its strength and its weakness.

Second, given its accomplishments, limits, and disappointments, on what grounds can liberal internationalism be defended? Here I argue that in the twenty-first century, it will need to be much more pragmatic and modest than it has recently been. It must learn from the ill-fated post–Cold War globalization of political and economic liberalism and reconnect itself to progressive versions of nationalism and the rebuilding of domestic coalitions around shared social purposes. Most important, it will need to build its intellectual and political foundations on the shifting grounds of rising global economic and security interdependence. To tackle the great challenges of twenty-first-century modernity, the world will need more liberal internationalism, not less.

The Arc of Liberal Internationalism

Liberal internationalism is a grand tradition in the study of international relations, which is built around a cluster of ideas, theories, narratives, and projects. Its ideas and arguments, as captured by founding thinkers and in classic texts, have been debated across generations. It is both a scholarly tradition and a set of ideological beliefs that find their way into real-world politics. It comes with narratives of "the global," stories and accounts of the rise of liberal democracy and the great struggles that have forged the modern world. It identifies a set of problems that recur across historical eras. Liberal internationalists share a genealogy, a sense that they are part of a larger intellectual and political enterprise. Sometimes the connections are faint—not all political actors wielding liberal internationalist ideas see themselves in this light. But when we step back and look across the past two centuries, the lineages and movements of the liberal international political project come clearly into view.

That political project has five defining features. First, the great question that liberal internationalism sets for itself is how it should understand and cope with the problems of modernity. Modernity, the ongoing transformation of societies and international relations driven by science, technology, and the industrial revolution, has put the entire world in motion, making all societies more complex and interdependent. As liberal internationalists have learned and relearned, modernity has two faces. The face of human advancement is technological change, economic growth, rising standards of living, and the constant revelation of shared interests and fates. But modernity's other face is economic depression, war, totalitarianism, reactionary backlash, and the sudden discovery of vulnerabilities. Liberal internationalism can be understood as the ideas and projects by which liberal democracies have responded to modernity's opportunities and dangers. It involves cooperation among states to capture the benefits of interdependence and guard against its perils. Shadowing the liberal international project is the ongoing debate about the character and consequences of modernity. At critical turning points—1918, 1945, 1991, and today—liberal internationalists have had to rethink their understandings of modernity and recast their ambitions and goals.

Specifically, I have drawn a contrast between the rationales for liberal internationalism as a political project at the two postwar junctures, depicting Woodrow Wilson and Franklin Delano Roosevelt as archetypes. Wilson and his contemporaries believed in the progressive potential of modernity and sought to enmesh the world in a liberal international system to draw out and thus to more steadily cultivate that potential. The dangers to peace in world politics were caused by states that had not yet become sufficiently modern. FDR and his contemporaries saw modernity as an ambiguous development that could be harnessed equally for progressive and regressive ends, so they turned to liberal internationalism as a way of fortifying and preserving those last remaining sparks of liberal democracy in an increasingly hostile world. Whereas Wilson's liberal internationalism was premised on nineteenth-century notions of international law, public opinion, and moral sanction, FDR's liberal internationalism incorporated new conceptions of political rights and social protections. If liberal democracy was to survive, it would need to be embedded in a more elaborate, club-like international order to coordinate relations between states so as to cope with the growing complexities and vulnerabilities of economic and security interdependence. For Wilson, the spread of liberal democracy was the glue that would hold together international order. For FDR and his generation, a new type of international order would need to be built to provide the glue to hold liberal democracies together.

The other great transformation of the past two centuries is the shift from a world of empires to a world of nation-states. Liberal internationalism emerged in the early nineteenth century in an era when empire provided the organizing logic of global order—and empire remained a looming presence well into the twentieth century. Yet by the end of the century, it had all but disappeared, and the Westphalian state system had spread to all corners of the world. Liberal internationalism has been shaped and reshaped by its efforts to navigate this global transformation. It adapted itself to empire by offering a variety of impulses and rationales for liberal imperialism. During the nineteenth century and the era of Woodrow Wilson, imperial and liberal internationalism were often hard to tell apart. Yet ultimately, liberal internationalism came to tie itself to self-determination and Westphalian sovereignty. In important respects, world politics in the twentieth century was an extended global struggle over whether and how the world would transition from an empire-based order to something new. Many forces— geopolitical, technological, ideological—shaped the outcome. Liberal internationalism initially found itself on both sides of this contest, but by the end of World War II, it squarely premised its vision of global order on the Westphalian system of states.

Third, liberal internationalism in the nineteenth century was a bundle of different internationalisms. It was not a full-blown political project but a scattering of movements and activities. In the early and mid-nineteenth century, Britain's struggle over the Corn Laws gave birth to the free trade movement. The peace movement also emerged in these decades. Later, jurists and other activists championed international law, and the arbitration movement was launched. Other internationalists put their efforts into convening congresses and parliamentary assemblies. Prominent nineteenth-century figures such as Richard Cobden led movements that merged free trade with campaigns for peace. By the end of the century, these various strands of internationalism were beginning to merge. The two Hague Peace Conferences and other forums provided occasions for groups and movements to meet. Not all of them were obvious coalition partners, and part of the drama of nineteenth-century internationalism was the political struggle that brought these groups together or pulled them apart. Woodrow Wilson's contribution was not the originality of his ideas, it was his bringing together of liberal internationalism's various strands into a relatively coherent political project. In the century since Wilson, the strands have continued to combine, fray, and recombine. There is an ongoing debate about what the liberal international coalition does and does not contain. The movement's crisis today is partly the breakdown of the old postwar coalition.

Fourth, liberal internationalism has always affiliated itself with and relied on other forces to generate political outcomes. It has never been sufficiently coherent and broad-gauged to push away or overpower other movements and projects. This is in part because it is itself a coalition of causes and movements rather than a unified programmatic agenda. The ideas and projects of liberal internationalism are also open and flexible enough to lend themselves to other agendas. Over the past two centuries, these agendas have included nationalism, capitalism, imperialism, great-power politics, and British and American hegemony. Liberal internationalism is woven into these ideologies and projects and has been variously in alignment or tension with them. It has been intellectually and politically linked not only to Western imperialism but also to anti-imperialism. It arose in the West just as liberal democracy was emerging, and it became associated with the building of modern nation-states and national governments. Nationalism and internationalism have been opposite sides of the same modernizing coin. Some internationalists rejected nationalism as a source of illiberalism and war, but the nation-state has remained liberal internationalism's center of gravity.

These affiliations have been a source of both strength and weakness. Liberal international ideas would have left a far smaller mark on the global order if they had been disconnected from other forces and movements. But these affiliations have also generated a stream of dilemmas, contradictions, compromises, and hypocrisies that unsettle the liberal project's grander aspirations.

Finally, liberal internationalism has been deeply tied to the domestic social and economic agendas of liberal democracy. For two hundred years, a central aim of liberal order building has been to protect liberal societies and generate capacities for their governance. This explains liberal internationalism's affiliation with nationalism and the nation-state. Its goal has not been to undermine or overturn the nation-state but to facilitate the realization of progressive goals. This logic is most clearly evident in the Western system created after World War II, in which the Bretton Woods institutions and the wider array of regimes and partnerships provided tools for governments to stabilize their economies and offer social protections. But there is a more general pattern: in each era, liberal internationalism was pushed forward by progressive movements. In the nineteenth century, these consisted of reform movements tied to trade and liberal party politics across the Western world. Wilson-era liberal internationalism was supported by the progressive movement in the United States and reform liberalism in Western Europe. The postwar liberal order was built from the New Deal coalition in the United States and liberal and social democratic movements in Great Britain, France, West Germany, and other European states. As I argued in the previous chapter, it is the erosion of these progressive coalitions that has brought this liberal order to its recent crisis.

Liberal internationalism evolved out of the confluence of these forces and circumstances over the past two centuries. In the nineteenth century, liberals saw a world transformed by capitalism, empire, and the expansion of international society, and they associated modernity with the progress of industrial society. World War I, which revealed modernity's dangerous side, forced internationalists to rethink their views and spell out a program for a reformed international order guided in new ways. The trauma of the 1930s and World War II forced another rethinking, and then a reworking of the liberal internationalist agenda under American hegemonic leadership. As the "problems of interdependence" changed, so too did notions of social security and national security. In each era, thinking shifted in regard to the sources and character of liberal international order. The ideas and principles of liberal internationalism became less entangled with race and empire but more entangled in American hegemony and the Cold War. The necessity of building the postwar liberal order within the Western bloc of the bipolar world system was turned into a virtue. Those inside the order benefited from the dense ties of economic and security cooperation. In the post–Cold War decades, that order both globalized and fragmented—and now, delivering less security and less community, it is at a crossroads.

Where Do We Plant the Liberal Internationalist Flag?

On what grounds can we defend liberal internationalism? This question can be answered by looking at six major debates that liberal internationalists have had among themselves over their project's scope and character. In these debates, they have grappled with the trade-offs between efficiency and social stability, sovereignty and interventionism, and global openness and political community. They have debated the nature of "the global"—the forces and logic shaping the modern world and their implications for the security and well-being of liberal democracy. As they did in past crises, liberal internationalists must again debate the character, limits, and possibilities of their project.

Efficiency versus Social Stability

A core strand of liberal internationalism has been a commitment to open trade. Countries linked by trade and open markets gain both economically and politically. Ideally, trade generates efficiency and welfare gains for countries that participate, thus facilitating their growth and advancement. These mutual gains and interdependence have political effects, including heightened incentives to settle disputes peacefully. From the British repeal of the Corn Laws to the post-1945 building of a multilateral trading system, liberal democracies have consistently looked for ways to realize the gains of trade. Winners win more than losers lose, so if the winnings are distributed in ways that compensate the losers, everyone comes out ahead. But open trade is a disruptive threat to workers and communities, and the social bargains that soften the impact of economic dislocation are imperfect. In giving national governments space and policy tools to pursue economic stabilization and development, the "embedded liberalism" behind the reconstruction of the postwar Western world tried to reconcile open trade and free-market capitalism with social protections and economic security.

As we saw in chapter 8, this compromise has broken down. The embrace of neoliberal policies and the deregulation and global integration of capital markets that accompanied the post–Cold War spread of economic and political liberalism have been driving forces. The Western governments' capacity and willingness to maintain their social democratic commitments has waned. Even under the best of conditions, the model of international trade at the heart of economic liberalism oversimplifies reality. "It neglects all the noneconomic considerations that so often turn governments away from its prescriptions, such as the social and cultural side-effects of trade, or the frequent neglect of public goods, collective equipments, and education," writes Stanley Hoffmann. "Above all, it ignores factors of inequality: the benefits from free trade spread slowly, if at all, and unevenly through the formidable barriers of privilege, class, and status within societies (in which small groups often monopolize the rewards) and the obstacles of unequal endowments and levels of development in the world."[1] Not all the rise in inequality or the breakdown in economic and social protections is traceable to the liberalization of trade and capital flows. Technological changes in the workplace and shifts from manufacturing to services also play a role.[2] But efficiency gains from deeper economic integration seem to be slowing relative to the rise of economic insecurity and inequality. Dani Rodrik argues that the advanced industrial countries have already passed the point beyond which expanded trade does more to redistribute wealth within their societies than to increase efficiency and growth. Although economic globalization is intensifying the gaps between the winners and losers, it is not generating sufficient economic gains to compensate the losers.[3]

In making the case for economic openness, liberal internationalists will need to reestablish the foundations of embedded liberalism—that is, managed openness that reconnects trade and markets with social security and shared gains. The industrial world cannot return to the early decades of the Bretton Woods system, but it can look for new ways to balance openness and social protections. The aim of reforming international rules and institutions should be to enable national governments to make good on their social democratic commitments. "Democracies have a right to protect their social arrangements," Rodrik argues, "and when this right clashes with the requirements of the global economy, it is the latter that should give way."[4] Economic openness can last in liberal democracies only if it is tied to a social ethic of fairness and shared benefits. Without inaugurating a new era of protectionism, liberal democracies have to reestablish the multilateral system of rules and institutions that allows states to manage openness, guided by the liberal norms of multilateralism, reciprocity, and nondiscrimination. They need to rebuild the social contract at home and renew the international rules and norms that balance openness with social stability.

Sovereignty versus Interventionism

The norms of sovereign equality and national self-determination are integral to the modern liberal international vision. As we have seen, by the second half of the twentieth century, the liberal international project was firmly built on a Westphalian foundation. To be sure, the United States and other liberal states have repeatedly practiced all the dark arts of power politics. Throughout the Cold War and post–Cold War decades, they have transgressed sovereignty norms through military intervention, covert action, and coercive regime change. But the norms and principles of state sovereignty remain firmly embedded in the institutions and legitimating rationale of the post–World War II liberal international order.

American military interventionism during the Cold War played out as part of the geopolitical and ideological struggle with the Soviet Union. The Korean and Vietnam Wars were the most tragic and costly of the dozens of armed interventions carried out by the United States across the Cold War periphery. Since the Soviet Union fell, the reasons for interventions have expanded to include humanitarian disasters, human rights violations, and nonstate terrorist threats. In areas of humanitarianism, economic policy, and democracy promotion, the Western liberal states look increasingly as if they are trying to impose their own values and interests on weaker states.[5] In this regard, it is useful to distinguish between two versions of liberal internationalism: defensive and offensive.[6] Defensive liberalism is the older liberal orientation anchored in the norms of self-determination and the right of countries to maintain their own institutions and doctrines. Offensive liberalism is the more recent universalizing agenda that involves the reordering of other societies.[7] Rising states such as China, India, and Brazil tend to embrace defensive liberalism and resist the intrusiveness of the newer liberalism. In accommodating these rising powers, liberal internationalism will need to rethink their offensive liberal impulses. Gaining agreement on the broader principles of order—sovereignty and multilateral rules and institutions that allow states to manage their interdependence—should take precedence over efforts to force convergence on the details of development or governance.

In the areas of human rights and transnational terrorism, the dilemmas are less about the imposition of liberal values on unwilling states than about the circumstances under which the international community needs to act.[8] When a state commits mass domestic violence such as genocide or ethnic cleansing, the outside world cannot simply look away. If a state is collapsed or unable to prevent transnational terrorist groups from operating on its territory, these circumstances might also require the international community's intervention. The response proposed for these occasions is the evolving norm of "responsibility to protect" (R2P), which was adopted by the United Nations in 2005 and remains controversial.[9] R2P is not a license for great powers to unilaterally intervene in weaker states. It is meant to stimulate international agreement on the circumstances under which agents of the international community—authorized by the United Nations—are morally obliged to prevent or stop atrocities. The burden of the norm is actually Westphalian in implication. Its goal is to strengthen the presumption that national governments must make good on their obligations as sovereign states and that the international order should help them do so. Only in the absence of this Westphalian state capacity—and under extreme conditions defined by the international community—do outside powers intervene. The goal for liberal internationalists should be to seek as wide an agreement as possible on the legal bases for intervention.[10]

Clubs and Open Systems

The postwar liberal international order was built around exclusive groupings of states, such as NATO and the European Union, as well as wider multilateral organizations with more open membership, such as the United Nations. When the Cold War broke the world into bipolar blocs, the United States and its partners put their efforts into building the Western economic and security order. This Western political grouping resembled a club. It was a clearly defined, exclusive group of like-minded states with a shared identity based on their regime characteristics, geography, and historical experience. There was little doubt about who was inside and who was outside the order.[11] As I argued in chapter 6, the club character of the postwar liberal order was important for its functioning. To be inside was to have rights and responsibilities. The club offered protection and provided governments with institutions and capacities to facilitate cooperation and problem solving. The compromises of embedded liberalism were organized within its confines. That there were barriers to entry only reinforced commitment and cooperation. In chapter 8, I argued that the erosion of this club-like nature is a defining feature of the current crisis.

Open systems of multilateral cooperation, which reflect the Westphalian norms of sovereign equality and nondiscrimination that are embedded in the wider global order, are also integral to the liberal international vision. Membership in these organizations is predicated not on regime character, but only on recognition of a state's sovereign status and its commitment and ability to carry out the responsibilities of membership. If the legitimacy of the club of liberal democracies lies in their shared social purposes, the legitimacy of open systems of order derives from the universalism inherent in Westphalian principles of sovereignty. An open system's strength is its inclusiveness. For many realms of international relations—including arms control, pandemic disease prevention, environmental regulation, and management of the global commons—regime type is not relevant to cooperation. Addressing these problems requires as wide a participation of states as possible. The weakness of open systems is in enforcement. If the rules say that any state can be in or out as it chooses, the benefits of membership cannot be predicated on embracing a suite of values and responsibilities.

Liberal internationalists, including Woodrow Wilson, have spoken up for both types of order. Initially, in offering American support for a postwar organization, Wilson argued in favor of open and universal membership. In his speech to the League to Enforce the Peace in May 1916, Wilson said the United States "shall be as much concerned as the nations at war to see peace assume an aspect of permanence." This was why it would be in the nation's interest to participate in a "universal association of the nations . . . to prevent any war begun either contrary to treaty covenants or without warning and full submission of the causes to the opinion of the world—a virtual guarantee of territorial integrity and political independence." Eager not to be seen as committing the United States to upholding an unjust status quo, Wilson advanced general principles that would guide the settlement, including famously asserting that "every people" had "a right to choose the sovereignty under which they shall live," and small states were entitled to "the same respect for their sovereignty and for their integrity that great and powerful nations expect and insist upon."[12] During the years of American neutrality, Wilson did not once mention that the peace settlement would be linked to the way states were internally governed or the character of their regimes.[13] In January 1917, Wilson's "peace without victory" speech explicitly called for a settlement between existing states and regimes. It was only after Wilson brought the United States into the war that he shifted the focus to freedom and democracy as prerequisites for peace. In his War Address in April 1917, Wilson now asserted that "a steadfast concert of peace can never be maintained except by a partnership of democratic governments. No autocratic state government could be trusted to keep faith within it or observe its covenants."[14] Wilson was now envisaging a more exclusive grouping of democracies that would be bound together ideologically and oriented toward building a democratic peace. After the war was over, Wilson essentially reverted back to the open and universal version of his program. For Wilson, in the end, the establishment of a League of Nations was more important than the specific logic of its membership.

The question today for liberal internationalism is: How much of the club-like character of liberal order should and can be rebuilt? The goal is not to undermine or ignore the Westphalian principles that set the terms of wider global cooperation. But what is the future of the deeper, more exclusive cooperation among liberal democracies? In security relations, human rights, and the political economy of industrial society, liberal democracies have specific interests and values that illiberal states do not. Exclusive groupings within the wider international order are still an important means for advancing these values. So too is it important to strengthen the mechanisms of conditionality and the enforcement of norms and principles within the club. The European Union is struggling to respond to member states that transgress its common standards. NATO has also found itself struggling to deal with alliance members that lose their democratic character.[15] The irony of the rise of China and Russia as overt challengers to Western liberal democracy is that it may strengthen the identity and functioning of the liberal democratic world as a political grouping, even as it gives illiberal states an alternative club to join.

Relations with the Illiberal World

Dealing with illiberal great powers is one of the oldest problems facing the liberal international order. Do you invite them in, anticipating that they will become socialized and move toward liberal democracy? Do you exclude them? Do you actively seek to confront their revisionist agendas, or seek peaceful coexistence? At different times over the past two centuries, liberal states have pursued all these strategies. The underlying reality is that the liberal international order—open, rules-based, and organized around a core of liberal democracies—is a threat to illiberal states. From their perspective, the United States and the liberal capitalist order are revisionist.

The American grand strategy at the end of the Cold War was to invite the illiberal states into the liberal order. Once China and Russia gained the benefits of trade and exchange, went the reasoning, they would understand that it was in their interest to become "responsible stakeholders." Implicit in this logic was the expectation that these states would engage in self-initiated regime change. They would slowly shed their autocratic and authoritarian institutions and move closer to the Western liberal democratic model. This has not happened, and liberal internationalists must now reassess their assumptions and consider new approaches.

One option is to seek accommodation with these illiberal states by making the liberal international order less revisionist. This might mean curtailing efforts to promote "offensive" liberalism"—that is, efforts to push and pull these states toward the liberal democratic model. In effect, this strategy calls for making the liberal international order friendly to China and Russia by stepping back from the vision of a one-world liberal order. The emphasis instead would be on coexistence, building on the "defensive" liberal principles of self-determination, tolerance, and ideological pluralism. Liberal internationalism would be made more conservative.[16]

Another option is to confront illiberal states more aggressively. The assumption here is that China and Russia are the vanguard of a broader long-term challenge to the liberal international order. If it cannot contain the ambitions of these countries, the liberal order itself is threatened. This view hinges on a key claim about China: that it hopes to perfect an authoritarian model of industrial society that can compete with—and even surpass—the long-term growth capacity of liberal democracy. The jury is still out.[17] But if China does succeed in offering the world an illiberal pathway to modernity, the stakes for the liberal democratic world rise and the rivalry can easily become a Cold War–style struggle between deeply antagonistic ideological and political projects.

Finally, liberal internationalists might pursue a mixed strategy of looking for opportunities to cooperate with China and Russia on the playing field of Westphalian internationalism, focusing on shared functional problems such as arms control, environment, and the global commons, while actively seeking to consolidate and strengthen cooperation across the liberal democratic world. Here the assumption is that the liberal democracies—particularly if they are organized worldwide—have long-term advantages that will bend the grand struggle in their favor. The key is to renew and defend liberal democracy within like-minded states and to strengthen the institutions, functionality, and legitimacy of the liberal international order.[18]

Hegemony and Restraint on Power

Over the past century, the liberal international project has become deeply entangled with the exercise of American power. Woodrow Wilson carried liberal internationalist ideas to the Paris Peace Conference. After World War II, the United States built a liberal hegemonic order organized around open, rules-based relations and a core of Western liberal democracies. As I argued in chapter 6, this liberal hegemonic order both amplified and legitimated American power as well as shaped and restrained it. The United States tied itself to the other leading liberal states and exercised power through an array of economic, political, and security institutions. How restrained it was during the postwar era is a subject of much debate. Institutional restraints were certainly not an iron cage, and the United States reserved the right to act unilaterally when it chose. Power politics was hardly eliminated from the democratic world. Nonetheless, this liberal hegemonic order did manifest important features of consent. The United States and the other Western liberal democracies used institutions to establish restraint and commitment, and in doing so, they created an order that was somewhat independent of balance-of-power and imperial logics. The presence of liberal institutions allowed these states to dampen the two forces that typically shape international order—anarchy and empire. These forces never totally disappeared, of course, but they retreated enough to define the Western order as a hierarchical order with liberal characteristics.[19]

Liberal internationalism has both benefited and suffered under American hegemony. Like Great Britain in the nineteenth century, the United States in the twentieth century incorporated liberal internationalist ideas and projects into its hegemonic order building while pursuing other great-power strategies. Great Britain held on to its empire, and the United States engaged in crude imperial ventures and cultivated close relations with illiberal states. But particularly after 1945, it is difficult to see how liberal internationalism—

defined as open and rules-based order with progressive social purposes—
would have fared any better if it were not closely tied to America's efforts to
organize and dominate the postwar international order. As I argued in chapter 6, American postwar leaders recognized the value of binding the nation
to other liberal democracies and operating within the postwar system of multilateral institutions. This strategy made American power more legitimate
and enduring. The liberal great power's pursuit of enlightened self-interest
was integral to the rise and spread of liberal ideas and projects. Yet the United
States also demonstrated, repeatedly, that it can be an unfaithful steward of
liberal internationalism. Under the Trump administration, it is actively seeking to undermine the liberal features of the existing global order.

The challenge for liberal internationalists is to try to recover the connections between hegemony and liberal order. The reasons powerful liberal
states might want to build and operate within a system of open, rules-based
relations are clear enough. As I argued in chapter 8, the hollowing out of
the security-community character of the existing liberal order is one reason it is now in crisis: today it is easier for leaders to offer alternative narratives of the American national interest. The Trump administration's claims
that the liberal order generates more costs than benefits for the United
States also register with some voters. Yet the costs that the United States
incurs from seeking to operate outside the rules and norms of liberal international order are also real—and over the long term, they are much greater.
They include the loss of influence, credibility, and the cooperation of
friends and allies. America's democratic allies clearly want the United
States to remain within this order. During the high tide of American unipolarity, it was possible for US officials to see less value in liberal rules and
institutions. But in an era of declining American power, the value of cooperation with other liberal democracies should grow. Roles, responsibilities,
expectations, bargains—these aspects of the postwar liberal order draw our
attention precisely because the Trump administration ignores and under-
mines them. Yet lurking in this new danger is an opportunity to renegoti-
ate the hegemonic character of liberal internationalism or, short of this,
build a post-hegemonic consortium of like-minded states that could collectively underwrite a reformed liberal order.

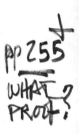

Narratives of Modernity

Liberal internationalists have offered many grand accounts of modernity and its implications for liberal democracy. As I argued in chapter 2, they have built their project around the assumption that deep forces of modernization are moving the world forward whether we will it or not. On this assumption, liberal internationalists have built a view of long-term political change as the product of accumulated knowledge, discovery and innovation, interdependence and mutual gain, and evolved social institutions. The forces of development are not necessarily laws of motion, and development does not always proceed in a progressive or enlightened direction, but the character and logic of modernity can be understood. As Anthony Giddens argues, modernity has a "grand narrative."[20] Over two centuries, however, liberal internationalists have seen this grand narrative in many ways. The view of modernity as understood by many Europeans on, for example, 14 April 1900, the occasion of the opening of the Paris Universal Exposition, was very different from the way it was viewed on 16 April 1945, when Stalin's armies began their final brutal destruction of Berlin. In the same way, modernity does not look the same today as it looked on 9 November 1989, when the Berlin Wall was smashed open. So what is today's liberal internationalist narrative of modernity?

Three versions have been offered. One is the grand Enlightenment narrative in which the deep forces of modernity are inexorably moving societies toward liberal democracy. There is movement and direction in human affairs. God, reason, moral imperative—thinkers have invoked a variety of "hidden hands" moving societies toward a more enlightened future. A world revolution—the Enlightenment project—is transforming societies and carrying them all in the direction of greater wealth, knowledge, and humane moral values. Thomas Paine and the American founders had such ideas. Cold War–era modernization theorists offered a political economic version of this universalist vision, and so did Francis Fukuyama in his famous essay "The End of History."[21] The cards in the deck of politics and economics are stacked in favor of the liberal democratic world. Its principles, institutions, and moral foundations give it advantages over alternative ideologies and projects. Liberal democracy itself is in a sense the self-fulfilling agent of progress. Political agency is not entirely missing in this vision of liberal modernity; societies can move backward and miss historical openings. But the grand forces of modernity are the wind at liberal democracy's back as it forges the modern world order.

Another view offers a more tempered outlook. Liberal democracies can "bend the arc" of history in their direction, but this requires a struggle filled with contingency, compromises, and tragic choices. This narrative is reflected in the liberalism of Reinhold Niebuhr. There is a dark side to human nature that thwarts liberalism's idealist aspirations, but there is also a human capacity for moral reasoning and enlightened self-reflection that can inform the search for a more decent world.[22] President John F. Kennedy gave voice to this view in a speech at American University in 1963. Describing the conditions of world peace, he rejected the idealized vision of a liberal march of history. Peace, he said, could not be based on a "sudden revolution of human nature but on the gradual evolution in human institutions."[23] President Barack Obama echoed this view. Speaking in Hiroshima, Japan, he argued that "technological progress without an equivalent progress in human institutions can doom us."[24] The task of modern states—the liberal democracies especially—was to take on the difficult task of strengthening international norms and institutions. Modernity is relentlessly improving technology and the capacity for violence, but "progress in human institutions" is less certain. Reason and moral principles can define the path forward, but they must do so in a world where unreason and reactionary movements never fully disappear. This narrative is less universal and less optimistic about the future than the high Enlightenment vision. The violence and catastrophes of the past weigh heavily on it. The liberal democratic capacity to create a better world must be realistically understood, constantly cultivated, and wisely employed.

A third view, notably advanced by the philosopher Isaiah Berlin, is even bleaker. Here, tragedy and struggle are never vanquished and human history is not inherently progressive. Humans' universal attributes will not direct them to a common set of political ideals and institutions. This strain of liberalism acknowledges the "value pluralism" of societies and peoples and argues that they have no common pathway or destination. There is no "true path," Berlin argued, on which to "drive the human caravan."[25] His liberalism is built around respect for difference and the search for rules and norms that can allow people of good will to manage their differences. John Gray describes this view as "agonistic"—referencing *agon*, the Greek word for conflict and struggle.[26] Liberalism—and by extension liberal internationalism—seeks to create stable political orders that allow people and societies to define their own identities and values. A different minimalist strain is Judith Shklar's "liberalism of fear." Her liberalism is shorn of universalist or progressive aspirations and is not about moving human society forward. Instead, she argues, it "has only one overriding aim: to secure the political conditions that are necessary for the exercise of political freedom."[27] Liberalism cannot remake societies, perfect human nature, or overcome, in any grand systemic sense, the destructive and violent forces of repression, tyranny, and violence. Liberal societies must struggle simply to protect individual rights and freedoms. All that people have in common is their shared vulnerability to forces that seek their ruin. Berlin's and Shklar's visions radically shift the terms of the liberal project. It is no longer a grand march into a better future, only a search for autonomy, stability, and survival.

Every generation of liberal internationalists has debated and advanced versions of these grand narratives. Today, Berlin's agonistic liberalism has an appeal, if only because it offers a needed corrective to liberalism's tendency toward grandiosity. Nothing guarantees a future defined by the progressive march of democratic societies. "History has no libretto," Berlin wrote in one of his last letters to a friend.[28] Quite the opposite. The liberal project must be grounded on the fragility—indeed the radical uncertainty—of liberal democracy, not on an assumption of inevitability. Modernity does not privilege liberalism; liberalism is an approach to tackling modernity's challenges. But this agonistic view is not necessarily incompatible with the liberalism of "bending the arc" of history. Tragedy, unintended consequences, political decay, catastrophe and collapse—history is not liberal Whiggery. But humans have both a political and moral capacity to "make things better" through the incremental and pragmatic reform of their institutions. This is the liberalism of Philadelphia in 1789 more than that of West Berlin in 1989. It is a view in which political institutions—starting with national constitutions—are needed to protect "the people" from themselves, their leaders, and the upheavals of modernity. Modernity will constantly and inevitably throw up new problems. Liberal democracy—and by extension liberal international order—creates the institutions and working relationships needed to address these problems.

The Road Ahead

If liberal internationalism is to remain relevant in the twenty-first century, it must return to its roots. It must define itself less as a grand vision of a global march toward an ideal society, and more as a pragmatic, reform-oriented approach to making liberal democracies safe. This reformist view sets liberal internationalism apart from other internationalist traditions. It is what Woodrow Wilson had in mind when he argued that the relations among states are "corrigible." John Maynard Keynes noted this orientation in an open letter to FDR in the early years of the New Deal: "You have made yourself the trustee for those in every country who seek to mend the evils of our condition by reasoned experiment within the framework of the existing social system."[29] Roosevelt and his advisers took office in the 1930s not fully understanding the scope or nature of the crises that beset the nation or the world. FDR's specific policies mattered less than his administration's experimental style. They tried various measures; some worked and others failed. Over time, their pragmatic, empirical, problem-solving approach paid off with reforms that put the American system, and thus the wider democratic world, on a more stable footing. Liberal internationalism would do well to recapture this orientation.

To make liberal democracies safe, reasoned experimentation will also need to have an internationalist outlook. This is because liberal democracies, like orchids, do better in some environments than others. They need a stable and cooperative international order to flourish. Liberal principles are vulnerable to demagogues and to the usurpation of state power triggered by foreign threats and wartime emergencies. Liberal democracies are not billiard balls on a pool table. They are more complex and vulnerable polities that require a protective international setting. In essence they are more like eggs, which require the protection of egg cartons. Liberal order building is fundamentally a project to build egg cartons. Likewise, liberal democracies are organized around principles and values that are in deep tension with each other: liberty and equality, individualism and community, sovereignty and interdependence. Liberal order building is in part a project to create a framework of institutions and capacities that help states manage these tensions and trade-offs. In these various ways, liberal internationalism is not some sort of rarefied "globalism" that seeks to rob states of their sovereignty. It is a pragmatic, reform-minded endeavor to strengthen the ability of liberal democracies to survive and flourish.

Across two centuries, liberal internationalism has been manifest as a bundle of internationalisms. It is a cluster of ideas and agendas, not one grand ideological doctrine. The crisis of liberal internationalism is partly the unraveling of the cluster of internationalisms that the Cold War era braided together. It was a coalition that fused ideas about free trade, social democracy, national security, multilateralism, democratic solidarity, and hegemonic leadership. In the 1990s, just when economic and political liberalism were spreading around the world, this coalition broke down. Liberal internationalism became in large part a neoliberal project aimed at expanding and integrating market capitalism. The embedded character of the liberal order eroded. The challenge for the twenty-first century is to rebuild the coalition with an eye to reestablishing the connections between international order and the life opportunities of liberal democratic peoples. This core element of liberal internationalism was hinted at by Norman Angell in 1918 when he coined the term *democratic internationalism* to describe what he hoped would be a new era of cooperation among the Western countries.[30] Liberal internationalism must be defined as a project that seeks to promote the security and well-being of the broad segments of liberal democratic society.

Liberal internationalism also needs to reclaim its legacy as a set of ideas and programs for managing economic and security interdependence. Its aim should not be to open and integrate the world system but to cooperatively shape the terms of openness. This means embedding markets and exchange relations in rules and institutions that balance the trade-offs between efficiency and social protection. Achieving this balance may mean a reduction, at the margin, in trade openness and integration. The goal is less about building or eliminating borders than about agreeing upon principles and institutions for the cooperative management of borders. When the liberal democracies in the 1930s and 1940s attempted to dig themselves out from a collapsed world economy, the degree of openness was less important than the effort to rebuild economic relations around multilateral mechanisms and principles of reciprocity and nondiscrimination. Today, the task is not to champion "globalization" but to agree on a way of managing it.

This book draws a contrast between Wilson and FDR as alternative approaches to liberal internationalism. I argue that Wilson's great contribution to liberal internationalism was to synthesize divergent strands of internationalist thought—to bring together and assemble various mechanisms into one grand structure, whereas FDR's fundamental contribution was to pragmatically reshape and adapt Wilson's synthesis. The question naturally arises: which of the two offers the better prescription for today? At first glance, FDR should command our favor. Wilson essentially misdiagnosed his era. FDR, in contrast, presided over a revolution in thinking about rights and protections within liberal democratic societies and offered a more pragmatic and operational vision of a security community of liberal states. His genius was in the experimental ethos he brought to order building. But I would argue that both are correct and needed—but in different ways. In looking into the future, what is needed is our own, twenty-first-century Wilsonian moment of grand synthesis of new techniques and mechanisms, developed to address problems with which neither Wilson nor FDR would have been familiar, such as climate change, supersonic nuclear weapons, drug-resistant bacteria, the effects of rapid automation of global production chains on the class structure in developed societies, and artificial intelligence to name a few. After this, it is Roosevelt's spirit of pragmatic experimentation and institutional innovation that should inspire a new generation of liberal order building, guided by the goal of making liberal democracies safe.

At each turn over the past two centuries, liberal democracies have had to discover what sort of international order they wanted to build. Now they face this challenge again. Liberal internationalists have always been ambivalent and inconsistent about the character of their preferred order: some have sought to build an exclusive realm for the liberal democracies, leaving the rest of the world on the periphery, while others have imagined a global liberal order built around an ambitious vision of integration and convergence. The virtue of the "small and thick" vision of order is that it is easier for an exclusive grouping to agree upon and pursue expansive social purposes. Liberal order designed as a club creates roles and responsibilities that facilitate the functioning of order. This was the great insight of the post-1945 liberal order: because membership was conditional, states had incentives to act in the interests of the larger group. On the other hand, the virtue of the "large and thin" vision of order is that most of the problems that liberal democracies face are not unique to liberal democracies. All states are vulnerable to global warming, the spread of infectious disease, nuclear proliferation, cyber warfare, and terrorism. This is the essential insight of Westphalian internationalism.

This does raise the question—anticipated in the debates over the "grand area" during the Roosevelt years—of whether, in a purely Westphalian world where liberal internationalism is forced into a subglobal domain, the social, economic, and political security and welfare of liberal democracies can be reasonably maintained. The uncomfortable counterfactual, reminiscent of the interwar years, would be that once a Westphalian order comes to be dominated by illiberal rather than liberal states, the very viability of liberal democracies may be compromised—in other words, there is some "critical proportion" of illiberalism that liberal internationalism may not be able to survive in a Westphalian order. After all, this is precisely the worry that led FDR and his advisers to conclude that the United States could survive and prosper as a democracy only in a unified world in which the liberal democracies held sway.

In the end, with precisely this worry in mind, liberal democracies must work at building both types of order. Liberal democracies have unique interests and values that bring them together. They need each other in order to act together in a way that gives them a critical mass in world politics. But in the twenty-first century, the storms of modernity are also global. Liberal internationalists will need to gather their two hundred years of ideas and projects into a grand effort—illuminated by ideals but grounded in pragmatism—to ensure not just the future of democracy but the survival of the planet.

NOTES

1. Cracks in the Liberal World Order

1. A telling moment came early in the new administration at a meeting President Trump had with his secretaries of defense and state. "'The postwar, rules-based international order is the greatest gift of the greatest generation,' [James] Mattis told the president, according to two meeting attendees. The secretary of defense walked the president through the complex fabric of trade deals, military agreements and international alliances that make up the global system the victors established after World War II, touching off what one attendee described as a 'food fight' and a 'free for all' with the president and the rest of the group. Trump punctuated the session by loudly telling his secretaries of state and defense, as several points during the meeting, 'I don't agree!'" *Politico*, 3 March 2018.
2. See G. John Ikenberry, "The Plot against American Foreign Policy: Can the Liberal Order Survive?," *Foreign Affairs*, Vol. 96, No. 3 (May/June 2017), pp. 2–9.
3. Donald Tusk, quoted in Michael Shear, "Trump Attends G-7 with Defiance, Proposing to Readmit Russia," *New York Times*, 8 June 2018. Tusk made these comments in the aftermath of the G-7 summit, the annual gathering of the leaders of the seven major industrial democracies, gathered in Toronto, Canada, in June 2018. For over forty years, these G-7 summits have been a fixture of the Western liberal order, a moment when the United States and its closest democratic allies meet to discuss economic and security affairs and reaffirm their historic ties and commitment to common values and interests. But the 2018 summit took a different turn. The US president, Donald Trump, arriving late and leaving early to signal his distaste for the event, attacked his allies for unfair trade practices and inadequate alliance contributions, while also restating his determination to leave the Paris climate accord and the Iran nuclear agreement. In negotiations over the

summit communiqué, Trump's team objected to including the time-honored statement of their shared commitment to the "rules-based order." The delegation eventually backed down, agreeing to a compromise that expressed support for "a" rules-based order rather than "the" rules-based order. In the end, however, after leaving the conference, Trump withdrew his support for the communiqué.

4. See Ivan Krastev and Stephen Holmes, *The Light That Failed: A Reckoning* (New York: Pegasus Books, 2020); and Edward Luce, *The Retreat of Western Liberalism* (New York: Atlantic Monthly Press, 2017).

5. See Timothy Snyder, *The Road to Unfreedom: Russia, Europe, America* (New York: Penguin, 2018).

6. Ross Douthat, "Cracks in the Liberal Order," *New York Times*, Sunday Review, 26 December 2015.

7. Many observers have noted the growing troubles facing the US-led liberal international order, emphasizing, variously, crises besetting American hegemony, Western political order, the deeper foundations of liberalism and liberal internationalism, and liberal modernity itself. See, for example: Gideon Rose, "The Fourth Founding: The United States and the Liberal Order," *Foreign Affairs*, Vol. 98, No. 1 (January/February 2019), pp. 10–21; Hanns W. Maull, "The Once and Future Liberal Order," *Survival*, Vol. 61, No. 2 (April/May 2019), pp. 7–32; Kori Schake, "The Trump Doctrine Is Winning and the World Is Losing," *New York Times*, 15 June 2018; Richard Haass, "Liberal World Order, R.I.P.," *Project Syndicate*, 21 March 2018, https://www.project-syndicate.org/commentary/end-of-liberal-world-order-by-richard-n--haass-2018-03?barrier=accesspaylog; Francis Fukuyama, "US against the World? Trump's America and the New World Order," *Financial Times*, 11 November 2016; Ian Buruma, "The End of the Anglo-American Order," *New York Times Magazine*, 29 November 2016; Ulrich Speck, "The Crisis of Liberal Order," *The American Interest*, 12 September 2016; Michael J. Boyle, "The Coming Illiberal Era," *Survival*, Vol. 58, No. 2 (2016), pp. 35–66; Charles A. Kupchan and Peter L. Trubowitz, "Dead Center: The Demise of Liberal Internationalism in the United States," *International Security*, Vol. 32, No. 2 (Fall 2007), pp. 7–44; Georg Sørensen, *A Liberal World Order in Crisis: Choosing between Imposition and Restraint* (Ithaca, NY: Cornell University Press, 2011); Rebekka Friedman, Kevork Oskanian, and Ramon Pacheco Pardo, eds., *After Liberalism? The Future of Liberalism in International Relations* (New York: Palgrave Macmillan, 2013); Amitav Acharya, *The End of American World Order* (London: Polity Press, 2014); Stanley Hoffmann, "The Crisis of Liberal Internationalism," *Foreign Policy*, No. 98 (Spring 1995), pp. 159–77; and John Gray, *False Dawn: The Delusions of Global Capitalism* (New York: New Press, 2000). For a collection of alternative views, see G. John Ikenberry, Inderjeet Parmar, and Doug Stokes, eds., "Ordering the World? Liberal Internationalism in Theory and Practice," special issue, *International Affairs*, Vol. 94, No 1 (January 2018).

8. See Miles Kahler, "Who Is Liberal Now? Rising Powers and Global Norms," in Amitav Acharya, ed., *Why Govern: Rethinking Demand, Purpose, and Progress in Global Governance* (Cambridge: Cambridge University Press, 2016), pp. 55–73.

9. For surveys of mid-1970s Western debates over the future of liberal democracy, see Jan-Werner Müller, *Contesting Democracy: Political Thought in Twentieth-Century Europe* (New Haven, CT: Yale University Press, 2011), chap. 6; and Niall Ferguson, Charles S. Maier, Erez Manela, and Daniel J. Sargent, eds., *The Shock of the Global: The 1970s in Perspective* (Cambridge, MA: Harvard University Press, 2010). The Trilateral Commission published perhaps the most famous study of 1970s-era problems of liberal democracy. See Michel Crozier, Samuel P. Huntington, and Joji Watanuki, *The Crisis of Democracy: On the Governability of Democracies* (New York: New York University Press, 1975).

10. On the crisis of authority in the Western liberal order, see G. John Ikenberry, *Liberal Leviathan: The Origins, Transformation, and Crisis of the American World Order* (Princeton, NJ: Princeton University Press, 2011).

11. See Robert Kagan, *The Jungle Grows Back: America and Our Imperiled World* (New York: Alfred A. Knopf, 2018).

12. See Martin Jacques, *When China Rules the World: The End of the Western World and the Birth of a New Global Order* (New York: Penguin, 2009).

13. See Charles A. Kupchan, *No One's World: The West, The Rising Rest, and the Coming Global Turn* (Oxford: Oxford University Press, 2012).

14. Pankaj Mishra, *Age of Anger: A History of the Present* (New York: Farrar, Straus and Giroux, 2017), p. 25. For a similar argument, see Patrick J. Deneen, *Why Liberalism Failed* (New Haven, CT: Yale University Press, 2018). Yuval Noah Harari argues that the liberal millennium is giving way to a posthumanist future, driven by artificial intelligence and technologies that reengineer human minds. Harari, *Homo Deus: A Brief History of Tomorrow* (New York: Random House, 2016). For critiques, see Adam Gopnik, "The Illiberal Imagination: Are Liberals on the Wrong Side of History?," *New Yorker*, 20 March 2017, pp. 88–93; and Michael Ignatieff, "Which Way Are We Going?," *New York Review of Books*, Vol. 64, No. 6 (6 April 2017), pp. 4–6.

15. Ira Katznelson, *Desolation and Enlightenment: Political Knowledge after Total War, Totalitarianism, and the Holocaust* (New York: Columbia University Press, 2003).

16. Wilson cited in Lloyd Gardner, *The Anglo-American Response to Revolution, 1913–1923* (Oxford: Oxford University Press, 1984), p. 1.

17. Traditions are, as Eric Hobsbawm argues, constructed—or invented—by social actors seeking to connect their current circumstances to ideas and events in the past, thereby creating lineages and continuities that impart meaning and direction to their pursuits. See Hobsbawm, "Introduction: Inventing Traditions," in Hobsbawm and Terence Ranger, eds., *The Invention of Tradition* (Cambridge: Cambridge University Press, 1983), pp. 1–14.

18. Ideology can be thought of as ideas that are converted into social forces or organized agendas for political action; programmatic worldviews that fuse the interests of actors with beliefs and ideals. See George Lichtheim, "The Concept of Ideology," *History and Theory*, Vol. 4 (1964), pp. 164–95.

19. The political project of liberal internationalism is built around stories of thinkers, ideas, activists, leaders, movements, breakthroughs, triumphs, and failures. In this sense, liberal internationalism can be depicted as what George Egerton calls "political myth," that is, "a dramatic didactic narrative or projection of events, social conditions, and human actions, an imaginative presentation of history and destiny with intense meaning for a social group or class." George W. Egerton, "Collective Security as Political Myth: Liberal Internationalism and the League of Nations in Politics and History," *International History Review*, Vol. 4 (1983), p. 498.

20. The term *liberal internationalism* began to appear in scholarly writings in the 1930s and 1940s and came into widespread use in the 1970s and after. See Tim Dunne and Matt MacDonald, "The Politics of Liberal Internationalism," *International Politics*, Vol. 50, No. 1 (January 2013), pp. 1–17; and Beate Jahn, *Liberal Internationalism: Theory, History, Practice* (New York: Palgrave, 2013). Foreshadowing the term, Norman Angell introduced the idea of "democratic internationalism" in a 1918 book on Western postwar cooperation. See Angell, *The Political Conditions of Allied Success: A Plea for a Protective Union of the Democracies* (New York: G. P. Putnam's Sons, 1918). The term *liberal international order* came into use more recently. The first scholarly use of the term appears to be in a 1999 article that I coauthored with Daniel Deudney. See Deudney and G. John Ikenberry, "The Nature and Sources of Liberal International Order," *Review of International Studies*, Vol. 25, No. 2 (April 1999), pp. 179–96. Harold Quigley, a US Far Eastern expert writing in 1943, used the term in outlining a strategy for promoting postwar order in the Far East after the (hoped for) defeat of Japan. See Quigley, "The Far East and the Future," *Virginia Quarterly Review*, Vol. 19, No. 1 (Winter 1943). I thank Michael Doyle for this reference. The term did not appear in the *New York Times* until 2012. See Thomas Wright, "The Return of Great-Power Rivalry Was Inevitable," *Atlantic Monthly*, 12 September 2018, https://www.theatlantic.com/international/archive/2018/09/liberal-international-order-free-world-trump-authoritarianism/569881/. *Liberal international order*—or just *liberal order*—is now invoked frequently as a shorthand term for the America-led international order, which is generally defined by the alliances, institutions, and rules created and upheld by the United States and other states after World War II. In this book, I use the term in the more generic sense, as a general type of international order, of which the American-led liberal hegemonic order is but one specific manifestation.

21. Daniel Deudney, *Bounding Power: Republican Security Theory from the Polis to the Global Village* (Princeton, NJ: Princeton University Press, 2007), p. 2.

22. For accounts of liberal internationalism that explore various historical and thematic aspects, see Hans Kundnani, "What Is the Liberal International Order?," Policy Essay, No. 17 (Washington, DC: The German Marshall Fund, 2017); Casper Sylvest, *British Liberal Internationalism, 1880–1930* (Manchester: Manchester University Press, 2009); Sondra R. Herman, *Eleven against War: Studies in American Internationalist Thought, 1898–1921* (Stanford, CA: Stanford University Press, 1969); Michael W. Doyle, *Liberal Peace: Selected Essays* (New York: Routledge, 2012); Michael Howard, *War and the Liberal Conscience* (London: Temple Smith, 1978); Tony Smith, *America's Mission: The United States and the Worldwide Struggle for Democracy* (Princeton, NJ: Princeton University Press, 1994); Tony Smith, *Why Wilson Matters: The Origins of American Liberal Internationalism and Its Crisis Today* (Princeton, NJ: Princeton University Press, 2017); Michael Mandelbaum, *The Ideas that Conquered the World: Peace, Democracy, and Free Markets in the Twenty-First Century* (New York: PublicAffairs, 2004); Timothy Garton Ash, *Free World: America, Europe, and the Surprising Future of the West* (New York: Random House, 2004); Elizabeth Borgwardt, *A New Deal for the World: America's Vision for Human Rights* (Cambridge, MA: Harvard University Press, 2005); Stewart Patrick, *The Best Laid Plans: The Origins of American Multilateralism and the Dawn of the Cold War* (New York: Rowman and Little-field, 2008); Frank Ninkovich, *Modernity and Power: A History of the Domino in the Twentieth Century* (Chicago: University of Chicago Press, 1994); Tim Dunne and Trine Flockhart, eds., *Liberal World Orders* (Oxford: Oxford University Press, 2013); and Ikenberry, *Liberal Leviathan*. For an influential portrait of liberalism within the wider array of classical theories of international relations, see Michael Doyle, *Ways of War and Peace: Realism, Liberalism, and Socialism* (New York: Norton, 1997).

23. I thank Edward Keene for helping me clarify this point.

24. For the classic statement of realism, defined in terms of the problem of anarchy, see Kenneth Waltz, *Theory of International Politics* (New York: Random House, 1979).

25. The major modern statements of these two varieties of realism are, respectively, Waltz, *Theory of International Politics*; and Robert Gilpin, *War and Change in World Politics* (New York: Cambridge University Press, 1981). For a portrait of these two branches of realist theory and their diverging scholarly trajectories in the 1980s, see William Wohlforth, "Gilpinian Realism and International Relations," *International Relations*, Vol. 25, No. 4 (2011), pp. 499–511.

26. For a discussion of cyclical and developmental logics in international relations theory, see Robert Jervis, "The Future of World Politics: Will It Resemble the Past?," *International Security*, Vol. 16, No. 3 (Winter 1991/92), pp. 39–73.

27. Ernest Gellner, *Nations and Nationalism* (Ithaca, NY: Cornell University Press, 1983), p. 112.

28. For important historical accounts of the rise of modern societies and international relations, see Barry Buzan and George Lawson, *The Global Transformation: History, Modernity and the Making of International Relations* (Cambridge: Cambridge University Press, 2015); C. A. Bayly, *The Birth of the Modern World, 1780–1914* (Oxford: Blackwell, 2004); and Jürgen Osterhammel, *The Transformation of the World: A Global History of the Nineteenth Century*, trans. Patrick Camiller (Princeton, NJ: Princeton University Press, 2014).

29. On the logic and dynamics of modernizing industrial societies and implication for international relations, see Daniel Deudney, "Liberal Historical Materialism," in Deudney, *Bounding Power*, chap. 7.

30. See Hans J. Morgenthau, *Politics among Nations: The Struggle for Power and Peace*, 5th ed. (New York: Alfred A. Knopf, 1973); E. H. Carr, *The Conditions of Peace* (London: Macmillan, 1942); and Carr, *Nationalism and After* (London: Macmillan, 1945).

31. G. Lowes Dickinson, *The International Anarchy, 1904–1914* (New York: The Century Co., 1926), p. 47. I am grateful to Mick Cox for this reference.

32. As Stanley Hoffmann puts it: "There are forces capable of ensuring a minimum of order. They result from common sociability (Locke's notion) or mutual interests (Hume's); and they can result in common norms." Hoffmann, *Primacy or World Order: American Foreign Policy since the Cold War* (New York: McGraw-Hill, 1978), p. 108.

33. These divergent emergent and contractarian conceptions of order have been at the heart of recent debates between realists and liberal internationalists over anarchy and the role of institutions in fostering cooperation between states. See Waltz, *Theory of International Politics*; and Robert O. Keohane, *After Hegemony: Coöperation and Discord in the World Political Economy* (Princeton, NJ: Princeton University Press, 1984). The debate is showcased in David Baldwin, ed., *Neorealism and Neoliberalism: The Contemporary Debate* (New York: Columbia University Press, 1993).

34. See Ikenberry, *Liberal Leviathan*, chap. 2.

35. See John Ruggie's discussion of different types of "institutional forms" of international order. Ruggie, *Multilateralism Matters: The Theory and Praxis of an Institutional Form* (New York: Columbia University Press, 1993). For a survey of types of international order, see Stephen A. Kocs, *International Order: A Political History* (Boulder, CO: Lynne Rienner, 2019); Matthew D. Stephen and Michael Zurn, eds., *Contested World Orders: Rising Powers, Non-Governmental Organizations, and the Politics of Authority beyond the Nation-State* (Oxford: Oxford University Press, 2019), chap. 1; and Ikenberry, *Liberal Leviathan*, chap. 2.

36. Famously, Isaiah Berlin captured this point in his distinction between negative and positive concepts of liberty. Negative liberty is the protection of life and property against the intrusions of others. Its realization involves resisting the infringements and impositions of others on one's own freedom. Positive liberty involves the realization of qualities of life that one does not yet possess, which requires active collaboration with others to bring them forth. See Isaiah Berlin, "Two Concepts of Liberty," in Berlin, *Four Essays on Liberty* (Oxford: Oxford University Press, 1969), pp. 118–72.

37. See Helena Rosenblatt, *The Lost History of Liberalism: From Ancient Rome to the Twenty-First Century* (Princeton, NJ: Princeton University Press, 2018). For an incisive account of the intellectual origins and foundations of modern liberalism, emphasizing its social and moral first principles, see Adam Gopnik, "The Rhinoceros Manifesto: What Is Liberalism?," in Gopnik, *A Thousand Small Sanities: The Moral Adventure of Liberalism* (New York: Basic Books, 2019), pp. 23–82. For recent histories of the liberal tradition, see Edward Fawcett, *Liberalism: The Life of an Idea* (Princeton, NJ: Princeton University Press, 2014); and James Traub, *What Was Liberalism? The Past, Present, and Promise of a Noble Idea* (New York: Basic Books, 2019).

38. Rosenblatt, *The Lost History of Liberalism*, p. 40.

39. See Sylvest, *British Liberal Internationalism, 1880–1930*.

40. E. H. Carr, *The Twenty-Years Crisis, 1919–1939: An Introduction to the Study of International Relations* (London: Macmillan, 1951), p. 103. For a liberal critique of Carr, see Robert O. Keohane, "Twenty Years of Institutional Liberalism," *International Relations*, Vol. 26, No. 2 (June 2012), pp. 125–38.

41. See Graham Allison, "The Myth of the Liberal Order: From Historical Accident to Conventional Wisdom," *Foreign Affairs*, Vol. 97, No. 4 (July/August 2018), pp. 124–33; and Patrick Porter, "A World Imagined: Nostalgia and Liberal Order," *Policy Analysis*, no. 843 (Washington, DC: CATO Institute, 2018). For a critique, see Rebecca Friedman Lissner and Mira Rapp-Hooper, "The Liberal Order Is More than a Myth: But It Must Adapt to the New Balance of Power," *Foreign Affairs*, 31 July 2018, https://www.foreignaffairs.com/articles/world/2018-07-31/liberal-order-more-myth.

42. John Mearsheimer, *The Great Delusion: Liberal Dreams and International Realities* (New Haven, CT: Yale University Press, 2018), p. 219.

43. For other critiques of liberalism and liberal hegemony for this perspective, see Stephen M. Walt, *The Hell of Good Intentions: America's Foreign Policy Elite and the Decline of U.S. Primacy* (New York: Farrar, Straus and Giroux, 2018); Barry Posen, *Restraint: A New Foundation for U.S. Grand Strategy* (Ithaca, NY: Cornell University Press, 2015); Patrick Porter, *The False Promise of Liberal Order: Nostalgia, Delusion, and the Rise of Trump* (Cambridge: Polity Press, 2020); and Michael Desch,

"America's Liberal Illiberalism: The Ideological Origins of Overreaction in U.S. Foreign Policy," *International Security*, Vol. 32, No. 3 (Winter 2007/8), pp. 7–43.

44. For critiques of liberal internationalism along these lines, see Samuel Moyn, "Beyond Liberal Internationalism," *Dissent*, Winter 2017, pp. 108–14; and Perry Anderson, *The H-Word: The Peripeteia of Hegemony* (London: Verso, 2017).

45. Samuel Moyn, "Soft Sells: On Liberal Internationalism," *The Nation*, 3 October 2011, p. 43.

46. Mark Mazower, *No Enchanted Palace: The End of Empire and the Ideological Origins of the United Nations* (Princeton, NJ: Princeton University Press, 2009), p. 17. See also Jeanne Morefield, *Covenants without Swords: Idealist Liberalism and the Spirit of Empire* (Princeton, NJ: Princeton University Press, 2005).

47. Samuel Moyn, *Not Enough: Human Rights in an Unequal World* (Cambridge, MA: Harvard University Press, 2018). See also Richard A. Falk, *Achieving Human Rights* (New York: Routledge, 2009), and Falk, *Human Rights Horizons* (New York: Routledge, 2000). For many decades, Falk has been a leading voice in normative debates about world order and struggles over social justice, sustainable development, and nuclear disarmament. See Falk, *A Study of Future Worlds* (New York: Free Press, 1975).

48. For thoughtful reflections of the economic and political failings of liberal internationalism, see Jeff Colgen and Robert Keohane, "The Liberal Order Is Rigged: Fix It Now or Watch It Wither," *Foreign Affairs*, Vol. 96, No. 3 (May/June 2017), pp. 36–44; Eric Posner, "Liberal Internationalism and the Populist Backlash," University of Chicago working paper no. 606 (11 January 2017); and Stephan Haggard, "Liberal Pessimism: International Relations Theory and the Emerging Powers," *Asia & Pacific Policy Studies*, Vol. 1, No. 1 (January 2014), pp. 1–17.

49. Compare, for example, Andrew J. Bacevich, *American Empire: The Realities and Consequences* (Cambridge, MA: Harvard University Press, 2002); and Perry Anderson, *American Foreign Policy and Its Thinkers* (London: Verso, 2015).

50. Mark Mazower, *Governing the World: The History of an Idea* (London: Penguin, 2012), p. xv.

2. Liberal Democracy and International Relations

1. Arthur Schlesinger Jr., "Has Democracy a Future?," *Foreign Affairs*, September/October 1997, p. 11.

2. Montesquieu, *Considerations on the Causes of the Grandeur and Decadence of the Romans*, trans. Jehu Baker (New York: D. Appleton and Co., 1882), p. 378.

3. Björn Wittrock, "Modernity: One, None, or Many? European Origins and Modernity as a Global Condition," *Dadealus*, Winter 2000, pp. 55–56.

4. Anthony Giddens, *The Consequences of Modernity* (Stanford, CA: Stanford University Press, 1990), p. 2.

5. Immanuel Kant, "The Idea of a Universal History with a Cosmopolitan Intent" [1784], in Kant, *Perpetual Peace and Other Essays*, trans. Ted Humphrey (Cambridge, MA: Hackett, 1983). For a discussion of this point, see Andrew Hurrell, "Kant and the Kantian Paradigm in International Relations," *Review of International Studies*, Vol. 16, No. 3 (July 1990), pp. 183–205.

6. Adam Smith, *An Inquiry into the Nature and Causes of the Wealth of Nations* [1776] (Oxford: Clarendon Press, 1976).

7. Smith developed these ideas in his earlier and lesser-known book *The Theory of Moral Sentiments*. Smith's philosophical views were greatly influenced by David Hume. See Dennis C. Rasmussen, *The Infidel and the Professor: David Hume, Adam Smith, and the Friendship That Shaped Modern Thought* (Princeton, NJ: Princeton University Press, 2017). For an exploration of Smith's moral theory as it relates to international relations, see Andrew Wyatt-Walter, "Adam Smith and the Liberal Tradition in International Relations," *Review of International Studies*, Vol. 22, No. 1 (January 1996), pp. 5–28.

8. Jeremy Bentham, *A Fragment on Government and An Introduction to the Principles of Morals and Legislation* [1776], ed. with an introduction by Wilfrid Harrison (Oxford: Basil Blackwell, 1948), p. 3. See David Armitage, "Globalizing Jeremy Bentham," *History of Political Thought*, Vol. 32, No. 1 (2011), pp. 63–82.

9. These internationalist thinkers worried about whether states would constrain their actions in the face of international law. But, as F. H. Hinsley argues, they based their optimism on the belief that states would obey the law because of enlightened understanding of their interests and the pressure of public opinion, which "should be an adequate restraint on civilized states as it should be within them." F. H. Hinsley, *Power and the Pursuit of Peace* (Cambridge: Cambridge University Press, 1963), p. 87.

10. The lineages of this view can be traced to earlier centuries. A particularly influential statement is Bernard de Mandeville's *The Fable of the Bees*, published in 1705, which consists of a poem, along with commentary, with these famous lines: "Thus every Part was full of Vice, / Yet the whole Mass a Paradise; / Flatter'd in Peace, and fear'd in Wars, / They were th' Esteem of Foreigners, / And lavish of their Wealth and Lives, / The Balance of all other Hives." Mandeville, *The Fable of the Bees: Or Private Vices, Publick Benefits*, with an introduction by Phillip Harth (London: Penguin, 1989). David Hume reaches a similar conclusion in "Of the Independencey of Parliament," in Hume, *Essays: Moral, Political and Literary* [1777] (Indianapolis: Liberty Fund, 1987), p. 42: "Political writers have established it as a maxim, that, in contriving any system of government, and fixing the several checks and controuls of the constitution, every man ought to be supposed a knave,

and to have no other end, in all his actions, than private interest. By this interest we must govern him, and, by means of it, make him, notwithstanding his insatiable avarice and ambition, co-operate to public good." Similarly, Rousseau begins his *Social Contract* by promising to "take men as they are and laws as they can be." The best theoretical statement of these arguments is in Albert Hirschman, *The Passions and the Interests: Political Arguments for Capitalism before Its Triumph* (Princeton, NJ: Princeton University Press, 1977).

11. John Robertson, *The Case for the Enlightenment: Scotland and Naples, 1680–1760* (Cambridge: Cambridge University Press, 2005), p. 28.

12. Not all Enlightenment thinking pointed in a liberal direction or led to optimistic pronouncements about the future. See Isaiah Berlin, "The Bent Twig," in Berlin, *The Crooked Timber of Humanity: Chapters in the History of Ideas* (London: John Murray, 1990), and Berlin, "The Counter-Enlightenment," in Berlin, *Against the Current: Essays in the History of Ideas* (Harmondsworth, UK: Penguin, 1982), pp. 1–24.

13. Dennis C. Rasmussen, *The Pragmatic Enlightenment: Recovering the Liberalism of Hume, Smith, Montesquieu, and Voltaire* (Cambridge: Cambridge University Press, 2014).

14. Peter Gay, *The Enlightenment: An Interpretation* (New York: Alfred A. Knopf, 1966), p. 179. Margaret C. Jacob provides a sweeping portrait of the everyday ways in which Europeans and American colonists, from the second half of the eighteenth century, experienced the effects of Enlightenment thinking, allowing them to "imagine entirely human creations such as republics and democracies." Jacob, *The Secular Enlightenment* (Princeton, NJ: Princeton University Press, 2019), p. 3.

15. See Nils Gilman, *Mandarins of the Future: Modernization Theory in Cold War America* (Baltimore: Johns Hopkins University Press, 2003); Clark Kerr, *The Future of Industrial Societies: Convergence or Continued Diversity?* (Cambridge, MA: Harvard University Press, 1983); and Shmuel N. Eisenstadt, ed., *Multiple Modernities* (New Brunswick, NJ: Transaction Publishers, 2012).

16. Liberal international order can and has coexisted with these other varieties of order; indeed, there is a lively debate about whether liberal international order—organized within the Western or liberal democratic world—leads to and depends upon imperialism and empire elsewhere. For an important statement, see Atul Kohli, *Imperialism and the Developing World: How Britain and the United States Shaped the Global Periphery* (Oxford: Oxford University Press, 2020).

17. Smith claimed that this was the most important (but "least observed") effect of free trade and commercial society, put forward as his culminating argument in book 3 of *The Wealth of Nations*.

18. There are many qualifications and complexities to this claim. The theory of import substitution argues that the selective use of protectionism can be useful to

developing countries seeking to foster domestic industry in key sectors, which can make a country wealthier in the long run—for example, the United States in the nineteenth century and China in the twenty-first century. Modern formulations of these insights include the Stolper–Samuelson theorem and the broader Heckscher–Ohlin trade theory. For a survey, see Robert Gilpin, *The Political Economy of International Relations* (Princeton, NJ: Princeton University Press, 1987), chap. 5.

19. Hirschman, *The Passions and the Interests.*

20. Jeremy Bentham, *An Introduction to the Principles of Morals and Legislation* [1780] (Oxford: Clarendon Press, 1907).

21. This is not a vision of world government, but of rules and institutions that facilitate cooperation. This is captured by Montesquieu when he argued that international law is "based by nature upon this principle: that the various nations ought to do, in peace, the most good to each other and, in war, the least harm possible, without detriment to their genuine interests." Charles de Secondat, Baron de Montesquieu, *The Spirit of the Laws* [1748], trans. Anne M. Cohler, Basia C. Miller, and Harold S. Stone (Cambridge: Cambridge University Press, 1989), book 1, p. 3.

22. John Gerard Ruggie, "Multilateralism: The Anatomy of an Institution," in Ruggie, ed., *Multilateralism Matters: The Theory and Praxis of an Institutional Form* (New York: Columbia University Press, 1993), p. 11.

23. The distinction—although difficult to fully separate in reality—is between rule *of* law and rule *by* law. The specific theories that liberal internationalists have offered to describe and explain the functions and efficacy of international rules and institutions have varied across eras and intellectual schools of thought.

24. Robert O. Keohane, *After Hegemony: Cooperation and Discord in the World Political Economy* (Princeton, NJ: Princeton University Press, 1984).

25. John Rawls, *The Law of Peoples* (Cambridge, MA: Harvard University Press, 1999), p. 35. On the connections between the domestic rule of law and international legal regimes, see Ian Hurd, *How to Do Things with International Law* (Princeton, NJ: Princeton University Press, 2017).

26. See G. John Ikenberry, *After Victory: Institutions, Strategic Restraint, and the Rebuilding of Order after Major War* (Princeton, NJ: Princeton University Press, 2001).

27. *Foreign Relations of the United States: Lansing Papers*, Vol. 2 (Washington, DC: US Department of State, 1939–1940), p. 118. I am grateful to Tolya Levshin for this reference.

28. Clarence Streit, writing in 1938, appears to be the first modern writer to point out the empirical tendency of liberal democracies to maintain peace among themselves. See Streit, *Union Now: A Proposal for a Federal Union of the Leading Democracies* (New York: Harper, 1938), pp. 90–92. This is noted by Michael W. Doyle in "The

Voice of the People: Political Theorists on the International Implications of Democracy," in Doyle, *Liberal Peace: Selected Essays* (New York: Routledge, 2012), p. 123. As Duncan Bell argues, there was already a belief in the pacific tendencies of democracies in the nineteenth century. See Bell, "Before the Democratic Peace: Racial Utopianism, Empire and the Abolition of War," *European Journal of International Relations*, Vol. 20, No. 3 (2014), pp. 647–70.

29. Charles Lipson, *Reliable Partners: How Democracies Have Made a Separate Peace* (Princeton, NJ: Princeton University Press, 2005).

30. Autocracies often have more stable leadership than liberal democracies, which replace leaders through regular elections, and this stability can be useful in securing international agreements. Scholars have recently begun to explore the varying capacities of autocratic states to engage in cooperation, finding that some of the institutional features that facilitate cooperation among democracies (greater leader accountability, limited policy flexibility, and greater transparency) can also be found in some autocratic states. See Michaela Mattes and Mariana Rodríguez, "Autocracies and International Cooperation," *International Studies Quarterly*, Vol. 58, No. 3 (September 2014), pp. 527–38. A recent line of argument focuses on the ways in which the domestic vulnerability of authoritarian states to nationalist protests can be used by leaders to gain bargaining advantages in international conflicts with other states, including democracies. See Jessica L. Weeks, "Autocratic Audience Costs: Regime Type and Signaling Resolve," *International Organization*, Vol. 62, No. 1 (2008), pp. 35–64; Weeks, "Strongmen and Straw Men: Authoritarian Regimes and the Initiation of International Conflict," *American Political Science Review*, Vol. 106, No. 2 (2012), pp. 326–47; and Jessica Chen Weiss, *Powerful Patriots: Nationalist Protest in China's Foreign Relations* (Oxford: Oxford University Press, 2014).

31. Lipson, *Reliable Partners*.

32. See, for example, David Lake, "Power Pacifists: Democratic States and War," *American Political Science Review*, Vol. 46, No. 1 (March 1992), pp. 24–37.

33. See Michael W. Doyle, "Liberalism and World Politics," *American Political Science Review*, Vol. 80, No. 4 (December 1986), pp. 1151–69, which argues that democracies behave on the "assumption of amity" toward one another and on the "assumption of enmity" toward authoritarian regimes.

34. For studies of the "sociability" of Western liberal democracies in the nineteenth century, see Frank Thistlethwaite, *America and the Atlantic Community: Anglo-American Aspects, 1790–1850* (New York: Harper Torchbooks, 1963); Robert Kelley, *The Transatlantic Persuasion: The Liberal-Democratic Mind in the Age of Gladstone* (New York: Knopf, 1969); and John M. Owen, *Liberal Peace, Liberal War: American Politics and International Security* (Princeton, NJ: Princeton University Press, 1997).

35. Michael W. Doyle, "Kant, Liberal Legacies, and Foreign Affairs, Part I," in Doyle, *Liberal Peace*, pp. 20–21.
36. Daniel Deudney and G. John Ikenberry, "The Nature and Sources of Liberal International Order," *Review of International Studies*, Vol. 25 (1999), pp. 179–96. See also Deudney, "The Philadelphian System: Sovereignty, Arms Control, and Balance of Power in the American States-Union, 1787–1861," *International Organization*, Vol. 49, No. 2 (Spring 1995), pp. 191–228; Deudney, "Binding Sovereigns: Authority, Structure, and Geopolitics in Philadelphian Systems," in *State Sovereignty as Social Construct*, ed. Thomas Biersteker and Cynthia Weber (New York: Cambridge University Press, 1996), pp. 190–239; Deudney, *Bounding Power: Republican Security Theory from the Polis to the Global Village* (Princeton, NJ: Princeton University Press, 2007); and Ikenberry, *After Victory*, chap. 1.
37. Paul W. Schroeder, "Alliances: 1815–1945: Weapons of Power and Tools of Management," in Klaus Knorr, ed., *Historical Dimensions of National Security Problems* (Lawrence: University Press of Kansas, 1975), p. 230.
38. Although liberal states have pioneered and built the most elaborate co-binding security institutions, it is a strategy that can also be pursued more generally between geopolitical rivals. This idea of "enmeshment in institutions" to mitigate security rivalry was raised by a British diplomat, Edward Wood, Earl of Halifax, in a letter to a colleague, Lord Robert Cecil, in reference to British relations with Russia in 1927: "Do not let the Cabinet break with the Soviet[s] if you can help it. I cannot see that it would do the slightest good, and I have an uneasy feeling that there is something in the whole Russian problem that is not clearly revealed to those who would abruptly break off all relations. It may be that you will never alter Russia by appeals to a correct theory of international relations, but that the process will be much slower and will only come about through Russia itself no longer wanting to be a bother to everybody, and that this in turn will only come about when she has been, by trade and otherwise, drawn out of her isolation. *If you stand sufficiently far away from a single horse he can give you a very effective kick; but if you are among a dozen horses in a railway-truck, they cannot hurt you.*" Halifax to Cecil, 6 April 1927, Add MS 51084, Cecil of Chelwood Papers, British Library (emphasis added). I am grateful to Tolya Levshin for this reference.
39. Karl Deutsch et al., *Political Community and the North Atlantic Area: International Organization in the Light of Historical Experience* (Princeton, NJ: Princeton University Press, 1957). See also Emanuel Adler and Michael Barnett, *Security Communities* (Cambridge: Cambridge University Press, 1998).
40. Hedley Bull, *The Anarchical Society: A Study of Order in World Politics* (London: Macmillan, 1977), p. 4.

41. John Gerard Ruggie, "International Regimes, Transactions and Change: Embedded Liberalism in the Postwar Economic Order," *International Organization,* Vol. 36, No. 2 (1982), pp. 379–415.

42. China may be in this position today: seeking to participate in parts of the liberal international order, but worried about—and seeking to guard against—its "corrosive" effects on authoritarian rule at home. See Thomas Christensen, *The China Challenge: Shaping the Choices of a Rising Power* (New York: Norton, 2015).

43. E. H. Carr, *The Twenty Years' Crisis, 1919–1930: An Introduction to the Study of International Relations* (London: Macmillan, 1951), pp. 22–23, 27.

44. This reformist ethos of liberal internationalism is captured in Martin Wight's description of "rationalism," which he distinguishes from realism and revolutionism. See Wight, *International Theory: The Three Traditions* (Leicester: Leicester University Press, 1991).

45. See G. John Ikenberry, "Liberal Internationalism 3.0: America and the Dilemmas of Liberal World Order," *Perspectives on Politics,* Vol. 7, No. 1 (March 2009), pp. 71–87.

46. On the dimensions of sovereignty, see Stephen Krasner, *Sovereignty: Organized Hypocrisy* (Princeton, NJ: Princeton University Press, 1999).

47. See David Lake, *Hierarchy in International Relations* (Ithaca, NY: Cornell University Press, 2009); and Ian Clark, *The Hierarchy of States: Reform and Resistance in the International Order* (Cambridge: Cambridge University Press, 2009).

48. See Josiah Ober, "The Original Meaning of 'Democracy,'" *Constellations,* Vol. 15, No. 1 (2008), pp. 3–9. The term *democracy* as a description of an institutional form emerged in the sixteenth and seventeenth centuries in the works of thinkers such as Jean Bodin in France and Thomas Hobbes in England, both defenders of absolutist monarchy.

49. The root of the word *liberal* is the Latin word *liber,* which refers to a free person, as opposed to a slave.

50. The tradition of republican political theory runs from Polybius in antiquity to Machiavelli in the Renaissance to Montesquieu in the mid-eighteenth century and on to Jefferson, Madison, and Adams of the American founding. See Montesquieu, *The Spirit of the Laws.* For a restatement by its leading modern theorist, see Philip Pettit, *On the People's Terms: A Republican Theory and Model of Democracy* (Cambridge: Cambridge University Press, 2012).

51. Liberal democracy is a sort of conceptual portmanteau, and its two parts— liberalism and democracy—do not inevitably go together. Indeed, they are often in tension. Liberalism refers to principles of individual rights and juridical limits on state power, while democracy refers to principles of popular sovereignty and majority rule. States can be democratic, with leaders gaining office through

popular vote, but states lack the rule of law and constitutional checks on governmental power. This is what has been called "illiberal democracy"—and today, this
type of regime can be found in countries such as Russia, Egypt, and Turkey.
Conversely, states can have liberal characteristics—rule of law and constitutions—
but lack the institutions of a competitive electoral democracy. Singapore tilts in
this direction. In the modern era, however, liberalism and democracy—at least
until recently—have tended to go together. Whether labeled as "republics" or
"liberal democracies," these polities seek a balance, however uneasily, between
representative democracy and institutions that protect rights and restrain the state.
See Yascha Mounk, *The People vs. Democracy: Why Our Freedom is in Danger and
How to Save It* (Cambridge, MA: Harvard University Press, 2018); and Fareed
Zakaria, *The Future of Freedom: Illiberal Democracy at Home and Abroad* (New
York: Norton, 2007).

52. Great Britain has neither a formal separation of powers nor an independent judiciary, yet its parliamentary institutions and norms operate to divide and limit state
power. The classic statement of the logic and significance of divided and limited
government in the English political system is found in book 11 of Montesquieu,
The Spirit of the Laws.

53. As Michael Doyle observes, in liberal democracies, property can be "justified by
individual acquisition (for example, labor) or by social agreement or social utility."
State socialism and state capitalism are outside this definition. Doyle, *Ways of War
and Peace: Realism, Liberalism, and Socialism* (New York: Norton, 1997), p. 207.

54. Alexis de Tocqueville, *Democracy in America*, 2 vols. (New York: Vintage Books,
1945).

55. Thomas Paine, *The Rights of Man, Common Sense, and Other Political Writings*,
ed. Mark Philip (Oxford: Oxford University Press, 1995).

56. The US Declaration of Independence of 1776 and the Constitution of 1787 do not
mention the word *democracy*. In this period, the term *representative system* was
commonly used to describe representative government, while *democracy* continued to be a label associated with direct popular rule. As late as 1819, James Mill
described "the representative system" as "the grand discovery of modern times" in
his *Essay on Government.* Soon thereafter the term *representative system* became
synonymous with *democracy.* Mill's essay is reprinted in James Mill, *Political
Writings*, ed. Terence Ball (Cambridge: Cambridge University Press, 1992).

57. The historian Herbert Fisher captures the multifaceted and ongoing struggles that
followed the American and French Revolutions: "The spirit of liberty took many
forms, constitutional with Mirabeau, revolutionary with Danton, romantic with
Schiller, Shelley, and Lamartine, prophetic with Mazzini, intellectual with
Condorcet and J. S. Mill, practical with Cobden and Cavour, militant and
adventurous with Cochrane and Garibaldi; but once aroused it embarked on a

contest which is still unconcluded. Surviving the crimes of the French Revolution and the terror of Napoleon, it succeeded by the end of the nineteenth century in founding parliamentary institutions in every important European country with the exception of Russia." Fisher, A *History of Europe* (London: Edward Arnold, 1945), p. 791.

58. William McNeill, A *World History* (New York: Oxford University Press, 1967), p. 409.

59. David Armitage, *The Declaration of Independence: A Global History* (Cambridge, MA: Harvard University Press, 2008).

60. Christopher Hobson, *The Rise of Democracy: Revolution, War and Transformations in International Politics since 1776* (Edinburgh: University of Edinburgh Press, 2015). See also Francis Fukuyama, *Political Order and Political Decay: From the Industrial Revolution to the Globalization of Democracy* (New York: Farrar, Straus and Giroux, 2014), chaps. 27 and 28. For an exploration of the deeper and longer-evolving identities and purposes of sovereign states within international society, see Christian Reus-Smit, *The Moral Purpose of the State: Culture, Social Identity, and Institutional Rationality in International Relations* (Ithaca, NY: Cornell University Press, 1999).

61. Quoted in James T. Kloppenberg, *Toward Democracy: The Struggle for Self-Rule in European and American Thought* (New York: Oxford University Press, 2016), p. 753.

62. Quoted in Margaret MacMillan, *The War That Ended Peace: The Road to 1914* (New York: Norton, 2013), p. 33.

63. James Mayall, "Democracy and International Society," *International Affairs*, Vol. 64, No. 1 (2000), p. 64.

64. These democratic and republican constitutional ideals can be traced back to earlier eras, including the Italian Renaissance, to ideas about polities in which rule is not justified on the basis of heredity or divine mandate but on promotion of the general well-being of people and glory of the city. See J. G. A. Pocock, *The Machiavellian Moment: Florentine Political Thought and the Atlantic Republican Tradition* (Princeton, NJ: Princeton University Press, 1975); and Quentin Skinner, *Liberty before Liberalism* (Cambridge: Cambridge University Press, 1998).

65. See Seva Gunitsky, "Democracy's Future: Riding the Hegemonic Wave," *Washington Quarterly*, Vol. 41, No. 2 (Summer 2018), pp. 115–35; Gunitsky, *Aftershocks: Great Powers and Domestic Reforms in the Twentieth Century* (Princeton, NJ: Princeton University Press, 2017); and Samuel Huntington, *The Third Wave: Democratization in the Late 20th Century* (Norman: University of Oklahoma Press, 1993).

66. See Freedom House's *Freedom in the World 2000,* https://freedomhouse.org/report /freedom-world/freedom-world-2000. Free countries are those that exhibit a high degree of political and economic freedom and respect for civil liberties. In their 2020 annual survey, Freedom House reports that average worldwide scores for

political rights and civil liberties have declined each year after reaching a peak in 2005. The largest declines in scores have come from "third wave" democracies. Despite the weakening of global averages, eighty-six countries, or about 44 percent of the world's total, still qualify as "free" in 2019.

67. Carles Boix, "Democracy, Development, and the International System," *American Political Science Review*, Vol. 105, No. 4 (November 2011), pp. 809–28. For an effort to disentangle the relationship between the hierarchy of great-power relations, postwar settlements, regime characteristics, and democratic peace, see Patrick J. McDonald, "Great Powers, Hierarchy, and Endogenous Regimes: Rethinking the Domestic Causes of Peace," *International Organization*, Vol. 69, No. 3 (2015), pp. 557–88.

68. See Boix, "Democracy, Development, and the International System." Seva Gunitsky also traces democratic and authoritarian waves to shifts in the distribution of hegemonic power, emphasizing the role of the upheavals of economic depression and world war that produced "bursts of reform that influenced many states around the world." Gunitsky, "Democracy's Future," p. 117.

69. Some scholars have used the metaphor of an "egg carton" or "egg box" to depict how states have sought to organize international order. Hidemi Suganami, and later John Vincent, two scholars in the English school tradition, coined the "egg box" view of international society: "States/domestic societies are the eggs, full of nutrients inside, and the primary role of the international system (or 'international society') is to keep them apart safely in their respective shells (or borders) so that one egg does not end up crushing another." Email correspondence with Hidemi Suganami. See also the discussion in John Vincent, *Human Rights and International Relations* (Cambridge: Cambridge University Press, 1987), p. 123; and Robert Jackson, "Martin Wight, International Theory and the Good Life," *Millennium*, Vol. 19 (1990), p. 267. As Nicholas Wheeler puts it, in contrast to the "billiard ball" metaphor of international relations, which sees states as hard-shelled entities bumping into each other on a pool table, the "egg-box" conception of international society is one in which "the sovereign states are the eggs, the box is international society and the purpose of the box is to 'separate and cushion, not to act.'" Wheeler, "Guardian Angel or Global Gangster: A Review of the Ethical Claims of International Society," *Political Studies*, Vol. 44 (1996), p. 126. Daniel Deudney uses the "egg carton" metaphor to describe republican security theory and the challenge of constructing international regimes to cooperatively isolate and protect their nuclear capabilities. See Deudney, *Bounding Powers: Republican Security Theory from the Polis to the Global Village* (Princeton, NJ: Princeton University Press, 2007).

70. A vast literature explores the impact of liberal democracy on war and international cooperation. For major statements, see Doyle, *Ways of War and Peace*; and John M.

Owen, *Liberal Peace, Liberal War: American Politics and International Security* (Ithaca, NY: Cornell University Press, 1997). For a survey of the debate, see Dan Reiter, "Is Democracy a Cause of Peace?," in *Politics* (Oxford: Oxford Research Encyclopedia, 2017), https://oxfordre.com/politics/view/10.1093/acrefore/9780190 228637.001.0001/acrefore-9780190228637-e-287.

71. Barry Buzan, "From International System to International Society: Structural Realism and Regime Theory Meet the English School," *International Organization*, Vol. 47, No. 3 (Summer 1993), p. 351.

72. Ernst B. Haas refers to this evolving political formation as "liberal nationalism." See Haas, *Nationalism, Liberalism, and Progress: The Rise and Decline of Nationalism* (Ithaca, NY: Cornell University Press, 1997).

73. Jeffrey M. Chwieroth and Andrew Walter illuminate these evolving and fraught connections between the rise of democratic polities and international conflict and cooperation in the area of banking and finance. Examining banking crises since the nineteenth century, they find a democratic "wealth effect." The long-term rise of the middle class in democratic countries with growing economic assets has created "great expectations" that their governments will take responsibility to protect this wealth, leading these governments during financial crises to engage in increasingly extensive and costly efforts at financial stabilization and bailouts. The resulting instabilities caused by democratic political pressures make international cooperation both more difficult and more necessary. See Chwieroth and Walter, *The Wealth Effect: How the Great Expectations of the Middle Class Have Changed the Politics of Banking Crises* (Cambridge: Cambridge University Press, 2019).

74. Armitage notes that "until at least the late nineteenth century, and in many places for decades after, most of the world's population lived in the territorially expansive, internally diverse, hierarchically organized political communities called empires." But by the end of the twentieth century, "it is a striking feature of our political world that humanity is now divided into so many states but it is equally significant that there is no longer any self-styled empires." David Armitage, *Foundations of Modern International Thought* (Cambridge: Cambridge University Press, 2013), p. 191. See also Hendrik Spruyt, *The Sovereign State and Its Competitors* (Princeton, NJ: Princeton University Press, 1994).

75. See Jennifer Welch, "Empire and Fragmentation," in Tim Dunne and Christian Reus-Smit, eds., *The Globalization of International Society* (Oxford: Oxford University Press, 2017), pp. 145–65; and Daniel Gorman, *The Emergence of International Society in the 1920s* (Cambridge: Cambridge University Press, 2012).

76. Cemil Aydin, "Regions and Empires in the Political History of the Long Nineteenth Century," in Sebastian Conrad and Jurgen Osterhammel, eds., *An Emerging Modern World, 1750–1870* (Cambridge, MA: Harvard University Press, 2018), p. 85.

77. For an argument about how "the global" was constructed by empire, see Tony Ballantyne and Antoinette Burton, *Empires and the Reach of the Global, 1870–1945* (Cambridge, MA: Harvard University Press, 2012).

78. Jane Burbank and Frederick Cooper, *Empires in World History: Power and the Politics of Difference* (Princeton, NJ: Princeton University Press, 2010), pp. 3–4.

79. These historical patterns are described in Daniel Deudney and G. John Ikenberry, "America's Impact: The End of Empire and the Globalization of the Westphalian System" (unpublished paper, 2016).

80. Among many accounts, see John A. Hall, *Powers and Liberties: The Causes and Consequences of the Rise of the West* (Berkeley: University of California Press, 1986); and Walter Scheidel, *Escape from Rome: The Failure of Empire and the Road to Prosperity* (Princeton, NJ: Princeton University Press, 2019).

81. For depictions of the Westphalian state system, see F. H. Hinsley, *Power and the Pursuit of Peace* (Cambridge: Cambridge University Press, 1963); and Hedley Bull, *The Anarchical Society: A Study of Order in World Politics* (London: Macmillian, 1977).

82. On settler colonialism, see Duncan Bell, *Reordering the World: Essays on Liberalism and Empire* (Princeton, NJ: Princeton University Press, 2016).

83. The rise of nation-states in Europe and the rise to global power of European empire were deeply connected. In the period after the Napoleonic Wars, the states of Europe increasingly became nation-states, with citizenries that actively supported empire. "During this period of imperial expansion," Cemil Aydin argues, "there also arose active publics in Europe that embraced the empire as their own in various participatory processes, partly in the name of nationalism and patriotism." Nationalism, Christianity, and racialism in the metropolitan centers of European empire created constituencies and impulses for the pursuit of empire. See Aydin, "Regions and Empires in the Political History of the Long Nineteenth Century," in Conrad and Osterhammel, *An Emerging Modern World, 1750–1870*, p. 112.

84. Edward Keene, *Beyond the Anarchical Society: Grotius, Colonialism and Order in World Politics* (Cambridge: Cambridge University Press, 2002), p. 6.

85. See Andreas Wimmer and Yuval Feinstein, "The Rise of the Nation-State across the World, 1816 to 2001," *American Sociological Review*, Vol 75, No. 5 (2010), pp. 764–90.

86. This theme is developed in Neta Crawford, *Argument and Change in World Politics: Ethics, Decolonization, and Humanitarian Intervention* (Cambridge: Cambridge University Press, 2002). On the role of Westphalian norms of sovereignty in twentieth-century decolonization struggles, see Jan C. Jansen and Jürgen Osterhammel, *Decolonization: A Short History* (Princeton, NJ: Princeton University Press, 2019).

87. I explore this theme in chapter 7.

88. On the deepening of Western security interdependence, see Michael Howard, *War in European History* (Oxford: Oxford University Press, 2009). On the interaction of security interdependence and economic interdependence, see Frederick Hinsley, "The Rise and Fall of the Modern International System," *Review of International Studies*, Vol. 8, No. 1 (1982), pp. 1–8.

89. Recent historical treatments of the industrial revolution emphasize its global character and the ways in which agrarian civilizations across Eurasia were undergoing evolutionary shifts in markets, technologies, and productive activities in the centuries preceding the British boom. Bayly calls these worldwide shifts "industrious revolutions." See C. A. Bayly, *The Birth of the Modern World, 1780–1914* (Oxford: Blackwell, 2004), chap. 2.

90. For accounts, see Peter Mathias, *The First Industrial Nation: An Economic History of Britain, 1700–1914* (London: Methuen, 1969); Eric J. Hobsbawm, *Industry and Empire* (London: Penguin 1990); and Michael W. Flinn, *Origins of the Industrial Revolution* (London: Longman, 1966).

91. Barry Buzan and George Lawson, *The Global Transformation: History, Modernity and the Making of International Relations* (Cambridge: Cambridge University Press, 2015), p. 33.

92. On the global dimensions of the industrial revolution, see Bayly, *The Birth of the Modern World, 1780–1914*, chap. 5.

93. Ian Morris, *Why the West Rules—For Now: The Patterns of History and What They Reveal about the Future* (New York: Farrar, Straus and Giroux, 2010), p. 503.

94. Britain had 44 percent of its workforce employed in industrial production in 1881, compared to 26 percent for the United States and 36 percent for Germany.

95. Bayly, *The Birth of the Modern World, 1780–1914*, p. 238.

96. See Jeffry Frieden, *Global Capitalism: Its Fall and Rise in the Twentieth Century* (New York: Norton, 2006), p. 395.

97. Steve Biddle, *Military Power: Explaining Victory and Defeat in Modern Battle* (Princeton, NJ: Princeton University Press, 2006).

98. Trevor N. Dupuy, *The Evolution of Weapons and Warfare* (Indianapolis: Bobbs-Merrill, 1981). See also Archer Jones, *The Art of War in the Western World* (Champaign-Urbana: University of Illinois Press, 2000).

99. Robert Keohane and Joseph Nye, *Power and Interdependence: World Politics in Transition* (Boston: Little, Brown, 1977); Barry Buzan and Richard Little, *International Systems in World History* (Oxford: Oxford University Press, 2000); Barry Buzan, Charles Jones, and Richard Little, *The Logic of Anarchy: Neorealism to Structural Realism* (New York: Columbia University Press, 1993); and John Gerard Ruggie, "Continuity and Transformation in the World Polity: Toward a Neorealist Synthesis," *World Politics*, Vol. 35, No. 2 (1983), pp. 261–85.

100. Buzan and Lawson, *The Global Transformation*, p. 69.

101. For important early functionalist scholarship, see Leonard Woolf, *International Government* (New York: Brentano's, 1916); and David Mitrany, *A Working Peace System: An Argument for the Functional Development of International Organization* (London: Royal Institute of International Affairs, 1943).

102. The standardization of time was certainly one of the most important markers of the emergence of the modern world. As Vanessa Ogle argues: "In an arduous and drawn-out process, local times were abolished in favor of time zones and countrywide mean times; the Gregorian calendar spread to parts of the non-Western world; time was eventually severed from natural and agricultural rhythms and instead assumed more abstract qualities, a grid to be grafted onto natural rhythms; time was increasingly linked up with occupational notions—work time, leisure time, recreational time, time for acquiring useful knowledge." Ogle, *The Global Transformation of Time, 1870–1950* (Cambridge, MA: Harvard University Press, 2015), pp. 1–2.

103. As John Darwin observes, the "long equilibrium of cultures and continents was swept away," and the European states "gained for the first time a commanding lead over the rest of Eurasia and acquired the means to project their power into the heartlands of the great Asian empires." Darwin, *After Tamerlane: The Rise and Fall of Global Empires, 1400–2000* (New York: Bloomsbury, 2008), p. 160. See also Kenneth Pomeranz, *The Great Divergence: China, Europe, and the Making of the Modern World Economy* (Princeton, NJ: Princeton University Press, 2000).

104. David Cannadine, *Victorious Century: The United Kingdom, 1800–1906* (New York: Viking, 2017), p. 45.

105. See John R. Ferris, "'The Greatest Power on Earth': Great Britain in the 1920s," *International History Review*, Vol. 13, No. 4 (November 1991), pp. 726–50.

106. For a new historical portrait, see A. G. Hopkins, *American Empire: A Global History* (Princeton, NJ: Princeton University Press, 2018).

107. Paul Kennedy, *The Rise and Fall of the Great Powers: Economic Change and Military Conflict from 1500 to 2000* (New York: Random House, 1987), p. 243.

108. For studies that explore lineages and parallels in British and American hegemonic eras, see Joseph Nye, *Bound to Lead: The Changing Nature of American Power* (New York: Basic Books, 1990); Patrick Karl O'Brien and Armand Cleese, eds., *Two Hegemonies: Britain 1846–1914 and the United States 1941–2001* (Aldershot: Ashgate, 2002); Julian Go, *Patterns of Empire: The British and American Empires, 1688 to the Present* (New York: Cambridge University Press, 2011); and Kori Schake, *Safe Passage: The Transition from British to American Hegemony* (Cambridge, MA: Harvard University Press, 2017).

109. This logic and pattern of postwar order building is explored in G. John Ikenberry, *After Victory: Institutions, Strategic Restraint, and the Rebuilding of Order after Major War* (Princeton, NJ: Princeton University Press, 2001).

110. See Carr, *The Twenty Years' Crisis, 1919–1930*; Robert Gilpin, *War and Change in World Politics* (Cambridge: Cambridge University Press, 1981); William Wohlforth, "The Stability of a Unipolar World," *International Security*, Vol. 24, No. 1 (1999), pp. 5–41; and Stephen D. Brooks and Wohlforth, *The World Out of Balance: International Relations and the Challenge of American Primacy* (Princeton, NJ: Princeton University Press, 2008).

111. For a survey of these debates, see Charles S. Maier, *Among Empires: American Ascendancy and Its Predecessors* (Cambridge, MA: Harvard University Press, 2006).

112. The seminal statement is John Gallagher and Ronald Robinson, "The Imperialism of Free Trade," *Economic History Review*, Vol. 6, No. 1 (1953), pp. 1–15. See also Gallagher's Ford Lectures, *The Decline, Revival, and Fall of the British Empire* (Cambridge: Cambridge University Press, 1982); and Ronald Hyam, "The Primacy of Geopolitics: The Dynamics of British Imperial Policy, 1763–1963," *Journal of Imperial and Commonwealth Studies*, Vol. 27, No. 2 (1999), pp. 27–52.

113. John Lewis Gaddis, *Strategies of Containment: A Critical Appraisal of Postwar American National Security Policy* (Oxford: Oxford University Press, 1982).

114. This point is made by John Ruggie in his seminal observation that "the fact of American hegemony . . . was decisive after World War II, not merely American hegemony." Ruggie, "Multilateralism at Century's End," in *Constructing the World Polity: Essays on International Institutionalisation* (New York: Routledge, 1998), p. 127.

3. The Nineteenth-Century Origins of Internationalism

1. Perry Anderson, "Internationalism: A Breviary," *New Left Review*, Vol. 14 (March/April 2002), pp. 5–25.

2. Mark Mazower, *Governing the World: The History of an Idea* (London: Allen Lane, 2012), pp. 21–22. See also Martin H. Geyer and Johannes Paulmann, eds., *The Mechanics of Internationalism: Culture, Society, and Politics from the 1840s to the First World War* (Oxford: Oxford University Press, 2001); Akira Iriye, *Global Community: The Role of International Organizations in the Making of the Contemporary World* (Berkeley: University of California Press, 2004); Davide Rodogno, Bernhard Struck, and Jakob Vogel, eds., *Shaping the Transnational Sphere: Experts, Networks, and Issues from the 1840s to the 1930s* (New York: Berghahn Books, 2015); and F. S. L. Lyons, *Internationalism in Europe, 1815–1914* (Leyden: A. W. Sythoff, 1963).

3. On the contribution of French intellectuals, policymakers, and statesmen to the internationalist project, see Sudhir Hazareesingh, *Intellectual Founders of the Republic: Five Studies in Nineteenth-Century French Republican Political Thought*

(Oxford: Oxford University Press, 2001); and Peter Jackson, *Beyond the Balance of Power: France and the Politics of National Security in the Era of the First World War* (Cambridge: Cambridge University Press, 2013).

4. This distinction between "regulatory" and "revisionary" models of internationalism, particularly as it relates to the nineteenth-century international law and arbitration movements, is made in Duncan Bell, *Dreamworlds of Race: Utopia, Empire, and the Destiny of Anglo-America* (Princeton, NJ: Princeton University Press, 2020), chap. 2.

5. Inis L. Claude Jr., *Swords into Plowshares: The Problems and Progress of International Organization*, 4th ed. (New York: Random House, 1971), p. 22.

6. Edward Keene, *Beyond the Anarchical Society: Grotius, Colonialism and Order in World Politics* (Cambridge: Cambridge University Press, 2002), p. 98.

7. See Charles Maier, *Once within Borders: Territories of Power, Wealth, and Belonging since 1500* (Cambridge, MA: Harvard University Press, 2016).

8. This definition of empire draws from the model of the European maritime powers who built transoceanic colonial empires. They embodied principles that included, as Dominic Lieven notes, "autarchy, protectionism and the unblushing and consistent exploitation of the colonial economy in the cause of metropolitan prosperity and power." Lieven, *Empire: The Russian Empire and Its Rivals* (New Haven, CT: Yale University Press, 2000), p. 1. Lieven extends his discussion of this point in *The End of Tsarist Russia: The March to World War I and Revolution* (New York: Viking, 2015). For a leading exposition of this conception of empire as the relationship between an imperial core and colonial periphery, marked by economic exploitation and cultural domination, see Michael Doyle, *Empires* (Ithaca, NY: Cornell University Press, 1986). I develop these ideas further in chapter 7.

9. Jürgen Osterhammel, *The Transformation of the World: A Global History of the Nineteenth Century* (Princeton, NJ: Princeton University Press, 2014), p. 394.

10. For discussions of empire and hegemony, see Charles Maier, *Among Empires: American Ascendancy and Its Predecessors* (Cambridge, MA: Harvard University Press, 2006); John Darwin, *The Empire Project: The Rise and Fall of the British World-System, 1830–1970* (Cambridge: Cambridge University Press, 2009); and David Lake, *Entangling Relations: American Foreign Policy in Its Century* (Princeton, NJ: Princeton University Press, 1999). See also A. G. Hopkins's inaugural lecture as Smuts Professor at Cambridge, published as a pamphlet, Hopkins, *The Future of the Imperial Past* (Cambridge: Cambridge University Press, 1997).

11. See Barry Buzan and Richard Little, *International Systems in World History: Remaking the Study of International Relations* (Oxford: Oxford University Press, 2000).

12. For discussion of these distinctions, see G. John Ikenberry, *Liberal Leviathan: The Origins, Crisis, and Transformation of the American World Order* (Princeton, NJ: Princeton University Press, 2011).

13. This term was suggested to me by Tolya Levshin. See G. John Ikenberry and Tolya Levshin, "Liberal Internationalism and Empire" (unpublished paper, 2018). The term *preclusive control* comes from Glenn H. Snyder's study *Alliance Politics* (Ithaca, NY: Cornell University Press, 2007), p. 14. "Any alliance will have a preclusive effect, that is, it will block the ally from entering into a contradictory agreement with someone else, in particular an alliance with the opponent." Robert Gilpin also makes use of the term *preclusion*. "When Great Britain was no longer able to contain the imperialist ambitions of its continental European rivals because of its relative decline in power, it engaged in a massive effort of 'preclusive' imperialism; the object of colonialism, in other words, was to minimize potential losses more than to maximize potential gains." See Gilpin, *War and Change in World Politics* (Cambridge: Cambridge University Press, 1981), pp. 140–41.

14. There is no agreed definition of internationalism. E. H. Carr saw internationalism as "a special form of the doctrine of the harmony of interests," which he dismissed as utopian. Carr, *The Twenty Years' Crisis, 1919–1939: An Introduction to International Relations* (London: Macmillan, 1951), p. 85. In a widely cited definition, Fred Halliday sees internationalism as the idea that "we both are and should be part of a broader community than that of the nation or the state." He argues that internationalism carries with it the themes of growing interdependence between political entities, the resulting need for cooperation, carried out by various sorts of actors, such as governments, unions, and activists, and the belief that these forms of cooperation are desirable because they produce "an international interest beyond that of nations"—that is, outcomes such as peace, prosperity, and stable order that cannot be supplied by states or nations acting alone. See Halliday, "Three Concepts of Internationalism," *International Affairs*, Vol. 64, No. 2 (1988), p. 187. Perry Anderson echoes this view, arguing that "historically, the term may be applied to any outlook, or practice, that tends to transcend the nation towards a wider community, of which nations continue to form the principal units." Anderson, "Internationalism," p. 6.

15. Cemil Aydin has described the middle decades of the nineteenth century as an "era of self-strengthening of various empires, kingdoms, and states. . . . This self-strengthening of kingdoms and empires was accompanied by attempts to gain legitimacy through the performance of new practices of international diplomacy and international law, such as royal visits, bilateral treaties, the exchange of medals, and participation in international associations." See Aydin, "Regions and Empires in the Political History of the Long Nineteenth Century," in Sebastian

Conrad and Jürgen Osterhammel, eds., *An Emerging Modern World, 1750–1870* (Cambridge, MA: Harvard University Press, 2018), p. 41.

16. For an important study of America's role in Britain's imperial decline, see Wm. Roger Louis, *Imperialism at Bay: The United States and the Decolonization of the British Empire, 1941–1945* (New York: Oxford University Press, 1978).

17. Indeed, one of the leading forces of internationalism was European imperialism, which was instrumental in building global transportation systems and communication networks as well as the other infrastructural aspects of late nineteenth-century globalization. For accounts of empires as globalizers, order builders, and rule makers, see Osterhammel, *The Transformation of the World*, chap. 9; C. A. Bayly, *The Birth of the Modern World, 1780–1914* (Oxford: Blackwell, 2004); and Barry Buzan and George Lawson, *The Global Transformation: History, Modernity and the Making of International Relations* (Cambridge: Cambridge University Press, 2015).

18. Jennifer Pitts, *Boundaries of the International: Law and Empire* (Cambridge, MA: Harvard University Press, 2018), p. 2.

19. See Duncan Bell, *The Idea of Greater Britain: Empire and the Future of World Order, 1860–1900* (Princeton, NJ: Princeton University Press, 2007).

20. See Stephen Legg, "An International Anomaly? Sovereignty, the League of Nations and India's Princely Geographies," *Journal of Historical Geography*, Vol. 43 (January 2014), pp. 96–110.

21. Mark Mazower, *No Enchanted Palace: The End of Empire and the Ideological Origins of the United Nations* (Princeton, NJ: Princeton University Press, 2009), p. 46.

22. Susan Pedersen, *The Guardians: The League of Nations and the Crisis of Empire* (Oxford: Oxford University Press, 2015), pp. 4–5.

23. This argument is developed in chapter 7.

24. Leo Gross, "The Peace of Westphalia, 1648–1948," *American Journal of International Law*, Vol. 42 (1948), p. 28.

25. Osterhammel, *The Transformation of the World*, p. 394.

26. Daniel Philpott, *Revolutions in Sovereignty: How Ideas Shaped Modern International Relations* (Princeton, NJ: Princeton University Press, 2001).

27. See Kalevi J. Holsti, *Peace and War: Armed Conflicts and International Order, 1648–1989* (Cambridge: Cambridge University Press, 1991); Andreas Osiander, *The States System of Europe, 1640–1990* (Oxford: Oxford University Press, 1994); Ian Clark, *Legitimacy in International Society* (Oxford: Oxford University Press, 2005); Ian Clark, *International Legitimacy and World Society* (Oxford: Oxford University Press, 2007); and G. John Ikenberry, *After Victory: Institutions, Strategic Restraint, and the Rebuilding of Order after Major War* (Princeton, NJ: Princeton University Press, 2001).

28. Jennifer Mitzen, *Power in Concert: The Nineteenth-Century Origins of Global Governance* (Chicago: University of Chicago Press, 2013), p. 28.

29. Paul Schroeder, "The Transformation of Political Thinking, 1787–1848," in Jack Snyder and Robert Jervis, eds., *Coping with Complexity in the International System* (Boulder, CO: Westview Press, 1993), p. 48. See also Schroeder, *The Transformation of European Politics, 1763–1848* (Oxford: Oxford University Press, 1994).

30. Claude, *Swords into Plowshares*, p. 26.

31. Quoted in F. H. Hinsley, *Power and the Pursuit of Peace: Theory and Practice in the History of Relations between States* (Cambridge: Cambridge University Press, 1963), p. 255. What was lacking in the concert system was an agreement that defined the cases and circumstances under which the collective mediation of conflict would be mandated. These efforts would be attempted by governments at the end of the century. The geopolitics of this case and its implications for human rights as a political project are explored in Gary Bass, *Freedom's Battle: The Origins of Humanitarian Intervention* (New York: Vintage, 2009), part 4.

32. See Madeleine Herren, "Governmental Internationalism and the Beginning of a New World Order in the Late Nineteenth Century," in Geyer and Paulmann, *The Mechanics of Internationalism*, pp. 121–44.

33. See Daniel Deudney, "Hegemonic Disarray: American Internationalisms and World Disorder," in Hanns W. Maull, ed., *The Rise and Decline of the Post-Cold War International Order* (Oxford: Oxford University Press, 2018), pp. 199–216.

34. See Robert Keohane, *Power and Governance in a Partially Globalized World* (New York: Routledge, 2002); Peter Haas, *Epistemic Communities, Constructivism, and International Eonvironmental Politics* (New York: Routledge, 2015); and John Gerard Ruggie, "The New Institutionalism in International Relations" and "Multilateralism at Century's End," in Ruggie, *Constructing the World Polity: Essays on International Institutionalization* (New York: Routledge, 1998), pp. 45–61 and 102–30. Hedley Bull made the argument that Westphalian internationalism can, in principle, handle functionalist challenges arising from complex interdependence better than any feasible alternatives. See the final chapters of Bull, *The Anarchical Society: A Study of Order in World Politics* (London: Macmillan, 1977). For a skeptical perspective on the capacity of Westphalian internationalism to cope with functionalist challenges, such as climate change, see Richard Falk's critique in "Ordering the World: Hedley Bull after Forty Years," in Hidemi Suganami, Madeline Carr, and Adam Humphreys, eds., *The Anarchical Society at 40: Contemporary Challenges and Prospects* (Oxford: Oxford University Press, 2017), pp. 41–55.

35. Anthony Howe, "Free Trade and Global Order: The Rise and Fall of a Victorian Vision," in Duncan Bell, ed., *Victorian Visions of Global Order: Empire and*

International Relations in Nineteenth-Century Political Thought (Cambridge: Cambridge University Press, 2007), pp. 35–36.

36. On the evolving connections between nationalism, liberalism, and international order across the nineteenth and twentieth centuries, see Ernst B. Haas, *Nationalism, Liberalism, and Progress: The Rise and Decline of Nationalism* (Ithaca, NY: Cornell University Press, 1997).

37. Later, in the 1930s, fascist internationalism would make an appearance. See Jens Steffek, "Fascist Internationalism," *Millennium: Journal of International Studies*, Vol. 44, No. 1 (2015), pp. 3–22. For a survey of nineteenth- and twentieth-century far-right "nationalist internationalism," see David Motadel, "The Surprising History of Nationalist Internationalism," *New York Times*, 3 July 2019.

38. Glenda Sluga, *Internationalism in the Age of Nationalism* (Philadelphia: University of Pennsylvania Press, 2013), p. 7.

39. H. A. L. Fisher, *A History of Europe* (London: Edward Arnold, 1945), pp. 901–2.

40. "Richard Cobden," in Arnold Wolfers and Laurence Martin, eds., *The Anglo-American Tradition of Foreign Affair* (New Haven, CT: Yale University Press, 1956), pp. 193–95. See also Donald Read, *Cobden and Bright: A Victorian Partnership* (London: Edward Arnold, 1967).

41. Howe, "Free Trade and Global Order," p. 34.

42. Cheryl Schonhardt-Bailey, *From Corn Laws to Free Trade: Interests, Ideas, and Institutions in Historical Perspective* (Cambridge, MA: MIT Press, 2006).

43. The Anti–Corn Law League that emerged out of this moment was one of the most successful pressure groups of the nineteenth century. See Norman McCord, *The Anti–Corn Law League, 1838–1846* (London: Allen and Unwin, 1968); and Paul A. Pickering and Alex Tyrrekk, *The People's Bread: A History of the Anti–Corn Law League* (Leicester: Leicester University Press, 2000).

44. Howe, "Free Trade and Global Order," p. 27. As David Cannadine observes, "such peace-loving internationalists as Cobden and Bright believed that free trade would of itself produce equitable relations and peace and concord throughout the world." Cannadine, *Victorious Century: The United Kingdom, 1800–1906* (New York: Viking, 2017), p. 267.

45. Cannadine, *Victorious Century*, p. 267. See also Anthony Howe, *Free Trade and Liberal England, 1846–1946* (Oxford: Clarendon Press, 1997).

46. Charles P. Kindleberger, "The Rise of Free Trade in Western Europe, 1820–1875," *Journal of Economic History*, Vol. 35, No. 1 (March 1975), p. 36.

47. For an authoritative account of nineteenth-century European and global trade relations, see Ronald Findlay and Kevin H. O'Rourke, *Power and Plenty: Trade, War, and the World Economy in the Second Millennium* (Princeton, NJ: Princeton University Press, 2007), chap. 7.

48. See Howe, "Free Trade and Global Order," pp. 38–39.

49. John A. Hobson, *Richard Cobden: The International Man* [1919] (London: Ernest Benn, 1968), p. 21.

50. For a vivid portrait of the nineteenth-century peace movement and its various and shifting beliefs, see Michael Howard, *War and the Liberal Conscience* (London: Temple Smith, 1978), chap. 2. F. H. Hinsley chronicles the history of the peace movement in the Anglo-American world in *Power and the Pursuit of Peace: Theory and Practice in the History of Relations between States* (Cambridge: Cambridge University Press, 1963), chaps. 6 and 7. See also Martin Ceadel's comprehensive multivolume account, *The Origins of War Prevention: The British Peace Movement and International Relations, 1730–1854* (Oxford: Oxford University Press, 1996), and *Semi-Detached Idealists: The British Peace Movement and International Relations, 1854–1945* (Oxford: Oxford University Press, 2001); see also Peter Brock's trilogy, *Pacifism in the United States: From the Colonial Era to the First World War* (Princeton, NJ: Princeton University Press, 1968); *Pioneers of a Peaceable Kingdom: The Quaker Peace Testimony from the Colonial Era to the First World War* (Princeton, NJ: Princeton University Press, 1971); and *Pacifism in Europe to 1914* (Princeton, NJ: Princeton University Press, 1972). On the French peace movement, see Jackson, *Beyond the Balance of Power.*

51. Arthur C. F. Beales, *The History of Peace* (London: Bell, 1931), p. 48.

52. Quoted in Beales, *The History of Peace*, p. 53.

53. Brock, *Pacifism in Europe to 1914*, pp. 396–97.

54. John Morley, *The Life of Richard Cobden*, Vol. 1 (London: Fisher Unwin, 1879), p. 230.

55. Hobson, *Richard Cobden*, pp. 399–400.

56. Cecelia Lynch, "Peace Movements, Civil Society, and the Development of International Law," in Bardo Fassbender and Anne Peters, eds., *The Oxford Handbook of the History of International Law* (Oxford: Oxford University Press, 2012), p. x.

57. The Paris meeting is best remembered for Victor Hugo's opening address calling for a federation of European states—a future in which war would be replaced by "the universal suffrage of nations, by the venerable arbitration of a great sovereign senate."

58. Beales, *The History of Peace*, p. 79.

59. Quoted in Beales, *The History of Peace*, p. 75.

60. Cooper, *Internationalism in Nineteenth Century Europe*, pp. 13–14. See also Claude, *Swords into Plowshares*, chaps. 1 and 2.

61. See John Forrest Dillon, "Bentham's Influence in the Reforms of the Nineteenth Century," in Association of American Law Schools, ed., *Select Essays in Anglo-American Legal History*, Vol. 1 (Boston: Little, Brown, and Company, 1907), pp. 492–515.

62. Martti Koskenniemi, *The Gentle Civilizer of Nations: The Rise and Fall of International Law, 1870–1960* (Cambridge: Cambridge University Press, 2001).

63. Pitts, *Boundaries of the International*, p. 3.

64. Pitts, *Boundaries of the International*, p. 10.

65. Mazower, *Governing the World*, p. 66.

66. Cemil Aydin, "Regions and Empires in the Political History of the Long Nineteenth Century," in Conrad and Osterhammel, *An Emerging Modern World, 1750–1870*, p. 121.

67. See Arnulf Becker Lorca, "Universal International Law: Nineteenth Century Histories of Imposition and Appropriation," *Harvard International Law Journal*, Vol. 51, No. 2 (2010), pp. 475–552.

68. See R. P. Anand, "Family of 'Civilized' States and Japan: A Story of Humiliation, Assimilation, Defiance, and Confrontation," in Anand, ed., *Studies in International Law and History: An Asian Perspective* (New York: Springer, 2004).

69. Quoted in Beales, *The History of Peace*, p. 150.

70. Irwin Abrams, "The Emergence of the International Law Societies," *Review of Politics*, Vol. 19 (1957), pp. 361–80; and George Finch, "The American Society of International Law, 1906–1956," *American Journal of International Law*, 50 (1956), pp. 293–312.

71. Martha Finnemore, *The Purposes of Intervention: Changing Beliefs about the Use of Force* (Ithaca, NY: Cornell University Press, 2003), p. 25.

72. Finnemore, *The Purposes of Intervention*, p. 26.

73. Alfred Zimmern offers a detailed survey of the legalist turn in the internationalist movement and a powerful theoretical critique of its conclusions. See *The League of Nations and the Rule of Law, 1918–1935* (London: Macmillan, 1936). See also Oona A. Hathaway and Scott J. Shapiro, *The Internationalists: How a Radical Plan to Outlaw War Remade the World* (New York: Simon and Schuster, 2017).

74. Inis Claude has termed this form of multilateral diplomacy the "Hague System," reflecting the legalistic-oriented principles and forms of cooperation established in the two Hague Conferences. See Claude, *Swords into Plowshares*, pp. 28–34.

75. Finnemore, *The Purposes of Intervention*, pp. 38–41.

76. See Sondra R. Herman, *Eleven against War: Studies in American Internationalist Thought* (Stanford, CA: Hoover Institution Press, 1969). For historical background, see Stephen Wertheim, "The League of Nations: A Retreat from International Law," *Journal of Global History*, Vol. 7, No. 2 (July 2012), pp. 210–32.

77. Sluga, *Internationalism in the Age of Nationalism*, p. 19.

78. For example, in 1862, London hosted the International Industrial Exhibition. The International Council of Women was established in 1888.

79. Henryk Katz, *The Emancipation of Labor: A History of the First International* (Westport, CT: Greenwood Press, 1992).

80. See C. DeBenedetti, *Origins of the Modern American Peace Movement, 1915–1978* (Millwood, NY: KTO Press, 1978).

81. Iriye, *Global Community*, p. 14.

82. Iriye, *Global Community*, p. 13.

83. See Geyer and Paulmann, *The Mechanics of Internationalism.*

84. Iriye, *Global Community*, p. 10.

85. Osterhammel, *The Transformation of the World*, p. 510.

86. Claude, *Swords into Plowshares*, p. 34.

87. Craig Murphy, *International Organization and Industrial Change: Global Governance since 1850* (Cambridge: Polity Press, 1994).

88. Cornelia Navari, *Internationalism and the State in the Twentieth Century* (New York: Routledge, 2000), pp. 132–33.

89. Navari, *Internationalism and the State in the Twentieth Century*, p. 133.

90. Claude, *Swords into Plowshares*, pp. 35–36.

91. Bayly, *The Birth of the Modern World*, p. 243.

92. Beales, *The History of Peace*, p. 128.

93. Beales, *The History of Peace*, p. 238.

94. Proposals for international institutional structures often directly mirrored domestic democratic systems. For example, the Inter-Parliamentary Conference of 1905 formed a committee to discuss the creation of a Permanent Congress of Nations. In its report, the committee proposed the creation of a World Congress with two houses, with the Hague Conference as the Upper House and the Inter-Parliamentary Union itself as the Lower House. This proposal got no further than the committee report.

95. Beales, *The History of Peace*, p. 110.

4. Wilsonian Internationalism

1. Quoted in Arthur S. Link, *Wilson The Diplomatist: A Look at His Major Foreign Policies* (New York: New Viewpoints, 1974), p. 5.

2. Woodrow Wilson, "An Address to a Joint Session of Congress," 8 January 1918, in *The Papers of Woodrow Wilson* (hereafter *PWW*), 69 vols. (Princeton, NJ: Princeton University Press, 1984), Vol. 45, pp. 534–39.

3. Woodrow Wilson, "An Address in the Minneapolis Armory," 9 September 1919, in *PWW*, Vol. 63 (Princeton, NJ: Princeton University Press, 1990), p. 134.

4. Wilson, "An Address in the Minneapolis Armory," p. 133.

5. See Thomas W. Zeiler, David K. Ekbladh, and Benjamin C. Montoya, eds., *Beyond 1917: The United States and the Global Legacies of the Great War* (Oxford: Oxford University Press, 2017); Jay Winter, *Sites of Memory, Sites of Mourning: The Great War in European Cultural History* (Cambridge: Cambridge University Press,

1995); and David Reynolds, *The Long Shadow: The Great War and the Twentieth Century* (New York: Simon and Schuster, 2013).

6. See Daniel Gorman, *The Emergence of International Society in the 1920s* (Cambridge: Cambridge University Press, 2012).

7. In 1916, John Maynard Keynes, serving in the British Treasury, noted that "it is hardly an exaggeration to say that, in a few months time, the American executive and the American public will be in a position to dictate to this country in matters that affect us more nearly than them." Quoted in James Joll, *Europe since 1870: An International History* (London: Weidenfeld and Nicolson, 1973), p. 422.

8. Adam Tooze, *The Deluge: The Great War, America, and the Remaking of the Global Order, 1916–1931* (New York: Viking, 2014), p. 12.

9. I explore the United States' relationship with empire, including the British Empire, in chapters 6 and 7.

10. This theme is developed in Peter Clark, *The Last Thousand Days of the British Empire: Churchill, Roosevelt, and the Birth of the Pax Americana* (London: Bloomsbury, 2009).

11. See G. John Ikenberry, *After Victory: Institutions, Strategic Restraint, and the Rebuilding of Order after Major War* (Princeton, NJ: Princeton University Press, 2001).

12. Woodrow Wilson, "An Address to a Joint Session of Congress," 2 April 1917, in *PWW*, Vol. 41 (Princeton, NJ: Princeton University Press, 1983), p. 523.

13. See Arthur Herman, *1917: Lenin, Wilson, and the Birth of the New World Disorder* (New York: Harper, 2017); and Arno J. Mayer, *Wilson vs. Lenin: Political Origins of the New Diplomacy, 1917–1918* (New York: Meridian Books, 1964).

14. Speech by Prime Minister David Lloyd George at Wolverhampton, 24 November 1918, http://ww1centenary.oucs.ox.ac.uk/body-and-mind/lloyd-georges-ministry-men/. This same sentiment—that the costs and sacrifices of world war had created a moral obligation on political leaders to seek a better world—was echoed after World War II. On the twentieth anniversary of the D-Day landing, former president Dwight Eisenhower, speaking at the Normandy American Cemetery, told journalist Walter Cronkite: "These people gave us a chance, and they bought time for us, so that we can do better than we have before." See "Eisenhower Recalls the Ordeal of D-Day Assault 20 Years Ago," *New York Times*, 6 June 1964. The most moving expression of this sentiment might be Lincoln's Gettysburg Address, delivered only fifteen years after the failures of the 1848 revolutions in Europe.

15. Norman Angell, *The Great Illusion: A Study of the Relation of Military Power in Nations to Their Economic and Social Advantage* (London: William Heinemann, 1910). Quote taken from Michael Bentley, *The Climax of Liberal Politics* (London: Edward Arnold, 1987), p. 121.

16. See J. D. B. Miller, "Norman Angell and Rationality in International Relations," in David Long and Peter Wilson, eds., *Thinkers of the Twenty Years' Crisis: Inter-War Idealism Reassessed* (Oxford: Oxford University Press, 1995), pp. 100–121. Angell was not entirely original in articulating this argument. The Russian-Polish banker Ivan Bloch popularized the point in a series of publications, which he collected in *Is War Now Impossible?* (London: Richards, 1899).

17. Quoted in Frank Trentmann, *Free Trade Nation: Commerce, Consumption, and Civil Society in Modern Britain* (Oxford: Oxford University Press, 2008), pp. 148–50.

18. For a survey of the legacies of Cobden and nineteenth-century liberalism, see Anthony Howe and Simon Morgan, eds., *Rethinking Nineteenth Century Liberalism: Richard Cobden Bicentenary Essays* (New York: Routledge, 2006).

19. Historians offer various accounts of the Open Door policy. William Appleman Williams sees it as "America's version of the liberal policy of informal empire or free trade imperialism." Williams, *The Tragedy of American Diplomacy* (New York: Norton, 1959), p. 157. Frank Ninkovich emphasizes liberal ideology and not imperialism as the motivation. Ninkovich, "Ideology, the Open Door, and Foreign Policy," *Diplomatic History*, Vol. 6, No. 2 (September 1982), pp. 185–208. Walter LaFeber argues that the Open Door policy was a way to protect Chinese territorial and administrative integrity, a precondition for the United States to maintain "most favored nations" status in trade relations with China on the same terms as other major states. LaFeber, *The American Age: U.S. Foreign Policy at Home and Abroad*, Vol. 1 (New York: Norton, 1994), p. 103. See also Michael H. Hunt, *The Making of a Special Relationship: The United States and China to 1914* (New York: Columbia University Press, 1983), pp. 143–68.

20. See Tooze, *The Deluge*, pp. 15–16.

21. Benjamin F. Trueblood, "International Arbitration at the Opening of the Twentieth Century," *Advocate of Peace*, Vol. 67, No. 4 (April 1905), p. 80. For surveys of this history, see Alfred Zimmern, *The League of Nations and the Rule of Law, 1918–1935* (London: Macmillan, 1936); and Sir James Headlam-Morley, *Studies in Diplomatic History* (New York: Alfred King, 1930). The authors draw on their work for the British Foreign Office and the Phillimore Committee during the war and the peace conference. For a more recent survey, see Martti Koskenniemi, *The Gentle Civilizer of Nations: The Rise and Fall of International Law, 1870–1960* (Cambridge: Cambridge University Press, 2001).

22. See Nelson M. Blake, "The Olney-Pauncefote Treaty of 1897," *American Historical Review*, Vol. 50, No. 2 (January 1945), pp. 228–43.

23. Martha Finnemore, *The Purposes of Intervention: Changing Beliefs about the Use of Force* (Ithaca, NY: Cornell University Press, 2003), pp. 33–35.

24. See F. H. Hinsley, *Power and the Pursuit of Peace* (Cambridge: Cambridge University Press, 1963); and Paul Kennedy, *The Parliament of Man: The Past, Present, and Future of the United Nations* (New York: Random House, 2006).

25. A. C. F. Beales, *The History of Peace* (London: Bell, 1931), p. 238.

26. Inis L. Claude Jr., *Swords into Plowshares: The Problems and Progress of International Organization*, 4th ed. (New York: Random House, 1971), p. 30.

27. The Court of Arbitration was actually a permanent panel of arbitrators of high repute who were available for states desiring to make use of their services for any particular dispute. The Court of International Justice, established under the League of Nations and renamed the Permanent Court of International Justice under the United Nations, was the first international court in the proper sense of the word.

28. See Calvin DeArmond Davis, *The United States and the First Hague Peace Conference* (Ithaca, NY: Cornell University Press, 1962); Davis, *The United States and the Second Hague Peace Conference: American Diplomacy and International Organization, 1899–1914* (Durham, NC: Duke University Press, 1975); and Sandi Cooper, *Internationalism in Nineteenth Century Europe: The Crisis of Ideas and Purpose* (New York: Garland, 1976).

29. The British Foreign Office solicited the historian Charles Webster to conduct a study of the Congress of Vienna in preparation for the Paris Peace Conference—a good example of the awareness on the part of policymakers of the historical lineages in institutional forms. The study was later published as Webster, *The Congress of Vienna, 1814–1815* (Oxford: Oxford University Press, 1919). Webster privately complained that his colleagues at the Foreign Office made no use of his work, but he later came to play a prominent role in designing the postwar order on the British side during World War II. See Ian Hall, "The Art and Practice of a Diplomatic Historian: Sir Charles Webster, 1886–1961," *International Politics*, Vol. 42, No. 4 (December 2005), pp. 470–90.

30. This declaration was also the first multilateral attempt to codify during peacetime maritime rules that would be applicable during times of war. I am grateful to Adam Roberts for pointing out this agreement to me.

31. See Martha Finnemore and Michelle Jurkovich, "Getting a Seat at the Table: The Origins of Universal Participation and Modern Multilateral Governance," *Global Governance*, Vol. 20 (2014), pp. 361–73. On the role of Japan and Germany in the Hague Peace Conferences, see Klaus Schlichtmann, "Japan, Germany, and the Idea of the Hague Peace Conferences," *Journal of Peace Research*, Vol. 40, No. 4 (2003), pp. 377–94.

32. Finnemore and Jurkovich, "Getting a Seat at the Table," p. 365.

33. Elihu Root, "Instructions to the American Delegates to the Hague Conference of 1907," Department of State, Washington, DC, 31 May 1907, in James Brown Scott,

ed., *Instructions to the American Delegates to the Hague Peace Conferences and Their Official Reports* (New York: Oxford University Press, 1916), p. 72.

34. Claude, *Swords into Plowshares*, p. 31.

35. The long tradition of international ideas that lay behind this vision was noted on the British side in the report of its wartime committee on postwar order—the so-called Phillimore Committee report. Looking back to the settlements that followed the Thirty Years' War, the wars of Louis XIV, and the wars of the revolutionary and Napoleonic periods, the report sought to identify practical insights from the plethora of schemes and visions. See George W. Egerton, *Great Britain and the Creation of the League of Nations* (Chapel Hill: University of North Carolina Press, 1978).

36. One study reports that in the first six months of the war, over two thousand books in English alone were released on "the problems of preventing a repetition of a similar calamity in the future and of establishing a permanent peace." John Mez, *Peace Literature of the War: Material for the Study of International Polity, International Conciliation, Special Bulletin* (New York, 1916), pp. 3–4. Cited in Elizabeth Cobbs Hoffman, *American Umpire* (Cambridge, MA: Harvard University Press, 2013), p. 197.

37. For the distinction between conservative and progressive versions of liberal internationalism, see Thomas Knock, *To End All Wars: Woodrow Wilson and the Quest for a New World Order* (Oxford: Oxford University Press, 1992), chap. 4; Charles DeBenedetti, *Origins of the Modern American Peace Movement, 1915–1929* (Millwood, NY: KTO Press, 1978); Andrew Williams, *Failed Imagination? New World Orders of the Twentieth Century* (Manchester: Manchester University Press, 1998); and George Egerton, "Conservative Internationalism: British Approaches to International Organization and the Creation of the League of Nations," *Diplomacy & Statecraft*, Vol. 5, No. 1 (1994), pp. 1–20. Egerton's interpretation of Philip Kerr as a conservative internationalist is contested by Peter J. Yearwood in "'Real Security against New Wars': Official British Thinking and the Origins of the League of Nations, 1914–19," *Diplomacy & Statecraft*, Vol. 9, No. 3 (2007), pp. 83–109. For a rich discussion of the interplay of the two internationalisms within British officialdom during and after the war, see Yearwood, *Guarantee of Peace: The League of Nations in British Policy, 1914–1925* (Oxford: Oxford University Press, 2009).

38. See Martin David Dublin, "Toward the Concept of Collective Security: The Bryce Group's 'Proposals for the Avoidance of War,' 1914–1917," *International Organization*, Vol. 24, No. 2 (1970), pp. 288–318.

39. See Henry R. Winkler, *The League of Nations Movement in Great Britain, 1914–1919* (Metuchen, NJ: Scarecrow Press, 1952), pp. 18–20.

40. The Bryce Group was also influential in that subsequent work by later groups took the institutional architecture they produced as a sort of default model. This point is discussed in Winkler, *The League of Nations Movement in Great Britain.*

41. See Donald Birn, *The League of Nations Union, 1918–1945* (Oxford: Clarendon Press, 1981).

42. This point is stressed in Yearwood, *Guarantee of Peace*, especially in chaps. 2 and 3.

43. Quoted in Williams, *Failed Imagination?*, p. 30.

44. In a memorandum by Foreign Minister Lord Grey, this moderate case for the League of Nations was again restated. The nature of warfare had made a self-regulating system of balance of power and security untenable. See Williams, *Failed Imagination?*, p. 32.

45. The founding meeting of the LEP was held on 17 June 1915 in Philadelphia at Independence Hall in a gathering of some 120 conservatives from various fields and professions.

46. See Ruhl J. Bartlett, *The League to Enforce the Peace* (Chapel Hill: University of North Carolina Press, 1944), pp. 40–41.

47. See Sondra R. Herman, *Eleven against War: Studies in American Internationalist Thought, 1898–1921* (Stanford, CA: Hoover Institution Press, 1969).

48. Knock, *To End All Wars*, 56. These differences are also explored in Stephen Wertheim, "The League That Wasn't: American Designs for a Legalist-Sanctionist League of Nations and the Intellectual Origins of International Organization, 1914–1920," *Diplomatic History*, Vol. 35, No. 5 (November 2011), pp. 797–836.

49. Knock, *To End All Wars*, pp. viii–ix.

50. Knock, *To End All Wars*, p. 51.

51. Quoted in DeBenedetti, *Origins of the Modern American Peace Movement, 1915–1929*, pp. 8, 9.

52. See Dewey's influential book *The Public and Its Problem* (New York: Henry Holt, 1927). For a rich intellectual portrait of Dewey, see Alan Ryan, *John Dewey and the High Tide of American Liberalism* (New York: Norton, 1995).

53. Quoted in Bartlett, *The League to Enforce the Peace*, 221.

54. Woodrow Wilson, "An Address in Washington to the League to Enforce the Peace," 27 May 1916, in PWW, Vol. 37 (Princeton, NJ: Princeton University Press, 1981), pp. 113–16.

55. The actual drafting of the speech occurred on 5 January 1918 at the White House, when Wilson and Colonel House hammered it into shape. House records in his diary: "We actually got down to work at half past ten, and finished remaking the map of the world, as we would have it, by half past twelve-o-clock." Knock, *To End All Wars*, p. 142.

56. Walter Lippmann, "A Clue," *New Republic*, 14 April 1917, p. 317.

57. Quoted in Frank Ninkovich, *Power and Modernity: A History of the Domino Theory in the Twentieth Century* (Chicago: University of Chicago Press, 1994), pp. 39, 41.

58. Lloyd E. Ambrosius, *Woodrow Wilson and the American Diplomatic Tradition: The Treaty Fight in Perspective* (Cambridge: Cambridge University Press, 1987), p. 11.

59. Woodrow Wilson, "An Address at Bismarck," 10 September 1919, in *PWW*, Vol. 63 (Princeton, NJ: Princeton University Press, 1990), p. 155.

60. In his academic writings Wilson had made a similar point about the impact of the Civil War, which he saw as a decisive step forward in America's progress as a nation. In his five-volume history on the American people, Wilson sounded this theme: "The nation, shaken by those four never to be forgotten years of awful war, could not return to the thoughts or the life that had gone before them. An old age had passed away, a new age had come in, with the sweep of that stupendous storm. Everything was touched with the change it had wrought." Wilson, *A History of the American People*, 5 vols. (New York: Harper and Brothers, 1902), Vol. 4, p. 265. See also Ronald J. Pestritto, *Woodrow Wilson and the Roots of Modern Liberalism* (Lanham, MD: Rowman and Littlefield, 2005), chap. 3.

61. Quoted in Ninkovich, *Modernity and Power*, p. 52.

62. E. M. Hugh-Jones, *Woodrow Wilson and American Liberalism* (New York: Collier Books, 1962), 201.

63. David Kennedy, "The Move to Institutions," *Cardozo Law Review*, Vol. 8, No. 5 (April 1987), pp. 841–988. Kennedy argues that 1918 "executes a break between a preinstitutional and institutional moment" (p. 844). This is what John Ruggie has called "the twentieth-century discontinuity. . . . Above all, a completely novel form was added to the institutional repertoire of states in 1919: the multipurpose, universal membership organization, instantiated first by the League of Nations and then by the United Nations. Prior international organizations had but limited membership, determined by power, function, or both, and they were assigned specific and highly circumscribed tasks. In contrast, here were organizations based on little more than shared aspirations, with broad agendas in which large and small had a constitutionally mandated voice." Ruggie, "Multilateralism: The Anatomy of an Institution," *International Organization*, Vol. 46, No. 3 (Summer 1992), p. 583.

64. In his classic study of international organization, Inis Claude points to the Great War and the establishment of the League of Nations as the founding moment in the development of modern international institutions. "It is useful to consider the nineteenth century as the era of *preparation for* international organization, and, for this purpose, to treat 1815, the year of the Congress of Vienna, and 1914, the year of the outbreak of World War I, as its chronological boundaries. Starting thus, we establish the years which have passed since the momentous events of 1914 as the era of the *establishment of* international organization, which, in these terms, comes to be regarded as a phenomenon of the twentieth century." Claude, *Swords into Plowshares*, p. 41.

65. Tony Smith, *Why Wilson Matters: The Origins of American Liberal Internationalism and Its Crisis Today* (Princeton, NJ: Princeton University Press, 2017), p. 63.

66. Wilson, "An Address in Washington to the League to Enforce the Peace," pp. 113–16.
67. See Daniel T. Rogers, *Atlantic Crossings: Social Politics in a Progressive Age* (Cambridge, MA: Harvard University Press, 1998); and Rogers, "In Search of Progressivism," *Reviews of American History*, Vol. 10, No. 4 (December 1982), pp. 113–32.
68. For the most systematic study of Wilson's progressive roots, see Trygve Throntveit, *Power without Victory: Woodrow Wilson and the American Internationalist Experience* (Chicago: University of Chicago Press, 2017). In specific ways, Wilson drew upon the ideas of progressive thinkers: on the idea of "peace without victory" from Herbert Croly and language for his Fourteen Points from Walter Lippmann. For a survey of progressive-era thinkers, see James T. Kloppenberg, *Uncertain Victory: Social Democracy and Progressivism in European and American Thought, 1870–1920* (Oxford: Oxford University Press, 1986). On the connections between American progressivism and turn-of-the-century British "new liberalism" and continental liberal theorists of the reform of industrial society, see Helena Rosenblatt, *The Lost History of Liberalism: From Ancient Rome to the Twenty-First Century* (Princeton, NJ: Princeton University Press, 2018), chap. 7.
69. See Herman, *Eleven against War*.
70. See Knock, *To End All Wars*, p. 57.
71. "From the Diary of Raymond Blaine Fosdick," 11 December 1918, in *PWW*, Vol. 53 (Princeton, NJ: Princeton University Press, 1986), p. 366.
72. Quoted in DeBenedetti, *Origins of the Modern American Peace Movement*, p. 14.
73. DeBenedetti, *Origins of the Modern American Peace Movement*, p. 14.
74. Throntveit, *Power without Victory*.
75. See Throntveit, *Power without Victory*.
76. Woodrow Wilson, "An Address in the City Auditorium in Pueblo, Colorado," 25 September 1919, in *PWW*, Vol. 63 (Princeton, NJ: Princeton University Press, 1982), p. 504.
77. Wilson's lectures on international law were given at Princeton University in 1894. The record of these lectures survives in detailed notes taken by Andrew Clarke Imbrie, Mudd Library, Princeton University.
78. Woodrow Wilson, Imbrie notes from Lecture 2.
79. Quoted in Knock, *To End All Wars*, p. 9.
80. Quoted in Hugh-Jones, *Woodrow Wilson and American Liberalism*, pp. 137, 140.
81. World public opinion was the ultimate enforcer of the peace, or as Wilson put it in 1915, "If my convictions have any validity, opinion ultimately governs the world." Woodrow Wilson, "Remarks to the Associated Press in New York," 20 April 1915, in *PWW*, Vol. 33 (Princeton, NJ: Princeton University Press, 1980), p. 37.
82. Elihu Root, "Towards Making Peace Permanent," Nobel Peace Prize Address, 1912, https://www.nobelprize.org/prizes/peace/1912/root/lecture/.

83. Elihu Root, "The Pan American Cause . . . ," Washington, DC, 18 May 1907.

84. Woodrow Wilson to Edward M. House, 22 March 1918, in *PWW*, Vol. 47 (Princeton, NJ: Princeton University Press, 1984), p. 105. I thank John A. Thompson for this reference.

85. Smith, *Why Wilson Matters*, p. 115.

86. This belief in progressive organicism is something that Wilson shared with other liberal internationalists of the era, such as Jan Smuts, Gilbert Murray, and Alfred Zimmern. Jeanne Morefield traces this organicism to the communitarian liberalism of T. H. Green. Morefield, *Covenants without Swords: Idealist Liberalism and the Spirit of Empire* (Princeton, NJ: Princeton University Press, 2005). Morefield extends this argument to Smuts in *Empires without Imperialism: Anglo-American Decline and the Politics of Deflection* (Oxford: Oxford University Press, 2014).

87. Quoted in Knock, *To End All Wars*, p. 39. See Smith, *Why Wilson Matters*, pp. 92–93.

88. Woodrow Wilson, "An Address to the Senate," 22 January 1917, in *PWW*, Vol. 40 (Princeton, NJ: Princeton University Press, 1982), pp. 533–39.

89. Claude, *Swords into Plowshares*, p. 246.

90. Taft note of meeting with Wilson, 29 March 1918, in *PWW*, Vol. 47 (Princeton, NJ: Princeton University Press, 1984), pp. 200–201.

91. Taft note of meeting with Wilson, 29 March 1918, p. 201.

92. See John Milton Cooper Jr., *Woodrow Wilson: A Biography* (New York: Knopf, 2009), pp. 429–30.

93. "A Translation of a Memorandum by William Emmanuel Rappard," 1 November 1917, in *PWW*, Vol. 44 (Princeton, NJ: Princeton University Press, 1983), p. 488.

94. Woodrow Wilson, "An Address to the Senate," 10 July 1919, in *PWW*, Vol. 61 (Princeton, NJ: Princeton University Press, 1989), pp. 435–36.

95. Woodrow Wilson, "An Address in the City Auditorium in Pueblo, Colorado," 25 September 1919, in *PWW*, Vol. 63 (Princeton, NJ: Princeton University Press, 1990), p. 513.

96. Gary Gerstle, "Race and Nation in the Thought and Politics of Woodrow Wilson," in John Milton Cooper Jr., ed., *Reconsidering Woodrow Wilson: Progressivism, Internationalism, War, and Peace* (Baltimore: Johns Hopkins University Press, 2008), p. 93.

97. Kenneth M. Glazier, "W. E. B. Du Bois's Impression of Woodrow Wilson," *Journal of Negro History*, Vol. 58 (October 1973), p. 459.

98. See Jonathan D. Spence, *The Search for Modern China*, 2nd ed. (New York: Norton, 1999); and Rana Mitter, *A Bitter Revolution: China's Struggle with the Modern World* (Oxford: Oxford University Press, 2004).

99. Tooze, *The Deluge*, p. 16.

100. Naoko Shimazu, *Japan, Race and Equality: The Racial Equality Proposal of 1919* (New York: Routledge, 1998), p. 155.

101. Erez Manela, *The Wilsonian Moment: Self-Determination and the International Origins of Anticolonial Nationalism* (Oxford: Oxford University Press, 2007), p. 2.

102. Manela, *The Wilsonian Moment*, pp. 8–9.

103. See Frederick R. Dickinson, "More Than a 'Moment': Woodrow Wilson and the Foundations of Twentieth Century Japan," *Japanese Journal of Political Science*, Vol. 19, No. 4 (December 2018), pp. 587–99; and Dickinson, *World War I and the Triumph of a New Japan, 1919–1930* (Cambridge: Cambridge University Press, 2013). For studies of Japan's longer-term legacies and engagements with liberal internationalism, see the special issue: Takashi Inoguchi, "The Wilsonian Moment: Japan 1912–1952," *Japanese Journal of Political Science*, Vol. 19, No. 1 (December 2018).

104. Quoted in Knock, *To End All Wars*, p. 226.

105. See Arno J. Mayer, *Politics and Diplomacy of Peacemaking: Containment and Counterrevolution at Versailles, 1918–1919* (New York: Vintage, 1969), p. 368.

106. Laurence W. Martin, *Peace without Victory* (New Haven, CT: Yale University Press, 1958), chap. 3.

107. Wilson "The Modern Democratic State," ca. 1–20 December 1885, in *PWW*, Vol. 5 (Princeton, NJ: Princeton University Press, 1969), p. 63.

108. See John Maynard Keynes, *The Economic Consequences of the Peace* (New York: Harcourt Brace Jovanovich, 1920).

109. See Ninkovich, *The Wilsonian Century*, chap. 3.

110. Glenda Sluga, "Remembering 1919: International Organizations and the Future of International Order," *International Affairs*, Vol. 95, No. 1 (January 2019), p. 25. See also Daniel Laqua, "Transnational Intellectual Cooperation, the League of Nations, and the Problem of Order," *Journal of Global History*, Vol. 6, No. 2 (2011), pp. 223–47.

111. I thank Tolya Levshin for this insight.

112. Quoted in Lloyd Ambrosius, *Wilsonianism: Woodrow Wilson and His Legacy in American Foreign Relations* (London: Palgrave: 2002), p. 52.

5. Rooseveltian Internationalism

1. John Maynard Keynes, *The Economic Consequences of the Peace* [1919], with a new introduction by Michael Cox (London: Palgrave, 2019), p. 216.

2. See Eric Hobsbawm, *The Age of Extremes, 1914–1991* (London: Abacus, 1995), pp. 110–11.

3. Ira Katznelson, *Fear Itself: The New Deal and the Origins of Our Time* (New York: Liveright, 2013), p. 12.

4. At its largest, in 1934–35, the league had fifty-eight members, mostly from Europe, and two from Africa (Liberia and Ethiopia). For centennial assessments of the peacemaking of 1919, see Margaret MacMillan, Anand Menon, and Patrick Quinton-Brown, eds., "World Politics 100 Years after the Paris Peace Conference," special issue of *International Affairs*, Vol. 95, No. 1 (January 2019); and Alan Sharp, *Versailles 1919: A Centennial Perspective* (London: Haus, 2019). For a review of recent scholarship on the Versailles era, see John A. Thompson, "Review Article: American Power and Interwar Internationalism," *Historical Journal*, Vol. 61, No. 4 (2018), pp. 1137–48.

5. See Daniel Gorman, *The Emergence of International Society in the 1920s* (New York: Cambridge University Press, 2012).

6. Herbert Hoover, "Inaugural Address," 4 March 1929, https://avalon.law.yale.edu /20th_century/hoover.asp.

7. Adam Tooze, *The Deluge: The Great War and the Remaking of Global Order* (New York: Viking, 2014), p. 511.

8. Hobsbawm, *The Age of Extremes, 1914–1991.*

9. For surveys of European politics in the 1930s and the rise of fascism and authoritarianism, see Zara Steiner, *The Light That Failed: European International History, 1919–1933* (Oxford: Oxford University Press, 2007); Mark Mazower, *The Dark Continent: Europe's Twentieth Century* (London: Allen Lane, 1998); and Richard Overy, *The Inter-War Crisis* (New York: Routledge, 1994).

10. See Ian Nish, *Japanese Foreign Policy in the Interwar Period* (Westport, CT: Praeger, 2002).

11. For accounts of the rise of Hitler, see Richard Evans, *The Coming of the Third Reich: How the Nazis Destroyed Democracy and Seized Power in Germany* (London: Penguin, 2004); Thomas Childers, *The Third Reich: A History of Nazi Germany* (New York: Simon and Schuster, 2017); and Ian Kershaw's two-volume biography, *Hitler*, vol. 1, *1889–1936: Hubris* (New York: Norton, 1999), and vol. 2, *1936–1945: Nemesis* (New York: Norton, 2000).

12. Quoted in Evans, *The Coming of the Third Reich*, p. 197.

13. For a study of the diplomacy that preceded the signing of the pact, see Robert Ferrell, *Peace in Their Time: The Origins of the Kellogg-Briand Pact* (New Haven, CT: Yale University Press, 1952). For an idealist interpretation of the pact and its impact on the global legal order, see Oona Hathaway and Scott Shapiro, *The Internationalists and Their Plan to Outlaw War* (London: Allen Lane, 2017).

14. For an account of the arms race in the decade before the outbreak of World War II, see Joseph Maiolo, *Cry Havoc: The Arms Race and the Second World War, 1931–1941* (London: John Murray, 2010).

15. Quoted in Richard Overy, *The Twilight Years: The Paradox of Britain between the Wars* (New York: Viking, 2009), pp. 38, 43.

16. John Maynard Keynes, *The General Theory of Employment, Interest and Money* (London: Macmillan, 1936). Keynes, of course, began his critique of the Versailles settlement years before, with his 1919 polemic *The Economic Consequences of the Peace*. In this work, Keynes argued that the peacemakers in Versailles had failed to establish a stable framework for political and economic order. The war had "so shaken this system as to endanger the life of Europe altogether," but the absence of provisions for the reconstruction of Europe and the stabilization of new states, and the neglect of efforts to restore the finances of France and Italy, "will sow the decay of the whole of civilized life of Europe." For a reflection on Keynes's predictions, see Jonathan Kirshner, "The Man Who Predicted Nazi Germany," *New York Times*, 7 December 2019. For a survey of Keynes's evolving ideas on international relations, see Donald Markwell, *John Maynard Keynes and International Relations: Economic Paths of War and Peace* (Oxford: Oxford University Press, 2006).

17. See Mary Nolan, *The Transatlantic Century: Europe and America, 1890–2010* (New York: Cambridge University Press, 2012), pp. 108–11.

18. Keynes and Hayek never formally debated, instead arguing their differences in essays and opinion pieces. They met on occasion and developed a wary respect for each other. In a 1933 letter, Keynes wrote: "Hayek has been here [Cambridge] for the weekend. We get alone very well in private life. But what rubbish his theory is—I felt today that even he was beginning to disbelieve it himself." On various occasions, Hayek made similar remarks about Keynes, suggesting that the influence of his ideas had more to do with his charm and erudition than the cogency of his theory. See Alan O. Ebenstein, *Friedrich Hayek: A Biography* (New York: St. Martin's Press, 2001), p. 72.

19. Friedrich von Hayek, *The Road to Serfdom* (Chicago: University of Chicago Press, 1944).

20. Keynes, *The General Theory of Employment, Interest and Money*, p. 372.

21. Quinn Slobodian, *Globalists: The End of Empire and the Birth of Neoliberalism* (Cambridge, MA: Harvard University Press, 2018).

22. Karl Polanyi, *The Great Transformation: The Political and Economic Origins of Our Times* (New York: Farrar and Rinehart, 1944), p. 31.

23. Polanyi, *The Great Transformation*, p. 46.

24. E. H. Carr, *The Twenty Years' Crisis, 1919–1939* (London: Macmillan, 1940).

25. Carr, *The Twenty Years' Crisis, 1919–1939*, p. 29.

26. Carr, *The Twenty Years' Crisis, 1919–1939*, p. 224.

27. Carr's argument about the decline of British hegemony and the unraveling of international order influenced postwar theorists, most importantly Charles P. Kindleberger, *The World in Depression, 1929–1939* (Berkeley: University of California Press, 1973); and Robert Gilpin, *War and Change in World Politics* (Cambridge: Cambridge University Press, 1981).

28. In *Conditions of Peace,* written in 1942, Carr argued that liberal democracy will only be effective again when "economic power has been brought under control in exactly the same way as military power was brought under control in democratic countries before the nineteenth century." Carr maintained that liberal democracies would do well to learn from the planning experiences of fascist and communist states. E. H. Carr, *Conditions of Peace* (London: Macmillan, 1942), p. 33.

29. Vera Micheles Dean, *The Struggle for World Order* (New York: Foreign Policy Association, 1941), p. 22.

30. Dean, *The Struggle for World Order,* p. 25.

31. Dean, *The Struggle for World Order,* p. 94.

32. Carr, *Conditions of Peace,* p. 31.

33. In the past two decades, a growing body of scholarship has emerged that reassesses the ideas of Wilson-era and interwar internationalists. Broadly speaking, this revisionist literature takes issue with Carr's characterization of these thinkers as utopian, finding instead a diversity of views, variously idealist, pragmatic, and reformist. See Peter Wilson, "The Myth of the 'First Great Debate,'" *Review of International Studies,* Vol. 24, No. 5 (December 1998), pp. 1–16. See also David Long and Peter Wilson, eds., *Thinkers of the Twenty Years' Crisis: Inter-War Idealism Reassessed* (Oxford: Oxford University Press, 1995); and Lucian M. Ashworth, "Did the Realist-Idealist Great Debate Really Happen: A Revisionist History of International Relations," *International Politics,* Vol. 16, No. 1 (2002), pp. 33–51. Andreas Osiander finds "realist" thinking in the ideas of alleged "idealists," such as G. Lowes Dickinson, Leonard Woolf, Alfred Zimmern, and Norman Angell, seen in the use of the term *international anarchy.* See Osiander, "Rereading Early Twentieth-Century IR Theory: Idealism Revisited," *International Studies Quarterly,* Vol. 42, No. 3 (1998), pp. 409–32.

34. This argument is made by Michael Riemens, "The Scientific Study of International Affairs in the Inter-War Years: The International Studies Conference and the Netherlands Co-ordinating Committee for International Studies," in N. Nienke de Deugd, M. Drent, and P. Volten, eds., *Conference Proceedings: Towards an Autonomous European IR Approach—Relevance and Strategy: 20-Year Anniversary Conference of the Department of International Relations/International Organization of the University of Groningen, 4–5 October 2007* (Groningen: Groningen University Press, 2008), p. 3. I thank Barry Buzan for this reference.

35. For an illuminating portrait of the rise of international relations as a profession, see Jan Stöckmann, "The Formation of International Relations: Ideas, Practices, Institutions, 1914–1940" (PhD diss., Oxford University, 2017).

36. See Daniel Laqua, ed., *Internationalism Reconfigured: Transnational Ideas and Movements between the World Wars* (New York: I. B. Tauris, 2011).

37. For portraits of interwar Anglo-American debates about the crisis of international order, see Overy, *The Twilight Years*; Robert Boyce, *The Great Interwar Crisis and the Collapse of Globalization* (London: Palgrave, 2009); and Michael Pugh, *Liberal Internationalism: The Interwar Movement for Peace in Britain* (London: Palgrave, 2012).

38. See Kiran Klaus Patel, *The New Deal: A Global History* (Princeton, NJ: Princeton University Press, 2016), pp. 3–4.

39. Philip Kerr, "Liberalism in the Modern World," lecture to the Liberal Summer School, published as a pamphlet (London, 1933), reprinted in John Pinder and Andrea Bosco, eds., *Pacifism Is Not Enough: Collected Lectures and Speeches of Lord Lothian* (London: Lothian Foundation Press, 1990), p. 148.

40. Or Rosenboim, *The Emergence of Globalism: Visions of World Order in Britain and the United States, 1939–1950* (Princeton, NJ: Princeton University Press, 2017), pp. 3, 4.

41. Rosenboim, *The Emergence of Globalism*, p. 8.

42. See the discussion of Angell in the previous chapter.

43. See J. D. B. Miller, "Norman Angell and Rationality in International Relations," in Long and Wilson, *Thinkers of the Twenty Years' Crisis*, pp. 100–121. For a survey of Angell's responses to the altered circumstances of the post-1918 period, see Martin Ceadel, *Living the Great Illusion: Sir Norman Angell, 1872–1967* (Oxford: Oxford University Press, 2009), chaps. 7 and 8; and Lucian M. Ashworth, *Creating International Studies: Angell, Mitrany, and the Liberal Tradition* (Aldershot: Ashgate, 1999).

44. Norman Angell, *The Great Illusion, 1933* (London: Heinemann, 1933), pp. 369–70; and Angell, "The International Anarchy," in Leonard Woolf, ed., *The Intelligent Man's Way to Prevent War* (London: Victor Gollancz, 1933), pp. 19–66. Even as early as 1918, Angell hinted at the need for the liberal democracies to organize themselves into a system of cooperative security. "The survival of the Western democracies, in so far as that is a matter of the effective use of their force, depends upon their capacity to use it as a unit, during the War and after." See Angell, *The Political Conditions of Allied Success* (London: G. P. Putman's Sons, 1918), p. 4.

45. See Paul Rich, "Alfred Zimmern's Cautious Idealism: The League of Nations, International Education, and the Commonwealth," in Long and Wilson, *Thinkers of the Twenty Years' Crisis*, pp. 79–99; and D. J. Markwell, "Sir Alfred Zimmern Revisited: Fifty Years On," *Review of International Studies*, Vol. 12 (1986), pp. 279–92.

46. Quoted in Rich, "Alfred Zimmern's Cautious Idealism," p. 82.

47. Alfred Zimmern, *The League of Nations and the Rule of Law, 1918–1935* (London: Macmillan, 1936), pp. 283–84.

48. Alfred Zimmern, *Quo Vadimus?* (Oxford: Oxford University Press, 1934).

49. Zimmern advocated strong resistance to Nazi aggression, urging a policy of rearmament and alliance. Ironically, E. H. Carr favored a policy of appeasement. For the change in his views, see Jeanne Morefield, *Covenants without Swords: Idealist Liberalism and the Spirit of Empire* (Princeton, NJ: Princeton University Press, 2005).

50. For portraits of Cecil's internationalist thinking, see Peter Raffo, "The League of Nations Philosophy of Lord Robert Cecil," *Australian Journal of Politics and History*, Vol. 20, No. 2 (August 1974), pp. 186–96; and Gaynor Johnson, *Lord Robert Cecil: Politician and Internationalist* (London: Routledge, 2013).

51. As Cecil argued in 1941, "Indeed, the marked success of the League's non-contentious work followed by the recrudescence of European war, is glaring evidence of the mistake made by those who urged that the League could be made to work as a peace-keeping machine without its coercive powers." Robert Cecil, *A Great Experiment: An Autobiography by Lord Robert Cecil* (Oxford: Oxford University Press, 1941), p. 328.

52. Robert Cecil, "The Future of Civilization," Nobel Lecture, 1 June 1938, https://www.nobelprize.org/prizes/peace/1937/chelwood/lecture/.

53. Cecil spelled out this view in a pamphlet, *An Emergency Policy: An Urgent Proposal for the United Nations* (London: Hutchinson, 1948). In it, Cecil called for the creation of a nucleus of willing liberal democracies to police the peace as a complementary or substitute mechanism for the Security Council, which, he had already then realized, would be paralyzed on all essential questions by great power disagreement.

54. Cecil, *A Great Experiment*, p. 351.

55. For an overview of the struggles between American isolationists and internationalists, see Christopher McKnight Nichols, *Promise and Peril: America at the Dawn of the Global Age* (Cambridge, MA: Harvard University Press, 2011). For a portrait of internationalist movements in the interwar period, see Warren F. Kuehl and Lynne K. Dunn, *Keeping the Covenant: American Internationalists and the League of Nations, 1920–1939* (Kent, OH: Kent State University Press, 1997). For the standard account of FDR's internationalism, emphasizing its continuities with Wilsonian internationalism, see Robert Divine, *Second Chance: The Triumph of Internationalism during World War II* (New York: Atheneum, 1967). For more recent histories emphasizing discontinuities, see Andrew Johnstone, *Against Immediate Evil: American Internationalists and the Four Freedoms on the Eve of World War II* (Ithaca, NY: Cornell University Press, 2014); and John A. Thompson, *A Sense of Power: The Roots of America's Global Role* (Ithaca, NY: Cornell University Press, 2015).

56. See David Milne, "The Syndicated Oracle: Walter Lippmann," in *Worldmakers: The Art and Science of American Diplomacy* (New York: Farrar, Straus and Giroux, 2015), chap. 4.

57. Quoted in Townsend Hoops and Douglas Brinkley, *FDR and the Creation of the U.N.* (New Haven, CT: Yale University Press, 2000), chap. 1.

58. See Ronald Steel, *Walter Lippmann and the American Century* (Boston: Little, Brown, 1980), p. 327.

59. Steel, *Walter Lippman and the American Century*, pp. 335–36.

60. Lippmann, *U.S. Foreign Policy: Shield of the Republic* (Boston: Little, Brown and Co., 1943), p. 106.

61. Quoted in Steel, *Walter Lippmann and the American Century*, p. 407.

62. See Hathaway and Shapiro, *The Internationalists.*

63. James T. Shotwell, "Franklin Roosevelt, Cordell Hull, and the Birth of the United Nations," in *The Faith of an Historian and Other Essays* (New York: Walker, 1964), p. 280.

64. Harold Josephson, *James Shotwell and the Rise of Internationalism in America* (Madison, NJ: Fairleigh Dickinson University Press, 1975), pp. 207–11.

65. James T. Shotwell, *The Long Way to Freedom* (Indianapolis: Bobbs-Merrill, 1960), pp. 586–88.

66. Christopher D. O'Sullivan, *Sumner Welles, Postwar Planning, and the Quest for a New World Order, 1937–1943* (New York: Columbia University Press, 2009), p. xii.

67. O'Sullivan, *Sumner Welles, Postwar Planning and the Quest for a New World Order*, p. 12.

68. Sumner Welles, *Where Are We Heading?* (New York: Harper and Brothers, 1946), p. 27.

69. O'Sullivan, *Sumner Welles, Postwar Planning and the Quest for a New World Order*, pp. 43–44.

70. See Josephson, *James T. Shotwell and the Rise of American Internationalism in America*, p. 179.

71. For depictions of this transformation, see Alan Brinkley, *The End of Reform: New Deal Liberalism in Recession and War* (New York: Alfred A. Knopf, 1995); Mary Ann Glendon, *Rights Talk: The Impoverishment of Political Discourse* (New York: Free Press, 1993); and Michael Kazin, *American Dreamers: How the Left Changed a Nation* (London: Vintage, 2011). For its roots in the progressive era, see Daniel T. Rogers, *Atlantic Crossings: Social Politics in a Progressive Age* (Cambridge, MA: Harvard University Press, 1998), chap. 10.

72. Helena Rosenblatt argues that the transformation in American—and Western— liberalism in the 1930s is best seen as a move from an older vision of liberal society as moral community to a newer vision of liberalism based on individualism, political rights, and social protections. See Rosenblatt, *The Lost History of Liberalism: From Ancient Rome to the Twenty-First Century* (Princeton, NJ: Princeton University Press, 2018).

73. Roosevelt played an outsized role during these years as the single most important figure in salvaging the fortunes of liberal democracy and giving the liberal democratic model its modern shape. Roosevelt was the leader of the most powerful democracy during the era of its greatest crisis, and his policy activism and pragmatism—combined with a buoyant optimism—had a profound impact on the liberal imagination on both sides of the Atlantic for decades, and indeed it continues today. On the tenth anniversary of FDR's death, the philosopher Isaiah Berlin wrote an essay on what Roosevelt meant to a young man growing up in Europe during the depression. "When I say that some men occupy one's imagination for many years, this is literally true of Mr. Roosevelt's effect on the young men of my generation in England, and probably in many parts of Europe, and indeed in the entire world. If one were young in the thirties and lived in a democracy, then, whatever one's politics, if one had human feelings at all, or the faintest spark of social idealism, or any love of life, one must have felt very much as young men in Continental Europe probably felt after the defeat of Napoleon during the years of the Restoration: that all was dark and quiet, a great reaction was abroad, and little stirred, and nothing resisted. . . . The only light in the darkness was the administration of Mr. Roosevelt and the New Deal in the United States. At a time of weakness and mounting despair in the democratic world, Mr. Roosevelt radiated confidence and strength. He was the leader of the democratic world, and even today upon him alone, of all the statesmen of the thirties, no cloud has rested—neither on him nor on the New Deal, which to European eyes still looks a bright chapter in the history of mankind." Originally published in the *New Republic* in July 1955. Reprinted in Isaiah Berlin, "President Franklin Delano Roosevelt," in *Personal Impressions* (London: Hogarth Press, 1980), p. 23.

74. Franklin Roosevelt, "Acceptance of Renomination, June 27, 1936," in *The Public Papers and Addresses of Franklin D. Roosevelt*, Vol. 5, ed. Samuel I. Rosenman (New York: Random House, 1938), p. 236.

75. David Plotke, *Building a Democratic Political Order: Reshaping American Liberalism in the 1930s and 1940s* (New York: Cambridge University Press, 1996), p. 1.

76. Franklin Roosevelt, "Message to Congress on the Objectives and Accomplishments of the Administration," 8 June 1934, in *The Public Papers and Addresses of Franklin D. Roosevelt*, Vol. 3, ed. Samuel I. Rosenman (New York: Random House, 1938), p. 292.

77. James Joll, *Europe since 1870: An International History* (London: Weidenfeld and Nicolson, 1973), p. 442.

78. See Sherri Berman, *The Social Democratic Moment: Ideas and Politics in the Making of Interwar Europe* (Cambridge, MA: Harvard University Press, 1998).

79. Hobsbawm, *The Age of Extremes*, p. 140.

80. These terms, along with the term *international organization*, were entering the scholarly and popular lexicon during these decades. See Pitman B. Potter, "Origin of the Term International Organization," *American Journal of International Law*, Vol. 39, No. 4 (October 1945), pp. 803–6.
81. Patel, *The New Deal*, pp. 114–16.
82. See Wolfgang Schivelbusch, *Three New Deals: Reflections on Roosevelt's America, Mussolini's Italy, and Hitler's Germany, 1933–1939* (New York: Metropolitan Books, 2006).
83. David Caute, *The Fellow Travelers: Intellectual Friends of Communism* (New Haven, CT: Yale University Press, 1988). On Keynes's views, see Anthony Arblaster, *The Rise and Decline of Western Liberalism* (Oxford: Basil Blackwell, 1984), chap. 17.
84. FDR was reportedly motivated in part by an effort to counter Nazi Germany's "New Order" propaganda. It was thus a historical echo of Wilson's Fourteen Points, which offered a response to the Russian Revolution.
85. For accounts of the Atlantic Charter meeting, see Douglas Brinkley and David R. Facey-Crowther, eds., *The Atlantic Charter* (New York: St. Martin Press, 1994); and Theodore A. Wilson, *The First Summit: Roosevelt and Churchill at Placentia Bay 1941* (Boston: Houghton Mifflin, 1969).
86. Wilson, *The First Summit*, p. 205.
87. Quoted in Forrest Davis, *The Atlantic System: Story of Anglo-American Control of the Sea* (New York: Reynal and Hitchcock, 1941), p. 307.
88. Winston Churchill, "Broadcast Regarding his Meeting With Roosevelt," 24 August 1941, https://www.jewishvirtuallibrary.org/churchill-broadcast-regarding-his-meeting-with-roosevelt-august-1941.
89. The newspaper columnist Anne O'Hare McCormick argued in June 1942 that "the idea of a New Deal for the world" was the central theme of the Roosevelt administration's plans for postwar order. See O'Sullivan, *Sumner Welles, Postwar Planning, and the Quest for a New World Order*, p. 78. See also William Range, "A Global New Deal," in *Franklin D. Roosevelt's World Order* (Athens: University of Georgia Press, 1959), chap. 10.
90. Elizabeth Borgwardt, *A New Deal for the World: America's Vision for Human Rights* (Cambridge, MA: Harvard University Press, 2005), pp. 280–81.
91. Arthur H. Vandenberg Jr., ed., *The Private Papers of Senator Vandenberg* (Boston: Houghton Mifflin, 1952), pp. 3–4.
92. See Frank Ninkovich, *Modernity and Power: A History of the Domino Theory in the Twentieth Century* (Chicago: University of Chicago Press, 1994); Neil Smith, *American Empire: Roosevelt's Geographer and the Prelude to Globalization* (Berkeley: University of California Press, 2003); and Alan K. Henrikson, "FDR and the 'World-Wide Arena,'" in David B. Woolner, Warren F. Kimball, and David

Reynolds, eds., *FDR's World: War, Peace, and Legacies* (New York: Macmillan, 2008), pp. 35–62.

93. Franklin D. Roosevelt, "Quarantine Speech," 5 October 1937, The Miller Center, University of Virginia, https://millercenter.org/the-presidency/presidential-speeches /october-5-1937-quarantine-speech.

94. Franklin D. Roosevelt, "Annual Message to Congress," 4 January 1939, The American Presidency Project, https://www.presidency.ucsb.edu/documents/annual-mes sage-congress.

95. David Reynolds, *America, Empire of Liberty: A New History* (London: Allen Lane, 2009), p. 355.

96. FDR to Pope Pius XII, 23 December 1939, in *Roosevelt's Foreign Policy, 1933–1941: Franklin D. Roosevelt's Unedited Speeches and Messages* (New York: W. Funk, 1942), p. 29.

97. "President Roosevelt to Ambassador Grew, Letter of 21 January 1941," in US Department of State, *Foreign Relations of the United States*, Vol. 4 (Washington, DC: US Department of State, 1941), p. 8.

98. Franklin D. Roosevelt, "Statement by President Roosevelt to Members of the United Nations Monetary and Finance Conference," 29 June 1944, CVCE.EU, https://www.cvce.eu/en/obj/statement_by_franklin_d_roosevelt_29_june_1944-en -051f8720-94b9-4aee-991b-901dd926a578.html.

99. Jacob Viner, "Objectives of Post-War International Economic Reconstruction," in W. McKee and L. Wiesen, eds., *American Economic Objectives* (New Wilmington, PA: Economic and Business Foundation, 1942), p. 168.

100. President Roosevelt's Message to Congress on Bretton Woods Money and Banking Proposals, 12 February 1945, Richard H. Immerman, Temple University, https://sites.temple.edu/immerman/president-roosevelts-message-to-congress-on -bretton-woods-money-and-banking-proposals/.

101. Susan Pedersen, "Review Essay: Back to the League of Nations," *American Historical Review*, Vol. 112, no. 4 (October 2007), pp. 1091–117. See also Pedersen, *The Guardians: The League of Nations and the Crisis of Empire* (New York: Oxford University Press, 2015); and Patricia Clavin, *Securing the World Economy: The Reinvention of the League of Nations, 1920–1946* (New York: Oxford University Press, 2013).

102. Quoted in Ninkovich, *Modernity and Power*, p. 105.

103. See Michael Howard, *War and the Liberal Conscience* (London: Temple Smith, 1978), p. 96.

104. See Michael Fullilove, *Rendezvous with Destiny: How Franklin D. Roosevelt and Five Extraordinary Men Took America into the War and into the World* (New York: Penguin, 2013), p. 121. For an account of the drafting of FDR's ninth State of the

Union speech, which included the Four Freedoms as its peroration, see Samuel I. Rosenman, *Working with Roosevelt* (New York: Harper and Brothers, 1952), pp. 262–63.

105. See Borgwardt, *A New Deal for the World*.

106. For an overview, see Andrew Shonfield, *Modern Capitalism* (New York: Oxford University Press, 1965).

107. For a good account of the rise of the term *national security* in American foreign and defense planning circles before and during World War II, see Dexter Fergie, "Geopolitics Turned Inwards: The Princeton Studies Group and the National Security Imagination," *Diplomatic History*, Vol. 43, No. 4 (September 2019), pp. 644–70. See also Emily S. Rosenberg, "Commentary: The Cold War and the Discourse of National Security," *Diplomatic History*, Vol. 17, No. 2 (Spring 1993), pp. 277–84.

108. See Andrew Preston, "Monsters Everywhere: A Genealogy of National Security," *Diplomatic History*, Vol. 38, No. 3 (2014), pp. 477–500. For accounts of the rise of the doctrine of national security, see Daniel Yergin, *Shattered Peace: The Origins of the Cold War and the National Security State* (New York: Houghton Mifflin, 1977); John Lewis Gaddis, *Strategies of Containment: A Critical Appraisal of American National Security Policy during the Cold War*, rev. ed. (New York: Oxford University Press, 2005); and Melvyn P. Leffler, *A Preponderance of Power: National Security, the Truman Administration, and the Cold War* (Stanford, CA: Stanford University Press, 1992).

109. Preston, "Monsters Everywhere," p. 487.

110. Franklin D. Roosevelt, "On the Recession," Fireside Chat 12, 14 April 1938, The Miller Center, University of Virginia, https://millercenter.org/the-presidency /presidential-speeches/april-14-1938-fireside-chat-12-recession.

111. Quoted in Julian E. Zelizer, *Arsenal of Democracy: The Politics of National Security—From World War II to the War of Terrorism* (New York: Basic Books, 2010), p. 55.

112. See Maurizio Vaudagna, "Social Protection and the Promise of a Secure Future in Wartime Europe and America," in Marco Mariano, ed., *Defining the Atlantic Community: Culture, Intellectuals and Policies in the Mid-Twentieth Century* (New York: Routledge, 2010).

113. Preston, "Monsters Everywhere," p. 492.

114. See Anne-Marie Burley, "Regulating the World: Multilateralism, International Law, and the Project of the New Deal Regulatory State," in John G. Ruggie, ed., *Multilateralism Matters: The Theory and Praxis of an Institutional Form* (New York: Columbia University Press, 1993), pp. 125–56.

6. The Rise of Liberal Hegemony

1. Edward Mortimer, *The World That FDR Built: Vision and Reality* (New York: Charles Scribner's Sons, 1988), p. 4. A similar image was invoked by an observer to the 1919 peace conference: "The Paris of the Conference ceased to be the capital of France. It became a vast cosmopolitan caravanserai teeming with unwonted aspects of life and turmoil, filled with curious samples of the races, tribes, and tongues of four continents who came to watch and wait for the mysterious to-morrow. . . . All of them burned with desire to be near to the crucible in which the political and social systems of the world were to be melted and re-cast." E. J. Dillon, *The Inside Story of the Peace Conference* (New York: Harper and Brothers, 1920), pp. 4, 6.

2. Arthur Sweetser, Memorandum on Approaches to Postwar International Organization, 17 September 1941, War and Peace Studies of the Council on Foreign Relations, quoted in John A. Thompson, *A Sense of Power: The Roots of America's Global Role* (Ithaca, NY: Cornell University Press, 2015), p. 183.

3. This chapter builds on ideas presented in G. John Ikenberry, *Liberal Leviathan: The Origins, Rise, and Crisis of the American World Order* (Princeton, NJ: Princeton University Press, 2011), particularly "The Rise of the American System," pp. 159–219.

4. See Timothy Garton Ash, *Free World: America, Europe, and the Surprising Future of the West* (New York: Random House, 2004); James Huntley, *Pax Democratica: A Strategy for the 21st Century* (London: Palgrave Macmillan, 1998); Daniel H. Deudney, "The Philadelphian System: Sovereignty, Arms Control, and Balance of Power in the American States-Union, circa 1787–1861," *International Organization*, Vol. 49, No. 2 (Spring 1995), pp. 191–228; and Ikenberry, *Liberal Leviathan*.

5. For recent efforts by realist scholars to depict the Western postwar as an artifact of Cold War balancing, see John Mearsheimer, "Bound to Fail: The Rise and Fall of Liberal International Order," *International Security*, Vol. 43, No. 4 (Spring 2019), pp. 7–50; and Graham Allison, "The Myth of the Liberal Order," *Foreign Affairs*, Vol. 97, No. 4 (July/August 2018), pp. 124–33. For a debate among realists, liberals, and constructivists on the sources of cohesion and cooperation within the Western postwar order, see G. John Ikenberry, ed., *America Unrivaled: The Future of the Balance of Power* (Ithaca, NY: Cornell University Press, 2002).

6. The term *superpower* entered the political lexicon during these early years precisely to capture this new power reality. See William T. R. Fox, *The Super-Powers: The United States, Britain, and the Soviet Union* (New York: Harcourt, 1944).

7. Margaret MacMillan, "Rebuilding the World after the Second World War," *Guardian*, 11 September 2009. This reality of American power was not lost on the

world. It was a different type of power reality than had been seen in recent centuries. It was not simply a transition from British to American power—the disparities were greater this time, and the character of power was also more multifaceted. The United States stood, as Martin Wight observes, in relation to its allies, "not as Castlereagh's England stood to the other Powers of the grand alliance against Napoleon, but as the Roman Republic stood to the Hellenistic monarchies from the mid-second century B.C." Wight, "The Balance of Power and International Order," in Alan James, ed., *The Bases of International Order: Essays in Honor of C.A.W. Manning* (New York: Oxford University Press, 1973), p. 115.

8. See Paul Kennedy, *The Rise and Fall of Great Powers: Economic Change and Military Conflict from 1500 to 2000* (New York: Random House, 1987), p. 359.

9. This logic is explored in G. John Ikenberry, *After Victory: Institutions, Strategic Restraint, and the Rebuilding of Order after Major War* (Princeton, NJ: Princeton University Press, 2001).

10. On the range and complexity of issues facing postwar leaders, see Andrew Baker, *Constructing a Post-War Order: The Rise of U.S. Hegemony and the Origins of the Cold War* (New York: I. B. Tauris, 2011); Peter Clarke, *The Last Thousand Days of the British Empire: Churchill, Roosevelt, and the Birth of Pax Americana* (London: Bloomsbury, 2008); and Robert Hilderbrand, *Dumbarton Oaks: The Origins of the United Nations and the Search for Postwar Security* (Chapel Hill: University of North Carolina Press, 1990).

11. Warren F. Kimball, *The Juggler: Franklin Delano Roosevelt as Wartime Statesman* (Princeton, NJ: Princeton University Press, 1994), p. 17. See also Robert Divine, *Second Chance: The Triumph of Internationalism in America during World War II* (New York: Atheneum, 1971); and Robert Dallek, *Franklin Roosevelt and American Foreign Policy, 1932–1945* (Oxford: Oxford University Press, 1979).

12. For a portrait of the multiple voices and visions behind the Roosevelt administration's planning for postwar order, see Kenneth Weisbrode, "The Master, the Maverick, and the Machine: Three Wartime Promoters of Peace," *Journal of Policy History*, Vol. 21, No. 4 (2009), pp. 366–91.

13. Harry S. Truman, "Address on Foreign Economic Policy, Delivered at Baylor University," 6 March 1947, Harry S. Truman Library and Museum, https://www .trumanlibrary.gov/library/public-papers/52/address-foreign-economic-policy -delivered-baylor-university.

14. Harry S. Truman, "Message to Congress Recommending Assistance to Greece and Turkey," 12 March 1947, National Archives, https://www.archives.gov/historical -docs/todays-doc/index.html?dod-date=312.

15. See Odd Arne Westad, *The Global Cold War: Third World Interventions and the Making of Our Times* (Cambridge: Cambridge University Press, 2007).

16. For the doctrinal and strategic debates over Cold War policies, see John Lewis Gaddis, *Strategies of Containment: A Critical Appraisal of American National Security Policy during the Cold War* (Oxford: Oxford University Press, 2005).

17. For studies of Cold War liberalism, see Jan-Werner Müller, "Fear and Freedom: On 'Cold War Liberalism,'" *European Journal of Political Theory*, Vol. 7, No. 1 (January 2008), pp. 45–64; and Jason K. Duncan, *John F. Kennedy: The Spirit of Cold War Liberalism* (New York: Routledge, 2014). For the tensions between Cold War liberals and antiwar progressive internationalists, see Randall Bennett Woods, "The Rhetoric of Dissent: J. William Fulbright, Vietnam, and the Crisis of International Liberalism," in Martin J. Medhurst and H. W. Brands, eds., *Critical Reflections on the Cold War: Linking Rhetoric and History* (College Station: Texas A&M University Press, 2000), pp. 187–208. For a post-9/11 statement and reconsideration, see Peter Beinart, *The Good Fight: Why Liberals—and Only Liberals—Can Win the War of Terror and Make American Great Again* (New York: HarperCollins, 2006); and Beinart, *The Icarus Syndrome: A History of American Hubris* (New York: Harper, 2010).

18. These trade-offs are explored in a more contemporary context in Michael Ignatieff, *The Lesser Evil: Political Ethics in an Age of Terror* (Princeton, NJ: Princeton University Press, 2005).

19. NSC-68 as published in Ernest May, ed., *American Cold War Strategy: Interpreting NSC-68* (New York: St. Martin's Press, 1993), p. 40.

20. See John Baylis, *Diplomacy of Pragmatism: Britain and the Formation of NATO 1942–49* (Kent, OH: Kent State University Press, 1993); Marc Tractenberg, *A Constructed Peace: The Making of the European Settlement, 1945–1963* (Princeton, NJ: Princeton University Press, 1999); and Wallace Thies, *Why NATO Endures* (Cambridge: Cambridge University Press, 2009), chaps. 3 and 4.

21. This is a central theme of Robert Gilpin, *Political Economy of International Relations* (Princeton, NJ: Princeton University Press, 1987).

22. For classic statements of this power transition theory, see Robert Gilpin, *War and Change in World Politics* (New York: Cambridge University Press, 1981); and A. F. K. Organski, *World Politics* (New York: Knopf, 1967). For a sweeping historical portrait of great-power transitions, see Kennedy, *The Rise and Fall of the Great Powers*. The grand strategies of rising and falling great powers are surveyed in Randall L. Schweller, "Managing the Rise of Great Powers: History and Theory," in Alastair Iain Johnston and Robert Ross, eds., *Engaging China: The Management of an Emerging Power* (New York: Routledge, 1999), pp. 1–31.

23. See G. John Ikenberry, ed., *Power, Order, and Change in World Politics* (New York: Cambridge University Press, 2014).

24. The classic discussion of milieu-oriented strategies is Arnold Wolfers, *Discord and Collaboration: Essays on International Politics* (Baltimore: Johns Hopkins Univer-

sity Press, 1965). For a discussion of rule-by-rules and rule-by-relationships, see Ikenberry, *Liberal Leviathan*, chap. 3.

25. Harley Notter, *Postwar Foreign Policy Preparation* (Washington, DC: U.S. Department of State, 1950), p. 126.

26. Address at Yale University, 28 November 1939, in Dean Acheson, *Morning and Noon: A Memoir* (Boston: Houghton Mifflin, 1965), pp. 267–75.

27. George C. Marshall, "Commencement Speech at Princeton University," 22 February 1947, The George C. Marshall Foundation, https://www.marshall foundation.org/library/digital-archive/6-026-speech-princeton-university-february -22-1947/.

28. Stewart Patrick, *The Best Laid Plans: The Origins of American Multilateralism and the Dawn of the Cold War* (New York: Roman and Littlefield, 2009), p. 53.

29. Cordell Hull, "The Outlook for the Trade Program," speech delivered before the Twenty-Fifth National Foreign Trade Convention, New York City, 1 November 1938. See also Arthur W. Schatz, "The Anglo-American Trade Agreement and Cordell Hull's Search for Peace, 1936–1938," *Journal of American History*, Vol. 57, No. 1 (June 1970), pp. 85–103.

30. See Patrick, *The Best Laid Plans*, chap. 4.

31. This Council on Foreign Relations project, "Studies of American Interests in the War and Peace," consisted of a series of ongoing study groups, led by scholars and policy experts. The central figures in the "Economic and Financial Group," were Jacob Viner and Alvin H. Hansen, both leading international economists and former presidents of the American Economic Association.

32. Council on Foreign Relations, "Studies of American Interests in the War and the Peace," New York, "Methods of Economic Collaboration: The Role of the Grand Area in American Economic Policy," E-B34, 24 July 1941, p. 1.

33. Carlo Maria Santoro, *Diffidence and Ambition: The Intellectual Sources of U.S. Foreign Policy* (Boulder, CO: Westview Press, 1992), p. 94.

34. Nicolas J. Spykman, *America's Strategy in World Politics: The United States and the Balance of Power* (New York: Harcourt Brace, 1942). For a discussion of Spykman, see Or Rosenboim, *The Emergence of Globalism: Visions of World Order in Great Britain and the United States, 1939–1950* (Princeton, NJ: Princeton University Press, 2017).

35. See Thompson, *A Sense of Power*, chap. 6; Neil Smith, *American Empire: Roosevelt's Geographer and the Prelude to Globalization* (Berkeley: University of California Press, 2004); Andrew Baker, *Constructing a Post-War Order: The Rise of U.S. Hegemony and the Origins of the Cold War* (New York: I. B. Tauris, 2011); and Patrick J. Hearden, *Architects of Globalism: Building a New World during World War II* (Fayetteville: University of Arkansas Press, 2002).

36. Melvyn P. Leffler, "The American Conception of National Security and the Beginning of the Cold War," *American Historical Review,* Vol. 89, No. 2 (1984), p. 358.

37. Cordell Hull, "Our Foreign Policy in the Framework of Our National Interests," *Department of State Bulletin,* 18 September 1943, p. 178.

38. See Patrick, *The Best Laid Plans,* p. 54.

39. During the Cold War, this technocratic strand of internationalism lay behind American foreign aid, assistance programs, and the ideology of modernization and nation-building. See Michael E. Latham, *Modernization as Ideology: American Social Science and "Nation Building" in the Kennedy Era* (Chapel Hill: University of North Carolina Press, 2000).

40. The historian Stephen Wertheim argues that FDR and his advisers saw the United Nations in narrow instrumental terms, as a legitimating cover for the project of establishing American worldwide military supremacy, although his rich archival evidence shows broader instrumental designs, including the facilitation of collective security and the enshrining of norms of peaceful settlement of disputes. See Wertheim, "Instrumental Internationalism: The American Origins of the United Nations, 1940–1943," *Journal of Contemporary History,* Vol. 54, No. 2 (2019), pp. 265–83. Wertheim does not give attention to the "Declaration by United Nations," signed on 1 January 1942, a commitment by twenty-six (and later forty-seven) allies to build new forms of international cooperation across economic, social, and security areas, informed by the "common program of purposes and principles" outlined in the Atlantic Charter.

41. See essays in Dan Flesch and Thomas G. Weiss, eds., *Wartime Origins of the Future United Nations* (New York: Routledge, 2015). On the legacy influence of League of Nations activities during the 1930s in the area of economic planning and employment and agriculture policy, see Patricia R. Clavin, *Securing the World Economy: The Reinvention of the League of Nations, 1920–1946* (Oxford: Oxford University Press, 2013).

42. See Thomas Risse-Kappen, *Cooperation among Democracies: The European Influence on U.S. Foreign Policy* (Princeton, NJ: Princeton University Press, 1995).

43. Diane Kunz, *Butter and Guns: America's Cold War Economic Diplomacy* (New York: Free Press, 1997), p. 12.

44. I develop this argument in G. John Ikenberry, "Reflections on *After Victory,*" *British Journal of Politics and International Affairs,* Vol. 21, No. 1 (2019), pp. 5–19.

45. The classic statement of this point is Inis Claude, "Collective Legitimation as a Political Function of the United Nations," *International Organization,* Vol. 20, No. 3 (1966), pp. 367–79. See also Thomas M. Franck, *The Power of Legitimacy*

among Nations (Oxford: Oxford University Press, 1990); and M. Patrick Cottrell, *The Evolution and Legitimacy of International Security Institutions* (Cambridge: Cambridge University Press, 2016).

46. The classic statement of this dilemma is Karl Polanyi, *The Great Transformation: The Political and Economic Origins of Our Times* (Boston: Beacon Press, 1957).

47. John Gerard Ruggie, "International Regimes, Transactions, and Change: Embedded Liberalism in the Postwar Economic Order," in Stephen D. Krasner, ed., *International Regimes* (Ithaca, NY: Cornell University Press, 1983), pp. 195–232.

48. For accounts of these negotiations, see Benn Steil, *The Battle of Bretton Woods: John Maynard Keynes, Harry Dexter White, and the Making of a New World Order* (Princeton, NJ: Princeton University Press, 2013); Richard Gardner, *Sterling-Dollar Diplomacy in Current Perspective* (New York: Columbia University Press, 1980); Armand Van Dormael, *Bretton Woods: Birth of a Monetary System* (London: Macmillan, 1978); and Alfred E. Eckes Jr., *A Search for Solvency: Bretton Woods and the International Monetary System, 1944–71* (Austin: University of Texas Press, 1975).

49. Jacob Viner, "Objectives of Post-War International Economic Reconstruction," in William McKee and Louis J. Wiesen, eds., *American Economic Objectives* (New Wilmington, PA: Economic and Business Foundation, 1942), p. 168.

50. See G. John Ikenberry, "Creating Yesterday's New World Order: Keynesian 'New Thinking' and the Anglo-American Postwar Settlement," in Judith Goldstein and Robert O. Keohane, eds., *Ideas and Foreign Policy: Beliefs, Institutions, and Political Change* (Ithaca, NY: Cornell University Press, 1993), pp. 57–86.

51. For a discussion of security—or institutional—binding, see Ikenberry, *After Victory*, chap. 3. For a major statement of security co-binding, see Deudney, "The Philadelphia System"; and Daniel Deudney, *Bounding Power: Republican Security Theory From the Polis to the Global Village* (Princeton, NJ: Princeton University Press, 2007).

52. For the classic statement of alliances as a tool for managing relations of states within the security pact, see Paul W. Schroeder, "Alliances, 1815–1945: Weapons of Power and Tools of Management," in Klaus Knorr, ed., *Historical Dimensions of National Security Problems* (Lawrence: University Press of Kansas, 1975), pp. 227–62. For more recent explorations, see Patricia A. Weitsman, *Dangerous Alliances: Proponents of Peace, Weapons of War* (Stanford, CA: Stanford University Press, 2004); and Jeremy Pressman, *Warring Friends: Alliance Restraint in International Politics* (Ithaca, NY: Cornell University Press, 2008). In a new history of NATO, Timothy Andrews Sayle argues that postwar European and American government elites valued NATO as a sort of insurance mechanism against fickle democratic electorates that might too quickly give in to peace overturns and undermine Cold War deterrence and power balance. See Sayle, *Enduring*

Alliance: A History of NATO and the Postwar Global Order (Ithaca, NY: Cornell University Press, 2019).

53. Lloyd Gardner, *A Covenant with Power: America and World Order from Wilson to Reagan* (New York: Oxford University Press, 1984), p. 81.

54. This interlocking alliance logic is captured in Lord Ismay's apocryphal quip: NATO existed "to keep the Russians out, the Americans in, and the Germans down." While there is no record of Ismay making this comment, numerous NATO documents over the years refer to this statement as an explanation for NATO's purpose. See Sayle, *Enduring Alliance*, pp. 2–3.

55. See Ash, *Free World*.

56. Secretary of State Dean G. Acheson, Department of State, press release of address to television networks, 18 March 1949.

57. Anne Deighton, "The Remaking of Europe," in Michael Howard and Wm. Roger Louis, eds., *The Oxford History of the Twentieth Century* (Oxford: Oxford University Press, 1998), p. 192.

58. Quoted in Forrest Davis, *The Atlantic System*, p. 303.

59. See Wm. Roger Louis, *Ends of British Imperialism: The Scramble for Empire, Suez and Decolonization* (New York: I. B. Tauris, 2006); and Stanley Hoffmann, "Sisyphus and the Avalanche: The United Nations, Egypt and Hungary," *International Organization*, Vol. 11, No. 3 (Summer 1957), pp. 446–69.

60. John Lewis Gaddis, *Now We Know: Rethinking Cold War History*, rev. ed. (New York: Oxford University Press, 1998), pp. 201–2.

61. For a survey of the growing literature on the internal logic and political bargains behind hegemonic order, see G. John Ikenberry and Daniel Nexon, "Hegemony Studies 3.0: The Dynamics of Hegemonic Orders," *Security Studies*, Vol. 28, No. 3 (2019), pp. 395–421.

62. Michael Mastanduno has done pioneering work on Cold War and post–Cold War bargains among the major Western powers. See Mastanduno, "System Maker and Privilege Taker: US Power and the International Political Economy," in G. John Ikenberry, Michael Mastanduno, and William C. Wohlforth, eds., *International Relations Theory and the Consequences of Unipolarity* (New York: Cambridge University Press, 2011), pp. 140–77; and Mastanduno, "Partner Politics: Russia, China, and the Challenge of Extending U.S. Hegemony after the Cold War," *Security Studies*, Vol. 28, No. 3 (2019), pp. 479–504.

63. Carla Norrlof, *America's Global Advantage: U.S. Hegemony and International Cooperation* (New York: Cambridge University Press, 2010).

64. See Benjamin Cohen, *Organizing the World's Money: The Political Economy of International Monetary Relations* (New York: Basic Books, 1977).

65. Michael Mastanduno, "Preserving the Unipolar Moment: Realist Theories and U.S. Grand Strategy after the Cold War," *International Security*, Vol. 21, No. 4 (Spring 1997), p. 61.

66. Charles de Gaulle, *The Complete War Memoirs of Charles de Gaulle*, Vol. 3: *Salvation, 1944–1946*, trans. Richard Howard [1959] (New York: Simon and Schuster, 1960), p. 906.

67. Jeffry Frieden, *Global Capitalism: Its Fall and Rise in the Twentieth Century* (New York: Norton, 2006), p. 279.

68. See Andrew Rawnsley, "Brave New World: The Search for Peace after the Second World War," *Guardian*, 1 September 2019.

69. For studies of the effects of World War II on the emergence of new political coalitions and the birth of social democracy in Western Europe and the United States, see Arthur Marwick, *War and Social Change in the Twentieth Century: A Comparative Study of Britain, France, Germany, Russia, and the United States* (New York: St. Martin's Press, 1974); and Isser Woloch, *The Postwar Moment: Progressive Forces in Britain, France, and the United States after World War II* (New Haven, CT: Yale University Press, 2019).

70. John Bew and Michael Cox, "A Man for All Seasons: The Life and Times of Clement Attlee," London School of Economics blog post, 14 March 2017, https://blogs.lse.ac.uk/politicsandpolicy/the-life-and-times-of-clement-attlee/.

71. For surveys of Attlee's internationalism, see Raymond Smith and John Zametica, "The Cold Warrior: Clement Attlee Reconsidered, 1945–47," *International Affairs*, Vol. 61, No. 2 (1985), pp. 237–52; and Peter Weiler, "British Labour and the Cold War: The Foreign Policy of the Labour Governments, 1945–51," *Journal of British Studies*, Vol. 26, No. 1 (January 1987), pp. 54–82.

72. John Bew, *Clement Attlee: The Man Who Made Modern Britain* (Oxford: Oxford University Press, 2017).

73. The authoritative account for West Germany's engagement with the postwar Western system is Ludolf Herbst, Werner Bührer, and Hanna Sowade, eds., *Vom Marshallplan zur EWG: Die Eingliederung der Bundesrepublik Deutschland in die westliche Welt* (Munich: Oldenbourg, 1990).

74. Adam Tooze, "Democracy and Its Discontents," *New York Review of Books*, 6 June 2019, https://www.nybooks.com/articles/2019/06/06/democracy-and-its-discontents/.

75. Mary L. Hampton, *The Wilsonian Impulse: U.S. Foreign Policy, the Alliance, and German Unification* (Westport, CT: Praeger, 1996), p. 24.

76. See Hans-Jürgen Grabbe, "Konrad Adenauer, John Foster Dulles, and West German-American Relations," in Richard H. Immerman, ed., *John Foster Dulles and the Diplomacy of the Cold War* (Princeton, NJ: Princeton University Press, 1992), pp. 109–32.

77. Terry Edward MacDougall, "Yoshida Shigeru and the Japanese Transition to Liberal Democracy," *International Political Science Review*, Vol. 9, No. 1 (1988), pp. 55–69.

78. On the idea of "civilian" great powers, see Daniel Deudney and G. John Ikenberry, "The Nature and Sources of Liberal International Order," *Review of International*

Studies, Vol. 25, No. 2 (April 1999), pp. 179–96. See also Hanns W. Maull, "Germany and Japan: The New Civilian Powers," *Foreign Affairs*, Vol. 69, No. 5 (Winter 1990/91), pp. 91–106.

79. Kenneth B. Pyle, *Japan in the American Century* (Cambridge, MA: Harvard University Press, 2018), p. 175.

80. Pyle, *Japan in the American Century*, p. 209.

81. Richard Samuels, *Securing Japan: Tokyo's Grand Strategy and the Future of East Asia* (Ithaca, NY: Cornell University Press, 2007), p. 35.

82. See G. John Ikenberry, "The Stakeholder State: Ideology and Values in Japan's Search for a Post-Cold War Global Role," in Yoichi Funabashi and Barak Kushner, eds., *Examining Japan's Lost Decades* (New York: Routledge, 2015), pp. 296–313.

83. For the authoritative account, see John W. Dower, *Embracing Defeat: Japan in the Wake of World War II* (New York: Norton, 2000).

84. James Joll, *Europe since 1870: An International History* (London: Weidenfeld and Nicolson, 1973), p. 474.

85. See William I. Hitchcock, "The Marshall Plan and the Creation of the West," in Melvin P. Leffler and Odd Arne Westad, eds., *The Cambridge History of the Cold War* (London: Cambridge University Press, 2013), pp. 154–74.

86. Matthias Schmelzer, *The Hegemony of Growth: The OECD and the Making of the Economic Growth Paradigm* (New York: Cambridge University Press, 2016), pp. 254–58.

87. See William Glenn Gray, "Making Hirschman Multilateral: The United States, the OECD, and Trans-Atlantic Relations, 1945–1975" (unpublished paper, 2018).

88. See G. John Ikenberry, "Why the Liberal World Order Will Survive," *Ethics and International Affairs*, Vol. 32, No. 1 (Spring 2018), pp. 17–29.

7. Liberalism and Empire

1. The very large and rapidly growing literature on America and empire is marked by many disagreements. A large body of American historiography of the Wisconsin School follows the lead of William Appleman Williams in constructing narratives of American history as continuous imperial expansion. See Williams, *The Tragedy of American Diplomacy* (New York: World Publishing, 1959); and Williams, *The Contours of American History* (Chicago: Quadrangle Books, 1966). For works in this tradition, see Walter LaFeber, *The New Empire: An Interpretation of American Expansion, 1860–1898* (Ithaca, NY: Cornell University Press, 1963); Lloyd Gardner, *Imperial America: American Foreign Policy Since 1898* (New York: Harcourt Brace Jovanovich, 1976); Anders Stephanson, *Manifest Destiny: American Expansion and the Empire of Right* (New York: Hill and Wang, 1995); Richard H. Immerman, *Empire for Liberty: A History of American Imperialism from Benjamin Franklin to*

Paul Wolfowitz (Princeton, NJ: Princeton University Press, 2010); and A. G. Hopkins, *American Empire: A Global History* (Princeton, NJ: Princeton University
Press, 2018).

2. For studies of the imperial impulses behind liberal international projects, includ-
ing the League of Nations and the United Nations, see Jeanne Morefield, *Covenants
without Swords: Idealist Liberalism and the Spirit of Empire* (Princeton, NJ: Princeton
University Press, 2005); Morefield, *Empire without Imperialism: Anglo-American
Decline and the Politics of Deflection* (Oxford: Oxford University Press, 2014); and
Mark Mazower, *No Enchanted Palace: The End of Empire and the Ideological
Origins of the United Nations* (Princeton, NJ: Princeton University Press, 2009).
For a Gramscian perspective, see Inderjeet Parmar, "The U.S.-Led Liberal Order:
Imperialism by Another Name?," *International Affairs*, Vol. 94, No. 1 (January 2018),
pp. 151–72; and Parmar, *Foundations of the American Century: The Ford, Carnegie,
and Rockefeller Foundations and the Rise of American Power* (New York: Columbia
University Press, 2012).

3. See Perry Anderson, *American Foreign Policy and Its Thinkers* (London: Verso,
2014); and various essays by Samuel Moyn: "Beyond Liberal Internationalism,"
Dissent, Winter 2017, pp. 10–14; and "Soft Sells: On Liberal Internationalism," *The
Nation*, 14 September 2011, https://www.thenation.com/article/archive/soft-sells
-liberal-internationalism/.

4. For classic statements of this realist view, see George Kennan, *American Diplomacy, 1900–1950* (Chicago: University of Chicago Press, 1951); and Henry Kissinger, *Diplomacy* (New York: Simon and Schuster, 1994).

5. These thinkers are often described as "restraint realists." See John Mearsheimer,
The Great Delusion: Liberal Dreams and International Realities (New Haven, CT:
Yale University Press, 2018); Stephen M. Walt, *The Hell of Good Intentions: America's Foreign Policy Elite and the Decline of U.S. Primacy* (New York: Farrar, Straus
and Giroux, 2018); Walt, *Taming American Power: The Global Response to U.S.
Primacy* (New York: Norton, 2005); and Barry Posen, *Restraint: A New Foundation
for U.S. Grand Strategy* (Ithaca, NY: Cornell University Press, 2015).

6. Stephen Kinzer, *The True Flag: Theodore Roosevelt, Mark Twain, and the Birth of
American Empire* (New York: Henry Holt, 2017). See also Jackson Lears, "How the
United States Began Its Empire," *New York Review of Books*, 23 February 2017,
https://www.nybooks.com/articles/2017/02/23/how-the-us-began-its-empire/.

7. David C. Hendrickson, *Republic in Peril: American Empire and the Liberal
Tradition* (New York: Oxford University Press, 2018). See also Christopher A.
Preble, *The Power Problem: How American Military Dominance Makes Us
Less Safe, Less Prosperous, and Less Free* (Ithaca, NY: Cornell University
Press, 2009).

8. Michael Doyle, *Empires* (Ithaca, NY: Cornell University Press, 1991), p. 45.

9. John Darwin, *The Empire Project: The Rise and Fall of the British World-System, 1830–1970* (Cambridge: Cambridge University Press, 2009); and Charles S. Maier, *Among Empires: American Ascendancy and Its Predecessors* (Cambridge, MA: Harvard University Press, 2006). A good comparative historical survey of these instrumentalities can be found in Ronald Hyam, *Understanding the British Empire* (Cambridge: Cambridge University Press, 2010), chap. 3.

10. Duncan Bell, *Reordering the World: Essays on Liberalism and Empire* (Princeton, NJ: Princeton University Press, 2016), p. 20.

11. See Jennifer Pitts, "Political Theory of Empire and Imperialism," *Annual Review of Political Science*, Vol. 13 (2010), pp. 211–35.

12. Uday Singh Mehta, *Liberalism and Empire: A Study in Nineteenth Century British Liberal Thought* (Chicago: University of Chicago Press, 1999), p. 20.

13. John Stuart Mill, "Considerations on Representative Government" [1861], in John Gray, ed., *Liberty and Other Essays* (Oxford: Oxford University Press, 1998). See also Eileen P. Sullivan, "Liberalism and Imperialism: J. S. Mill's Defense of the British Empire," *Journal of the History of Ideas*, Vol. 44, No. 4 (October/December 1983), pp. 599–617.

14. See Bell, *Reordering the World*, pp. 104–5.

15. Sankar Muthu, *Enlightenment against Empire* (Princeton, NJ: Princeton University Press, 2003), p. 268.

16. Jennifer Pitts, *A Turn to Empire: The Rise of Imperial Liberalism in Britain and France* (Princeton, NJ: Princeton University Press, 2005), p. 1.

17. See Frederick Cooper's response to Mehta in Cooper, *Colonialism in Question* (Berkeley: University of California Press, 2005), p. 235.

18. Casper Sylvest, *British Liberal Internationalism, 1880–1930* (Manchester: University of Manchester Press, 2009), p. 43.

19. Quoted in David Gilmour, *The Ruling Caste: Imperial Lives in the Victorian Raj* (New York: Farrar, Straus and Giroux, 2006), p. 33.

20. See Duncan Bell's discussion of white settler colonialism, which he argues is a neglected topic in the broader historiography of the British Empire, in *Reordering the World*, chap. 2.

21. Quoted in Sylvest, *British Liberal Internationalism*, pp. 43–44.

22. This transition is richly documented in Daniel Gorman, *The Emergence of International Society in the 1920s* (Cambridge: Cambridge University Press, 2012); and John Edward Kendle, *The Round Table Movement and Imperial Union* (Toronto: University of Toronto Press, 1975).

23. Philip Kerr, "From Empire to Commonwealth," *Foreign Affairs*, Vol. 1, No. 2 (15 December 1922), p. 94.

24. Jan Smuts, *Draft Statement of War Aims*, British cabinet records, CAB 24/37 GT 3180.

25. Jan Smuts, *The League of Nations: A Practical Suggestion* (London: Hodder and Stoughton, 1918), p. vi. For background on Smuts's work at the Paris Peace Conference and the pamphlet's influence on Wilson, see Peter J. Yearwood, *Guarantee of Peace: The League of Nations in British Policy, 1914–1925* (Oxford: Oxford University Press, 2009), chaps. 2 and 3; and Mazower, *No Enchanted Palace*, chap. 1.

26. Mazower, *No Enchanted Palace*, p. 64.

27. See Alfred Zimmern, *The League of Nations and the Rule of Law, 1918–1935* (London: Macmillan, 1936).

28. Quoted in Morefield, *Covenants without Swords*, p. 15.

29. As Mazower notes, "Zimmern was convinced that moral rather than military or police power had kept the empire—the 'largest single political community in the world'—together and turned it into 'the surest bulwark against war in the present-day world.'" Mazower, *No Enchanted Palace*, pp. 89–90. Zimmern is quoted from a 1926 lecture at Columbia University. See Alfred Zimmern, *The Third British Empire: Being a Course of Lecture Delivered at Columbia University, New York* (London, 1926).

30. Robert Cecil, "The League of Nations and the Rehabilitation of Europe," in *Essays in Liberalism* [Being the Lectures and Papers which were delivered at the Liberal Summer School at Oxford, 1922] (London: W. Collins Sons & Co., 1922), p. 12.

31. See Hugh Cecil, "The Development of Lord Robert Cecil's Views on the Securing of a Lasting Peace, 1915–19" (PhD diss., 1971, Oxford University, Bodleian Library).

32. Quoted in Michael Pugh, *Liberal Internationalism: The Interwar Movement for Peace in Britain* (London: Palgrave Macmillan, 2012), p. 21.

33. Woodrow Wilson, "An Address in Washington to the League to Enforce Peace," 27 May 1916, in *The Papers of Woodrow Wilson*, 69 vols. (Princeton, NJ: Princeton University Press, 1981), Vol. 37, pp. 113–16.

34. Adam Tooze, *The Deluge: The Great War, America, and the Remaking of the Global Order, 1916–1931* (New York: Viking, 2014), p. 52.

35. See Pugh, *Liberal Internationalism*.

36. This theme is developed, combining global, imperial, and social history, in Helen McCarthy, *The British People and the League of Nations: Democracy, Citizenship, and Internationalism, c. 1918–45* (Manchester: Manchester University Press, 2012). See especially "Enlightened Patriots: League, Empire, and Nation," chap. 5.

37. Edward Keene, *Beyond the Anarchical Society: Grotius, Colonialism and Order in World Politics* (Cambridge: Cambridge University Press, 2002), p. xi.

38. Keene, *Beyond the Anarchical Society*, p. 7.

39. This is how the story is narrated in, for example, Walter Schiffer, *The Legal Community of Mankind: A Critical Analysis of the Modern Concept of World Organization* (Westport, CT: Greenwood Press, 1972).

40. Jennifer Pitts, *Boundaries of the International: Law and Empire* (Cambridge, MA: Harvard University Press, 2018); and Richard Tuck, *The Rights of War and Peace: Political Thought and the International Order from Grotius to Kant* (Oxford: Oxford University Press, 1999).

41. Lauren Benton, "From International Law to Imperial Constitutions: The Problem of Quasi-Sovereignty, 1870–1900," *Law and History Review*, Vol. 26, No. 3 (Fall 2008), pp. 595–619.

42. See Antony Anghie, *Imperialism, Sovereignty, and the Making of International Law* (Cambridge: Cambridge University Press, 2007), p. 81.

43. See Lauren Benton and Lisa Ford, *Rage for Order: The British Empire and the Origins of International Law, 1800–1850* (Cambridge, MA: Harvard University Press, 2014); Lauren Benton, *A Search for Sovereignty: Law and Geography in European Empires, 1400–1900* (Cambridge: Cambridge University Press, 2010); and Martti Koskenniemi, *The Gentle Civilizer of Nations: The Rise and Fall of International Law, 1870–1960* (Cambridge: Cambridge University Press, 2001).

44. Andrew Fitzmaurice, "Liberalism and Empire in Nineteenth-Century International Law," *American History Review*, Vol. 117, No. 1 (February 2012), p. 123. The seminal statement of this view is Edmund Burke's critique of Warren Hastings, which is documented and analyzed in David P. Fidler and Jennifer M. Welsh, *Empire and Community: Edmund Burke's Writings and Speeches on International Relations* (New York: Routledge, 2019).

45. For a discussion of the relationship between ideologies of liberalism and civilization, see Barry Buzan and George Lawson, *The Great Transformation: History, Modernity and the Making of International Relations* (Cambridge: Cambridge University Press, 2015), chap. 4.

46. See Frederick Cooper and Ann Laura Stoler, eds., *Tensions of Empire: Colonial Cultures in a Bourgeois World* (Berkeley: University of California Press, 1997).

47. See Brett Bowden, *The Empire of Civilization: The Evolution of an Imperial Idea* (Chicago: University of Chicago Press, 2009).

48. The American Declaration of Independence, USHistory.org, https://www.ushistory.org/declaration/document/.

49. Gerrit Gong, *The Standard of Civilization in International Society* (Oxford: Clarendon Press, 1984).

50. General Act of the Conference at Berlin (signed 26 February 1885), 165 CTS 485, https://loveman.sdsu.edu/docs/1885GeneralActBerlinConference.pdf. The act was signed by the representatives of the United Kingdom, France, Germany, Austria-Hungary, Belgium, Denmark, Spain, the United States of America, Italy, the Netherlands, Portugal, Russia, Sweden-Norway, and Turkey (Ottoman Empire).

51. Quoted in Bowden, *The Empire of Civilization*, p. 58.

52. A prominent example is Jan Smuts, *Holism and Evolution* (New York: Macmillan, 1926). For an extended discussion, see Morefield, *Empires without Imperialism*.

53. Frank Furedi, *The Silent War: Imperialism and the Change Perception of Race* (New Brunswick, NJ: Rutgers University Press, 1999); and Elazar Barkan, *The Retreat of Scientific Racism: Changing Conceptions of Race in Britain and the United States between the Wars* (Cambridge: Cambridge University Press, 1993).

54. Stephen Skowronek, "The Reassociation of Ideas and Purposes: Racism, Liberalism, and the American Political Tradition," *American Political Science Review*, Vol. 100, No. 3 (August 2006), p. 398.

55. Skowronek, "The Reassociation of Ideas and Purposes," p. 394.

56. More generally, the institutional discourse on human rights emerged only in the wake of World War II, a point made in Samuel Moyn, *The Last Utopia: Human Rights in History* (Cambridge, MA: Belknap Press of Harvard University Press, 2010). The league only established collective or corporate rights, such as self-determination, and provided regimes for their observance, such as the minorities and mandates commissions.

57. Naoko Shimazu, *Japan, Race and Equality: The Racial Equality Proposal of 1919* (New York: Routledge, 1998), p. 155. See also Lloyd Ambrosius, *Woodrow Wilson and the American Diplomatic Tradition: The Treaty Fight in Perspective* (New York: Cambridge University Press, 1987); and Paul Lauren, "Human Rights in History: Diplomacy and Racial Equality at the Paris Peace Conference," *Diplomatic History*, Vol. 3 (Summer 1978), pp. 257–79.

58. For conceptions of market capitalism and its implications for modern society, see Albert Hirschman, "Rival Interpretations of Market Society: Civilizing, Destructive, or Feeble?," *Journal of Economic Literature*, Vol. 20 (1982), pp. 1463–84.

59. John A. Hobson, *Imperialism: A Study* (London: James Nisbet and Co., 1902); Hobson, *The Crisis of Liberalism: New Issues of Democracy* (London: P. S. King, 1909); Norman Angell, *The Great Illusion: A Study of the Relation of Military Power to Their Economic and Social Advantage* (New York: G. P. Putnam's Sons, 1910); and Joseph A. Schumpeter, *Imperialism and Social Classes* (New York: Augustus M. Kelley, 1951).

60. See Bell, *Reordering the World*, p. 24.

61. Dipesh Chakrabarty, *Provincializing Europe: Postcolonial Thought and Historical Difference* (Princeton, NJ: Princeton University Press, 2000), p. 8.

62. Edward Keene, *Beyond the Anarchical Society: Grotius, Colonialism, and Order in World Politics* (Cambridge: Cambridge University Press, 2002), p. 135.

63. Keene, *Beyond the Anarchical Society*, p. 136.

64. See Robert Jackson, *The Global Covenant: Human Conduct in the a World of States* (Oxford: Oxford University Press, 2000), chaps. 7 and 13; and Neta Craw-

ford, *Argument and Change in World Politics: Ethics, Decolonization, and Humanitarian Intervention* (Cambridge: Cambridge University Press, 2002).

65. On the defeat of Nazism as a turning point in Western views of race and racial hierarchy as ordering ideas, see Furedi, *The Silent War.*

66. Keene, *Beyond the Anarchical Society*, p. 123.

67. Leonard Woolf, *Barbarians at the Gate* (London: Victor Gollancz, 1939), p. 83.

68. American and British political cultures were different in many ways, including in their images and attitudes toward empire. These differences were discovered by H. G. Wells in his travels in the United States in the years before World War I. Earlier in his career, Wells had conceived of a grand Anglo-American union that would support British Empire and liberal imperialism. After visiting the United States, Wells became skeptical that the United States had the political imagination to support an imperial union. See Duncan Bell, "Founding the World State: H. G. Wells on Empire and the English-Speaking Peoples," *International Studies Quarterly*, Vol. 62, No. 4 (December 2018), pp. 867–79.

69. See Wm. Roger Louis, *Imperialism at Bay: The United States and the Decolonization of the British Empire, 1941–1945* (New York: Oxford University Press, 1978); and David Reynolds, *Britannia Overruled: British Policy and World Power in the Twentieth Century* (New York: Longman, 1991).

70. The debate over the "grand area" is discussed in chapter 6.

71. See G. John Ikenberry, *Liberal Leviathan: The Origins, Crisis, and Transformation of the American World Order* (Princeton, NJ: Princeton University Press, 2011).

72. Ian Chong, *External Intervention and the Politics of State Formation: China, Indonesia, and Thailand, 1893–1952* (Cambridge: Cambridge University Press, 2012).

73. See Robert H. Jackson, *Quasi-States: Sovereignty, International Relations, and the Third World* (New York: Cambridge University Press, 1990).

74. See Julian Go, *Patterns of Empire: The British and American Empires, 1688 to the Present* (Cambridge: Cambridge University Press, 2011).

75. After the founding of NATO, some European governments expected the alliance to help protect their imperial possessions. Along with the Nordic countries and Canada, the United States was, as the historian Timothy Sayle notes, "unwilling to see NATO's thumb rest on the scales in support of colonial powers." Eisenhower made this point in August 1958 at a National Security Council meeting on the subject of African independence movements: "He would like to be on the side of the natives for once." See Timothy Andrews Sayle, *Enduring Alliance: A History of NATO and the Postwar Global Order* (Ithaca, NY: Cornell University Press, 2019), p. 25.

76. This point is developed theoretically with the notion of "discursive enmeshment." See a discussion in Andrew Hurrell, "Norms and Ethics in International Relations,"

in Walter Carlsnaes, Thomas Risse, and Beth A. Simmons, eds., *Handbook of International Relations* (Thousand Oaks, CA: Sage, 2002). Nina Tannenwald speculates that great powers may use discursive enmeshment strategically against one another in what she calls "normative geopolitics." See Tannenwald, "The Nuclear Taboo: The United States and the Normative Bases of Nonuse," *International Organization*, Vol. 53, No. 3 (Summer 1999), pp. 433–68.

77. Sumner Welles, speech at Panama Conference, 25 September 1930, reprinted in Welles, *The World of the Four Freedoms* (New York: Columbia University Press, 1943).

78. See Sumner Welles, *Where Are We Heading?* (New York: Harper and Brothers, 1946).

79. Rupert Emerson, "The New Higher Law of Anti-Colonialism," reprinted in Karl Deutsch and Stanley Hoffmann, eds., *The Relevance of International Law* (Garden City, NY: Anchor Books, 1968), p. 209. Erez Manela sees decolonization as the appropriation and extension of Western ideas and norms to the periphery. See Manela, *The Wilsonian Moment: Self-Determination and the International Origins of Anticolonial Nationalism* (Oxford: Oxford University Press, 2007). Others see the decolonization movement as a more creative act of turning the principle of self-determination into a right and reimagining global order. See Adom Getachew, *Worldmaking after Empire: The Rise and Fall of Self-Determination* (Princeton, NJ: Princeton University Press, 2019).

80. C. A. Bayly, *The Birth of the Modern World, 1780–1914* (Oxford: Blackwell, 2004), p. 3.

81. Robin W. Winks, *World Civilization: A Brief History* (San Diego: Collegiate Press, 1993), p. 506.

82. See Wm. Roger Louis, "The European Colonial Empires," in Michael Howard and Wm. Roger Louis, eds., *The Oxford History of the Twentieth Century* (Oxford: Oxford University Press, 1998), p. 93.

83. See Lucian M. Ashworth, *A History of International Thought* (New York: Routlege, 2014), pp. 125–26.

84. On Jane Addams, see Sondra R. Herman, *Eleven against War: Studies in American Internationalist Thought, 1898–1921* (Stanford, CA: Stanford University Press, 1969), chap. 5.

85. Beryl Haslam, *From Suffrage to Internationalism: The Political Evolution of Three British Feminists, 1908–1939* (New York: Peter Lang, 1999); Jo Vellacott, *Pacifists, Patriots, and the Vote: The Erosion of Democratic Suffragism in Britain during the First World War* (London: Palgrave Macmillan, 2007).

86. See Penny M. Von Eschen, *Race against Empire: Black Americans and Anticolonialism, 1937–1957* (Ithaca, NY: Cornell University Press, 1997); and Paul Gordon Lauren, *Power and Prejudice: The Politics and Diplomacy of Racial Discrimination* (Boulder, CO: Westview Press, 1998).

87. See the account in Christopher D. O'Sullivan, *Sumner Welles, Postwar Planning, and the Quest for a New World Order, 1937–1943* (New York: Columbia University Press, 2009), p. 138.

88. The text of the Appeal to the World can be found at https://www.blackpast.org /global-african-history/primary-documents-global-african-history/1947-w-e-b -dubois-appeal-world-statement-denial-human-rights-minorities-case-citizens-n/. See also David Levering Lewis, *W. E. B. Du Bois: A Biography* (New York: Henry Holt, 2009), pp. 672–77.

89. Mary L. Dudziak, *Cold War Civil Rights: Race and the Image of American Democracy* (Princeton, NJ: Princeton University Press, 2011), p. 12. See also Thomas Borstelmann, *The Cold War and the Color Line: American Race Relations in the Global Arena* (Cambridge, MA: Harvard University Press, 2003).

90. Von Eschen, *Race against Empire*.

91. See Ashworth, *A History of International Thought*, p. 125.

92. Susan Pedersen, "Back to the League of Nations," *American Historical Review*, Vol. 112, No. 4 (October 2007), p. 1092.

93. Susan Pedersen, *The Guardians: The League of Nations and the Crisis of Empire* (New York: Oxford University Press, 2015), pp. 4–5.

94. One example is the Institution Committee on Intellectual Cooperation (ICIC), founded by the League of Nations in 1922 and devoted to international scientific and cultural exchange. Daniel Laqua argues that the ICIC became a vehicle for the circulation of ideas about how to think about and pursue international cooperation, and it was thus a "tool for transforming the international order." Laqua, "Transnational Intellectual Cooperation, the League of Nations, and the Problem of Order," *Journal of Global History*, Vol. 6, No. 2 (2011), p. 226.

95. It was an Indian prince, the maharaja of Bikaner, who signed the Treaty of Versailles as one of the plenipotentiaries authorized to act on behalf of India.

96. R. P. Anand, "The Formation of International Organizations and India: A Historical Study," *Leiden Journal of International Law*, Vol. 23 (2010), p. 8. India had contributed more than a million soldiers to the war effort on numerous battlefields under British command, which strengthened its claim to representation at Versailles.

97. Anand, "The Formation of International Organizations and India," p. 12.

98. See T. A. Keenleyside, "The Indian Nationalist Movement and the League of Nations: Prologue to the United Nations," *India Quarterly: A Journal of International Affairs*, Vol. 39, No. 3 (July 1983), pp. 281–98.

99. Adam Roberts, "Towards an International Community? The United Nations and International Law," in Howard and Louis, *The Oxford History of the Twentieth Century*, pp. 310–11.

100. See David Armitage, *The Declaration of Independence: A Global History* (Cambridge, MA: Harvard University Press, 2007).

101. This is the conclusion reached by John Gallagher in *The Decline, Revival, and Fall of the British Empire* (Cambridge: Cambridge University Press, 1982), as well as by Wm. Roger Louis and Ronald Robinson in "The Imperialism of Decolonization," *Journal of Imperial and Commonwealth History*, Vol. 22, No. 3 (September 1994), pp. 462–511.

102. Christian Reus-Smit, *Individual Rights and the Making of the International System* (Cambridge: Cambridge University Press, 2013), pp. 22–23.

103. John Darwin, *Unfinished Empire: The Global Expansion of Britain* (London: Penguin, 2012), p. 384.

104. See Daniel Deudney and G. John Ikenberry, "America's Impact: The Decline of Empire and the Spread of the Westphalian State System" (unpublished paper, 2016).

105. Chalmers Johnson, *The Sorrows of Empire: Militarism, Secrecy, and the End of the Republic* (New York: Metropolitan Books, 2007). There is a large literature on the imperial characteristics of American foreign policy during and after the Cold War. For important statements, see Michael Mann, *Incoherent Empire* (London: Verso, 2005); and Andrew J. Bacevich, *American Empire: The Realities and Consequences of U.S. Diplomacy* (Cambridge, MA: Harvard University Press, 2002). For a survey of views, see Andrew Bacevich, *The Imperial Tense: Prospects and Problems of American Empire* (Chicago: Ivan R. Dee, 2003).

106. See Mearsheimer, *The Great Delusion*.

107. Jan-Werner Müller, "What Cold War Liberalism Can Teach Us Today," *New York Review of Books*, 26 November 2018, https://www.nybooks.com/daily/2018/11/26/what-cold-war-liberalism-can-teach-us-today/. See also Müller, *Isaiah Berlin's Cold War Liberalism* (London: Palgrave Macmillan, 2019).

108. Arthur Schlesinger Jr., *The Vital Center: The Politics of Freedom* (Boston: Houghton Mifflin, 1949).

109. For an exploration of Cold War liberalism and its impact on post–Cold War foreign policy, see Tony Smith, "National Security Liberalism and American Foreign Policy," in Michael Cox, G. John Ikenberry, and Takashi Inoguchi, eds., *American Democracy Promotion: Impulses, Strategies, and Impacts* (Oxford: Oxford University Press, 2003), chap. 4.

110. Kissinger, *Diplomacy*, p. 33.

111. Walter McDougall, *Promised Land, Crusader State: The American Encounter with the World Since 1776* (New York: Houghton Mifflin, 1997).

112. Michael C. Desch, "America's Liberal Illiberalism: The Ideological Origins of Overreaction in U.S. Foreign Policy, " *International Security*, Vol. 32, No. 3 (Winter 2007–8), pp. 7–43.

113. See James Lindley Wilson and Jonathan Monten, "Does Kant Justify Liberal Intervention?," *Review of Politics*, Vol. 73 (2011), pp. 633–47. For a response, see Michael Desch, "Benevolent Cant? Kant's Liberal Imperialism," *Review of Politics*, Vol. 73 (2011), pp. 649–56. Furthermore, it is also revealing that Kant himself retreated from his earlier conviction that perpetual peace was attainable in his later work, *The Metaphysics of Morals*, where he also argued that stability in relations among states—given that perpetual peace is not realistic—did not require homogeneity in domestic regimes.

114. See Michael Doyle, "Kant, Liberal Legacies, and Foreign Affairs, Part 2," *Philosophy and Public Affairs*, Vol. 12, No. 4 (1983), p. 330; and Doyle, "A Few Words on Mill, Walzer, and Nonintervention," *Ethics and International Affairs*, No. 23, No. 4 (2009), pp. 349–69.

115. Michael Doyle, *Ways of War and Peace: Realism, Liberalism, Socialism* (New York: Norton, 1997), p. 395. As Sankar Muthu shows, Kant evinced a profound opposition to imperialism, a belief rooted in his underlying moral commitments. See Muthu, *Enlightenment against Empire*, pp. 122–209.

116. Georg Sørensen, *A Liberal World Order in Crisis: Choosing between Imposition and Restraint* (Ithaca, NY: Cornell University Press, 2011). For other reflections on the divide between interventionist and noninterventionist strands of liberalism, see John Gray, *Two Faces of Liberalism* (Cambridge: Polity Press, 2000); Thomas Walker, "Two Faces of Liberalism: Kant, Paine, and the Question of Intervention," *International Studies Quarterly*, Vol. 52, No. 3 (September 2008), pp. 449–68; and Michael Doyle and Stefano Recchia, "Liberalism in International Relations," in Bertrand Badie, Dirk Berg-Schlosser, and Leonardo A. Morlino, eds., *International Encyclopedia of Political Science* (Thousand Oaks, CA: Sage, 2011), especially pp. 1437–38.

117. Sørensen, *A Liberal World Order in Crisis*, p. 2.

118. Gerry Simpson, "Two Liberalisms," *European Journal of International Law*, Vol. 12, No. 3 (2006), pp. 385–401.

119. Diversity is also accommodated because of the cost of addressing human rights violations by powerful states. This can be seen in the tepid liberal response to China's policy toward Muslims.

120. George W. Bush, "Second Inaugural Address," 20 January 2005, The Avalon Project at Yale Law School, https://avalon.law.yale.edu/21st_century/gbush2.asp.

121. For a debate among liberal internationalists on Bush's foreign policy, see G. John Ikenberry, Thomas J. Knock, Anne-Marie Slaughter, and Tony Smith, *The Crisis of American Foreign Policy: Wilsonianism in the Twenty-First Century* (Princeton, NJ: Princeton University Press, 2009).

122. See Tony Smith, *A Pact with the Devil: Washington's Bid for World Supremacy and the Betrayal of the American Promise* (New York: Routledge, 2007).

123. G. John Ikenberry, "America's Imperial Ambition," *Foreign Affairs*, Vol. 81, No. 5 (September/October 2002), pp. 44–60.

124. See Jonathan Monten, "The Roots of the Bush Doctrine: Power, Nationalism, and Democracy Promotion in U.S. Strategy," *International Security*, Vol. 29, No. 4 (Spring 2005), pp. 112–56.

125. This argument is developed in Daniel Deudney and G. John Ikenberry, "Realism, Liberalism and the Iraq War," *Survival*, Vol. 59, No. 4 (August/September 2017), pp. 7–26.

126. For an account of the ideas and officials behind this strategic guidance, see James Mann, *Rise of the Vulcans: The History of Bush's War Cabinet* (New York: Viking, 2004), pp. 208–15.

127. A statement opposing the war by thirty-three realist-oriented scholars was published in the *New York Times* on 22 September 2002.

128. Deudney and Ikenberry, "Realism, Liberalism and the Iraq War."

129. See Bruce Jones, Carlos Pascual, and Stephen John Stedman, *Power and Responsibility: Building International Order in an Era of Transnational Threats* (Washington, DC: Brookings Institution Press, 2009); and G. John Ikenberry and Anne-Marie Slaughter, *Forging a World of Liberty under Law* (Princeton, NJ: Woodrow Wilson School, 2016).

130. See Barry Posen, "The Case for Restraint," *American Interest*, Vol. 3, No. 1 (Fall 2007), pp. 7–17, https://www.the-american-interest.com/2007/11/01/the-case-for-restraint/; and G. John Ikenberry, "Debating the Strategy of Restraint," *American Interest*, Vol. 3, No. 1 (Fall 2007).

131. Peter Katzenstein and Robert Keohane, eds., *Anti-Americanism in World Politics* (Ithaca, NY: Cornell University Press, 2007).

8. The Crisis of the Post–Cold War Liberal Order

1. David A. Bell, "The Many Lives of Liberalism," *New York Review of Books*, 17 January 2019, https://www.nybooks.com/articles/2019/01/17/many-lives-of-liberalism/.

2. See Edward Luce, *The Retreat of Western Liberalism* (New York: Atlantic Monthly, 2017); and Bill Emmott, *The Fate of the West: The Battle to Save the World's Most Successful Political Idea* (New York: PublicAffairs, 2017).

3. Karl Polanyi, *The Great Transformation: The Political and Economic Origins of Our Times* (New York: Farrar and Rinehart, 1944).

4. E. H. Carr, *The Twenty Years' Crisis, 1919–1939* (London: Macmillan, 1940).

5. Adam Roberts, "An 'Incredibly Swift Transition': Reflections on the End of the Cold War," in Melvyn P. Leffler and Odd Arne Westad, eds., *The Cambridge History of the Cold War*, Vol. 3 (Cambridge: Cambridge University Press, 2010), p. 513.

6. For accounts of the end of the Cold War, see Robert Service, *The End of the Cold War: 1985–1991* (New York: PublicAffairs, 2015); Mary Elise Sarotte, *The Collapse: The Accidental Opening of the Berlin Wall* (New York: Basic Books, 2005); and Jacques Lévesque, *The Enigma of 1989: The USSR and the Liberation of Eastern Europe* (Berkeley: University of California Press, 1997). For portraits of American diplomacy at the end of the Cold War, see Robert D. Zelikow and Condoleezza Rice, *Germany Unified and Europe Transformed: A Study in Statecraft* (Cambridge, MA: Harvard University Press, 1995); and Robert L. Hutchings, *American Diplomacy and the End of the Cold War: An Insider's Account of U.S. Diplomacy in Europe, 1989–1992* (Baltimore: Johns Hopkins University Press, 1998).

7. Quoted in Daniel Hamilton, "A More European Germany, a More German Europe," *Journal of International Affairs*, Vol. 45, No. 1 (Summer 1991), pp. 127–49.

8. Thomas Bagger, "The World According to Germany: Reassessing 1989," *Washington Quarterly*, Vol. 41, No. 4 (Winter 2019), p. 54.

9. George H. W. Bush, "Inaugural Address," 20 January 1989, https://millercenter.org/the-presidency/presidential-speeches/january-20-1989-inaugural-address.

10. George H. W. Bush, "Address to the United Nations General Assembly," 25 September 1989, https://2009-2017.state.gov/p/io/potusunga/207266.htm.

11. Quoted in Tony Smith, *America's Mission: The United States and the Worldwide Struggle for Democracy* (Princeton, NJ: Princeton University Press, 1994), 315.

12. See Wallace J. Thies, *Why NATO Endures* (Cambridge: Cambridge University Press, 2009).

13. James A. Baker, *The Politics of Diplomacy: Revolution, War, and Peace, 1989–1992* (New York: Putnam, 1995), pp. 605–6.

14. Anthony Lake, "From Containment to Enlargement," *Vital Speeches of the Day*, Vol. 60, No. 1 (15 October 1993), pp. 13–19. See also Douglas Brinkley, "Democratic Enlargement: The Clinton Doctrine," *Foreign Policy*, No. 106 (Spring 1997), p. 116.

15. See White House, *A National Security Strategy of Engagement and Enlargement* (Washington, DC, July 1994).

16. For accounts of Clinton's strategy of expanding the community of market democracies, see Derek Chollet and James Goldgeier, *America between the Wars: From 11/9 to 9/11* (New York: PublicAffairs, 2008); and Smith, *America's Mission*, chap. 11.

17. See James Goldgeier, *Not Whether but When: The U.S. Decision to Enlarge NATO* (Washington, DC: Brookings Institution Press, 1999). For more recent evidence, see Mary Elise Sarotte, "How to Enlarge NATO: The Debate within the Clinton Administration, 1993–95," *International Security*, Vol. 41, No. 1 (Summer 2019), pp. 7–41.

18. On the creation of the WTO and its evolving relationship with China, see Paul Blustein, *Schism: China, America, and the Fracturing of the Global Trading System* (Waterloo, ON: CIGI Press, 2019).

19. Quoted in Strobe Talbott, *The Great Experiment: The Story of Ancient Empires, Modern States, and the Quest for a Global Nation* (New York: Simon and Schuster, 2008), p. 329.

20. See Talbott, *The Great Experiment*, pp. 329–30.

21. For a careful analysis of the assumptions and expectations behind the Clinton administration's engagement policy toward China, see Alastair Iain Johnston, "The Failures of the 'Failure of Engagement' with China," *Washington Quarterly*, Vol. 42, No. 2 (Summer 2019), pp. 99–114.

22. Bill Clinton, "Speech at the Paul H. Nitze School of Advanced International Studies," 8 March 2000, quoted in Michael Mandlebaum, *The Ideas That Conquered the World: Peace, Democracy, and Free Markets in the Twenty-First Century* (New York: PublicAffairs, 2002), p. 455.

23. Quoted in Chollet and Goldgeier, *America between the Wars*, p. 153.

24. George W. Bush, "Remarks to the Los Angeles World Affairs Council," 29 May 2001, https://www.govinfo.gov/content/pkg/PPP-2001-book1/pdf/PPP-2001-book1-doc-pg593.pdf.

25. Robert Zoellick, "Whither China? From Membership to Responsibility," remarks to the National Committee on US-China Relations, New York, 21 September 2005, https://2001-2009.state.gov/s/d/former/zoellick/rem/53682.htm.

26. Beth Simmons, Frank Dobbin, and Geoffrey Garrett, "Introduction: The Diffusion of Liberalization," in Simmons, Dobbin, and Garrett, eds., *The Global Diffusion of Markets and Democracy* (New York: Cambridge University Press, 2008), p. 3.

27. Anne O. Krueger, "The World Economy at the Start of the 21st Century," remarks by the first deputy managing director, International Monetary Fund (Annual Gilbert Lecture, Rochester University, New York), 6 April 2006, https://www.imf.org/en/News/Articles/2015/09/28/04/53/sp040606.

28. See Samuel P. Huntington, *The Third Wave: Democratization in the Late Twentieth Century* (Norman: University of Oklahoma Press, 1991).

29. Simmons, Dobbin, and Garrett, "Introduction," p. 3. See also Adam Przeworski, Michael E. Alvarez, José Antonio Cheibub, and Fernando Limongi, *Democracy and Development: Political Institutions and Material Well-Being in the World, 1950–1990* (Cambridge: Cambridge University Press, 2000).

30. The regional context is important in determining the incidence and success of democratic transitions. The greater the proportion of democracies already existing in a region, the greater the likelihood of democratic transitions by the remaining authoritarian regimes. See Kristian Skrede Gliditsch and Michael D. Ward, "Diffusion and the International Context of Democratization," *International Organization*, Vol. 60, No. 4 (2006), pp. 911–33.

31. See Stephan Haggard and Robert R. Kaufman, "Democratization during the Third Wave," *Annual Review of Political Science*, Vol. 19 (2016), p. 127.

32. Haggard and Kaufman emphasize the uniqueness of the international setting that facilitated the diffusion of liberalism and democracy. "The expectation of strong diffusion processes was associated with a particular moment in world history: the collapse of an authoritarian superpower, the dissolution of its empire, a brief moment of unchallenged American supremacy, and a strong belief in the combined power of economic interdependence, international institutions, and democracy." Haggard and Kaufman, "Democratization during the Third Wave," p. 137.

33. As Carles Boix finds, in historical periods when the international system is dominated by a liberal or authoritarian hegemon, the great powers are more likely to promote like-minded regimes. The most pronounced manifestation of this international setting occurred in the two decades after the end of the Cold War. See Boix, "Democracy, Development, and the International System," *American Political Science Review*, Vol. 105, No. 4 (2011), pp. 809–28.

34. On definitions of polarity, see G. John Ikenberry, Michael Mastanduno, and William C. Wohlforth, "Introduction: Unipolarity, State Behavior, and Systemic Consequences," in Ikenberry, Mastanduno, and Wohlforth, eds., *International Relations Theory and the Consequences of Unipolarity* (New York: Cambridge University Press, 2011), pp. 1–32.

35. Anne-Marie Slaughter argues that power and influence are created by countries that act as hubs of global networks. See Slaughter, *The Chessboard and the Web: Strategies of Connection in a Networked World* (New Haven, CT: Yale University Press, 2017).

36. G. John Ikenberry, "The Liberal Sources of American Unipolarity," in Ikenberry, Mastanduno, and Wohlforth, *International Relations Theory and the Consequences of Unipolarity*, pp. 216–51.

37. On the "club benefits" of liberal order, see Ikenberry, "The Liberal Sources of American Unipolarity"; and Daniel Drezner, *All Politics Is Global: Explaining International Regulatory Regimes* (Princeton, NJ: Princeton University Press, 2007).

38. This argument is made in G. John Ikenberry, *After Victory: Institutions, Strategic Restraint, and the Rebuilding of Order after Major War* (Princeton, NJ: Princeton University Press, 2001).

39. See John Mearsheimer, "Back to the Future: Instability in Europe after the Cold War," *International Security*, Vol. 15, No. 1 (Summer 1990), pp. 5–56; and my rebuttal in *After Victory*, chap. 7. For a survey of realist theories and their expectations about the post–Cold War international order, see Michael Mastanduno, "A Realist View: Three Images of the Coming International Order," in T.V. Paul and John A. Hall, eds., *International Order and the Future of World Politics* (London: Cambridge University Press, 1999), pp. 19–40. See also the debate in G. John Ikenberry, ed.,

America Unrivaled: The Future of the Balance of Power (Ithaca, NY: Cornell University Press, 2002).

40. The term *security community* was introduced by Karl Deutsch to capture the unique character of highly like-minded and consensual groupings of states. What defines a security community, according to Deutsch, is the complete absence of the perception of security threats between states within the community. See Deutsch, *Political Community and the North Atlantic Area: International Organization in the Light of Historical Experience* (Princeton, NJ: Princeton University Press, 1957). The term here is used slightly differently to refer to a political order in which its members actively establish institutions and agreements that create a community of shared risk and mutual protection. See also Emanuel Adler, "Seasons of Peace: Progress in Postwar International Security," in Emanuel Adler and Beverly Crawford, eds., *Progress in Postwar International Relations* (New York: Columbia University Press, 1991), pp. 128–73. Adler wrote this piece at the end of the Cold War and anticipated a progressive trajectory in which the Western security community would eventually expand to cover other regions of the world, especially Eastern Europe—though in perhaps less stable, less intimate arrangements (which he terms *common security*). It is interesting to note that Adler did not anticipate the weakening of the North Atlantic security community with its expansion.

41. Francis Gavin, *Gold, Dollars, and Power: The Politics of International Monetary Relations, 1958–71* (Chapel Hill: University of North Carolina Press, 2004).

42. See Michael Mastanduno, "System Maker and Privilege Taker: US Power and the International Political Economy," in Ikenberry, Mastanduno, and Wohlforth, *International Relations Theory and the Consequences of Unipolarity*, pp. 142–47; David Lake, *Entangling Relations: American Foreign Policy in Its Century* (Princeton, NJ: Princeton University Press, 1999), chaps. 5 and 6; and Lake, *Hierarchy in International Relations* (Ithaca, NY: Cornell University Press, 2011), which covers both the economic and security dimensions of American hegemony.

43. See G. John Ikenberry, *Liberal Leviathan: The Origins, Crisis, and Transformation of the American World Order* (Princeton, NJ: Princeton University Press, 2011), chap. 5.

44. Mastanduno, "System Maker and Privilege Taker," p. 171.

45. See Nicholas Lardy, *The State Strikes Back: The End of Economic Reform in China?* (Washington, DC: Peterson Institute for International Economics, 2019).

46. Avery Goldstein, *Rising to the Challenge: China's Grand Strategy and International Security* (Stanford, CA: Stanford University Press, 2005); and Thomas Christensen, *The China Challenge: Shaping the Choices of a Rising Power* (New York: Norton, 2016).

47. Michael Mastanduno, "Partner Politics: Russia, China, and the Challenge of Extending U.S. Hegemony after the Cold War," *Security Studies*, Vol. 28, No. 3 (Summer 2019), p. 501.

48. White House, "Statement by the President on the Trans-Pacific Partnership," 5 October 2015, https://obamawhitehouse.archives.gov/the-press-office/2015/10/05/statement-president-trans-pacific-partnership.

49. For a bellwether statement of this shifting view within the Washington foreign policy establishment about China, see Kurt M. Campbell and Ely Ratner, "The China Reckoning: How Beijing Defied American Expectations," *Foreign Affairs*, Vol. 97, No. 2 (March/April 2018), pp. 60–70.

50. See Ikenberry, *Liberal Leviathan*. For debates about American unipolarity, see Stephen Walt, *Taming American Power: The Global Response to US Primacy* (New York: Norton, 2005); and Stephen G. Brooks and William C. Wohlforth, *World Out of Balance: International Relations and the Challenge of American Primacy* (Princeton, NJ: Princeton University Press, 2008).

51. See Kori Schake, *America vs the West: Can the Liberal World Order Be Preserved?* (Sydney: Penguin, 2018).

52. For an overview of these governance challenges, see Amitav Acharya, *Why Govern? Rethinking Demand and Progress in Global Governance* (Cambridge: Cambridge University Press, 2016).

53. This idea of a security community as a response to mutual vulnerability is hinted at in the concept of the "risk society" put forward by the sociologists Ulrich Beck and Anthony Giddens. Their argument is that the rise of modernity—of an advanced and rapidly developing global system—has generated growing awareness of and responses to "risk." Modernization is an inherently unsettling march into the future. A risk society is, as Beck defines it, "a systematic way of dealing with hazards and insecurities induced and introduced by modernization itself." Beck, *Risk Society: Towards a New Modernity* (London: Sage, 1992). See also Anthony Giddens and Christopher Pierson, *Making Sense of Modernity: Conversations with Anthony Giddens* (Palo Alto, CA: Stanford University Press, 1998).

54. John G. Ruggie, "International Regimes, Transactions, and Change: Embedded Liberalism in the Postwar Economic Order," *International Organization*, Vol. 36, No. 2 (Spring 1982), pp. 379–415.

55. Ruggie, "International Regimes, Transaction, and Change," p. 393.

56. Rawi Abdelal and John G. Ruggie, "The Principles of Embedded Liberalism: Social Legitimacy and Global Capitalism," in David Moss and John Cisternino, eds., *New Perspectives on Regulation* (Cambridge, MA: Tobin Project, 2009), p. 153.

57. David Harvey, *A Brief History of Neoliberalism* (Oxford: Oxford University Press, 2005). For a sweeping historical portrait of transformations in Western industrial societies, beginning in the 1970s, and the rise of neoliberalism, broadly defined,

see Simon Reid-Henry, *Empire of Democracy: The Remaking of the West since the Cold War, 1971–2017* (New York: Simon and Schuster, 2019). For a trenchant early critique of the neoliberal project, see Susan Strange, *Casino Capitalism* (Oxford: Basil Blackwell, 1986).

58. For a portrait and critique of the Washington Consensus, see Narcis Serra and Joseph E. Stiglitz, eds., *The Washington Consensus Reconsidered: Towards a New Global Governance* (Oxford: Oxford University Press, 2008). See also John Williamson, "The Strange History of the Washington Consensus," *Journal of Post Keynesian Economics*, Vol. 27, No. 2 (Winter 2004/5), pp. 195–206.

59. Jeff D. Colgan and Robert O. Keohane, "The Liberal Order Is Rigged: Fix It Now or Watch It Wither," *Foreign Affairs*, Vol. 96, No. 3 (May/June 2017), p. 37.

60. For evidence of stagnant and declining incomes among the working and middle class in the United States and Europe, and connections to the election of Donald Trump and Brexit, see Ronald Inglehart and Pippa Norris, "Trump, Brexit, and the Rise of Populism: Economic Have-Nots and Cultural Backlash," Research Working Paper 16-026 (Cambridge, MA: Harvard Kennedy School, 19 July 2016).

61. See "Decline of Global Extreme Poverty Continues but Has Slowed," World Bank, Washington, DC, 19 September 2018, https://www.worldbank.org/en/news/press -release/2018/09/19/decline-of-global-extreme-poverty-continues-but-has-slowed -world-bank.

62. Branko Milanović, *Global Inequality: A New Approach for the Age of Globalization* (Cambridge, MA: Harvard University Press, 2016), chap. 1.

63. On the unraveling of postwar social democratic coalitions, see Paul Collier, *The Future of Capitalism: Facing the New Anxieties* (London: Allen Lane, 2019), chap. 3; and Carles Boix, *Democratic Capitalism at the Crossroads: Technological Change and the Future of Politics* (Princeton, NJ: Princeton University Press, 2019).

64. See Mark Blyth, *Austerity: A History of a Dangerous Idea* (Oxford: Oxford University Press, 2013); and Blyth, "Capitalism in Crisis: What Went Wrong," *Foreign Affairs*, Vol. 95, No. 4 (July/August 2016), pp. 172–79. For a wider portrait of the economic and social consequences of neoliberalism and its impact on global political and Western grand strategy, see Adam Tooze, *Crashed: How a Decade of Financial Crises Changed the World* (New York: Viking, 2018).

65. See Daniel Deudney and G. John Ikenberry, "Democratic Internationalism: An American Grand Strategy for a Post-Exceptionalist Era," working paper (New York: Council on Foreign Relations, November 2012).

66. For arguments that the Western post–Cold War policies of NATO enlargement, democracy promotion, and other pressures and encroachments were responsible for Russia's illiberal turn, see Stephen F. Cohen, *Failed Crusade: America and the Tragedy of Post-Communist Russia* (New York: Norton, 2002); Cohen, *Soviet Fates and the Lost Alternatives: From Stalinism to the New Cold War* (New York:

Columbia University Press, 2009); Dimitri K. Simes, "Losing Russia: The Costs of Renewed Confrontation," *Foreign Affairs*, Vol. 86, No. 6 (November/December 2007), pp. 36–52; and John Mearsheimer, "Why the Ukraine Crisis Is the West's Fault: The Liberal Delusions That Provoked Putin," *Foreign Affairs*, Vol. 93, No. 5 (September/October 2014), pp. 77–89. This is also the interpretation advanced by Mikhail Gorbachev in his recent memoir that retraces the history of post-Soviet Russia through the prism of international transformations in the early 1990s. See Gorbachev, *The New Russia* (Cambridge: Polity Press, 2016).

67. See Daniel Deudney and G. John Ikenberry, "The Unravelling of the Cold War Settlement," *Survival*, Vol. 51, No. 6 (December 2009/January 2010), pp. 39–62.

68. For a skeptical assessment of the role of Western policies on Russia's reversion to authoritarianism, see Kathryn Stoner and Michael McFaul, "Who Lost Russia (This Time)? Vladimir Putin," *Washington Quarterly*, Vol. 38, No. 2 (2015), pp. 167–87.

69. See Rosemary Foot and Andrew Walter, *China, the United States, and Global Order* (New York: Cambridge University Press, 2011).

70. See Christopher A. McNally, "Sino-Capitalism: China's Reemergence and the International Political Economy," *World Politics*, Vol. 64, No. 4 (2012), pp. 741–76; and Jessica Weiss, "A World Safe for Autocracy? China's Rise and the Future of Global Politics," *Foreign Affairs*, Vol. 98, No. 4 (July/August 2019), pp. 92–98. For a study of China's institutional strategies, see Phillip Lipscy, *Renegotiating the World: Institutional Change in International Relations* (Cambridge: Cambridge University Press, 2017).

71. See G. John Ikenberry, "Why the Liberal World Order Will Survive," *Ethics and International Affairs*, Vol. 32, No. 1 (Spring 2018), pp. 17–29.

72. See Richard Woodward, *The Organization for Economic Co-operation and Development (OECD)* (New York: Palgrave, 2009).

73. On the difficulties of accommodating rising non-Western states in global institutions, see Robert Wade, "Protecting Power: Western States in Global Organization," in David Held and Charles Roger, eds., *Global Governance at Risk* (Cambridge: Polity Press, 2013), pp. 77–110.

74. For portraits of this expanding system of multilateral governance, see Fen Osler Hampson and Paul Heinbecker, "The 'New' Multilateralism of the Twenty-First Century," *Global Governance*, Vol. 17, No. 3 (July/September 2011), pp. 299–310; Dries Van Langenhove, "The Transformation of Multilateralism: Mode 1.0 to Mode 2.0," *Global Policy*, Vol. 1, No. 3 (October 2010), pp. 263–70; Richard Cooper, "The G-20 as an Improvised Crisis Committee and/or a Contested 'Steering Committee,'" *International Affairs*, Vol. 86, No. 3 (2010), pp. 741–57; and Andrew Cooper and Vincent Pouliot, "How Much Is Global Governance Changing? The

G20 as International Practice," *Cooperation and Conflict*, Vol. 50, No. 3 (2015), pp. 334–50.

75. There is a literature that explores "who benefits" from empire. But there is less systematic work that explores the distribution of economic gains across the wider global and regional orders in different historical eras. D. K. Fieldhouse has done some of the best work on the economics of empire. See Fieldhouse, *Economics and Empire, 1830–1914* (London: Weidenfeld and Nicolson, 1973); and Fieldhouse, *The West and the Third World: Trade, Colonialism and Development* (Oxford: Blackwell, 1999). On the American case, see William Woodruff, *America's Impact on the World: A Study of the Role of the United States in the World Economy, 1750–1970* (London: Macmillan, 1975).

76. Arthur Stein argues that hegemonic leadership requires the hegemon to incur relative decreases to its economic growth to support the functioning of the broader order. See Stein, "The Hegemon's Dilemma: Great Britain, the United States, and the International Economic Order," *International Organization*, Vol. 38, No. 2 (Spring 1984), pp. 355–86.

77. For the classic portrait of the varieties of postwar capitalism, see Andrew Shonfield, *Modern Capitalism: The Changing Balance of Public and Private Power* (Oxford: Oxford University Press, 1965).

78. See Alice H. Amsden, *The Rise of the "Rest": Challenges to the West from Late-Industrializing Economies* (Oxford: Oxford University Press, 2001). For a discussion of the struggles between the United States and developing countries over development and economic policies, see Amsden, *Escape from Empire: The Developing World's Journey through Heaven and Hell* (Cambridge, MA: MIT Press, 2007).

79. See Bentley B. Allan, Srdjan Vucetic, and Ted Hopf, "The Distribution of Identity and the Future of International Order: China's Hegemonic Prospects," *International Organization*, Vol. 72, No. 4 (Fall 2018), pp. 839–69.

80. On the growing and diverse constituencies that are committed to the ongoing functioning of an open and multilateral governance system, see Miles Kahler, "Global Governance: Three Futures," *International Studies Review*, Vol. 20 (2018), pp. 239–46.

81. This argument is developed in Daniel Deudney and G. John Ikenberry, "Liberal World: The Resilient Order," *Foreign Affairs*, Vol. 97, No. 4 (July/August 2018), pp. 16–24.

9. Mastering Modernity

1. Stanley Hoffmann, *Primacy or World Order: American Foreign Policy since the Cold War* (New York: McGraw-Hill, 1978), p. 166. See also Robert Gilpin, *The Challenge of Global Capitalism: The World Economy in the 21st Century* (Princeton, NJ:

Princeton University Press, 2000), which foresaw many of our present discontents. For a more Marxist-oriented critique, see David Harvey, *A Brief History of Neoliberalism* (Oxford: Oxford University Press, 2007), and Thomas Piketty, *Capital in the Twenty-First Century* (Cambridge, MA: Harvard University Press, 2017), which emphasizes the historical tendencies of unregulated capitalism to heighten and accentuate distributional inequalities. Some popular works of political philosophy reach similar conclusions. See Patrick J. Deneen, *Why Liberalism Failed* (New Haven, CT: Yale University Press, 2019); Richard Sennett, *The Corrosion of Character: The Personal Consequences of Work in the New Capitalism* (New York: Norton, 2000); and Michael Sandel, *Democracy's Discontent: America in Search of a Public Philosophy* (Cambridge, MA: Harvard University Press, 1998), which anticipated even more profoundly than Gilpin the social, spiritual, and political dislocations of unfettered neoliberalism.

2. For an extended meditation on the broader implications of automation for the shape of human societies, see Yuval Noah Harari, *21 Lessons for the 21st Century* (New York: Spiegel and Grau, 2018), esp. chaps. 2 and 4.

3. Dani Rodrik, *The Globalization Paradox: Democracy and the Future of the World Economy* (New York: Norton, 2012).

4. Rodrik, *The Globalization Paradox*, p. xix. See also Robert Skidelsky, *Money and the Government: The Past and Future of Economics* (New Haven, CT: Yale University Press, 2018).

5. See John Gray, *The Two Faces of Liberalism* (Cambridge: Polity Press, 2000).

6. A similar contrast is made in the English School tradition between pluralist and solidarist understandings of international society. See Andrew Linklater and Hidemi Suganami, *The English School of International Relations: A Contemporary Reassessment* (Cambridge: Cambridge University Press, 2006); and John Vincent, *Human Rights and International Relations* (Cambridge: Cambridge University Press, 1986). Nicholas J. Wheeler offers a reasoned defense of the solidarist conception in *Saving Strangers: Humanitarian Intervention in International Society* (Oxford: Oxford University Press, 2001). For a more general discussion, see Andrew Linklater, *The Problem of Harm in World Politics: Theoretical Investigations* (Cambridge: Cambridge University Press, 2011).

7. Miles Kahler refers to these two liberal impulses as, respectively, "macro-liberalism" and "micro-liberalism." See Kahler, "What Is Liberal Now? Rising Powers and Global Norms," in Amitav Acharya, ed., *Why Govern? Rethinking Demand and Progress in Global Governance* (Cambridge: Cambridge University Press, 2016), p. 71. See also Georg Sørensen's distinction between the liberalism of "imposition" and the liberalism of "restraint": Sørensen, *A Liberal World Order in Crisis: Choosing between Imposition and Restraint* (Ithaca, NY: Cornell University Press, 2011).

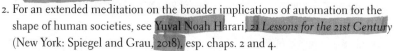

8. See Michael Walzer, *A Foreign Policy for the Left* (New Haven, CT: Yale University Press, 2018); and Michael W. Doyle, *The Question of Intervention: John Stuart Mill and the Responsibility to Protect* (New Haven, CT: Yale University Press, 2015). See also Stewart Patrick, *The Sovereignty Wars: Reconciling America with the World* (Washington, DC: Brookings Institution Press, 2018).

9. On the R2P norm, see Gareth Evans, *The Responsibility to Protect: Ending Mass Atrocity Crimes Once and for All* (Washington, DC: Brookings Institution Press, 2008).

10. This reformist ethos is very similar to the conclusion reached by Hedley Bull in his Hagey Lectures, marking a departure from his staunch defense of pluralism in *The Anarchical Society: A Study of Order in World Politics* (London: Macmillan, 1977), or his critiques of Richard Falk. For the Hagey Lectures, see Bull, *Justice in International Relations* (Waterloo, ON: University of Waterloo Press, 1984).

11. See Tristen Naylor, *Social Closure and International Society: Status Groups from the Family of Civilised Nations to the G20* (New York: Routledge, 2018).

12. Woodrow Wilson, "An Address in Washington to the League to Enforce Peace," 27 May 1916, in *The Papers of Woodrow Wilson,* 69 vols. (hereafter *PWW*), Vol. 37 (Princeton, NJ: Princeton University Press, 1981), pp. 113–16.

13. I thank John A. Thompson for this insight.

14. Woodrow Wilson, "An Address to a Joint Session of Congress," 2 April 1917, in *PWW*, Vol. 41 (Princeton, NJ: Princeton University Press, 1983), pp. 519–27.

15. See Alina Polyakova, *The Anatomy of Illiberal States: Assessing and Responding to Democratic Decline in Turkey and Central Europe,* special report (Washington, DC: Brookings Institution Press, 2019).

16. See Jennifer Lind and William Wohlforth, "The Future of Liberal International Order Is Conservative: A Strategy to Save the System," *Foreign Affairs,* Vol. 98, No. 2 (March/April 2019), pp. 70–80.

17. See Martin Wolf, "Xi Jinping's China Seeks to be Rich and Communist," *Financial Times,* 9 April 2019.

18. This strategy echoes the one advocated by George Kennan in the final paragraphs of his famous Long Telegram, https://nsarchive2.gwu.edu//coldwar/documents/episode-1/kennan.htm. See also Daniel Deudney and G. John Ikenberry, "Liberal World: The Resilient Order," *Foreign Affairs,* Vol. 97, No. 4 (July/August 2018), pp. 16–24.

19. For reflections on the debate over the logic and character of liberal hegemony, see the new preface in G. John Ikenberry, *After Victory: Institutions, Strategic Restraint, and the Rebuilding of Order after Major War* (Princeton, NJ: Princeton University Press, 2019).

20. Anthony Giddens, *The Consequences of Modernity* (Stanford, CA: Stanford University Press, 1990), p. 2.

21. Francis Fukuyama, "The End of History," *The National Interest*, No. 16 (Summer 1989), pp. 3–18. See also Fukuyama, *The End of History and the Last Man* (New York: Free Press, 1992).

22. See, for example, Reinhold Niebuhr, *Moral Man and Immoral Society: A Study of Ethics and Politics* (New York: Charles Scribner's Sons, 1932). Hans Morgenthau offers a similar line of argument in *Scientific Man versus Power Politics* (Chicago: University of Chicago Press, 1952), drawing heavily on Niebuhr.

23. John F. Kennedy, "Address at American University," Washington, DC, 10 June 1963, https://www.npr.org/documents/2006/oct/american_speeches/kennedy .pdf. See Jeffrey Sachs, *To Move the World: JFK's Quest for Peace* (New York: Random House, 2013).

24. "Text of President Obama's Speech in Hiroshima, Japan," *New York Times*, 27 May 2016, https://www.nytimes.com/2016/05/28/world/asia/text-of-president-obamas -speech-in-hiroshima-japan.html.

25. Isaiah Berlin, "The Pursuit of the Ideal," in Berlin, *The Crooked Timber of Humanity: Chapters in the History of Ideas* (London: Pimlico, 2013), pp. 1–19. Other writings by Berlin also distill his agonistic liberalism. See his magisterial essay, "John Stuart Mill and the Ends of Life," reprinted in Henry Hardy, ed., *Liberty: Incorporating the Four Essays on Liberty* (Oxford: Oxford University Press, 2002), pp. 173–206, and his unrivaled survey of Alexander Herzen ("Herzen and Bakunin on Individual Liberty," and "Part 4: Alexander Herzen," in "A Remarkable Decade"), reprinted in Henry Hardy, ed., *Russian Thinkers* (London: Penguin Classics, 2008), pp. 93–129 and 212–39. Indeed, John Gray argues that Berlin is most clear and eloquent in articulating his own view of liberalism in his essays on Herzen, with whom Berlin identified very intimately. See Gray, *Isaiah Berlin* (Princeton, NJ: Princeton University Press, 1996), pp. 30–33.

26. Gray, *Isaiah Berlin*.

27. Judith Shklar, "The Liberalism of Fear," in Nancy L. Rosenblum, ed., *Liberalism and the Moral Life* (Cambridge, MA: Harvard University Press, 1989), p. 21. For a portrait of liberal internationalism that draws on Shklar's "liberalism without illusions," see Stanley Hoffmann, "Liberalism and International Affairs," in Hoffmann, *Janus and Minerva: Essays in the Theory and Practice of International Politics* (Boulder, CO: Westview Press, 1987), pp. 394–417. For another illuminating essay by Hoffmann on these themes, see Hoffmann, "Sisyphus and the Avalanche: The United Nations, Egypt and Hungary," *International Organization*, Vol. 11, No. 3 (Summer 1957), pp. 446–69.

28. The phrase is originally Alexander Herzen's. Berlin uses it extensively in *Russian Thinkers* with attributions to various passages in Herzen's memoirs, *My Past and Thoughts* (Berkeley: University of California Press, reissue, 1982).

29. "An Open Letter to the President," *New York Times*, 31 December 1933.

30. See Norman Angell, *The Political Conditions of Allied Success: A Plea for a Protective Union of the Democracies* (New York: G. P. Putnam's Sons, 1918). With a similar meaning, Daniel Deudney and G. John Ikenberry use this term in "Democratic Internationalism: An American Grand Strategy for a Post-Exceptionalist Era," International Institutions and Global Governance working paper (New York: Council on Foreign Relations, 2012).

Page numbers in *italics* indicate figures.